Riccardo Antonangeli

The Fascist Character as Enigma in Post-World War II Italian Literature, Cinema, and Historiography

Crossovers: New Perspectives on CompLit

Edited by: Emilia Di Rocco & Beata Waligorska-Olejniczak

1   Riccardo Antonangeli
    The Fascist Character as Enigma in Post-World War II Italian Literature, Cinema, and Historiography
    ISBN (Print): 978-3-8382-2013-0
    ISBN (E-Book [PDF]): 978-3-8382-8013-4

This book series is part of the *European Society of Comparative Literature / Société Européenne de Littérature Comparée*. It publishes monographs that fall within the broadly understood category of Comparative Literature, exploring the interdisciplinary and transnational relationships between literature, society, science, art and other media. Reflecting the mission of the society, the series treats Europe as its focal point, using its cultural archives, intellectual history, and the intersections of ideas and phenomena—naturally intertwined with non-European forms of artistic creation—as its field of exploration.

Riccardo Antonangeli

THE FASCIST CHARACTER AS ENIGMA IN POST-WORLD WAR II ITALIAN LITERATURE, CINEMA, AND HISTORIOGRAPHY

Bibliografische Information der Deutschen Nationalbibliothek
Die Deutsche Nationalbibliothek verzeichnet diese Publikation in der Deutschen Nationalbibliografie; detaillierte bibliografische Daten sind im Internet über http://dnb.d-nb.de abrufbar.

Bibliographic information published by the Deutsche Nationalbibliothek
The Deutsche Nationalbibliothek lists this publication in the Deutsche Nationalbibliografie; detailed bibliographic data are available on the Internet at http://dnb.d-nb.de.

Cover picture: Illustration (Detail) by Tony Johannot and Maurice Sand for the reissue of Spiridion in "Œuvres illustrées de George Sand, volume IX" (Hetzel: Paris, 1856). Source: Bibliothèque nationale de France.

ISBN (Print): 978-3-8382-2013-0
ISBN (E-Book [PDF]): 978-3-8382-8013-4
© *ibidem*-Verlag, Hannover • Stuttgart 2025

Alle Rechte vorbehalten

Leuschnerstraße 40
30457 Hannover
info@ibidem.eu

Das Werk einschließlich aller seiner Teile ist urheberrechtlich geschützt. Jede Verwertung außerhalb der engen Grenzen des Urheberrechtsgesetzes ist ohne Zustimmung des Verlages unzulässig und strafbar. Dies gilt insbesondere für Vervielfältigungen, Übersetzungen, Mikroverfilmungen und elektronische Speicherformen sowie die Einspeicherung und Verarbeitung in elektronischen Systemen.

All rights reserved. No part of this publication may be reproduced, stored in or introduced into a retrieval system, or transmitted, in any form, or by any means (electronic, mechanical, photocopying, recording or otherwise) without the prior written permission of the publisher. Any person who commits any unauthorized act in relation to this publication may be liable to criminal prosecution and civil claims for damages.

Printed in the EU

Table of Contents

Introduction
Nel raggio delle distanze finte 9

CHAPTER 1
The Palimpsest of *Il conformista*: from Moravia to Bertolucci .. 45

    1.1 A Mysterious Object Difficult to Aim at: Marcello Emplots his Life. 45

    1.2 The Recognition Scene: The Disruption of Marcello's Plot. 55

    1.3 The Fascist Character as *failed* Stereotype and Dynamic Hero. 60

    1.4 Author and Hero: the Fascist as 'Other' and the Collapse into Affect. 68

    1.5 Ambiguity of Genres: Melodrama, *Bildungsroman* and Tragedy. 77

    1.7 Against Godard? Bertolucci's *Il conformista* as the formal resolution of two contrasting ideas of cinema: the idealist and the materialist one. 101

    1.8 *Cahiers du Cinéma* and *Cinéthique*: the Debate on Cinema in France between 1968 and 1969. Perspective, Depth of Field, Spectatorship. 106

    1.9 Theory in Practice: 'Inside the Gaze' of *Il conformista*. ... 122

    List of Figures 139

CHAPTER 2
The *Bildungsroman* of Italian Antifascism. Spontaneity and Organization as Narrative Motifs in Antifascist Historiography on the Resistance. 161

    2.1 A Sacred Story 161

    2.2 The Desire to Know 164

    2.3 The Interpretations of Fascism: Parenthesis, Autobiography or Counterrevolution? 167

2.4 The Myths of the Resistance: History as Romance, Tragedy and Comedy 173

2.5 Resistance as Comedy in the Epic Frame of Roberto Battaglia's *Storia della resistenza italiana* 177

2.6 Resistance as Tragedy: the 'Betrayed Revolution' of the *Azionisti*. The 'Civil War' Thread from Massimo Salvadori's *Storia della resistenza italiana*, to Claudio Pavone's *Una guerra civile*. 195

2.7 Education Through Terrorism: Enigma and Self-Evidence in Framing Violence. 210

2.8 The nexus between Spontaneity and Organization as a Problem of Education: the Two Bildungsroman of Italian Antifascism. 218

CHAPTER 3
Behind the Screen. The Fascist Enframed: *Un eroe del nostro tempo* and *Il prete bello* 233

3.1 The Organization of Space in the *Bildungsroman* of Sandrino. 233

3.2 The Enigma of *don Gastone*: The Fascist Character as the Ineffable Object of 'Hysterical' Storytelling and Voyeurism. 251

CHAPTER 4
The Excess of Demarcation. The Fascist Character and the Disruption of the Profilmic Space. 265

4.1 Daniela/Lili Marleen: *femme fatale* and collaborator in *Caccia tragica* 265

4.2 Pinin the Spy: the Fascist Character and Reality Effect in *Il Cristo proibito* 279

4.3 The Death of Tarcisio: *Era notte a Roma* as nemesis of *Roma città aperta* 286

4.4 The End of Ciano as Tragedy: History in *Il processo di Verona*. 298

4.5 'Rear Window' in Ferrara: Gaze and Space in *La lunga notte del '43*. 309

4.6 The Plot of Athos Magnani: Perspectives and Frames in *Strategia del ragno* 333

CHAPTER 5
Standing in the Way of Narrative Exchange and Desire:
a Reading of the Fascist Character in *Una questione privata*
by Beppe Fenoglio. 349

BIBLIOGRAPHY 383

    FILMOGRAPHY 391

Introduction
Nel raggio delle distanze finte

Fascist characters in Italian literature and films produced after the fall of the fascist regime seem to share, first of all, one recurrent epithet: they are 'mysterious.' By fascist character, I will refer, in the present work, not only to the classic figure of the *gerarca* but also, and mainly, to its more ambiguous variations: the female collaborator, often a prostitute, the spy, the *voltagabbana*, the informer, the traitor and the *repubblichino* (the adherent of the Repubblica Sociale Italiana, allied with Nazi Germany, 1943–45). No matter what degree of guilt, what involvement with fascism and with the occupying German forces these characters have, the authors of the texts that contain them see a veil of absurdity covering their aspect and conduct. To the eyes of the protagonist and of the author, they always appear as interpretative and *visual* enigmas, deforming the everyday cognitive abilities and usual perspective of the gaze, which attempts to frame them as objects.

Two examples, taken from autobiographical narratives written in the immediate postwar years respectively by Gianna Manzini and Franco Fortini, will help clarify the nature of the mystery of the fascist character. In Manzini's text, when two former Italian army barracks in Rome are occupied by the Nazis and then turned into prisons, the narrator notices a sort of uncanny deformation of time and space in the usual, familiar, everyday aspect of the nearby Roman avenue she lives in. The two large buildings and their new purpose and meaning seem to trigger a sort of estrangement:

> È incredibile come le cose più consuete, gli aspetti più affabili di un paesaggio invecchiato dall'abitudine, possano essere trasformati senza che avvenga alcun mutamento reale. Un luogo comune di cotidiane avventure si cangia ad un tratto in uno speciale deserto, ove le usuali misure di tempo e di spazio non sono più valide; diventa una scena che accenna un mistero, allestita per gli espatriati del vivere umano. Così, quasi per uno scarto nell'orbita della terra, ci sembrò ad un tratto di vivere altrove, costretti ad accettare una catena di eventi assurdi e logicissimi, i quali, pur contrastando

con gli elementi della vita cotidiana, continuavano ad essere intessuti di codesti elementi.¹

This defamiliarization, which turns everyday space and time into a scene alluding to a mystery and the normal causal chain of events into an at once *absurd* and logical sequence, perfectly exemplifies two textual deformations that the fascist character seems to enable with their presence: the disruption of the coherent, teleological progression of a narrative plot (as a logical cause-effect series) and the deformation of the profilmic space in cinema, of the symmetrical configuration within the limits of the frame.

Fortini's *Diario di un giovane borghese intellettuale* contains a report of a curious story told to him by a doctor. When he was the commissar of a partisan group, the doctor—Doctor M. in the story—had sentenced to death a 17-year-old fascist spy who had been captured some hours earlier. Just before everything was ready for the execution, a German battalion attacked the partisans, who were forced to escape into the forest. While surrounded, wounded and chased by the Germans, the doctor was saved by the person he would never have expected to be rescued by: the fascist spy. Change of setting. Some time afterward, the doctor is in Milan for a clandestine mission. One day, he is arrested. Someone recognized him in the street and reported him. Who? Precisely that young spy who saved him, who now tells the fascist police that he was the partisan commissar who ferociously tortured him while he was kept captive. This is how Fortini reports the end of the doctor's account, where he tells of the young fascist's accusations:

«Ha ripetuto queste accuse più di una volta, con una quantità di particolari inventati. Ho saputo che, preso dai tedeschi poco dopo l'episodio del nostro

---

1 Gianna Manzini, "Aspetti di un viale," in Mercurio, December 1945, 209. «It is unbelievable how the most usual things, the most affable aspects of a view that daily routine made look older, might be transformed without any actual mutation. A common place of everyday adventures suddenly turns into a special desert where the usual measures of time and space are not valid anymore; it becomes a scene that alludes to a mystery, set for those who expatriated from human existence. Thereby, almost as if a swerve from earth's orbit took place, we felt like living somewhere else, forced to accept a chain of absurd yet extremely logical events which, although in contrast with the aspects of daily life, continued to consist of these same elements.» [translation mine]

incontro nel bosco, aveva ripetuto a loro le medesime menzogne ed era stato così la causa diretta della morte orribile di una decina di amici miei seviziati e massacrati. In conseguenza della sua denunzia, fui condannato a morte; e scampai alla fucilazione in modo miracoloso, liberato dai miei stessi compagni. Durante la mia detenzione, in una cella prossima alla mia, c'era il giovane che mi aveva denunciato, trattenuto anch'egli dalla polizia fascista per sottrarlo a probabili vendette dei miei amici. Accadeva così che, ogni giorno, mi incontrassi con lui nel corridoio. Ci guardavamo. Naturalmente, non gli ho mai rivolto la parola».

M. aggiunge di aver saputo, a liberazione avvenuta, che quel giovane era stato fucilato dai partigiani per altre sue colpe, non avendo egli voluto, per un motivo a lui stesso inesplicabile, denunciarlo. *Dice che quel giovane è rimasto un mistero, il ricordo più enigmatico di tutto quel suo periodo.* [Italics mine][2]

The young fascist spy is the most mysterious and enigmatic memory the doctor has kept of the Resistance. Moreover, in the above short 'framed' narrative, past and present are linked by means of a recognition scene in the streets of Milan. Recognition is, in itself, an enigma, the difficult synthesis of past and present, of the present reality with the image-*eikon* that our memory has kept of the past reality. In fact, as Paul Ricœur writes:

> On se rapprochera plus encore de ce que j'aime appeler le petit miracle de la reconnaissance si on y discerne la solution de la plus vieille énigme de la problématique de la memoire, à savoir celle de la représentation présente d'une chose absente. La reconnaissance consiste dans la résolution effective de cette énigme de la présence de l'absence à la faveur de la certitude qui l'accompagne : «C'est bien elle ! C'est bien lui ! […] C'est l'énigme tout

---

2   Franco Fortini, "Diario di un giovane borghese intellettuale," in *Il Politecnico*, 39 (December 1947), 34; reproduced in Marco Forti and Sergio Pautasso (ed.) *Il Politecnico. Antologia critica* (Milano: Lerici, 1960), 773-774. «He repeated those accusations more than once, with a series of completely made-up details. I heard that, having been caught by the Germans right after the episode of our encounter in the forest, he had told them the very same lies, therofore becoming the direct cause of the horrible death of some of my tortured and massacred friends. As a consequence of his report, I was sentenced to death; and escaped the execution in a miraculous way, thanks to my companions who freed me. During my detention, in a prison cell next to mine, there was the young kid that reported me: the fascist police decided to keep him in order to protect him from the possible vengeance of my friends. Hence, everyday we bumped into each other in the corridor. We glanced at each other. Obviously, I never talked to him.» M. adds that somebody told him that, after the Liberation, the kid was executed by the partisans because of other crimes he committed. In fact, M. did not want, for reasons still inexplicable to him, report him. He says that that kid is still a mystery, the most enigmatic memory of that entire period of his life. [Translation mine]

> entière réaffirmée de la présence de l'absence : trancher *sur* le présent, reconnaître *pour* un souvenir.³

Fascism appears not as a repressed memory but rather as a cognitive and epistemological challenge. This book will try to unravel this enigma, show what lies behind it, and explain why an enemy is portrayed as a mystery.

Fascist characters are 'entertaining.' Entertaining, and not only *fascinating*, because the captivation they trigger has more to do with storytelling than eroticism, more with the *plaisir du texte* than with the guilty pleasures of perverted sexuality, as famously claimed by Susan Sontag in her 1974 essay "Fascinating Fascism." This means that their essential quality perhaps lies not so much in their representation, in the completed, finalized *image* with which they appear in a text—as sadomasochistic closeted homosexual torturers, for example—but in the *process* of their very aestheticization as fictional characters. How are stories with a fascist character told? How does an author describe the enemy? What type of storytelling practice is needed in order to give historical evil a narrative shape?

One of my central propositions in this study is that what readers and spectators find immediately striking in their first encounter with a fascist character is a sense of their pure literariness compared to the rest of the surrounding text. Fascist characters trigger a sort of block, a halt of reading, caused by the recognition of their somehow expanded, self-evident nature as fiction. There is at stake the perception of an inherent difference between them and the way other characters are portrayed, between their overdramatic figuration and the supposedly autobiographical, almost first-hand testimony, documentary nature of the rest of the story, as in the two examples above. The present book will be an attempt to problematize and clarify what I, for now, simply, tentatively called an emphasis on fictionality, these 'entertaining' and gap elements that fascist characters seem to enable in the texts hosting them.

The representation of fascism has been a widely explored research topic, and it is not my aim here to propose a further analysis of how fascism was portrayed in Italy in the years after 1945 and

---

3   Paul Ricœur, *Percours de la reconnaissance* (Paris: Stock, 2004), 200, 202.

even less to infer from the recurrent features of this representation an indication of deeper social and political upheavals characterizing national life and identity. This is by now a well-trodden research path, one that has brought significant and now universally acquired results, including, for example, the essays in the volume edited by R.J.B. Bosworth and Patrizia Dogliani, *Italian Fascism: History, Memory and Representation*. Among the conclusions that investigations of this kind have reached is that the fascist character is a demonstration of, first, the war as a traumatic experience that Italian collective memory has tried to cover, thereby betraying a sense of guilt and responsibility for having chosen to be on the 'wrong' side of history; second, the attempt to transfer that guilt and responsibility to the non-Italian ally, the Nazi outsider, making Italians appear as naïve, passive objects at the mercy of fate and the real criminals; third, the will to create a positive foundational myth for the newborn nation, idealizing the memory of the Resistance as a revolution unifying and redeeming the whole country, and demonizing the Nazi-fascists as the absolute evil that, once eradicated, would allow Italy to have a fresh and innocent start. Works such as *Il cattivo tedesco e il bravo italiano* by Filippo Focardi and *Uomini in nero. Il fascismo nel cinema italiano* by Maurizio Zinni describe the fascist character as a melodramatic caricature, as the stereotypical embodiment of absolute evil, regularly depicted with recurrent psychological and physical traits: bodily deformations (limp, one-eyed, with a sexually-transmitted disease, etc.) and psychic disturbances (deviant, perverted sexuality, sadistic tendencies, irrational violence, etc.). The result is a gallery of 'freaks' that serves to bolster a largely psychological interpretation of the legacy of fascism in postwar Italian history, resulting in a narrative of trauma, guilt, oblivion, and redemption (see F. Baldasso, *Against Redemption*, Fordham University Press, 2022). One narrative gets substituted by another: the first one told its addressees to forget that fascism was part of the national history; the second one brings fascism back into official history but does so mainly by making sense of fascism through a linear narrative of a society in 'bad faith,' one that could never really come to terms with its shameful past, since the price would have been the uncanny recognition of fascism's ongoing, latent persistence long after the end of the war.

Ruth Ben-Ghiat ends her essay "Liberation: Italian Cinema and the Fascist Past, 1945-50" with the following remarks:

> At a time of crisis in national identity and widespread shame about the Fascist regime, the films of De Santis offered Italians a vision of a nation that was cohesive and purposeful. Along with many other texts of the reconstruction period, they laid down a path for the collective memory of the dictatorship that exonerated ordinary Italians who had 'just been following orders' and projected responsibility for Fascism on to foreign powers. Although the crisis of national identity and variety of diplomatic, political, economic and social factors conspired to limit state-sponsored efforts at retribution, the wish of individual Italians to perceive themselves as victims, not perpetrators, also complicated the process of coming to terms with the Fascist past.[4]

This reading is, to various degrees, extended to all Italian literature and film on fascism, the Resistance and the 1943–45 civil war up until the 1960s, when, following, first, the indignation against the Tambroni government in 1960 and second, the student and worker protests of the late 1960s, a general rethinking and reassessment of that past is undertaken by the new generation born in the 1940s. The myth of the Resistance is questioned, and the memory of fascism is rescued from *taboo* status in order to highlight the *continuity* between the dictatorship and the postwar democracy under the common sign of bourgeois capitalism. As Dominic Gavin explains in commenting on *Strategia del ragno* (Bernardo Bertolucci, 1970):

> Bertolucci's film can be viewed in connection to a crucial phase for antifascist identity in postwar Italy. The film's release — and that of *Il conformista* — coincides with a turning point in the memory and interpretation of antifascism. On the one hand, the 1970 film recalls the impatient criticism of the so-called *antifascismo di stato* that had been voiced by various groups on the left over the previous decade. Yet it also coincides with the beginning of the season of widespread antifascist militancy that marked the 1970s, when fascism

---

4   Ruth Ben-Ghiat, "Liberation: Italian Cinema and the Fascist Past, 1945-50," in R. J. B. Bosworth and Patrizia Dogliani, (eds.), *Italian Fascism. History, Memory and Representation* (Macmillan, St. Martin's Press: Basingstoke, New York, 1999), 97.

and antifascism returned as pressing contemporary themes, as keys to interpret current political realities.⁵

After a decade-long period of repression of fascism from official memory and the parallel myths of *antifascismo di stato*, the younger generation revisited the lost, unknown past as a fantasy imbued with erotic meanings. Directors such as Liliana Cavani and Bernardo Bertolucci and historians like Guido Quazza and Claudio Pavone problematized historical memory by contesting the clear-cut polarization between bad fascism and good anti-fascism. Sadism becomes, at this point, the main individual connotation of the fascist character who drags the anti-fascist good character in an ambiguous circle of desire that perverts clear-cut and Manichean distinctions between victim and perpetrator, good and evil. As David Forgacs writes, questioning Susan Sontag's equation of fascism and sadism:

> The fascination with fascism as perversion that marked the cinema of the late 1960s and early 1970s seems to have had two main causes. One of them, perhaps a condition more than a cause, was the very rapid process of sexual liberalization in the 1960s. [...] the other cause was the more or less simultaneous lifting of restrictions on historical memory, and this was in large part an effect of the challenge mounted by the post-war generations to the collective repression and the channeling of historical memory into approved grooves that had characterized Italian society throughout the 1950s. This, too, led to a hot eruption of pseudo-history, or history crossed with fantasy, from which it would be wise now to keep a cool, critical distance.⁶

Repression and resurfacing, disappearance and reappearance. The representation of fascism and antifascism follows a pretty much teleological 'narrative' of maturation from unconsciousness to a more evolved, more or less conscious, recognition of the national past as a problematic event. Also, the fascist character becomes an object worthy of critical attention mainly thanks to film and/or historical analysis that greatly favored works from the late 1960s and early 1970s, given maybe the greater international resonance of Italian

---

5 Dominic Gavin, "Myths of the Resistance and Bernardo Bertolucci's *Strategia del ragno* (1970)" in *California Italian Studies*, 4 (2), 2013): 24.
6 David Forgacs, "Days of Sodom: The Fascism-Perversion Equation in Films of the 1960s and 1970s" in R. J. B. Bosworth and Patrizia Dogliani, (eds), *Italian Fascism*, 233.

cinema over Italian literature. What is in focus is the social and political content they are signs of, the historical context that originated them and that they refer back to; while their form as specific literary and filmic characters is almost never taken seriously, the formal analysis is limited to their caricatural and melodramatic nature. However, what if the fascist character enables a kind of textual perversion of the formal structure of a work of art?

I do not think another study on the historical, social and political value and resonance of fascism and antifascism could have added much more to what has been already achieved by the scholarship I have briefly and schematically sketched above. I do think, though, that a serious, formal analysis of these characters is scarce both in literary and film criticism. My essay aims to fill this gap and, at the same time, to contribute to a reassessment of some of the conclusions that scholarship on the subject has reached, starting from the teleological periodization in two macro periods of shadow and light. For this reason, I decided to focus most of my critical investigation on plots of novels and films from a limited time frame, roughly 1945 up until 1960. However, I do also include two films from a later period, Bernardo Bertolucci's *Strategia del ragno* and *Il conformista*, both released in 1970. In this way, my purpose was to question the above periodization, highlighting how, during the period of so-called oblivion, fascism and antifascism were far from being objects of a clear-cut Manichean distinction. In a word, what happened in the 1970s was already latent and working its way to the surface in the immediate postwar years. This can be observed only by means of going back to the texts, taking seriously and as worthy of close critical attention exactly those marginal parts and secondary characters that were rapidly dismissed as stereotypical representations and clichés. I am not trying to propose a formal analysis in contrast to the historical and political interpretations of the character, but, rather, a different approach and angle to the text, one that can perhaps revive the discussion around the cultural value of some works—and of some specific characters in them—that were previously dismissed as minor or as unworthy of the attention of 'academic research.' Specific storytelling patterns, narrative functions and motives might then be recognized as other constant and recurrent characteristics of fascist characters throughout Italian literature and cinema, besides the already familiar ones of sadism, perverse sexuality, and unmotivated violence.

The cliché and stereotypical appearance of these types is, in my opinion, the symptom of a different linguistic configuration that the narrativization of the enemy, of the *other*, requires. The fascist character is the manifestation of an epistemological problem, the narrative shape resulting from the attempt, the will to come to terms with, and assign a meaning to, an ambiguous, and not absolute, evil. The fascist, in fact, has the ambiguous nature of the enemy in a time of civil war: at once outsider and insider. This is an object that forestalls total exclusion and objectivization because they share the same national identity as those who fight them. The recognition of sameness in difference complicates both storytelling and classification. Hence, it does not seem totally correct to define as more or less uninterrupted 'oblivion' the representation of fascism before the 1960s. *Anni facili* (Luigi Zampa, 1953), *Gli sbandati* (Francesco Maselli, 1955), *Il Generale Della Rovere* (Roberto Rossellini, 1959), or the novels *Fausto e Anna* (Carlo Cassola, 1952), *Il prete bello* (Goffredo Parise, 1954), *Il segreto di Luca* (Ignazio Silone, 1956), the collection of short stories *Cinque storie ferraresi* (Giorgio Bassani, 1956), are only the major examples of how the continuity of fascism after the war, and thus the collaboration of the majority of Italians, was a phenomenon that was already a matter of analysis and 'material' for stories. The literature on the subject has always and constantly been extremely prolific, so much so that the fascist 'type' might as well be defined as one of the main and most original creations of Italian literature and film of the second half of the 20th century, or at least as the character that had the most fortune and influence also in the wider European context. Fascist characters have always been present in mainstream and 'alternative' literature and cinema. Comedies, caricatures, low-brow melodramas as well as auteurist cinema and 'official' literature—besides the will to 'forget' and 'unburden' from the guilt of collaboration—are all precious documents of how an ambiguous object that triggers disturbing recognition as well as distance, shapes and deforms the language and narrative through which the subject tries to make sense of it. Would it be possible, then, to identify certain rhetorical strategies and narrative genres enabled by the fascist character? With this in view, I would like to propose an enquiry that tries to open discussions rather than close them.

Maria Corti asks in her *Il viaggio testuale* why out of neorealism—given its roots in the Resistance's popular, oral tradition of storytelling and first-hand chronicles—there did not emerge «a national-popular epic.»[7] One reason, she argues, is the inherently contradictory nature of neorealism, characterized on the one hand by its faith in the exemplarity of personal experience and by faith «nelle cose che parlano da sé»[8] and on the other by the reluctance of this objectivity, and oral tradition, to be displaced into *sjužet*, i.e., into plot. While the first-hand popular, chronicle-like or journal-style and oral documentation on the Resistance is extremely rich, authors who try to use that material for narratives and stories inevitably transform their popular sources into myth because of their nature as intellectuals formed in 'traditional' culture and thus both inside and outside the object they want to narrate. There is, then, a contradictory imbalance between objectivity and myth due, among other things, to the ambiguous identity of the authors, who, while they did participate in the Resistance, cannot get rid of the fact that their status as outsiders to the culture of the masses makes them reframe the stories they re-narrate within the thematic and semantic fields of traditional literature:

> Mentre la documentazione ricchissima intorno alla Resistenza offre un certo numero di testi memorialistici dovuti a non letterati, magari a proletari, dove il raccontare viene veramente dal basso, da chi ha vissuto certe esperienze dall'interno, e riesce a farle parlare con precisa coerenza, molto più ardua e spesso stilisticamente contraddittoria diviene l'operazione sul reale quando chi racconta scende dall'alto, cioè dalla sua cultura, come dire dalla cultura tradizionale; allora gli accade di essere insieme dentro e fuori della materia. Scrive giustamente Asor Rosa: «è da notare, innanzitutto, che il populismo della letteratura resistenziale appare mosso, più che da una frequentazione diretta degli strati popolari interessati al processo di rinnovamento, da un forte impulso moralistico e ideologico: l'intellettuale va verso

---

7   Maria Corti, *Il viaggio testuale* (Torino: Einaudi, 1978), 36.
8   Ibidem. «faith in self-evident things that speak by themselves.» [translation mine]

il popolo, ma *il più delle volte, prima ancora di raggiungerlo concretamente e seriamente lo trasforma in mito in immagine rovesciata di sé*» Cioè può allora aversi con la pratica scrittoria una produzione rischiosa di senso anteriore al vero senso, di reale anteriore al vero reale: l'esito qualche volta è scontato o velleitario, sempre è lungi dal programma dell'oggettività, è fornito di funzione segnica diversa dalla prevista.[emphasis mine][9]

The reality of the present, which needs new structural models, gets translated instead into the old models that cause the elimination of all ambiguity and a resulting clear-cut classification into opposite semantic fields, which pave the way not to objectivity but to symbolization and myth. Through the hero, the author communicates their moral judgments. Maria Corti produces in the form of a chart this antithetical Manichean model, which necessarily reorders the real material into literary form:[10]

resistenti	fascisti
uomini integri	semiuomini o belve
popolani	borghesi
campagna	città
quartiere cittadino povero	città
strada dei poveri	città

---

9   Idem., 37-38. «On the one hand, the very rich documentation on the Resistance provides a certain number of memoirs written by non-intellectual, sometimes even by proletarians, in which the story is told from below, by someone who has directly lived certain experiences from the inside, and thereby can let these experiences talk with precise coherence. On the other, when the narrator comes from above, from his/her culture, i.e., from traditional culture, the operation on the real is much more complicated and stylistically contradictory: s/he is both inside and outside the material. Asor Rosa correctly writes: «the populism of the literature of the Resistance seems to be activated more by a strong moral and ideological impulse, rather than from a direct participation side by side with the masses involved in the process of renewal: the intellectual goes towards the people, but, most of the times, even before joining it really and seriously, s/he turns it into myth, into the reversed image of itself.» That is to say, the storytelling practice might consist of a risky superimposition of a meaning preexisting the actual meaning, of a reality that anticipates the actual reality: the outcome is sometimes predictable, and it is always very far from the program of objectivity, being endowed with a semantic function different from the expected one.» [translation mine.]
10 Idem., 63.

The narratological and semantic approach—here exemplified by Maria Corti's fundamental essay—has been the starting point of my research. It is historically justified also by the fact that the so-called 'resurgence' of a demystifying discourse on the fascist and antifascist past during the late 1960s and early 1970s coincided with the diffusion of the tenets of narratology and a simultaneous revival of Russian formalism. I intend to follow up on Maria Corti's formal analysis of that period's literature and attempt to investigate how the contradictory encounter between reality and myth, between a supposedly self-evident truth and literary form, between hero and author, takes shape in the films and novels analyzed. Often, the result, as we will see, does not allow the uncomplicated categorization shown above but instead reveals ambiguity and relativity, already in works produced in the late 1940s.

That a gap between facts and words, popular and traditional, was at the heart of neorealism and the reason for its unsuccessful attempt to create a national epic is already made clear in the famous preface written by Italo Calvino to the 1964 edition of his first novel, *Il sentiero dei nidi di ragno* (1947). First of all, the preface is in itself an exercise in proto-narratological style. The author continuously refers to the form itself of the preface as a genre, confessing his inability to write one altogether and the impossibility of deciding how and when to begin. The discourse results, then, as a postponement of the beginning and a preface that does not exactly refer to just one text but that, rather, opens the text to a potentially infinite chain of intertextuality. Instead of introducing the reader to the meaning of the text, the author hides and fragments the unity of meaning into multiple possible significations. By writing that book, Calvino destroyed the unique reality he wanted to capture. By writing this preface, he changes the nature of the book itself, turning it into an 'open work'. The transfiguration into literary form is paid at the high price of an irreversible loss of truth, described by Calvino as a very Bergsonian conflict between a memory as quality and flux and a memory as quantity and static, completed point. He defines neorealism as neo-expressionism, as the grotesque exaggeration of a fleeting reality:

> E poi il modo di figurare la persona umana: tratti esasperati e grotteschi, smorfie contorte, oscuri drammi visceral-collettivi. L'appuntamento con l'espressionismo che la cultura letteraria e figurativa italiana aveva mancato nel Primo Dopoguerra, ebbe il suo grande momento nel Secondo. Forse il vero nome per quella stagione italiana, più che «neorealismo» dovrebbe essere «neo-espressionismo.»
> Le deformazioni della lente espressionistica si proiettano in questo libro sui volti che erano stati di miei cari compagni. Mi studiavo di renderli contraffatti, irriconoscibili, «negativi», perché solo nella «negatività» trovavo un senso poetico.[11]

The most evident example of this expressionism and negativity is the fascist character, especially in the variants of the female or male, collaborator, traitor and spy. Only negativity seems to retain a poetic sense, thus implying that only through a deformation could reality function as material for a poetically sound and coherent literary work. The fascist character becomes, then, the textual location of the utmost *poiesis* of emphasized fiction, as I mentioned earlier. The moralistic categorization of the fascist as absolute evil is also the clearest manifestation of that contradiction between popular oral tradition and traditional moral classification into the roles of myth that Maria Corti identified as one of the reasons for the neorealist 'failure' to create a veritable epic. The fascist seems to embody the gap between facts and words, to constitute the disruption of an objective, popular tendency by a subjective, authorial one. Even the only epic tale that the literature on the Resistance ever produced — Fenoglio's *Una questione privata* according to Italo Calvino; *Il partigiano Johnny* for Maria Corti — is an "absurd and mysterious" book that seems to be praised by Calvino more for its post-structuralism *avant la lettre* than for its effective capturing of the past reality: «ed è un libro assurdo, misterioso, in cui ciò che si insegue, si insegue per inseguire altro, e quest'altro per inseguire altro ancora e

---

11   Italo Calvino, "Preface" to *Il sentiero dei nidi di ragno* (Torino: Einaudi, 1964), 12. «there was the manner of depicting characters: they all had exaggerated, grotesque features, twisted grimaces, dark, deep-rooted psychological scars. If Italian literature and art had missed out on expressionism after the First World War, it made up for it at the end of the Second. Perhaps the correct label for that artistic epoch in Italy ought to be 'Neo-expressionism' rather than 'Neo-realism.'» [Calvino, "Preface" to *The Path to the Spider's Nests* translated by Martin McLaughlin (London: Jonathan Cape, 1998), 13.]

non si arriva al vero perché.»[12] *Una questione privata* is defined, then, as the epic of the chain of signifiers, of truth, always unattainable and forever sliding a step away, like Achilles's tortoise in Zeno's paradox. In between the uncovering of truth in both *Una questione privata* and *Il sentiero dei nidi di ragno*, there is a fascist minor character: Alarico in the former text and Pelle in the latter. Alarico is the 'currency of exchange' that the protagonist, Milton, needs if he wants to free his friend and hear from him a decisive truth. Pelle finds the place where Pin hid the pistol, thus involuntarily causing the final murder of the protagonist's sister and her Nazi lover. In both instances, the fascist has a key structural function in the plot, standing in the way or accelerating the *dénouement* of the events until the end. In both cases, the fascist character is involved in a covering/uncovering of truth, and by having a very marked, evident narrative function as a sort of ambiguous helper/villain, in Propp's terms (he is a villain only insomuch as the lack of his help would be detrimental for the hero) this character also makes more manifest the plot structure of the novel, its narrative mechanism and its nature as *sjužet* deforming/covering the *fabula*. If, at the structural and thematic level, the fascist is what the partisan good hero needs to eliminate in order to preserve himself from the corruptions and perversions of evil, at the level of narrative discourse, the fascist is precisely what the hero needs to have around. Alex Woloch locates the minor character precisely at the intersection between an implied person and narrative form, «in the shadow-space between narrative position and human personality».[13]

> In this sense, the minor character, by calling attention to character-space, helps establish the relationship of "story" and "discourse" — the events in the novel and the rendition of these events in the narrative itself. […] I am arguing that narratives themselves allow and solicit us to construct a story — a distributed pattern of attention — that is at odds with, or divergent from, the formed pattern of attention in the discourse. This strikes near the

---

12   Ibidem, 24. «it is also an absurd, mysterious book, in which the object of pursuit is only pursued in order to pursue something else, and this something else is in turn pursued for the sake of something else again, and we never reach the ultimate goal.» [Calvino, *The Path of the Spider's Nests*, trans. by Martin McLaughlin 28.]
13   Alex Woloch, *The One vs. the Many* (Princeton: Princeton UP, 2005), 40.

essential openness of the literary text. The literary text solicits reinterpretation; it creates disjunctions between story and discourse that facilitate the production of meaning, the production of significance. It creates, more specifically, disjunctions between the attention the discourse grants certain characters and the attention that they would grant themselves and that the reader might grant them.[14]

The fascist character is at once a grotesque, expressionist deformation of reality and, as a minor character, they embody this fracture between stories and discourse and that between truth and language. The characteristic of this type of character is, then, precisely, the gap, the activation in the text of a sort of disjunction that produces meaning by emphasizing the split between signifier and signified historical past reality and 'myth.' With this in view, I aim to investigate the possibility of a form of gap specific to the fascist 'minor' character, reinterpreting the texts in which they appear by bringing them to the center of the critical reading. Also, the purpose of my research is to attempt a possible extension and further problematization of the above discourses on the contradiction inherent to neorealism as a gap between story and discourse, reality and myth, and also to genre criticism. Enabling with them the gap, the fascist character might also trigger an ambiguity at the level of genres and a consequent clash of different narrative types, thus concretizing that contradictory coexistence of tendencies toward the real, the *fabula* and their deformation-configuration in literary and film form. Alex Woloch has identified in the synecdoche the trope that best describes the minor character's function in a text (*Pride and Prejudice* in this case) as they get converted into one single characteristic «just as the whole gets filtered through the essential part, so the full person is squeezed into the flat character, a flatness motivated and sustained by the characteristic that gets derived from the individual only to subsume her».[15] Following this, I will propose that the fascist character functions as an *enigma* or 'riddle', a rhetorical figure which, according to Aristotle, triggers an ambiguous relationship between myth and reality, fable and truth, and thereby stimulates the reader to know more. Enigmas lead to knowledge by

---

14   Ibidem, 38,41.
15   Idem, 69.

means of obscurity. In this case, the thwarting of objectivity and the disruption of the usual connections between things create a language that, by covering truth, actually provides it as a result of a pleasurable cognitive process.

In *Poetics*, Aristotle defined enigmas or riddles as «impossible combinations of words (which can be done with a combination of metaphors).»[16] Riddles are difficult metaphors that at first seem to frustrate the reader with obscurity, only to give pleasure later and higher wisdom to the reader who is forced to get to meaning through a convoluted and indirect path. Aristotle develops this argument further in *Rhetoric*:

> Metaphor above all give perspicuity, pleasure and a foreign air, and it cannot be learnt from anyone else [...] And generally speaking, clever enigmas furnish good metaphors; for metaphor is a kind of enigma, so that it is clear that the transference is clever. [...]
> A riddle may mislead the listener at first, but only for the sake of good metaphor and wider knowledge: for the mind seems to say, 'How true it is! But I missed it.' And clever riddles are agreeable for the same reason; for something is learnt, and the expression is also metaphorical.[17]

Riddles, then, are complicated metaphors that express a truth that could not be represented otherwise, in plain language. The uncommon, tortuous sequence and the junction of two 'distant' metaphors, on the one hand, complicate and seem to forestall the attainment of wisdom completely, but, on the other — and herein lies the unique fascination that has always accompanied this trope — it allows the reader to have a hint, a sense of the hidden meaning thanks to the decipherment of a combination of words that only allude to, but never directly refer to, the message. If, as we have seen, between language and the real, there is always an unsurpassable gap, riddles turn that gap into an opportunity not only to know but to reach knowledge with pleasure, thanks to that very same deformation imposed by words on facts. Enigmas make use of the disjunction and find in it the way to truths that would be impossible to grasp otherwise. If, in antiquity and the Middle Ages, enigmas were used

---

16 Aristotle, *Poetics* xxii in Eleanor Cook, *Enigmas and Riddles in Literature* (Cambridge: Cambridge UP, 2006), 32.
17 Aristotle, *Rhetoric* III.ii. 9, 12, III.xi. 6, in Cook *Enigmas and Riddles,* 33.

to convey the perfect knowledge of divine wisdom, the same rhetorical strategy might also work for traumas and difficult memories, such as fascism, the Resistance, and the civil war have been, and continue to be, for Italy.

Riddles are typical in Greek tragedies, and Gloria Ferrari, in analyzing Aeschylus's use of metaphor, defines enigma as not simply a more complex kind of metaphor but as a discursive mode in its own right with specific rules and structure. The particular manipulation of metaphor is only one of the operations that the riddle requires to work. What makes the tragic riddle unique is the presence of a 'block' between the two conjoined metaphors. This gap halts the comprehension of the reader/listener, who perceives something 'off' between the two sets of images used to expose the 'fabled narrative' of the riddle. This moment of crisis in the interpretation of the enigmatic sequence is, in fact, due to a shift in the frame of reference entailed by the passage from the initial metaphoric expression to the second one. The frustration is generated by the dark intuition that the images that make sense in the second context are not the same ones that made sense in the first. The solution lies in realizing that a shift from the literal to a metaphorical code, and vice versa, has been taking place. Ferrari's in-depth analysis of the riddle of the 'vultures' in Aeschylus' *Agamemnon* is worth quoting, as it is one of the models for my reading of plots with fascist characters:

> The vultures metaphor has, in fact, the characteristic structure of the riddle: an opening frame of reference (the gathering of the host); descriptive elements, both literal and metaphorical (the war-cry, the oared wings); the "block," or elements that are in conflict with the preceding (the *goos,* "these" metics); and a concluding frame of reference, different from the initial one, in which the conflict is resolved (the sacrifice of Iphigenia and the revenge of Clytemnestra). Solving the puzzle depends on the ability to recognize that certain features—the pains "on untrodden ground," the *gods* of the metics, the Erinyes—are a block. They refer to a different subject: not the rape of Helen leading to the destruction of Troy, but the sacrifice of Iphigenia, the choir of Furies and the imminent murder of Agamemnon. In order to respond to the clues given in the "block," the audience must realize that at that point the context has become unstable, as regards both the subject at hand and the mode of discourse. With a switch in terms of the metaphor, the vultures are described just as Atreidae did. In moving from the initial frame to the final one, the ambiguous items mentioned above, are points of transition,

being applicable to one as well as the other, that produce a moment of hesitation between two equally viable solutions.[18]

The riddle, then, causes in the audience a "moment of hesitation," a cognitive crisis that frustrates at first but only bolsters the wisdom later attained, now with a gain in pleasure. The richness in dissonance and incoherence of the enigmatic structure has the power to disrupt both the audience's certainties and fixed static meanings and to make meaning dynamic, relative and ambiguous.

Also influential on my approach has been Peter Dronke's rethinking of fables as more than fabled narratives, as having a cognitive function and value of their own. Dronke reformulates fables as «speculations about man and his place in the universe.»[19] In *Fabula*, he traces the history of the 'defense' of the realm of imagination that culminated eventually in the 12th century thanks to Platonist thinkers. Signals in that direction were already present in the patristic period and in the new meanings assigned to the rhetorical concepts of *integumentum* (covering) and *involucrum* (wrapping), both suggesting how «hidden meanings may lurk in imagery and story matter.»[20] This concept began to counter the prevailing, older tendency to evaluate those two tropes as obscurity and mystification. Augustine first and then Scotus Eurigena renewed the relevance that Dionysius the Areopagite (c. 500) had given to *aenigma* and *symbolum*.

Nevertheless, it was in the 12th century that William of Conches and Peter Abelard almost equated *fabula, integumentum* and *involucrum* with myth, «but with a special emphasis on the 'inner' meaning of the mythic narrative, which is the philosopher's task to discover.»[21] Fabled narratives became then an effective linguistic solution to relate human knowledge to divine knowledge, dealing with figures belonging to the higher, heavenly spheres such as cosmic timeless and eternal gods and spirits. Enigma is not an allegory, as Isidore of Seville specified, insomuch as the former

---

18 Gloria Ferrari, "Metaphors and Riddles in the Agamemnon," in *Classical Philology*, Vol. 92, No. 1 (Jan., 1997), 34-35.
19 Peter Dronke, *Fabula* (Leiden and Köln: E.J. Brill, 1974), 2.
20 Idem., 4.
21 Idem., 5.

does not allude to a second meaning as the latter does. Enigmas have only one dark meaning, adumbrated by means of images; they do not link together one meaning with an allegorical second level of signification:

> As an enigma 'means more' than the images that adumbrate it, so too such 'meaning more' is implied in the twelfth-century Platonists' concept *integumentum*. Literally a covering, *integumentum* is used both for a myth that conceals hidden meanings and for the hidden meanings themselves, that lie covered beneath its narrative surface. In principle there is no limit to the meanings that an *integumentum* can conceal and generate; like a *symbolum*, it can 'show invisible forms', taking the reader to the unfathomable realm of the intelligible and the divine. This holds even if the literal meaning of the myth should be a scandalous account of pagan gods and goddesses—indeed, in the mystical Platonic tradition that Dionysius had transmitted to the medieval West, the unfitting and the monstrous is, by its sheer bafflement of human attempts to imagine the divine, most apt to convey truly how far the divine is beyond all imagining.[22]

"The unfitting and the monstrous" might reveal good coverings to pass on listeners' divine wisdom. The turpitude of a fabled narrative of adultery, for example, might be an *integumentum*, a way of expressing holy truths about souls and planets with rhetorical beauty and dignity. Also, the darker and more mystified the enigma, the more 'carnal' and debased the fable's material, the more enriched with multiple meanings the listener might be at the end of their 'textual journey:'

> And that men might come away from it the more enriched, finding something enclosed that could be opened in many ways, more than if they had found it, already open, in one way only. [...] Thus the writer's use of *involucra*, enclosing meaning within a wrapping or covering it by veils, is significantly linked with the possibility of a richer range of meanings for his reader. Both for the poet (David) and the prophet (Isaiah), the sacrifice in immediate clarity may entail a gain in multivalent meaning, which is suggestive rather than fixed.[23]

The monstrous fable, as a cognitive and speculative practice that results in a dynamic openness to a multiplicity of meanings that

---

22 Peter Dronke, *Dante and Medieval Latin Traditions* (Cambridge: Cambridge UP, 1986.), 25.
23 Dronke, *Fabula*, 57.

counter fixed classification, is one of the qualities of the rhetorical trope enigma-*integumentum* that works particularly well with the fascist character and its narrative function in the plot-*sjužet*. The truth about the past of the Resistance, fascism and civil war is unattainable, but the expressionist and grotesque character might have a cognitive function pointing to reality through channels different from those of an objective, realist account of those same facts.

Hesitation, disruption, monstrous and polysemy. These qualities granted to riddles and enigmas have also had an important social and educative function since the primitive stages of civilization. Riddles, in fact, were often linked with taboo and threatening items that were possibly disruptive of both the individual and collective identity. Functionally, riddles question the established order by playing with conceptual borderlines and giving pleasure by this crossing and blurring of boundaries that reveals the festive relativity and instability of all things and how their supposed stability and fixity are just an appearance. Most likely to be tabooed are the ambiguous spaces between different categories, those equivocal characteristics that are shared by multiple sets of categories. Enigmas thus disrupt classification by means of the ambiguity of certain components of their configuration, as Ian Hamnett explains:

> Riddles are one form of ambiguity or ambivalence, and they can be understood in the light of the social and cognitive function of ambiguous or ambivalent utterances, concepts and actions. An ambivalent word, concept or item of behavior can be considered as belonging to any of two or more frames of reference according to the interpretation brought to bear upon it, or indeed to several or all such frames at once. It can therefore operate as a point of transition between these different frames of reference or classificatory sets. It can indeed mediate between sets that are not only different, but in many aspects opposed, and in this way it can form the basis for a differing system of classification, or allow contrasting classifications and conceptual frameworks to co-exist at the same time.[24]

Therefore, ambiguous and ambivalent objects put the stability of any classificatory system in danger, as shown by riddles that refer to processes of social change or the qualities of alien, newly

---

24 Ian Hammet, "Classification and Change: The Function of Riddles," in *Man*, New Series, Vol. 2, No. 3, (Sep, 1967): 381-382.

introduced objects, or bodily excretions. For the same reason, though, they can be used to mediate and compromise between opposite categories of concept, person or object. They reinforce the gap by turning ambiguity into a taboo, but at the same time, they allude to and reveal that same ambivalence, bringing to the surface all its disruptive and confusing relativity that destabilizes classificatory distinctions between things, ideas and also—maybe more importantly—between self and other:

> Ambiguous and ambivalent items threaten the integrity of the system and are, therefore, especially likely to be subject to taboo. Nowhere is the 'danger' inherent in classificatory confusion so intense, nor the prohibitions therefore so stringent, as in the separation of the thinking subject from his environment—of 'ego' from 'not ego.' It has been suggested that bodily excretions are objects of taboo, at least partly because they are a potential threat to this primary discrimination, being ambiguous in so far as they are part of a person's body and at the same time separate from him. (Both A and not A). Riddles in general, therefore, and riddles concerning the body or its parts and functions in particular, can be said to threaten a breakdown in cultural segregation of conceptual categories and might be expected to fall under taboo.[25]

The rhetorical structure and procedure of the enigma mirrors its social and cognitive function. The "block" first confirms the distance and incoherence between fixed, static categories, and second, the compromise and shift between them that disrupt and relativize the previous classification.

I suggest that the fascist character brings the ambiguity of riddles to the formal, cognitive discourse of the plot and also seems to share its social and educative function. By reading the fascist as an enigma, it is possible to identify some recurrent formal patterns in the plots of a selected group of novels and films from 1945 until 1970. In fact, besides the already formulated characteristic physical and psychical features of the fascist—a sadist with some sort of bodily deformity or disease—the character appears to enable some formal modifications, some *topoi* that, in my opinion, allow us to group plots with fascist types into a sort of subgenre, with its own rules and structure, of Italian literature and cinema. The most frequent

---

25   Idem., 389.

plot structure is based upon rational plans gone wrong. It is clear that the hero has acted in a certain way and that their actions have caused a definite effect. However, in the end, there is the sudden, unexpected revelation that those actions were never committed, and thus, the expected effects did not take place at all. A plot configured in this fashion also inevitably entails the problem of human agency and responsibility, the contrast of voluntarism and determinism being one of the main controversial areas of the philosophical and political debate between liberalism and socialism.

A disruption of the logic sequence cause-effect—beginning-middle-end—has occurred, and the author has kept from both the audience and hero some key information necessary to postpone the solution to the puzzle until the very end. The problem is that, from the perspective of the hero and the reader, there was no riddle whatsoever until the entire plot is revealed as a riddle only retrospectively from the final point of view. It is, then, what Roland Barthes defined as a lure when the author intentionally hides—for reasons that exceed the inner dynamic of the events as reconfigured by the plot—information only to surprise the reader. The narrative structure of Ennio Flaiano's *Tempo di uccidere* (1947) turns on the belief, the certainty that the hero has about a crime he did not commit, and the final astonishment in finding out that the crime *mysteriously* actually happened, but that nevertheless the agency is uncertain and that he cannot be blamed. The story is set in Ethiopia during the fascist colonial war. The protagonist first robs a major who kindly offers him a lift and then sabotages the wheel of his truck in order to kill him so he cannot report the theft. He carries the missing screw in his hand, so he is certain that the wheel will eventually detach, thereby letting the truck precipitate from the road. However, he observes the truck through his binoculars as it continues its journey without problems until it gets lost from his view. At the end of the novel, he is sure that the major has reported him, but he is told that the truck never actually reached its destination.

Alberto Moravia's *Il conformista* (1951) has a similar structure: the hero is sure of being a murderer, and then, in the end, he finds out that he actually never committed the crime. Also, in Renata

Viganò's *L'Agnese va a morire* (1949), the protagonist thinks she killed a Nazi officer—and there are, once again, no textual clues to doubt it—and at the end, after having been arrested because of her role in the Resistance, she sees him alive. Both in *Il conformista* and *L'Agnese va a morire* the truth about the initial crime, and then its hidden nonexistence, is uncovered through a recognition scene, the *anagnorisis* of Greek tragedy, which itself works as the moment of truth in which the protagonist faces the riddle of time, the mystery of what was thought dead and is now alive, the recognition of the identity between what was and what is. Another recurrent *topos* is the emphasis on voyeurism, on scenes with characters spying, peering through keyholes or half-closed doors, overhearing behind screens or trying to gaze at almost invisible silhouettes hidden behind veiled windows and semitransparent curtains. Calvino's *Il sentiero dei nidi di ragno* begins precisely with the protagonist spying on his sister while she is in bed with a German soldier. Also, *Il conformista,* both film and novel, reiterates on many occasions the theme of voyeurism. In Vasco Pratolini's *Un eroe del nostro tempo* (1947), Goffredo Parise's *Il prete bello* (1953) and Florestano Vancini's film *La lunga notte del '43* (1960), the very layout of space where the story takes place favors a voyeuristic dynamic with many characters frequently depicted spying or overhearing each other. In all these cases, the subject finds the way to truth barred by all sorts of screens that, like *enigmas*, both frustrate and arouse the desire to know. Cesare Pavese's *La luna e i falò* (1949), Fenoglio's *Una questione privata*, Curzio Malaparte's *Il Cristo proibito* (1951), and Bertolucci's *Strategia del ragno* all share the same plot structure with an enigma that needs to be deciphered and a secret that awaits to be unearthed. In Pavese's novel, Nuto waits until the very end to confess to Anguilla the difficult, monstrous truth about what happened to Santina; in Fenoglio, Milton desperately tries to seize a fascist officer to offer in exchange for his captured partisan friend Giorgio to ask the latter the truth about Fulvia finally; in Malaparte the protagonist comes back to his hometown after the war, with the priority of finding and then killing the person who betrayed his partisan brother by consigning him to the Germans. The people in the hometown, even his mother, know who the traitor is but are still too wounded by the atrocities and conflicts of the war. Therefore, they place a veil of silence over the spy's identity, forestalling the hero's quest for truth and the final uncovering of how the past events actually occurred. In Bertolucci's film, the son of a local partisan martyr comes back to his hometown to enquire about the circumstances of his father's death. He will eventually discover the ambiguous nature of his father, who, instead of the partisan hero everyone thinks he was, may have actually been a traitor and a spy.

There seems always to be a gap and a disjunction between the subject and the reality of things, and in all the plots sketched above and in the many others, I will analyze in the chapters that follow how the fascist character has precisely this barring and mystifying function of standing in the way of the unveiling of truth. In most cases, they are the very object of that search. Nevertheless, in all these instances, the only attainable truths seem to be incomplete, shattered, ambiguous ones. The interpretation of the fascist type as a riddle also allows us to challenge and invert the commonly accepted view of the fascist character as a stereotype, cliché and mere villain of a melodrama. If we approach the fascist as an enigma, the clear-cut Manichean classification that grounds the 'melodramatic imagination'—as in Peter Brooks' famous work—suddenly collapses and is replaced by that multiplicity of meanings, ambivalence and ambiguity disruptive of categorizations that underlies the very social and cognitive function of riddling practices. Athos Magnani, Marcello Clerici, Sandrino, Virginia, Don Gastone, Santina, Alarico, Lucini, Pelle, Daniela/Lili Marleen, and Pino Barillari are both thematic and semantic enigmas, characters whose ambiguity thwarts the clear-cut classification of identities in fixed categories of good and evil, victim and perpetrator, fascist and antifascist, helper and villain. The expressionist caricature and grotesque mask works as a riddle that, after blocking the detection of truth and reality, actually multiplies meanings, favoring a relativity that mediates between categories, thus revealing the unsuspected and unexpected ambivalence of a certain demarcation between fascism and antifascism themselves. Through the obscurity and opacity of the riddle, a dialogizing compromise might be found between opposite and clashing concepts and political ideals. I suggest that this new approach would allow other alternative readings of those same texts, until now too frequently 'marked' by psychoanalytical interpretative narratives that, while being necessary and still mostly undeniably pertinent and valid, risk on many occasions to crystallize and limit them to discourses of repressed memory and mourning.

My work suggests that, by enabling in the text a riddling structure, the fascist might also be read as a dynamic and carnivalesque character that escapes finalization and brings ambiguity and relativity to the plot rather than a fixed and static stereotypical, uncomplicated coherence. I draw here on Mikhail Bakhtin's formulations of the carnivalesque and grotesque, as much as from his early investigations of heroes who seem to escape finalization into a coherent, 'consummated' aesthetic form. The eccentricity and festive relativity of the carnivalesque destroys the integrity of the subject's identity, revealing it to be unfinalizable in a stable form and its noncoincidence between image and meaning: «scandals and eccentricities destroy the epic and tragic wholeness of the world, they make a breach in the stable, normal ("seemly") course of human affairs and events, they free human behavior from the norms and motivations that predetermine it.»[26] Absolute contingency takes the place of necessity, as happens in the recognition scenes briefly sketched above. A similar disruption of the logical, causal sequence of cause-effect, beginning-middle-end — that forms the basis also of the narrative plot itself, as analyzed by Brooks in *Reading for the Plot* — characterizes the grotesque, that, as Bakhtin claims:

> liberates man from all the forms of inhuman necessity that direct the prevailing concept of the world. This concept is uncrowned by the grotesque and reduced to the relative and the limited. Necessity, in every concept which prevails at any time, is always one-piece, serious, unconditional, and indisputable. But historically the idea of necessity is relative and variable. The principle of laughter and the carnival spirit on which grotesque is based destroys this limited seriousness and all pretense of an extratemporal meaning and unconditional value of necessity. It frees human consciousness, thought, and imagination for new potentialities.[27]

---

26 Mikhail Bakhtin, *Problems of Dostoevsky's Poetics* (Minneapolis, London: University of Minnesota press, 1984), 117.
27 Mikhail Bakhtin, *Rabelais and His World* (Bloomington: Indiana University Press, 1984), 49.

The carnivalesque and grotesque characteristics of the fascist type make them a difficult 'hero' to finalize and enframe as *other*. The past of more or less active collaboration with the fascist regime of certain authors and the inescapable degree of sameness of the fascist as fellow Italians turn these characters into ambiguous items that the author fails to take a step back from and look at from an external, transcendental, detached perspective which would grant them that 'excess of seeing' necessary to endow the hero with a coherent, causal destiny with finalized form and meaning. As Ilya Kliger and Michael Holquist explain, at the end of an investigation of the Kantian gap opened between the self and the world by the inevitable need for language as a filter for human experience and contact with the surrounding reality:

> According to Bakhtin, the *self* perceives the world as the horizon for its activity. It is spatially, temporally, and "meaningfully" open to the surrounding world. It always projects in space toward the object of its intentionality, in time, toward the ever-receding goal in the absolute future. In a way, the *self* is contemporaneous not with its time but with its meaning: it cannot die or be born, cannot be temporally bound, but exists insofar as it continues to project itself meaningfully into the future.
> The *other*, as *other-for-me*, stands in a very different relation to the surrounding world, a relation of an object to its surroundings. In space, the other is externalized as a bounded body among other physical objects; in time, the other is temporally bound by birth and death, as if already dead and brought to life again as a hero of a biography. The bounded space and biographical time of the other is, furthermore, filled with a stable meaning, a determinate, unchangeable manner of comportment in the surrounding world.[28]

Out of the above epistemological basis, Bakhtin structures an aesthetics of narrative founded on the author-hero duality that would lead to a disruption of all synthesis and the final unveiling of all unity of either object or subject as a metaphoric configuration. In this sense, enigmas and riddles, as particularly complicated, 'looping' metaphors, deepen the gap even further. In fact, as Michael Holquist and Ilya Kliger notice, the hero, conceived as absolute projectuality, transforms the act of aesthetic contemplation from a passive, detached and disinterested one into a dynamic, vivified

---

28 Michael Holquist and Ilya Kliger, "'Minding the Gap:' Toward a Historical Poetics of Estrangement," in *Poetics Today*, Vol. 26, No. 4 (Winter, 2005), 633.

knowing process that, in a way, is perhaps adumbrated in the conception of knowledge entailed in the medieval trope of *integumentum* as analyzed by Peter Dronke. For Kliger, Bakhtin's aesthetics occupies an ambivalent position *vis-à-vis* Kant's:

> The hero can be understood as a *self*, forward-looking, project-directed and, within the parameters of his own consciousness, forever incomplete. It is only the external perspective of an *other* – the author, in possession of an essential "excess of seeing" – that endows the hero and his path with fate-like completeness and stable meaning. [...] If in Kant, the aesthetic experience of disinterested pleasure was paradigmatically conceived as a confrontation of a contemplative subject (author, producer of a coherent whole) with the object of contemplation, here, a third element is inserted between the two: the hero's pre-formative activity, vivifying the contemplated word, rendering the object of contemplation dynamic. Stable, static knowing is supplemented by a kind of knowing-in-motion, a vision of the object world as it appears to a valuating, striving, self-transcendent self-consciousness. [...] The dual synthesis of self-other that comes to replace Kant's transcendental synthesis of apperception reappears, in the realm of aesthetics, as the two-headed author-hero, the subject of contemplation-empathy supplanting the unified subject of mere disinterested contemplation.[29]

That inescapable *quid,* that inherent impossibility of capturing, remembering and communicating to an audience of non-witnesses the reality, the truth about the Resistance, about the 1943–45 civil war between fascism and antifascism, seems to be a constant 'thorn,' the recurrent regret of neorealism. Natalia Ginzburg will later talk in these terms: «Ma poi avvenne che la realtà si rivelò complessa e segreta [...]; e si rivelò ancora situata di là dal vetro, e l'illusione di aver spezzato quel vetro si rivelò effimera.»[30] Secrecy and revelation are the two poles toward which the literature of the period oscillates. The 'spirit' of those events, as in the words of Calvino, seems to be doomed to escape indeterminately just for a tiny bit to the author, who wants to approach reality with an objective stance. They occupy a position on the threshold, both inside the events as witnesses side by side with 'the masses' and outside as an author, a bourgeois intellectual inevitably linked to Tradition.

---

29 Ilya Kliger, "On Genre Memory in Bakhtin," in Ilya Kliger and Boris Maslov, edited by, *Persistent Forms. Explorations in Historical Poetics* (New York: Fordham University Press, 2016), 233.
30 Natalia Ginzburg, *Lessico famigliare* (Torino: Einaudi, 1963), 32.

Through the duality of author-hero and the introduction of a dynamic role of the hero, I aim to propose a type of approach that can 'free' certain melodramatic caricatures from the dangers of too static readings. It is a critical operation that intends to involve the reader as well as the character, casting a renewed focus on characters who are often overlooked, if not downright despised, as lowbrow, and thereby opening the way to new interpretations of both the formal and social functioning of the texts taken into consideration.

The conflict between fascism and antifascism is displaced in fiction as a conflict of formal tendencies: a realist vocation inherited from the popular oral tradition of the Resistance and expressionism derived from more traditional literature. If the vividness and closeness to the reality of things of the oral accounts get lost in the literariness of more traditional and fixed literary forms, I believe that the oral source still retains traces in 'neorealism,' as the orientation of those texts remains, in a sense, oratorical. This is an orientation which, in the words of Yuri Tynianov, commenting on Lomonosov's *Rhetoric*, consists of «diversity, surprise and unexpectedness.»[31] The final discourse in *La casa in collina* or the 'ideological' dialogue in *Il sentiero dei nidi di ragno* are examples of a tendency to speak directly to the reader and — since there is the perception of a gap between author and reality — to try to persuade, communicate, win over them by a straightforward address rather than objective representation. Therefore, the enigmatic or riddling structure might also be seen in view of this oratorical orientation toward the audience, functioning as an effective rhetorical strategy to catch the reader's attention toward that lost truth by means of frustration, surprise and finally, enriched pleasure. The fascist character is the structural element whose function is precisely to break, to create a block and then allow the junction of distant ideas and forms. Drawing again on Tynianov, we could say that this character functions as a dynamic structural component of the text, «renewing the dynamics in the relationship of factors. Such is the dialectical

---

31 Yuri Tynianov, "The Ode as an Oratorical Genre," in *New Literary History*, Vol. 34, No. 3, (Summer, 2003), 576.

development of form, modifying the correlation between the constructive principle and that which is subordinated to it.»[32] The fascist enables a sort of ambiguity of genres, transforming the text into a sort of hybrid form that borrows formal tendencies from different genre traditions. In two interesting separate remarks, Calvino notices how the two most widely diffused tendencies of postwar Italian literature were, first, the creation of a political *Bildungsroman* and, second, the fabrication of melodramatic fascist villains. The *Bildungsroman* is, in fact, the most recurrent plot structure in the period I examine.

On the one hand, authors such as Moravia in *Il conformista*, Pratolini in *Un eroe del nostro tempo,* Fenoglio in *Primavera di bellezza* and the historians in the area of the *Partito d'azione* seem to refer to its 19th century "Stendhalian" version. In contrast, Pavese in *Il compagno,* Viganò in *L'Agnese va a morire* and the historians of Marxist inspiration appear to look back at the social realist version of the genre. In the former case, the spontaneity of the hero wins over the organization by means of a higher entity (destiny, history, party). In the second instance, the organization enframes the hero's spontaneity within its caged trajectory and collective, universal goals and values. Katerina Clark draws attention to the shared structure between *bildungsroman* and social realist novels, precisely through this dynamic between spontaneity and organization, which also dominated the historiographical and political debate on the Italian resistance within the Left:

> As is generally true of ritual forms, the master-plot personalizes the general processes outlined in Marxist-Leninist historiography by encoding them in biographical terms: the positive hero passes in stages from a state of relative "spontaneity" to a higher degree of "consciousness," which he attains by some individual revolution.[33]

According to Franco Moretti, the hero of the 'classic' 18th century *bildungsroman* reaches at the end of the plot a sort of compromise between his inner, true ideals and the current social values, which

---

32 Yuri Tynianov, *The Problem of Verse Language,* (Ardis: Ann Arbor, 1981), 35.
33 Katerina Clark, *The Soviet Novel: History as Ritual* (Bloomington: Indiana University Press, 2000), 16.

are in total opposition and contrast with them. There is not, then, in the 18th century *Bildungsroman* a preference over spontaneity and organization, but a sort of accord between the two poles of individual freedom and inclusion in a collective, universal perspective. In the Stendhalian *bildungsroman,* though — and there are many 'heirs' of Julien Sorel and Fabrizio del Dongo in the works examined in this essay — the hero never actually 'buys' the imposed, external rules of social organization, and his faith in his own beliefs disrupts his formation and development. The hero is left somehow in isolation and disjointed from the rest of society: the junction between two different sets of values does not lead to a 'working' compromise but to the recognition of a gap between the two. The absorption of spontaneity into the organization is rejected, and it results in a mismatch. Postwar Italian *bildungsromane* follow this thread and are, in fact, mostly accounts of failed formations, educations, and inclusions within the social frame of the newborn republic. This is particularly evident in those *bildungsromane* that have a fascist character not as a marginal figure but as a protagonist: *Il conformista* and *Un eroe del nostro tempo*. In both cases, the fascist is a 'stranded' object whose entrance into postwar society fails. Marcello and Sandrino are *others* who, despite their attempt to conform, remain ambiguous, tabooed objects that refuse classification. They are examples of carnivalesque and dynamic heroes who refuse finalization and a clear-cut assignation of meaning. Borrowing from Hayden White, in my book, I will try to argue that the many examples of disrupted *Bildung* are the narrative shape of a parallel historiographical failure of the 'emplotment' of the fascist character within a linear, coherent scheme and categorization. The fascist past and its narrative embodiment in the fascist type are always an *enigma*. At the structural level, this means that what the riddle does with metaphors, the fascist character does with different narrative types: joining together different genres and creating hybrid texts characterized by formal ambiguity.

Moravia 'emplots' Marcello Clerici in a structure that is at once *bildungsroman* and tragedy. His great intuition was, in my opinion, to make a structural choice also work as a critical tool since Marcello's tragedy intertwines with that of Professor Quadri, whose character was 'inspired' by the exiled antifascist and leader of Giustizia e Libertà Carlo Rosselli. Marcello, I will argue, is, in fact, enframed not only in his *bildungsroman* but also in the tragedy of Professor Quadri. The emplotment of both Quadri and Marcello in a common tragic destiny—culminating in *anagnorisis* and *deus ex machina* scenes—hides a precise ideological response to, and judgment of, Carlo Rosselli and his social liberalism. Moravia, Rosselli's cousin, opposed and criticized Rosselli's antifascism as corrupt and counterproductive—Marcello is a former student of Quadri's in the fiction—given its historical roots in bourgeois liberalism and the Risorgimento nationalist tradition. Tragedy, then, becomes the narrative shape of a precise political criticism, translating, by means of the tragic fate, a determinism of Marxist inspiration. The ambiguity of genres mirrors an ideological interpretation that saw fascism, and also a type of antifascism, as two ambiguous intertwined categories.

Therefore, I am suggesting a use of narrative genres that draws from Fredric Jameson's use of generic categories «as mere ad hoc experimental constructs, devised for a specific textual occasion and abandoned like so much scaffolding when the analysis has done its work.»[34] His formulation of realism as dissymmetry, as a non-genre always on the brink of collapsing into something else, and thus of genre as an imaginary solution to real conflicts, as formal resolution of actual social contradictions, and as «a symbolic act that must reunite or harmonize heterogeneous narrative paradigms which have their own specific and contradictory ideological meaning,»[35] directed my research toward an in-depth investigation of the generic patterns characteristic of texts with fascist figures, too often considered as monolithic static traditional genres, which often use melodramatic categories. Besides the stereotype of the 19th-century melodramatic villain, the fascist activates complex generic discontinuities that might also lead to a reassessment and reconsideration of the ideological debates and contradictions that

---

34 Fredric Jameson, *The Political Unconscious* (New York: Cornell University Press, 1981), 145.
35 Ibidem, 144.

characterized postwar Italy. With this in view, my analysis proposes that observing the evolution of generic patterns and their interaction and coexistence in certain texts can lead to a more synchronic consideration of the ideological knot of fascism and antifascism—and behind it of Marxism and idealism, voluntarism and determinism—rather than 'framing' it only in the narrative of repression and resurgence that favored the products of the more mature critical and political consciousness of the 1970s over the works of two decades earlier. Through this kind of 'genre criticism,' it is possible to observe certain ideological tendencies in their latency as symbolically present in the text as specific generic categories or configurations, such as a type of character or a typical scene.

The gap between self and world, between the construction of a realist epic and historical events, is occupied by the fascist character, which—adapting Frye's terminology in *The Secular Scripture*—harmonizes the "then" narrative of romance and the "hence" one of myth. Italian literature and cinema about the fascist past might, then, be a fruitful case study to read in the light of Fredric Jameson's work on realism and his definition of the genre in *The Antinomies of Realism* as constantly menaced by melodrama, and therefore, as a battlefield between two temporalities, between the marked time of fate, of the *récit*, of the completed event, of the teleological succession of beginning-middle-end, and the 'open' unfinalized time before destiny of the eternal present, of the unnamable emotion, that is to say of affect.

In Calvino's first collection of short stories, published in 1949, there is one in particular, "Ultimo viene il corvo" (which gives the title to the whole collection), in which the fascist character reveals all of his enigmatic roles. This story, in its brevity and simplicity, yields the perfect example with which to start my inquiry. While trout fishing in a mountain stream, a group of partisans meets a young boy with an unerring aim. With one of their rifles, he is, in fact, able not only to kill one trout after the other but also a falcon up in the sky and pine cones on distant trees. Impressed by his aiming capacity, the group decides to let him join the fight. The story is told from the point of view of the young boy who seems to use the rifle as a sort of camera, a lens through which he can observe a new world unfolding in front of his eyes, and a measure with which to calculate distances between things:

> Si fece dare altre cartucce. Erano in tanti ormai a guardarlo, dietro di lui in riva al fiumicello. Le pigne in cima agli alberi dell'altra riva perché si vedevano e non si potevano toccare? Perché quella distanza vuota tra lui e le cose? Perché le pigne che erano una cosa con lui, nei suoi occhi, erano invece là, distanti? Però se puntava il fucile la distanza vuota si capiva che era un trucco; lui toccava il grilletto e nello stesso momento la pigna cascava, troncata al picciòlo. Era un senso di vuoto come una carezza: quel vuoto della canna del fucile che continuava attraverso l'aria e si riempiva con lo sparo, fin laggiù alla pigna, allo scoiattolo, alla pietra bianca al fiore di papavero. [...]
> Andare via era bello perché a ogni svolta si vedevano cose nuove, licheni sulle pietre, tutte cose nel raggio delle distanze finte, delle distanze che lo sparo riempiva inghiottendo l'aria di mezzo.[36]

Not only is the story told from his point of view, but the 'point of view' is the very object of the story. With the rifle, the young hero begins to be aware of perspective as an illusion and of the space that separates him from the surrounding world. The rifle makes him think that there is no distance between himself and things because the moment he presses the trigger, the target falls, and all that space and distance seem to be annihilated. Between the time of the shot and the space linking him as subject with the target as object of the shot, there seems to be a disjunction, a mysterious gap. Since the other partisans forbid him to shoot at whatever he sees moving, he decides to take the rifle with him and venture alone into the forest.

---

36 Italo Calvino, "Ultimo viene il corvo," in *Ultimo viene il corvo* (Milano: Mondadori, 2002), 126-127. «They gave him some more cartridges when he asked for them. Lots of men were looking on now from the bank behind him. Why, he thought, could he see the pine cones at the tops of the trees on the other bank and not touch them? Why was there this empty distance between things and himself? Why were the pine cones—which seemed part of him, inside his eyes—so far away instead? Surely it was an illusion when he aimed the gun into the empty distance and touched the trigger and at the same second a pine cone dropped in smithereens? The sense of emptiness felt like a caress—emptiness inside the rifle barrel continuing through the air and filling out when he shot; the pine cone up there, a squirrel, a white stone, a butterfly. [...] It was fine to leave, because there were new things to be seen at every turn, trees with cones, birds flying from branches, lichen on stones, all at those false distances, the distances that could be filled by a shot swallowing the air in between.» [Calvino, "The Crow Comes Last," in *Difficult Loves*, trans. by Archibald Colquhoun and Peggy Wright (New York: Harvest/HBJ Book, 1985), 96-97.

His journey proceeds aimlessly with no other logic than moving from target to target. He kills in sequence: one hare, partridges, a red mushroom, pine cones, jays, a dormouse, a lizard, a big snail, and a frog. Suddenly, warned by the gunshots, a group of German soldiers start running after him, and he kills one of them, aiming at one small button of his uniform. As the other partisans come to rescue him, he and another German soldier start a private duel, chasing and firing at each other and eventually ending in an isolated field. Tracked down by the fire of the young boy, the desperate Nazi soldier hides behind a rock, with no possible way out: if he tries to put his head out, the young boy will instantly kill him as he holds him up at gunpoint, not too far away. As soon as the soldier hides behind the rock, something curious happens in the story: a sudden, unexpected shift of point of view. The author, in fact, abandons the point of view and the viewfinder of the protagonist and now tells the story from the enemy's point of view, from the object's perspective. We are now dragged into the suspended time of the target's wait for the right moment to run away. In order to seize the right opportunity, the soldier begins, then, to interpret his enemy's behavior to find a logical and rational motivation for the order and cause behind his shots. In fact, the soldier notices — but we readers already know this — that the partisan, while waiting for him to come out, 'kills the time' by shooting at every bird he sees moving around the rock: a song thrush, a snipe, a cockerel. He infers from this a causal plot, a rational thread, motivating the boy's conduct. Therefore, when he sees a raven beginning to descend slowly in circles toward them, the soldier expects the partisan to aim at the raven and kill the bird. The boy, though, instead of shooting at the raven — which keeps descending and getting closer to the ground — shoots at pine cones:

> A ogni sparo il soldato guardava il corvo: cadeva? No, l'uccello nero girava sempre più basso sopra di lui. Possibile che il ragazzo non lo vedesse? Forse il corvo non esisteva, era una sua allucinazione. Forse chi stava per morire vede passare tutti gli uccelli: quando vede il corvo vuol dire che è l'ora. Pure, bisognava avvertire il ragazzo che continuava a sparare alle pigne. Allora il soldato si alzò in piedi e indicando l'uccello nero col dito, — Là c'è il corvo! — gridò, nella sua lingua. Il proiettile lo prese giusto in mezzo a un'aquila ad

ali spiegate che aveva ricamata sulla giubba.
Il corvo s'abbassava lentamente, a giri.³⁷

First, the mysterious shift of perspective, now the final riddle: why does the partisan not follow his previous logic and shoot at the raven? The change of perspective makes us readers, for just a little while, know more than the soldier. He needs to look at and infer the logic that seems to guide the shots. Once he understands that, the reader and the character are once again united, both sharing the same expectation and surprise: yes, from what we have seen, the young boy should shoot at the raven. The fact that he delays the shot is frankly illogical. What is even more so is that the partisan will kill the soldier by aiming at the eagle on his uniform. In a way, then, this final shot seems to follow once again the previous logic since he does aim at a bird. But if so, why then did he not aim at the raven, too? At once irrational and rational, the short story ends with a veritable enigma. Was his not shooting at the raven part of a strategy to fool the German soldier? It seems unlikely given his naïve 'hillbilly' nature and also given the fact that he at last points at the eagle. This last detail, in fact, seems to reconstruct the rational causality that structured the short tale from its beginning. The Nazi falls victim to his deductive operation because of the mismatch separating his expectations, the way his mind 'emplotted' the actions of his enemy, from the way the events betrayed his calculations, escaping the finalization of the mental scheme framing reality. The death of the fascist character is an enigma, and it is emplotted as a failure to frame reality within a coherent, completed series of events, as the disruption breaks the scheme and reveals it as a mere image and illusion of the subject's observation of reality.

---

37 Idem, 130. «At every shot the soldier looked at the crow; was he falling? No, the black bird was making lower and lower turns above him. Surely it was impossible the boy hadn't seen it? Perhaps the crow did not exist? Perhaps it was an hallucination of his? Perhaps when one is about to die one sees every kind of bird pass; when one sees the crow it means one's time has come. He must warn the boy, who was still going on firing at the pine cones. So the soldier got to his feet and pointed at the black bird. "There's a crow!" he shouted in his own language. The bullet hit him in the middle of an eagle with spread wings embroidered on his tunic. Slowly the crow came circling down.» [Calvino, *The Crow Comes Last*, trans. by Archibald Colquhoun and Peggy Wright, 101.]

Maybe the boy learned the lesson that by means of the viewfinder, by embracing his rifle as a film camera, perspectival vision is nothing but an illusion, a subjective distortion of space. The final riddle is activated precisely through an unexpected, because narratively unjustified, change of perspective. Through a perfect estrangement, the self is seen from the point of view of the other, and what was believed to be rational reveals its simultaneous irrationality. The gap separating self and other is inhabited by the illusionary organizing principles of the narrative, of the plot. The automatic process of the young boy advancing from target to target is disrupted by the estrangement that lays bare the boundaries between fiction and reality, enabling the subject to see reality once again. If Calvino had kept on narrating the story from the point of view of the boy, the tale would have stayed limited by the automatization of its logic. Paradoxically, it is the estrangement that allows the raven to be seen but not shot that allows the object to be different from all the preceding objects in the series. In a way, it is the estrangement that causes the death of the fascist. The young partisan, by aiming at reality through the lens of the rifle-camera, engages in a sort of miniature optics-*bildungsroman*—at the end of which he learns that his looking deforms the things he looks at, and then he is able to look at himself from the point of view of the other, guessing what the other is expecting from him—the fascist is killed by that *bildung* which has culminated in the estranged understanding of the world. Calvino enframes the duel between a fascist and a partisan as a riddle and as a playful reflection on perspective and on the unbridgeable "false distance" between the self and the world that narrative inhabits.

CHAPTER 1
The Palimpsest of *Il conformista*: from Moravia to Bertolucci

1.1 A Mysterious Object Difficult to Aim at: Marcello Emplots his Life.

Il conformista starts with a long prologue, almost a self-sufficient short story, which, I believe, is one of the clearest examples of Moravia's narrative style. Three are the key points in this sort of tragic introduction to the rest of the novel: first, a not clearly defined, underlying obscurity; second, the coquetry of the protagonist; third, his fallacious aim. The protagonist, Marcello Clerici, whom we first encounter in the prologue as a boy, is a synthesis of these three qualities.

Everything in the first fifty pages is mysterious and obscure; everything seems to happen obscurely to the eyes of the protagonist, who, himself, feels creeping inside his soul deep, dark passions and instincts. Two, among others, the impulse to kill and a still unaware homosexual desire. Marcello perceives the world obscurely; the relationship between the self and his surroundings is not direct, but a cloud of uncertainty and obliquity mediates it. He thinks almost exclusively through premonitions, presentiments, forebodings, and suspicions: «oscuramente pensava.»[38] Reality seems to hide the true meaning of things behind a screen, a veil: objects and events are perceived by the young mind as signs of something else, something yet to come or, in any case, never present. Marcello thinks that because he likes to kill animals, then he will be predisposed to kill human beings, too, and this murderous tendency means to him that he is, and will always be, evil by nature. His acts are «misteriosamente intrisi di colpevolezza.»[39] He recognizes

---

[38] Alberto Moravia, *Il conformista* in *Opere Complete vol. 8* (Milano: Bompiani, 1975), 7 «Dimly he thought» Moravia, *The Conformist*, translated by Tami Calliope (Hanover, New Hampshire: Zoland Books, 1999), 7
[39] Idem., «mysteriously soaked in guilt.» 5

himself guilty of killing the lizards, the cat, and, at last, his friend Roberto, but his acts are only vaguely guilty. Why? Because he feels that something else made him do those forbidden, immoral acts, an obscure energy:

> la forza oscura, malefica, astuta ed estranea, tutta colorata delle tinte brune della fatalità e della disgrazia, che l'aveva portato, quasi suo malgrado, dallo sterminio dei fiori alla strage delle lucertole e da questa al tentativo di uccidere Roberto.[40]

Marcello has, since the beginning, a melodramatic imagination. His world not only «bears the stamp of meaning»[41] in which everything is a «sign of something else,»[42] but it is also animated by what Brooks defines as «the moral occult,»[43] that is:

> the domain of operative spiritual values, which is both indicated within and masked by the surface of reality [...] It bears comparison to the unconscious mind, for it is a sphere of being where our most basic desires and interdictions lie, a realm which in quotidian existence may appear closed off from us but which we must accede to since it is the realm of meaning and value. The melodramatic mode in large measure exists to locate and to articulate the moral occult.[44]

The omnipresent, latent obscurity and mystery lurking in Marcello's world, as his young mind perceives it, is already typical of the melodramatic mode. A moral Manichaeism is already set in the prologue, and the whole novel will soon appear as the

> scene of dramatic choice between heightened moral alternatives, where every gesture, however frivolous or insignificant it may seem, is charged with the conflict between light and darkness.[45]

---

40 Ibidem., «the obscure, maleficent, astute, and extraneous force, colored completely with the dark shades of fatality and misfortune, that had carried him almost despite himself from the extermination of the flowers to the massacre of the lizards and from this to the attempt to murder Roberto.» 27
41 Peter Brooks, *The Melodramatic Imagination* (New Haven: Yale University Press, 1976), 10
42 Idem., 11
43 Idem., 5
44 Ibidem.
45 Ibidem.

Every crime is in a metonymic relation to the next and a more serious one. A sort of mysterious, inescapable necessity is perceived to guide his acts, linked by his imagination in a meaningful metonymic causal succession.

Having briefly noticed the curious frequency of words belonging to the semantic field of obscurity, mystery, and enigma, I will now introduce another key trait of Marcello's personality: he is a coquette. In fact, when approached by the chauffeur Lino and when his classmates forced him to wear a dancing tutu, he feels once again an obscure pleasure in letting them do what they want to him. He only weakly tries to resist. This is the definition of "civetteria" found in the *Vocabolario della lingua italiana Treccani:*

> l'abitudine del civettare, leggerezza, volubilità; anche più semplicemente, desiderio di attirare comunque l'attenzione su di sé e una benevola simpatia o ammirazione.

The word comes from the French *coquetterie,* and Lucien, the protagonist of Sartre's *L'Enfance d'un Chef* — one of the main sources of the novel — owns this same quality as well:

> «Tu as des belles fesses», dit soudain Bergère. Lucien croyait faire un cauchemar: «Elles vous plaisent?» Demanda-t-il avec coquetterie.[46]

In *Le Grand Robert de la langue française* "coquetterie" is the

> souci de se faire valoir pour plaire…souci de plaire aux personnes de l'autre sexe, attitude quelque peu provocante…Désir de susciter et d'entretenir chez quelqu'un un amour que l'on n'est pas disposé à partager, à contenter.

Civetteria is the typical and always recurrent feature of Moravia's characters, indistinctively related to men or women. It becomes the psychological tendency of a whole class: the Italian bourgeois and its guilt of flirting with the fascist regime. In its mixture of passivity and desire both to stimulate the other's action and to draw their attention, *civetteria* perfectly translates, within the psychology of the individual, the national problem of conformism with Fascism. Moreover, *civetteria* is an attitude that relieves one of the responsibilities by simultaneously foreshadowing guilt. It is a synthesis of difference and indifference, of responsibility and innocence, of

---

46 Jean Paul Sartre, *L'Enfance d'un Chef* (Paris: Gallimard, 1939), 201

desire and resistance, of innate volition and external constriction. It is, in a way, related to that very obscurity I described above. Both qualities imbue the hero's character with passivity and lack of personality, always ready to leave all responsibilities and the agency of his life to something other: an obscure, undefined impulse for both a denied and craved object of desire. The coquetry is the visible, bodily consequence of the obscure, mysterious impulses troubling the self that, at this point, risks losing all free will and power of decision-making. The *civetta* wants to conquer for the sake of the conquest alone, an undesired object, or, better, an object that becomes desirable only when it stimulates and incites the vanity of the subject. I do not see what I want, and I see what wants me. I desire a gaze on me. The perspective must be reversed. Looking obscurely at the world requires a gaze that goes from the subject to the object, while coquetry makes the subject invite the other to look. The trajectory is reversed.

The last part of the prologue is dominated by a problem of aim: Marcello's view towards the world and his object of desire is defective, and the targets he sees are always doubled or split. Given that Moravia read and wrote about Machiavelli, I believe the slingshot scene in the prologue to be a reference to *The Prince*.

In Book VI of *The Prince*, Machiavelli warns the founders of new monarchies against a too-ambitious imitation of the most excellent men and of their past perfection and exploits. He does so by means of the fascinating, highly ambiguous simile of the mindful archer: in order to hit an apparently distant target, he inclines his arch to raise the degree of his aim, not because he actually intends to reach that height, but because, before shooting the arrow, he first valued the virtue of his arch:

> Debbe uno uomo prudente intrare sempre per vie battute da uomini grandi, e quelli che sono stati eccellentissimi imitare, acciò che, se la sua virtù non vi arriva, almeno ne renda qualche odore: e fare come li arcieri prudenti; a' quali, parendo el loco dove disegnano ferire troppo lontano, e conoscendo fino a quanto va la virtù del loro arco, pongono la mira assai più alta che il loco destinato, non per aggiugnere con la loro freccia a tanta altezza, ma per potere con lo aiuto di sì alta mira pervenire al disegno loro.[47]

---

47 Niccolò Machiavelli, *Il Principe* (Torino: Einaudi, 1961), 26. «A prudent man must always enter by paths beaten by great men and imitate those who have

Thus, he imagines a second mark above the real one, and by this higher and fictive aim, Machiavelli implies that an imitation of those past virtuous princes cannot be fully fulfilled by the present ones. In their potentialities, after having considered the actual material quality of the means now at their disposal, there is only a kind of approximation: nothing can be added to the past perfect virtues: there will always be a missing surplus preventing the final, total overlapping. In other terms, here Machiavelli is saying both that those excellent examples should be imitated and that, at the same time, a complete imitation is not only impossible but also imprudent. Thus, the simile is not a real simile, or at the very least, it is an unorthodox one. In fact, it is stating its purpose only to deny it simultaneously. *Imitate! Not too mindlessly, though.* The archer diverts his imitative gaze from the real target to the higher and fictive one as a consequence of the much more tangible relationship with the material virtue of the arch. Hence, the resulting arched trajectory is already there, since the beginning, in the arch itself, and it is not a result of the *alta mira*'s object, of the transcendent and perfect end of its line of sight.

Il conformista opens with a similar "problem of aim." The scene represents not only a prologue within a prologue, anticipating the assassination of Lino but also the first and simplest form in which the main idea of the entire novel is translated and presented to the reader. The rest of the plot will be nothing but repetition and an imitation of the syllogistic exemplarity of this short episode.

As a child, Marcello was inclined to destroy the flowers and kill the small lizards in his garden. Even if he is a child, he suddenly perceives this disposition to be unusual, perverse, abnormal. One day, he confesses the killings to his friend Roberto in search of a comprehensive word that could suddenly straighten his

---

been most excellent, so that if his own virtue does not reach it, at least it might be able to yield some of its scent: and do like prudent archers who, the place where they intend to wound seeming too far, and knowing how far the virtue of their bow reaches, aim much higher than the destined place, not to reach such height with their arrow, but in order to be able to attain their design with the aid of such high aim.» Machiavelli, *The Prince,* translated by Angelo M. Codevilla (New Haven: Yale UP, 1997), 20.

abnormality. Contrary to his expectations and hopes, Roberto confirms his fears: to kill lizards is evil. In his imagination now, he is at war with Roberto, and, one day, armed with his slingshot, he climbs the wall covered with ivy that separates his garden from his friend's house, being ready to shoot at the first slight movement or noise his eye is able to perceive:

> Nella sua fantasia, la casa era un castello, la cancellata nascosta dal rampicante, le mura fortificate, e il pertugio una breccia pericolosa e facilmente valicabile. Allora, improvvisamente e questa volta senza possibilità di dubbio, vide le foglie muoversi da destra a sinistra, tremando e oscillando. Sì, ne era certo, le foglie si muovevano e qualcuno doveva pur farle muovere. Tutto in un sol momento pensò che Roberto non c'era, che era un gioco e che, visto che era un gioco, lui poteva tirare il sasso; e al tempo stesso che Roberto c'era e lui non doveva tirare il sasso se non voleva ammazzarlo. Poi, con subitanea e spensierata decisione, tese gli elastici e scagliò il sasso nel folto delle foglie. Non contento, si chinò, febbrilmente incastrò un altro sasso nella fionda, lo tirò, ne prese un terzo, tirò anche quello. Ormai aveva messo da parte scrupoli e timori e non gli importava più che Roberto ci fosse o non ci fosse.[48]

Shortly after, he peers through the ivy, checking whether or not he hit something or someone. The view of a big gray cat lying lifeless a few meters away suddenly fills his body with a strange feeling of uneasiness and terror:

> Uccidendo il gatto, in realtà, aveva avuto intenzione di uccidere Roberto. Soltanto il caso aveva voluto che il gatto fosse morto in luogo dell'amico. Un caso, però, non privo di senso; che non si poteva negare che ci fosse stata progressione dai fiori alle lucertole, dalle lucertole al gatto e dal gatto

---

48   Moravia, *Il Conformista*, 14. «In his fantasy, the house was a castle, the railings hidden by the creeper the fortified walls, and the opening a dangerous and easily crossed breach. Then, suddenly and this time without any possibility of doubt, he saw the leaves move from right to left, trembling and rocking. Yes, he was sure of it, the leaves were moving and someone must have made them move. All in the same moment he thought that Roberto was not there, that it was only a game and that, since it was only a game, he could hurl the stone; and at the same time, that Roberto was there and that he should not hurl the stone unless he wanted to kill him. Then, with instant and thoughtless decision, he pulled back the bands and let fly the stone into the heart of the leaves. Not content with this, he bent down feverishly inserted another stone in the slingshot, shot it, put in a third stone and shot that one, too. By now he had put fears and scruples aside and no longer cared whether Roberto was there or not.» (Moravia, *The Conformist*, 15-16.)

> all'omicidio di Roberto pensato e voluto seppure non eseguito ma tuttora eseguibile e, forse, inevitabile. [...] Guardava e, tutto ad un tratto, quasi per sovraimpressione, gli parve di vedere in luogo del gatto, Roberto, anche lui disteso tra gli iris.[49]

Like the archer in *The Prince*, Marcello, in order to hit the envisioned target, his friend Roberto, imagines a second, misaligned and, as we will see, actually non-existent one, the cat. That same night, in fact, while having dinner with his parents, he is struck by the fleeting appearance of the cat's silhouette on the windowsill. If the cat is still alive, that logical progression connecting the lizards to the cat and, in the end, to Roberto is nothing but an illusionary sequence and its supposed necessity is revealed as a contingency. Paraphrasing Machiavelli, Marcello did not consider well the material virtue of his arch, willing to impose on reality the perfect, logical symmetry of a scheme. His thinking provides an event that was simply an *accident*, with meaning within a system of cause and effect: the three homicides, in increasing order of importance, confirm his deviance.

The climax of the prologue is the assassination of Lino, the third and most important of the crimes he commits when still a child. One day, after having been seduced by the idea of possessing a real revolver, he responds to the veiled flirting of Lino, the older chauffeur of some aristocratic Roman family. Their ambiguous game of retraction and seduction, of coquetry and sexual desire, will tragically end after a second encounter: Marcello kills Lino with that same revolver that was supposed to be the reward of his sexual 'favors.' At this point of the novel, Marcello is sure, and we readers are too, that he actually killed Lino, even though his guilt will never come to light. Some ten years later, now an adult but still obsessed with the past crime, he finds the final proof of his innocence in an old newspaper's account of those facts: Lino, it is

---

[49] Idem., 15-16. «While killing the cat he had, in reality, intended to kill Roberto. It was only by chance that the cat had died in place of his friend. A not insignificant chance, however, since it was undeniable that there had been a progression from the flowers to the lizards, from the lizards to the cat, and from the cat to the murder of Roberto, thought about and desired and, although not executed, still possible and perhaps even inevitable. [...] He looked at it and all of a sudden, almost as if superimposed there, he seemed to see Roberto in place of the cat, he too stretched among the iris.» (Moravia, *The Conformist*, 17).

written, died while cleaning his revolver. The crime was archived as nothing but a tragic accident:

> Voltò in fretta la pagina e, nella cronaca nera, come si aspettava, trovò la notizia, con un titolo su una colonna: *mortale incidente*. [...] La notizia non avrebbe potuto essere più concisa né più convenzionale, pensò subito rileggendola. Tuttavia, pur con le formule logore del giornalismo più anonimo rivelava due fatti importanti. Il primo che Lino era morto davvero, cosa di cui era stato sempre convinto ma che non aveva mai avuto il coraggio di accertare; il secondo che questa morte era stata attribuita per evidente suggerimento del moribondo ad una *casuale disgrazia*.[50]

Marcello will make this 'accident' his original sin and the true beginning of his future life as a good man, a good husband and a 'good soldier' within the ranks of the fascist police. He sees the crime as a sign of his deviant personality and perversity, the homosexual desire and inclination towards evil that he needs now to sublimate and to keep silent. In the end, this difference needs to be changed into indifference, and then the crime is now elected by his mind as the perfect cause upon which a complete and unambiguous submission to fascism has to be grounded. From the beginning, he is drawn by his imagination into a «cerchio maledetto dei presagi e delle fatalità»[51] that gives his vision a tendency to

---

50 Moravia, *Il conformista*, 61. «He turned the page hurriedly and found the news in the crime reports, as he had expected, with a headline above one column that read: FATAL ACCIDENT. [...] The report could not have been more concise or conventional, he thought, rereading it. All the same, even the worn-out formulas of the most anonymous journalism revealed two important facts. The first was that Lino was really dead, something of which he had always been convinced but had never had the courage to confirm; the second was that this had been attributed, evidently by suggestion of the dying man, to *accident*.» (Moravia, *The Conformist*, 67-68.) In the above translation by Tami Calliope, both the Italian *incidente* and *disgrazia* are translated by the same word: *accident*. Even so, there is a slight, but significant, difference. *Disgrazia* more literally would mean *misfortune*, and in Italian has a religious meaning which in this particular case is very notable. *Disgrazie* usually come from God. In fact, Marcello thinks *casuale disgrazia* should have been suggested by Lino, and Lino is a defrocked priest. Moreover, to connote a *disgrazia* as *casual*, is a sort of oxymoron, since the loss of divine Grace cannot be, by definition, merely accidental. Then, Marcello ascribes to Lino the belief that Marcello's reaction and refusal was in reality the God's way to punish him for his sexual weakness and 'perverse' desire.

51 Idem., 24. «the cursed circle of presentiments and fate.» (Moravia, *The Conformist*, 28.)

homogenization: he sees reality as order, symmetry and progression, in which events are the cause and effect of other events, in which everything refers to everything for the sake of analogy and of mental association. In this case, the mind of a fascist functions as a kind of Proustian mind.[52] Marcello's first means of measuring reality and of giving it a readable meaning are metonymy and prolepsis. His main ambition was since he was a child, to «far entrare il suo atto in un *ordine* purchessia.»[53] The *purchessia,* the 'whatever it is,' is the key word here, indicating the absence of voluntary choice and the presence of indifference towards the kind of order to which he will give his preference. Potentially, any order would be fine. Every action or twist of fate at this point is traced back to a precise reason. His credo is: «affondare lo strumento del pensiero in un terreno fertile di analogie e di significati.»[54] Nothing can remain a mere coincidence, and, on the contrary, it must be turned into the anticipatory sign of a predestination. In other words, this first crime acquires meaning and 'normality' only insomuch as a prefiguration of a second murder that would finally transform its contingency into a necessity, into the beginning of an end:

> We reinterpret beginnings from the perspective of the end, eliciting from this totality a theme, thought or meaning. [...] Narrative activity is precisely the redemption, recuperation or transformation of succession into meaning.[55]

This second crime is the political assassination of Professor Quadri, an Italian antifascist leader and intellectual expatriated in Paris who is maneuvering resistance from over the Alps. Right after he is charged with the mission, Marcello suddenly perceives it as somehow obscurely referring back to his childhood's tragic crime: «in maniera oscura egli intuiva che un nesso sottile univa queste due

---

52 In this sense Bertolucci's 1970 adaptation refers back directly to *La Recherche* more than to Moravia's text.
53 Moravia, *Il conformista,* 11. «making some sort of sense of what he had done.» (Moravia, *The Conformist,* 12.)
54 Idem., 136. «sinking the tool of his reflection into soil fertile with analogies and significance.» (Moravia, *The Conformist,* 153.)
55 J. M. Bernstein, *The Philosophy of the Novel – Lúkacs, Marxism and the Dialectics of Form* (Minneapolis: University of Minnesota Press, 1984), 110.

cose.»[56] The international and universal motivation of the mission overlaps here with the wholly private meaning it acquires in relation to Marcello's innermost drive. Fascism becomes the *whatever*, the *purchessia* order in which his perversity can deviate back again into a normal, straight-lined purpose and trajectory. That crime would be canceled by the political and successive one.

When Quadri is finally killed, again in a *coquette* way, Marcello being not the material executor but just the passive observer, the end finally gives sense to the beginning. Earlier, with the proleptic projection of the past forward into a future purpose, and now with the retrospective meaning given to a past event, Marcello creates a plot through which his perverse life becomes the cause of a normal, meaningful autobiography: the story of a formation, an education, a *bildungsroman*. The adventitious death of Lino has to be repeated by the political death of Quadri in order to acquire a higher sense and, then, to be retrospectively justified. The space enclosed between the two crimes is the imagined time for a revelatory plot, in which Marcello passes from being a mere actor to being the «stage manager of his own destiny, constantly projecting the self into the future on the basis of hypothetical plots.»[57] Marcello, through his imagination, can grasp that his life as a whole has a progression temporally ordered and directed towards the repetition of the past in the future. Metonymy, time and repetition form the plot, which mediates between the I and a reality that, if it had been perceived with immediacy, would have appeared as chaos. It doubles reality by making an event the significant action with which it becomes possible to realize and accomplish the desired end:

> In repetition, then, the historicality of action is fully realized as thematised, action becoming what it always, tacitly, is: the taking up of the past as the sole locus of potentialities for future action. The extensiveness of human life as stretching between birth and death is gathered together in order that these natural boundaries of action become constitutive horizons for action, the meaning of action being the gathering and relating of beginning and end.[58]

---

56 Moravia, *Il conformista*, 98. «He intued dimly that a subtle link united these two things.» (Moravia, *The Conformist*, 109.)
57 Brooks, *Reading for the Plot* (Cambridge: Harvard University Press, 1992), 72.
58 J. M. Bernstein, *The Philosophy of the Novel*, 135.

Marcello projects that first accident through a temporal trajectory, imagining for it a sort of delay, of duration before the repetition of a crime that is both the same and different. His life now is a coherent whole which he holds together by «an act of temporal synthesis»[59] which casts upon its parts a common meaning. Lino and Quadri metonymically superimpose into one figure, and Marcello, while centering one mark, has to focus his aim on the other, 'six inches above' one, the imagined target of a totalizing plot. Once again, we are confronted here with a problem of aim.

From this succession, Marcello can finally imagine his own life as the result of a unique, totalizing inclination towards a destiny of crime and death:

> Finding the right sequence of events, putting together the revelatory plot, depends on uncovering that "line of sight", that aim and intention, that will show how incidents link together.[60]

1.2 The Recognition Scene: The Disruption of Marcello's Plot.

Both Lino and Quadri find here, in the cat scene, their prefiguration. Nevertheless, another vision will, on the very same night of the cat's death, question the solidity of Marcello's analogies and 'line of sight.' In fact, while sitting at the dinner table with his parents, he suddenly sees a shadow too rapidly appearing and disappearing on the windowsill: he is now convinced it must have been the cat he thought was dead. The consequence is as obvious and as potentially destructive as all of his narrative: if he did not kill the cat, he did not kill Roberto. This revelation of the crime to be nothing but an apparent crime will be the turning point not only in this episode but in the entire plot of the novel. Indeed, towards the end of the story, a recognition scene comes out of nothing, revealing all of Marcello's plot and narrative of repetition and justification to be an illusion founded on a fatal error, an error of sight indeed: after the war is over and the fascist regime has fallen, one night in the Roman

---

59 Idem, 115.
60 Brooks, *Reading for the Plot*, 35.

park of Villa Borghese, a notorious meeting place for male prostitutes, he again meets Lino who, evidently, did not die at all. Suddenly, the recognition collapses the entire narrative construction that, in Marcello's imagination, would have linked the two crimes: the first crime being nothing but the absence of a crime, thus revealing instead the inexistence of the beginning and, as the logical outcome, of its continuation too. «Ci fu un equivoco,»[61] Lino says to a surprised Marcello, who killed Quadri exactly as a direct consequence of his first 'murder' of Lino, which is now revealed to be nothing more than a «delitto immaginario.»[62] After the recognition of Lino, the execution of Quadri loses its necessity, its essence as a meaningful and predicted end, and it rests, on the contrary, as isolated contingency and misfortune. There is not a first, past crime already implying the second one as its cause. By creating his plot of prefiguration, prolepsis and analogy of conformism between two unrelated events, Marcello intended precisely to deny the contingent basis of his life, narrative and political engagement:

> In having followed a story we view all that has preceded from the point of view of the end, we view the sequence of events as a pattern, as parts belonging to a whole. Narrative understanding involves the cancelling out of the *contingency* of events and actions as revealed in the following of the story, and their retrieval in a whole which by fully coordinating them renders their meaning determinate.[63]

The death of Lino is an imaginary and necessary myth, starting from which Marcello can provide his life with a direction, a finality pointing to the subsequent death of Quadri. This second crime is the true encounter upon which both the plot of the novel and the political plot of conformism found their origin and cause. It is that second mark that is finally revealed as lacking any reference to reality, to the virtue of Marcello himself. The encounter has to remain isolated, a singular and immediate event. It does not acquire meaning through a metonymic and causal relation with a second copy, an event which, as repetition, gives meaning to the first part of the

---

61 Moravia, *Il conformista*, 276. «there was a mistake.» (*The Conformist*, 312.)
62 Idem., 277. «imaginary crime (*The Conformist*, 313.)
63 Bernstein, *The Philosophy of the Novel*, 132.

sequence. The encounter is not the end which can be anticipated, predicted and foreshadowed because: «every encounter is aleatory in its effects, in that nothing in the elements of the encounter prefigures, before the actual encounter, the contours and determinations of the being that will emerge from it.»[64]

If the political conformism of Marcello to fascism has its cause in the death of Quadri, as the outcome of a lifelong plot, the «rejection of all finality»[65] implied by the recognition of the contingency of that same crime unmasks that same conformism as lacking any necessary basis. Fascism is just a *purchessia* order, as Quadri was a *purchessia* target. After the recognition of Lino, everything seems to lose its definite contours; even Professor Quadri is described first with the connotations of Machiavelli's *Prince,* second with those of Dostoevsky's Great Inquisitor, and, third, the way his dead body is positioned, with that of his wife, exactly duplicates the infamous photography of the dead bodies of Mussolini and Claretta Petacci. Indeed, Quadri is associated with all these, both historic and fictional figures, thus looking more like a product of Marcello's imagination than of reality. This is the photographic description of how the two bodies were lying on the grass, with the head of his wife obliquely leaning on Quadri's chest:

> Quadri era disteso supino e di lui non si vedevano che le spalle e la testa, e di questa soltanto il mento con la gola attraversata dalla riga nera di un taglio. Invece, di Lina, gettata un po' di traverso sul marito, si scorgeva la persona intera.[66]

The face of his enemy blurs and overlaps with his prince's face, suggesting in this way the groundless nature of his faith and obedience to Fascism. Roberto, Lino, Quadri and Mussolini are all «empty configurations»[67] demonstrating the «instability of motivation in

---

64 Louis Althusser, *The Underground Current of the Materialism of the Encounter* (New York: Verso, 2006), 193.
65 Idem., 79.
66 Moravia, *Il conformista*, 246. «Quadri was stretched out on his back and all you could see of him were his shoulders and head, and of this only the chin and the throat, sliced across with the black line of a knife cut. You could see Lina's whole body, however, thrown partway across her husband's.» (Moravia, *The Conformist*, 280.)
67 Brooks, *Reading for The Plot*, 79.

relation to result.⁶⁸» and the necessity of appropriating those 'deaths', two imaginary and two real, to a common plot «which implies the rejection of merely contingent (or unassimilable) incident or action.»⁶⁹ Nothing can be valuable in itself:

> What makes the world intelligible are abstract, a priori concepts. Every account of life, every way of ordering empirical discourse which would make it intelligible is an interpretation of that discourse in terms of a conceptual, theoretical system not immanent to empirical discourse.⁷⁰

The encounter is, on the contrary, the rejection of all finality. It states the necessity of contingency. This is, I think, the ultimate meaning of the recognition scene between Lino and Marcello. Nevertheless, the scene hides more, being a problematic paradox: Marcello's illusionary plot is unmasked and deprived of its necessary foundation, precisely by means of one of the most important devices of plot, i.e., the Aristotelian, tragic *anagnorisis*. The metonymy, the contingency of the character's plot is interrupted, split by the intrusion of the outer plot of the author himself. The resurrection of Lino has no roots in the plot that can justify its occurrence. Resurrection and subsequent recognition, then, reveal all the preceding plot as a sort of *leurre*.⁷¹ Moravia's plot was a lie no less than Marcello's illusionary narrative. The author lied to his characters by omitting the nonexistence of what Marcello took as the cause of all his future behavior. Both plots are delays, dilatory spaces, and enigmas, described by Barthes as follows:

> narrativement, une énigme conduit d'une question à un réponse *à travers un certain nombre de retards*. De ces retards, le principal est sans doute la feinte, la fausse réponse, le mensonge, que nous appellerons la *leurre*. Le discours a déjà menti par prétérition [...] *la cause vraie*.[emphasis mine]⁷²

Il conformista is an unparalleled and overlooked metanarrative reflection on plot, first of all, because the main theme of the novel is its protagonist, Marcello, who tries to adapt his life to a coherent narrative whole. He imagines the two crimes of his life, Lino and

---

68 Ibid.
69 Idem., 91.
70 Bernstein, *The Philosophy of the Novel*, 98.
71 Barthes, Roland, *S/Z*, (Paris: Editions du Seuil, 1970), 39.
72 Ibidem.

Quadri, to be one the cause of the other. The true plot of *Il conformista* is, then, the invention of a plot as an intermediation between the self and his trajectory in the world. The hero, as we have seen, creates a plot in order to justify and make linear and clear his obscure, mysterious tendencies and predispositions. He needs to create a plausible, verisimilar story.

Nevertheless, he fails, and I believe he fails because Marcello is a fascist character and, as we will see, one of a unique kind. Moreover, the novel itself was considered to be a failure, one of Moravia's weakest works. Italian critics despised it in particular because of a narrative inaccuracy: the resurrection of Lino. The recognition scene was implausible, a narrative inconsistency that made the verisimilitude of the novel collapse all at once. I think that the two failures, the two plots of Marcello and Moravia, are to be analyzed in their interconnectedness. The author and the hero fail exactly because the protagonist of the novel is a fascist character, one of the few cases in the Italian second postwar literary scenario. What does this particular kind of character enable in the text in terms of genre, plot and authorship? What happens when such a problematic figure of recent, traumatic historical events is given narrative shape, that is, when someone with extremely denoted historical characteristics is displaced as a fictional character with a precise narrative function into the plot of a novel?

Il conformista is a novel about form and the relationship of form to life. Marcello tries to give his life an easily readable melodramatic form by turning it into a linear, causal destiny following a meaningful, symmetrical narrative plot. This attempt fails when Lino is resurrected, and Marcello recognizes him one night in Villa Borghese. The plot he imagined linking the first crime to the second suddenly fades away: it is impossible to impose on his life such a fixed, straightforward explanation. The fascist hero is a dynamic factor of the text, and he makes the novel fail. This failure coincides with the recognition scene because Marcello's biography, from being the unproblematic destiny of a static hero, turns into a dynamic, indefinable flow: his supposedly natural tendency to be evil was only a mistake, the result of a wrong interpretation of his self. When the fascist is displaced into the plot of the novel as character, he has been assigned certain recurrent, specific functions and traits easily readable and recognizable by the reader: he is a hero troubled by a perverse personality, a spy who betrays his old master and who cheats on his wife. Nevertheless, this static unity, which the assassination of Quadri will finally ratify once and for all, sanctioning its intactness, breaks into flow, a mix of different, multiple heterogeneous elements when Lino emerges back into the text.

1.3 The Fascist Character as a *failed* Stereotype and Dynamic Hero.

The distinction between a static and a dynamic hero is one of the fundamental themes of Russian formalism, and, in particular, the concept of dynamism, of dynamic poetic factors investigated and theorized by Yuri Tynianov:

> The unity of the work is not a closed, symmetrical intactness, but an unfolding, dynamic integrity. Between its elements is not the static sign of equality and addition, but the dynamic sign of correlation and integration.[73]

The plot invented by Marcello to make sense of his evil was working as the static sign of equality and addition, metonymically relating the childhood crimes to the political, adult one of Quadri. The recognition scene shows instead that between the two events, there is not repetition but only a metaphorical correlation. Marcello's life, his evil nature and consequent conformism to the fascist regime have not one necessary reason configurable as causal, teleological destiny-biography. His personality is a hybrid interaction of multiple traits, contingent and not absolute characteristic, a blending of guilt and fate, evil and good, coquetry and activity. The dynamic hero escapes categorization and static classifications; it has a variety of functions and not a specific one. From a logic and syllogistic unity to an "irregular flux:"

> On the oratorical and emotional level where the effect of the word was taken into account, a different way of unfolding the verbal material grew up in

---

[73] Yuri Tynyanov, *The Problem of Verse Language* (Ann Arbor: Ardis Publishers, 1981), 33.

place of the logical, syllogistical principle. This new way involved tension and release in a broken flow, in maximal tension and maximal release.[74]

Between the two crimes, a "semantic fracture" is established, and the logical, easy, normal semantic association between the two events is destroyed. Thereby, the structure of the novel might be read as an enigma based on an obscure metaphorical relation between two events. The recognition scene deforms the doublet and, with it, also the linearity of the plot Marcello was modeling his life on:

> the normal semantic associations of the word are destroyed, and in their place, there is a semantic *break* [*slom*]. The trope is felt to be a *conversion* or *perversion* – the expression is Lomonosov's, which supremely shows the broken semantic line of poetic discourse.[75]

Another formalist, Viktor Shklovsky, had a different, more static, definition of the hero. Don Quixote, in his *Theory of Prose*, is the perfect model of the hero that has mainly the function of a thread: it is a narrative device that serves to link together the narrative chain of events and episodes. The hero is the mere motivation for the succession of a novel's episodes in a series. Don Quixote's wisdom is not a quality of his personality but only a narrative device used to interpolate wise sayings into the texture of the novel. He is useful to the author:

> The hero integrates these episodes in exactly the same way that an observer integrates the pictures of an art gallery in his mind. [...] The Don Quixote type made famous by Heine and gushed over by Turgenev was not the author's original plan. This type appeared as a result of the novel's structure, just as a change in the mode of execution often created new forms in poetry.[76]

I believe that Marcello, throughout the novel, believes himself to be a static hero obeying the model of Shklovsky's Don Quixote, and, when he recognizes Lino, he unveils he discovers his true nature as

---

74 Yuri Tynyanov, "The Ode as an Oratorical Genre" in *New Literary History*, Vol. 34, No. 3, 568.
75 Idem., 167.
76 Viktor Shklovsky, *Theory of Prose* (Champaign & London: Dalkey Archive Press, 1990), 100, 80.

unstoppable flux, as the dynamic hero as described by Tynianov. In fact, the recognition makes impossible the previous categorization into a static definition of his personality. Marcello is not evil by nature, as he never killed Lino. His subjectivity is instead a dynamic entity that avoids unproblematic, melodramatic definitions and it is impossible to fix, to enclose into a stereotyping portrait.

It is now possible to read the failure of *Il conformista* as a novel more as the failed attempt to stereotype the fascist character. While Marcello gives meaning to his life by emplotting it, on the one hand, within a melodramatic universe of clear-cut moral opposites and, on the other, as a sort of political *bildungsroman* of his 'career' in the fascist party, Moravia enframes Marcello's story as tragedy and as a different type of *bildungsroman*. The political education of Marcello resembles, in fact, the socialist realist novel, a politicized variant of the *bildungsroman*. The recognition scene, instead, reveals his political trajectory to be ungrounded and based on a lie. Therefore, his *bildungsroman* seems more reminiscent of Stendhal's *Le Rouge et Le Noire*, i.e., the story of the impossibility of conforming and adapting his innermost drives to the surrounding society. The compromise between self and world, and between spontaneity and organization, is not reached, and this was the outcome of the *bildungsroman* in his classic, 18th-century version and of its later variation in the socialist realist novel. Tragedy and the Stendhalian *bildungsroman*, on the contrary, are genres that favor ambiguity and relativity of values over categorization and thus choice between one frame of reference or another.

Marcello, too, as we will see, is a hybrid, ambiguous hero whose personality draws its traits and functions from two kinds of "types." The recognition scene is the moment of truth that reveals the novel as a dynamic process of displacement of life into art, of the material into form. There is not one uncomplicated form or narrative shape that can capture the multiplicity and complexity of the historical figure of the fascist. The fascist, when displaced as a character into the plot of the novel, is an agent of dynamism: first, of the novel's genre; second, of the hero's function; third, of the relationship linking author and hero and, fourth, of the self with the surrounding world, both present and past.

Marcello Clerici, the fascist hero of *Il conformista,* is a curious blend. He is both the protagonist of the novel and a fascist, and this doublet is oxymoronic. In fact, the fascist, in post-war Italian novels and films, is traditionally a character with recurrent, exaggerated, stereotypical traits. Their function within the plot is either that of the melodramatic villain, the antagonist of the partisan hero, or that of one of the background figures or minor characters. In both cases, the fascist is normally a "type" over-characterized as evil, dominated by perverse, abnormal sexuality, and vicious and immoral.

The fascist is historically the enemy living and acting on the wrong side of history, as famously stated by Kim in Calvino's *Il sentiero dei nidi di ragno.* When the fascist is displaced from history into narrative form, the "natural" pre-determined narrative function ready for them is that of the villain, the rival of the good partisan, both in love and war. Regardless of the fascist's historical role as the enemy in the real world, the literary and narrative function which they have in the text preexists them because, as Propp wrote:

> It has already been shown that functions must be defined independently of the characters who are supposed to fulfill them. In following the enumeration of the functions, one becomes convinced that they must also be defined independently of how and in what manner they are fulfilled.[77]

The antagonist continues Propp, might be the dragon, the devil, the bandits, the witch or the stepmother and, I would add, the fascist, as far as Italian post war novels are concerned. It is not important *who* and *how* certain actions are completed throughout the plot, but *what* the characters do, i.e., their actions. The fascist, then, is only one of the various anthropomorphic personifications of the function of the villain of evil. In narrative terms, it is not a necessary union but a contingent, temporary embodiment of evil in one "type" of character drawn from recent historical events. Functions, as noted by Jameson in commenting on Propp's *Morphology of the Folktale,* are not fixed forms; they are only provisionally invested in anthropomorphic bearers:

---

77 Vladimir Propp, *Morphology of the Folktale* (Austin: University of Texas press, 1968), 66.

> The experience of the seme of evil can no longer be permanently assigned or attached to this or that human agent, it must find itself expelled from the realm of interpersonal or inner-worldly relations in a kind of Lacanian *forclusion* and thereby be projectively reconstituted into a free-floating and disembodied element, a baleful optical illusion.[78]

Marcello, then, is a fascist only momentarily, and his role as fascist and villain is only a "free-floating and disembodied element," not a necessary, absolute, natural trait of his personality. The recognition scene will exactly disembody the fascist aura from Marcello. The fascist Marcello is a contradictory doublet, both villain—and thus described with the recurrent, caricatural features typical of certain minor fascist characters—and the hero, the protagonist, of the novel. The recognition scene will show that what he perceived as an "evilness" by nature was, in reality, only a contingent embodiment of the free-floating function of a villain. From the villain's fixed form, here again, the function of the evil antagonist is given back to its disembodied dynamism.

Marcello, throughout the causal chain of events that leads from the crime of Lino to the second one of Quadri, acts both as a villain and as a protagonist, or, better, he is a hero who thinks he needs to act as a villain, traitor, or spy in order to erase his abnormality and evil nature. In the plot that his inner self imagines, he plays the literary function of villain in order not to be perceived as a villain anymore. It is a matter of optical illusion again, of switching the point of view and side of history from which he perceives his personality. The plot of *Il conformista* is, in this sense, the story of a literary character's desire to be a "type," the paradoxical plot of a protagonist who thinks he needs to be the "type" of villain in order to redeem himself. The protagonist, in fact, is abnormal compared to the mass of minor characters, different and distinguished from them. Then, his political conformism might also be read as a narratological conformism: a protagonist that wants to become fascist in order to lose his abnormality, his uniqueness, and finally be like any other fascist minor character, a type.

---

78 Fredric Jameson, *The Political Unconscious* (Ithaca: Cornell University Press), 119.

We can find an example of the fascist as a type and secondary character in one of Moravia's most famous and successful works in terms of plot and character complexity: *La romana*. The fascist here is Astarita, an officer of the regime's police driven by an almost satyr-like desire for the female protagonist. Astarita is the real trigger of the melodramatic plot, being both the villain-antagonist that tries not only to buy Adriana's love and thus steal her from the young communist Mino but also to force the latter to betray his companions, turning him into a spy. Both Mino and Astarita commit suicide at the end of the novel, after having been the two characters triggering the spy story plot and a melodramatic love triangle with Adriana in which none of the three can get the corresponding object of desire. Marcello is the synthesis of these two functions as villain: love antagonist nuanced with a disgusting perversity and traitor at once.

However, Marcello is more than Astarita, and in this surplus lies his unique complexity. In fact, Marcello is also the typical Moravian protagonist and, in this sense, not only is he Astarita and Mino, but also Adriana, the female protagonist of *La romana,* and Michele, the inept hero of *Gli indifferenti*. He is a type of man driven by the very same conflicts that repeat themselves, with certain variants, in all of Moravia's novels and short stories. He is troubled by that fracture between normality and abnormality, alienation and conformism, thought and indifference, which is the preferred and always recurring existential cross carried throughout their lives by the type of the Moravian protagonists. Now, being at the same time two kinds of types, the Moravian protagonist and fascist antagonist, with the caricatural traits of a minor figure, he could not be a static, one-dimensional and unproblematic character. Writing a fascist character and placing him as the protagonist of a plot could not be a simple task without specific narrative consequences. The fascist was not just any kind of character, especially during the immediate post-war years. Thus, also the creation and insertion of a figure imbued with such a special complexity must be considered a delicate narrative operation, likely bound, as we have seen, to failure.

The conflict between normality and abnormality, which troubles Marcello's personality, and that is the same one at the core of all Moravian heroes, is also perfectly translatable as the narrative, the formal conflict between the functions of antagonist and protagonist. Until the recognition scene, Marcello embodies both functions: he is the usual Moravian protagonist who, troubled by unnamed obscure, abnormal impulses, becomes the fascist and villain character of a melodrama in order to relinquish his abnormality and become like any other, the "stereotype" of *the* fascist. The plot that both Marcello and Moravia try to build is, thus, a path leading to the "stereotypification" of Marcello as fascist, the formation and narrative of *bildungsroman* of a fascist character. Moreover, here lies the paradox of a protagonist whose aim and goal in life is to become a melodramatic villain. Marcello, who has a natural propensity to kill, imposes on himself the narrative function of the villain in melodrama. If fascism wins, villainy will become normality, and his natural, abnormal, obscure tendencies will be justified by society and not condemned as immoral and evil. Marcello is an antagonist who tries to escape his typicality as the evil villain and fascist by imagining a plot in which the protagonist needs to be a villain in order to achieve normality and to make his desires socially acceptable. Marcello is, then, a unique, atypical version both of the fascist character and of the Moravian hero, and, as a result, his form will be a dynamic, unclassifiable doublet: the static roles of the hero and the villain/minor character mix with one another and break their boundaries after having been juxtaposed and synthesized in one paradoxical figure. It will be Moravia himself to split this atypical doublet of types into the dynamic, indefinite form of a character who is impossible to define with clear, absolute traits. The non-death of Lino, by many considered the main flaw of the novel because too unrealistic, is, in my opinion, the very moment in which the stasis is turned into dynamism and a fixed form collapses into flux. Marcello's stereotypical form as a fascist villain fragments itself, revealing the unity of the Moravian protagonist and of the fascist antagonist in the same hero to be an impossible one. Marcello is finally recognized as obscurity: neither villain nor good, neither hero nor antagonist. The recognition scene is, in a word, the moment of truth that melts into contingency, dynamism, relativity and relationality every defined, secured meaning and binary opposition of good and evil, realistic and unrealistic, hero and fascist.

Marcello is trying to fit himself into the contemporary world, to become part of it, at the same time constructing an image for himself and giving meaning to his fate. This image and this fate coincide with the model of the fascist type:

> At a certain moment in the process of his maturation, a person begins to orient himself toward one or another ideal image already present in the collective consciousness. He allies himself with a historical personality type, and sometimes this may be prepared for gradually, and sometimes it may come as a sudden break. Uncoordinated, unconscious, or semiconscious elements coalesce in a system.[79]

Following Lydia Ginzburg's words, I argue that the fascist represents a very complex, problematic «epochal personality type»[80] that finds its narrative shape in apparently stable, static «typological characteristics,» «schematic typification,» and «mechanically articulated qualities.»[81] The fascist character is a formula, a conventional image always dominated by recurrent features. Nevertheless, this is only a temporary truth, and, as I have already mentioned, the fascist cannot be considered as any kind of character given its traumatic origins in the historical actuality of war still too present. In fact, this typification of the protagonist as the fascist villain is nothing but the orientation of both the novel's plot written by the author and of Marcello's personality: both are only attempts to shape an otherwise obscure personality as a perfectly recognizable image, as an epochal stereotype. Both attempts fail, and what was oriented to become a type, thus enclosed into a predetermined, known, ideal form, ends up in the impossibility of being defined and absorbed into a fixed formula. The typification of the fascist as the fascist character and villain is only a structural orientation of the configuration of the narrative plot, and the fascist, conceived as a stereotype, hides behind its superficial immediacy and schematic

---

79 Lydia Ginzburg, *On Psychological Prose* (Princeton: Princeton University Press, 1991), 18.
80 Ibidem
81 Ibid.

function a dynamic complexity which, on the contrary, shows all formulaic categorizations to be impossible.

1.4 Author and Hero: the Fascist as 'Other' and the Collapse into Affect.

The form of the novel and the destiny of its protagonist coincide with this process of typification. Marcello, both as the character and human being, needs to become a typical, ordinary fascist bourgeois with a house and a spouse like everyone else. The narrative shape of Marcello's *bildung,* of his conformation with fascism, has the features and structural function of the fascist villain-antagonist. The typicality of such a character—that borrows some recurrent caricatural traits of fascist minor figures—will allow him to cover the inner, obscure abnormality of his soul under the straightforward, necessary destiny unfolding as a linear, teleological and causal sequence of events. Hero and author share at this moment of the novel the same "axiological context:" Marcello imagines his life as the plot of a novel, thereby seeing himself from the outside, as other, as the hero of a complete, 'consummated' logical sequence. Marcello needs to become a fascist type and projects his life as a narrative plot linking two crimes. Moravia, too, initially frames Marcello as other, as the hero of a socialist realist politicized *bildungsroman,* and as the typical alienated, indifferent protagonist of one of his works. They both, in a word, have the goal to form a fascist type, a personality without obscure, ambiguous traits: an easily recognizable form with features and functions that would support and ease the narrative impulse of the author and the conforming aspirations of the character itself. The type helps the plot created by the author and the one imagined by Marcello to have the unproblematic, linear, reified form of melodrama and politicized *bildungsroman.* The static hero, as we have seen, is, according to Shklovsky, a tool in the hands of the author, a technical device used to glue episodes together and insert the author's world and wisdom into the text. They are also the hero of the historical novel as described by Lukács, i.e., a minor character who is the "neutral ground"[82] and the "middle-of-the-road"[83] nucleus conceived as the mere point of encounter between extremes: the opposing poles of social forces, the individual and the national, the public and the private, the general and the empirical. His entire personality and destiny depend on one single and decisive event. It is, retrospectively, from the point of view of this "moment of truth" or "moment of collision" that the subject models his life. The assassination of Quadri is this moment, the event that «overshadows the human personality by its magnitude and importance.»[84] Such a destiny has, then, a closed, limited horizon that allows both author and hero to orient themselves in a world ruled by an unproblematic, Manichean, formulaic system of values and moral coordinates. The moment of truth-collision is the *conditio sine qua non* for the creation of both stories: Marcello's inner plot to become a fascist type and Moravia's external narrative plot of *Il conformista*. Marcello and Moravia act as if the event of the second crime, the killing of Quadri, has already occurred. They, in fact, see the second crime as an imitation of the first, as already foreshadowed by the childhood events narrated in the prologue. Fredric Jameson, in *The Antinomies of Realism*, defines this as "the narrative impulse:"

> The time of the *récit* is then a time of the preterite, of events completed, over and done with, events that have entered history once and for all. It will be clear enough what a philosophy of freedom must object to in such an inauthentic and reified temporality: it necessarily blocks out the freshness of the event happening, along with the agony of decision of its protagonists. It omits in other words, the present of time and turns the future into a dead future.[85]

Marcello's process of typification as a fascist and as a fascist character coincides with Moravia's narrative impulse. Both plot lines live in the time of the *récit* because the assassination of Quadri, the epic moment of truth and the dramatic moment of collision, is a

---

82   György Lukács, *The Historical Novel* (Lincoln: University of Nebraska Press, 1983), 36.
83   Ibidem.
84   Ibid.
85   Fredric Jameson, *The Antinomies of Realism* (New York: Verso, 2013), 18.

completed event, the imitation of a previous crime that already predetermined Marcello's destiny since the beginning. The connection between the two crimes constitutes the true *récit* of *Il conformista* and, most of all, it confers meaning on both events and Marcello as well. Marcello and his destiny mean something because of the allegorical relationship established between two otherwise disconnected events. There is no room for doubts or uncertainty: if Quadri gets killed, Marcello will be a Fascist villain and *so* a normal Fascist like everybody else. By absorbing the two crimes into the meaningful, coherent narrative system of a plot, the events of Marcello's life are sealed off, and time becomes nothing but destiny, anecdote, and an irrevocable past. He becomes what Todorov calls a *homme récit*, like the *Thousand and One Nights* characters that embody the stories they narrate. His identity is completed, marked by this irrevocable time of the decisive event, the moment of crisis that will shape his personality once and for all. Such a static hero, of course, facilitates the task of the writer, being the unproblematic motivation of a device and a type with predetermined systematic and formulaic features. Marcello's axiological context exactly coincides with its author's, thus allowing the possibility of configuring a coherent narrative whole with precise moral coordinates and clear-cut meanings. They share the same 'excess of seeing,' being Marcello's imaginary trajectory between one crime and the other, nothing but a tale within the tale. Marcello is his typical destiny and he is at the same time the plot of *Il conformista*. Both storylines stretch *a posteriori* from the assassination of Quadri, constricting all the previous events within a strict and syllogistic logic. Nevertheless, it is exactly this embodiment of the *récit* by Marcello, by the fascist character, that will eventually create a fracture between the points of view of the hero and of the author, making the latter lose his control on the former, his 'excess of seeing.' In fact, as Bakhtin writes in his early essay "The Author and the Hero in Aesthetic Activity":

> And history, likewise, knows no past, present, and future; it knows no long or short time, no "long ago" or "recently" — as absolutely unique and non convertible moments. The time of history is itself nonreversible, of course, but within it all relations are fortuitous and relative (and reversible), for there is no absolute center of value. History and geography are invariably

aestheticized to a certain degree. From the psycho-mathematical standpoint, the space and time of a human being's life constitute no more than negligible segments of one infinite space and time, and it is only this, of course that guarantees their univocity and determinateness with respect to meaning in any theoretical judgment. But, from within a human life, they acquire a unique center of value, in relation to which they gain body. In correlation with the "bodied" or consolidated time of human life, artistic time and space, nonconvertible and stably architectonic, acquire an emotional-volitional tonality and include eternity and extratemporality, and infinitude, the whole and the part—as such.[86]

The time of the *récit*, the allegorical time of the completed event, of the irrevocable past allows the author to impose a meaning on his character's life, that is, to mark his existence with a meaningful destiny. Moreover, this hero shares with his author the same belief in the plot connecting the *before* to the *after*, the first to the second crime, because his inner life is based on his belief in a necessary process of social conformation and narrative typification:

> In order to become consummated, i.e., to assume the form of a finished work, prose must utilize the aestheticized process of the creative individual who is its author, that is, it must reflect within itself the image of the finished *event* of his act of creation, inasmuch as from within its own meaning, abstracted from the author, prose is incapable of finding any consummating and architectonically integrating moments.[87]

The "type" helps the plot created by the author and that one imagined by Marcello to have the unproblematic, linear, reified form of melodrama and socialist realist *bildungsroman*. These forms need, in fact, the time of the narrative impulse, the time of the *récit*, which seals off the event once and for all, thus making it easily definable with absolute meaning.

Marcello would have succeeded in being a fascist type and Moravia in creating a plot with a perfectly symmetrical structure. However, the epilogue surprises the reader with an unannounced, unprepared *coup de théâtre*. By "unprepared," I mean here narratively unprepared, in other words, an episode that is not grounded in the previous episodes of the plot; and, curiously, the consequence of this unanticipated scene will be the revelation that one event, the execution of Quadri, was exactly lacking its supposed

---

86 Mikhail Bakhtin, "Author and Hero in Aesthetic Activity in Art and Answerability" (Austin: University of Texas Press, 1990), 208.
87 Idem., 210.

premise, i.e., once again event and narrative device share the same qualities: the recognition scene does not have a plausible cause, and it will make the cause upon which the second crime was grounded disappear. What precisely happens with the recognition scene?

Lino is alive, and this true resurrection out of nothing has structural consequences so far, completely unexplored and not unpacked, since the episode has always been considered an inexcusable authorial mistake. The recognition scene breaks all the rules of verisimilitude; it is the very point of failure of the novel: the failure of Marcello's plot and Moravia's as well because the recognition scene represents, then, the moment of the split, the fracture and subsequent collision between the two axiological contexts of the hero and of the author, until that moment unified and coinciding. The failure then might appear as a formal failure, the textual locus of the author's lost control of the material of his novel, of its character and plot. The recognition scene, first of all, says that Marcello is not a type. The process of typification abruptly stops, and this moment of crisis is also the point at which the plot of the novel and the plot imagined by Marcello detach from each other, destroying the necessary link between the two crimes. So, if, as I have said earlier, Marcello *is* the plot of *Il conformista* when this plot collapses, is he erased too as a character? Yes and no. What, in my opinion, the recognition scene really shows is the impossibility of the fascist character to be a type. Marcello loses his typicality as a fascist villain, but still, he remains a fascist character. When such a character is deprived of its typicality, it loses at the same time its static features, and it also escapes the limits of the closed, irrevocable absolute time of the *récit*. A character that was the story is now out of the story, the latter being broken into its discrete, disconnected contingent parts. Marcello loses his destiny and his *récit* and becomes pure openness and relativity, the eternal present of affect, the moment in itself:

> The temporal and spatial articulation and disposition of the parts of a discursive whole, even of such an elementary one as a syllogism (antecedents, consequents, etc.), reflect not the moment itself, but the temporal process of the progression of human thinking, although not the fortuitous, psychological process, to be sure, but the aestheticized, rhythmic process of thinking. [...] A thought as such contains, inherently, the energy of extraspatial and extratemporal infinitude, in relation to which anything concrete is merely

> fortuitous; a thought can provide no more than the direction for seeing something concrete, but a direction that is infinite, a direction incapable of *consummating* a whole.[88]

Now, the two events defining to Marcello's eyes his personality were nothing but fortuitous moments of his life and not completed, meaningful events marking his essence once and for all. His consciousness is not limited any longer by the coherence of a plot, by the meaningful and completed unity of its parts, because as Bakhtin writes, the unity of the consciousness is always still to be completed and invariably open, constantly unaccomplished.

The artistic creation is the event of the relationship and the encounter between the author and the hero. According to Bakhtin, the choice of every meaning, the structure of every image, and every rhythm tone are conditioned and determined by the two axiological contexts of the author and of the hero. The event of their collision and mutual contrast generates the stable architecture of artistic unity. Every word in the novel is the expression of a reaction to a reaction. The author reacts to the hero's reaction in relation to what is happening within the artistic composition. The author reacts aesthetically to the emotive-ethical response of the hero to an event. From this reaction, the choice of characters, the intonation, the rhythmic tone and other formal features are determined:

> In this sense, we could say that every word in narrative literature expresses a reaction to another reaction, the author's reaction to the reaction of the hero; that is, every concept, image, and object lives on two planes, is rendered meaningful in two value-contexts—in the context of the hero and in that of the author. [...] after all the hero's reaction and evaluation, his emotional-volitional attitude, have a cognitive-ethical and realistic (lived-life) character; the author reacts to the reaction of the hero and consummates it aesthetically. The essential life of a work is constituted by this event of the dynamic, living relationship of author and hero.[89]

The recognition scene is exactly the moment of crisis in which the relationship between author and hero shows all its dynamism and vitality. If, until the reappearance of Lino author and hero were sharing the same response and their contexts were then coinciding

---

88   Ibid., 175
89   Idem., 218.

perfectly, the recognition activates the dynamism of their relation, causing the fracture of the two reactions: in the recognition scene is the author's reaction, which prevails, transmitting his position in relation to the hero, his evaluation of the character's essence, personality, destiny. Marcello's plot, his belief in a destiny of conformity thanks to the second murder, causes the author to end it finally and to reveal it as a mere illusion of the hero. The author is the only one who could know that Lino is alive, a knowledge that was denied to both the hero and readers. The author shows his reaction to be predominant by means of a purely formal, aesthetic device: anagnorisis, one of the three key formal devices of tragedy since Aristotle's *Poetics*. The destiny that the hero, from his axiological context and perspective, thought to be inevitable and irrevocable is finally revealed by the author as only one possible, contingent embodiment and concretization among infinite others. The recognition scene reveals the plot as one possible aestheticization of one event, as the reaction of his hero to one event in his childhood. There is nothing absolute, complete and definite in the plot we just followed. It was so only if the hero imagined his life as the plot of the novel if the self saw himself as other. The recognition scene seems then as a moment of pure irony: the author claims back his dominant position and detaches himself from the context of the hero, reacting to his response. The aesthetic nature of the plot of the novel is now made perceivable to both the hero and reader because of the falsity and illusory character of Marcello's convictions and plot. Every event is already aesthetic even before any attempt to make sense of it:

> Even in life, where every word is intonated by us, this intonation is never purely realistic, but always includes an admixture of aesthetic intonation. An actual cognitive-ethical reaction is pure, but the utterance of it for another inevitably absorbs into itself an element that is aesthetic; any expression as such is aesthetic from the outset.[90]

The hero's destiny was only one possible embodiment of the "type" of the fascist villain, not an absolute, general type and model. That same theme could have been embodied differently by another hero,

---

90 Idem., 219.

and it could have had a different relation with the author. The plot woven by the hero in order to link two events becomes, then, only a moment of the aesthetic characterization of one single man.

The recognition scene opens the character, fragments its typicality and turns it into a dynamic, undefined identity. Also, the plot's linear, schematic temporality is broken because the two crimes at the extremities of the story do not mirror each other and do not have any causal relation between them. Marcello cannot any longer be clearly and definitively categorized as evil or traitor because his destiny as the melodramatic villain was founded on a mistake, an optical error due to his point of view. His abnormality, deprived of its aesthetic form and architecture, is now perceivable directly in its materiality as an unnamable affect. His personality loses its form as destiny, formula and schema and fades into the dynamic flux of an eternal present. The obscurity that in the prologue was only half-perceived and a recondite, infinitesimal hidden share of his inner self invades now all of his subjectivity. The enigma of his personality is now perceivable immediately and in an unarticulated manner. The fascist character is defamiliarized, not perceivable anymore under the systemic, completed clarity of the type, but immediately present to the eyes of the author and readers as dynamism before language or naming. The fascist is estranged from himself, from his named destiny and features, from his completed and recognizable typicality. Without the explanation of his plot, Marcello remains as pure data, not haunted anymore by meaning or ideological connotation, a floating and disembodied element left in all its strangeness and problematic essence. The novel has lost its hero, and its plot as affecting denarrativizes and dechronologizes the action so far narrated:

> Affects are singularities and intensities, existences rather than essences, which usually unsettle the more established psychological and physiological categories. [...] This irreconcilable divorce between intelligibility and experience, between meaning and existence, then can be grasped as a fundamental feature of modernity. [...] If it means something, it can't be real; if it is real, it can't be absorbed by purely mental or conceptual categories. [...] The regime of the past-present-future and of personal identities and destinies is as its outer limit the realm of the *récit*; while the impersonal consciousness of an eternal or existential present would at its outer limit govern pure

scene, a showing that was altogether divorced and separated from telling and purified of it.[91]

The plot that so far had the temporality of the past-present-future — and perfectly schematized as the temporality of three identical crimes Roberto-Lino-Quadri — must be now observed as something again not completed and closed, in other words not typical. The hero is now perceived in its potentiality and not in its necessity. Marcello is the potential hero of a story, and he is only one embodiment among many:

> Language or, rather, the world of language also has its own potential hero, as it were, who is actualized in an utterance of lived life within myself and within the other. And it is only when aesthetic directedness becomes specialized and detaches itself from other tendencies that, in the very process of detaching itself from and contending with the other tendencies, it begins to differentiate, a hero appears as well as his author, and the living event constituted by their differentiation, contention, and mutual relations spills over into a finished work of art and crystallizes in it.[92]

The Fascist character and the *récit* that was assigning it a plausible identity and a determined destiny of typicality are now split from its plot, estranged from any fixed and completed identity. The reader, surprised by an unprepared formal mistake in the general aesthetic architecture of the novel, can recognize now that identity to be a mistake, a *récit* imposed on an event and on one man. The melodramatic, and for some aspects, socialist realist *bildungsroman* of Marcello's fantasy is now read against the background of a truth that escapes the fixation of form, i.e., of the relative, ambiguous absence of compromise and absolute truth typical of other genres, such as tragedy and the Stendhalian later variation of the *bildungsroman*. The typical hero dies and leaves his place to the dynamic, potential hero of affect. The recognition scene precisely signs this moment of crisis, both of the novel's plot and the hero's consciousness, and of the shift from the hero conceived as function and as a static device — formulated as we have seen by Shklovsky in *Theory of Prose* — to the hero as conceived by Tynianov: a dynamic form,

---

91 Jameson, *The Antinomies of Realism*, 25, 36-37.
92 Bakhtin, *Author and Hero in Aesthetic Activity*, 230.

which is impossible to reduce to one, absolute formulaic typical model. *Il conformista* is a failure only because it represents the attempt to build a novel with a fascist as type and protagonist. The fascist character, though, reveals itself to be refractory to be completed and limited by a formula, an uncomplicated, reified and meaningful personality. The Fascist character is oriented to be a type throughout the plot of the novel. However, the recognition scene signifies a switch in the structural orientation of the work of art, a moment of tension in the stability of its realism:

> A tension between plot and scene, between the chronological continuum and the eternal affective present which, realized in quite distinct ratios in the various great realists, nonetheless marks out the space in which realism emerges and subsists, until one of the two antithetical forces finally outweighs the other and assures its disintegration.[93]

1.5 Ambiguity of Genres: Melodrama, *Bildungsroman* and Tragedy.

The recognition scene is a shock for the reader because any melodramatic, precise binary opposition between good and evil is pushed back into ambiguity, relativity and doubt. The hero's identity shifts from being a dramatic destiny defined by its temporal continuity and orientation towards a moment of collision-truth to being an open possibility still in becoming and free of any sort of predestination *a posteriori*. The moment of recognition might also be interpreted as the trigger of an estranged look at Marcello, at his adherence to the model of the fascist villain type. The fascist character that seemed to own the irrevocability and one-dimensionality of a dramatic destiny is now shattered into potentiality, confusion, and relativity. The recognition scene is the moment of estrangement and irony when the form of the novel and the hero are perceived as momentary, arbitrary, contingent aestheticizations. The fascist character cannot be automatically perceived as a type. It is, on the contrary, defamiliarized by Moravia, who breaks the meaningful plot and causal chain of events, denying Marcello the plausible

---

93 Jameson, *The Antinomies of Realism*, 83.

sense and normal identity he built for himself. The plot was only a device to make sense of a mystery, of the obscure enigma of a character's subjectivity. It is, then, possible to say that the novel begins as a socialist realist politicized *bildungsroman* and as melodrama and that it ends as tragedy — with *anagnorisis* and *deus ex-machina* — and as Stendhal's version of the *bildungsroman*. The recognition scene is the textual location of this crisis, of the dynamic tension between different narrative types; it is the moment of fracture and dynamic conflict between the axiological contexts of the hero and author when the author *reacts* to the hero's reaction to an event.

The fascist character is not a schema, a formula, or a type but, on the contrary, is a character imbued with a carnivalesque, dialogic energy. At the end of *Il conformista*, we are left with a character to whom the author, even though through a "dishonest" narrative device, denied the clear-cut limits of a dramatic destiny. The fascist character is still an open and dynamic entity that is formally and aesthetically difficult to fix into an always valid typical shape. The recognition scene shows, on the contrary, that the attempt to emplot the fascist caused the opposite result of generating tension between author and hero, character and genre, between form and life-material. All these aesthetic components are now reacting to each other in a state of pure, dynamic relationality. Even all moral values are now reversed, since it is impossible, or at least more complicated, to classify as good and evil the events and the characters of the novel. The recognition scene, following Bakhtin once again, is a grotesque moment, revealing the fascist character as a carnivalesque mask disrupting the temporality of a realist *récit*, the binary Manichean moral values of a melodramatic imagination, that is, the stability, stasis of the Fascist-villain equation. The recognition scene is an aesthetic scandal:

> Scandals and eccentricities destroy the epic and tragic wholeness of the world, they make a breach in the stable, normal ("seemly") course of human affairs and events, they free human behavior from the norms and motivations that predetermine it.[94]

---

94 Mikhail Bakhtin, *Problems of Dostoevsky's Poetics* (Minneapolis: University of Minnesota Press, 1984), 117.

The disruptive dynamism of the hero of *Il conformista* leads to the fragmentation of the epic and tragic integrity of his identity and destiny; he is estranged from them. The usual, habitual, familiar and automatic adhesion of the Fascist to a certain literary genre type is, at the end of *Il conformista,* put into question, left as an open enigma. The fascist character, so far perceiving the world and being perceived by the world through the symmetrical view of what Brooks calls "melodramatic imagination," now perceives and is perceived through a "carnivalesque sense" of the world which favors defamiliarization, estrangement, irony, deautomatization, and also the ambiguity of tragedy:

> Nothing conclusive has yet taken place in the world, the ultimate word of the world and about the world has not yet been spoken, the world is open and free, everything is still in the future and will always be in the future. [..] Opposites come together, look at one another, are reflected in one another, know and understand one another. [...] Therefore all things that are disunified and distant must be brought together at a single spatial and temporal "point."[95]

Marcello is a grotesque image, ambivalent, neither good nor evil, neither guilty nor innocent. He is a "not yet completed metamorphosis", an open and uncompleted form, and not the static characterization of a type:

> The last thing one can say of the real grotesque is that it is static; on the contrary it seeks to grasp in its imagery the very act of becoming and growth, the eternal incomplete unfinished nature of being. Its images present simultaneously the two poles of becoming: that which is receding and dying, and that which is being born. [...] Actually the grotesque liberates man from all the forms of inhuman necessity that direct the prevailing concept of the world. This concept is uncrowned by the grotesque and reduced to the relative and the limited.[96]

With the recognition scene, a carnivalesque sense of the world permeates *Il conformista* and its characters. If Lino is alive, the novel, thanks to the grotesque scandal of an unprepared anagnorisis, needs to be read as the awareness of the contingent, relative nature

---

95 Ibidem., 166, 177.
96 Mikhail Bakhtin, *Rabelais and His World* (Bloomington: Indiana University press, 1984), 49, 52.

of plots and narratives that try to give meaning and make sense of such traumatic historical events and personalities. After the recognition scene, both the plot and the character are estranged and recognized only as deformations of an eternal, dynamic truth.

> The fundamental mechanism of estrangement is decontextualization, perspective by incongruity. [...] A new context either creates or *is* a new point of view. Thus, the gap between thing (or word) and context that art is called upon to preserve, protect, and continuously reestablish is a gap between subject and object, the dilation of the space—the Kantian space of alienation—between self and world.[97]

Marcello projected himself meaningfully into the future, from one crime to a second one. He configured a plot ruled by a biographical linear time, thanks to which self and world would be combined in a determinate, irrevocable, meaningful destiny. The plot linking the two crimes both grounds his conformity to fascism and constitutes the main narrative plot of the novel; it is an act of synthesis that the hero shares with the author since, so far, the two contexts of hero and author are in perfect agreement. Nevertheless, the recognition scene signifies a fracture between the two syntheses, first, of the self with the surrounding world (the world and self were combined through the ineluctable tragic destiny), second, of the author with the hero of the novel. The dynamic, carnivalesque hero resists the finalization attempted by the author, and the coherent image of a self-guided by a straightforward, definite destiny in the world is revealed as pure narrative construction:

> Under such conditions, synthesis is rendered highly problematic, and we are indeed reminded that unity, either of object or of subject, is no more than an image, a metaphor.[98]

Alternatively, a plot that metaphorically linked one murder to another would have made the fascist character of Marcello adhere to the model of the fascist-villain type. This equation is finally broken, and the identity is left open, a dynamic incongruity. Fascist

---

97 Michael Holquist and Ilya Kliger, *Minding the Gap. Toward a Historical Poetics of Estrangement* in "Estrangement Revisited (I) ", Poetics Today 26, 4 Winter 2005: 629.
98 Idem., 634.

characters in Italian literature must be considered open questions and not closed answers.

Incongruity and dynamism do not fragment only the image of the character as type; they have the same disruptive function within the genre system of the novel. The recognition, once again, is the moment of crisis of the genre definition of *Il conformista*. Marcello, the fascist character, is portrayed to see the world as melodrama, which is still the stage of the Manichean conflict between good and evil. Nevertheless, another opposite genre might define the plot of *Il conformista* before the recognition scene. If Marcello has a melodramatic imagination and structures his life as melodrama and as a socialist realist *bildungsroman*, the recognition scene shows these structures—and the clear-cut moral and political categorizations they entail—to be mere illusions, thanks to the *anagnorisis* Moravia can reconfigure the wider plot of the novel more as a Stendhal's *bildungsroman* and as a tragedy, two genres that favor ambiguity of values over classification and compromise. According to Moretti, the classic 18th and 19th-century coming-of-age novel has the main goal of promoting the compromise between the abnormality of the truest but unattainable ideals of the self and the ordinary, middle-way kind of life that is required by society. Once again, we should remember that a type is exactly the result of a formal, structural compromise between the general and universal features with the particular and individual ones. The aesthetic goals of the author and the personal, individual ones of the hero mirror each other. The *bildungsroman* is the construction of a synthesis between the I and society:

> Work in the *Bildungsroman* creates a continuity between external and internal, between the 'best and the most intimate' part of the soul and the 'public' aspect of existence. Once again, we have the congruence of formation and socialization.[99]

Between self and world, a symbolic exchange takes place, a synthesis once again, which results in an allegorical construction that

---

99 Franco Moretti, *The way of the World* (London-New York: Verso, 2000), 30.

would give meaning to the hero's life and destiny in society. The hero of the *bildungsroman* is:

> A symbolic animal, man yearns for a symbolic form that may heal the gap between the values 'within' and the world 'without.'[100]

The goal of Marcello is the same as that of the classic coming of age novel and of the social Realist novel of political education: *"il superamento dell'alienazione."*[101] A symbolic exchange must take place between the subjective aspirations of the hero and the real objective possibilities of their realization in society. Spontaneity must be enframed within the precise collective goals of the organization. The plot of *Il conformista* has as its first objective the finalization of Marcello as a determinate type of man and, simultaneously, of character, a certain type of *villain*. He needs a story that would make sense of his primordial guilt with Lino, of his spontaneous tendency to violence, in order to exchange his mysterious, obscure deviance with a social role that would make some political use of that murderous impulse. Fascist society was a villain society, and conforming to it would have inevitably signified being a villain because villainy was the normal condition of everyone. Marcello knows that he is acting as a villain, a traitor and a spy, but he is also aware that this is what society asks of him in exchange for a normal life. Marcello imagines his life as a socialist realist *bildungsroman*, as a political education to become a fascist.

At the formal level, this translates into the attempted configuration of his character as the caricature of the melodramatic villain. The recognition scene — by revealing Marcello's plot as a contingent, illusory construction — also disrupts the Socialist Realist and melodramatic plot based, first, on a teleological, uncomplicated emplotment of spontaneity into an organization, second, on the compromise between the ideals of the Self and those of the surrounding society. The genre of the novel shifts, first, to the ambiguity of values typical of tragedy and, second, to the impossibility of compromise that characterizes Stendhal's *bildungsroman*, i.e.,

---

100 Idem., 68.
101 Ibidem

between the true inner beliefs of the hero and those that society expects him to conform with. Marcello's conformity to fascist society fails in the same way as Julien Sorel failed to keep under control his Napoleonic ideals in the France of the Bourbon Restoration. Somehow, and certainly in an indirect way, the years under the antifascist education of Professor Quadri have finally sabotaged Marcello's formation as a fascist. But who exactly is Professor Quadri?

1.6 Against Idealism?
Il conformista as imaginary solution of the ideological controversy between a liberal-socialist antifascism and a Marxist one.

The starting point of *Il conformista* is an act of estrangement. The main purpose of Moravia was, in fact, to describe and narrate fascism from the inside, from the opposite point of view of a fascist and not from his perspective as a political outsider, as an author more aligned with Marxism. What if, then, a similar estranging premise was the basis of the critical reading of the text? What if the figure of the antifascist Quadri becomes the starting point of the critical discourse on *Il conformista*? The character of the professor, in fact, was inspired by the historical figure of Carlo Rosselli, founder and intellectual guide of the antifascist movement of *Giustizia e Libertà*. This identification brings another layer of ambiguity and complexity to the novel and, in particular, to the relationship between the author and his text.

If the formal judgment of the work has, since then, practically never changed—the novel always takes up minor and marginal space in most of the critical analysis dedicated to Moravia—the text has generated a vast bibliography of a so-called 'biographical' criticism. It has been examined as a historical document about, first, the extent of Moravia's more or less passive participation in the fascist regime and, second, as an important and somehow coded, enigmatic testimony on the assassination of Carlo and Nello Rosselli, which happened in Bagnoles-sur-l'Orne on June 9th, 1937. Moreover, the nature of the text as testimony is made highly ambiguous and somehow uncanny by the fact that Alberto Moravia, born Pincherle, was the cousin of Carlo and Nello: their mother, Amelia, poet and playwright, was the sister of Carlo Pincherle, Alberto's father, and probably had a major role in guiding and inspiring the young Alberto during the early years of his intellectual apprenticeship. The uncanny piece of the puzzle is first of all represented by Moravia's reaction to the cousins' murder, a reaction of complete, mysterious and unjustified silence. Alberto never tried to contact his aunt or any of his other relatives until years after the war ended. Many interpretations have been given of his behavior, the most common and obvious being the one that saw in the acclaimed writer's silence a convenient move to protect his literary career by showing the fascist authorities his 'distance' from a leading antifascist enemy of the regime at the time of the Spanish Civil War. Another aspect that makes Moravia's involvement in the events and characters gravitating around the murder of the Rosselli brothers more equivocal and hazier is the relationship between the writer and the spy of the OVRA who was appointed to follow the moves of one of the most prominent members of *Giustizia e Libertà* during his Parisian exile, and eventually to point him to the hit men, the *cagoulards*. In fact, the spy, the fiduciary of the Fascist Police, was Giacomo Antonini, a well-known intellectual and important, well-connected figure in the literary circles of Paris. Moravia and Antonini knew each other very well since before the war; the latter was a very useful contact helping Moravia to promote and sell his work in the French literary market. Later on, during and after the war, Antonini became a Bompiani agent, directly charged to find publishing houses for the French editions of Moravia's novels. Their relationship and correspondence abruptly stopped right after the publication of *Il conformista,* whose main character, Marcello Clerici, was clearly inspired by the spy Antonini, confirming that Moravia was aware of the role he played in the murder of his cousins, adding another disturbing layer of ambiguity surrounding the plot of *Il conformista,* and the relationship of the author to the hero of the story.

I will now attempt to propose a perspectival change in the critical strategy to approach the text and to structure the analytical discourse around it. Instead of focusing on, and taking as a starting point, the figure of the main hero, I will take as the focal center of the work, as the true object of the aesthetic frame of the novel, the fact that the victim was Carlo Rosselli. *Il conformista* is not only a criticism of a certain type of antifascism of which Rosselli was considered to be the emblem; it is a much more nuanced and rich text tackling and directly targeting the entire philosophical and ideological background and tradition represented by Rosselli that had its roots in a hundred years of Italian political and intellectual history. The novel is, then, the aesthetic shape of an ideological *agon*, the testimony of a philosophical contest between two traditions, idealism and Marxism, that influenced enormously the political and intellectual debate surrounding the formation of the newborn Italian Republic in 1948. It embodied the clash of two contrasting theses and visions of Italian history and the present—Rosselli's and Moravia's—that would serve as the ideological backbone of Bernardo Bertolucci's adaptation of the novel in 1970. The critical target of the film is, once again, certain liberal antifascist ideals embodied by Rosselli. However, twenty years have passed, and the contest between a liberal and a Marxist antifascism is represented in the film in an altogether different form, entailing a somehow inverted dynamic. Criticism of Bertolucci's film—similar to what happened to Moravia's novel—has always insisted on the same predetermined tracks of the Oedipal interpretation, subsuming the ideological and political meaning of the film to its fundamental and self-evident psychological significance and its structure as a session of psychoanalysis. It is also well known that the film symbolically juxtaposes the father figures of Rosselli and Jean-Luc Godard, the latter being the indisputable artistic master and point of reference of the Italian director in the sixties. Just as Moravia symbolically 'killed' Rosselli, the structure and plot of the novel is itself the shape taken by a veritable ideological debate—in the manner of the medieval rhetorical *quaestio*—Bertolucci by killing Rosselli is in reality 'killing' Godard. Nevertheless, in my opinion, the film, like the novel, is not a direct, uncritical and irrefutable rejection of the master's ideology, but rather a dialogic encounter and attempt of compromise between two ideas of cinema: a well-defined one, as was that of Godard and the

Cahiers du cinéma critical circle, highly influenced by Althusser, and the evolving one of Bertolucci, influenced by the Italian, Gramscian tradition of Marxism. More than being a text on fascism, *Il conformista*, in both its novelistic and filmic variations, frames, on the one hand, an ideological contest all internal to the Italian antifascist tradition, split between a liberal and a Marxist faction and, on the other, an encounter between two tightly connected but diverging ideas of cinema, in years when the critical rethinking and questioning of the cinematic form was in continuous evolution after the end of Hollywood's 'golden age' and the normalization of its nemesis and deconstruction, the *Nouvelle Vague*.

Moravia's aversion for his cousins and the liberal, Jewish milieu of their family – among which the ideals of the *Risorgimento* tradition were strongly rooted – is well known and overtly 'confessed' by Moravia himself on various occasions. He despised in that family its atmosphere of moral and ideological snobbery, which exemplified, according to him, the liberal Jewish bourgeoisie convinced of its perfection, righteousness, of being on the right side and of the superiority of its patriotic, nationalistic ideals inherited from the Mazzinian tradition. Moravia's family, on the contrary, belonged to a bourgeoisie lacking strong political or ideological inspirations and any sense of civil activism:

> Moravia ricorda un'istintiva, non ideologica e non consapevole diffidenza, da ragazzo, verso lo stile di vita, le abitudini intellettuali e gli ideali politici dei parenti fiorentini. Essi gli apparivano "ingenui", non "attuali", "illusi e ottocenteschi e con un sacco di idee generose ma poco pratiche nella testa", gli facevano un "effetto strano come di gente veramente per bene e per questo destinata ad andare a gambe all'aria" (Moravia 1990, pp. 16 e 19). D'istinto percepisce un contrasto tra passato e moderno. "Avevo sedici anni e non mi occupavo di politica. Ma avevo sempre provato antipatia per il fascismo e al tempo stesso sentivo, in maniera contraddittoria, che gli antifascisti erano perdenti." Al loro confronto egli si sentiva paradossalmente più "smaliziato", dotato della sensibilità moderna che era propria anche dei fascisti" (Moravia 1990, p. 19).[102]

---

102 Simone Casini, edited by, *Alberto Moravia. Lettere ad Amelia Rosselli con altre lettere familiari e prime poesie* (Bompiani: Milano, 2009), 92. «Moravia remembers that as a boy he had an instinctive, non ideological and unconscious diffidence toward the life style, the intellectual habits and the political ideals of his

This was not a political opposition but a mostly emotional, biological, blind rejection and rage against the type of bourgeoisie that Rosselli exemplified. On top of this mysterious, almost affect-like, unnamable bodily 'biological' emotion, Moravia built, nevertheless, also a complex, refined and highly sophisticated antithetical discourse undermining the righteousness and highness of ideals inspiring the political action and social thought of the GL leader. The aesthetic process that will result in *Il conformista* is, then, a path that unites in a step-by-step progress, affect, ideological *quaestio* and the novel as the literary genre most apt to frame in its form this mysterious knot of emotion and politics. Borrowing from Fredric Jameson's conception of the novel as a sort of experimental battlefield for the dialogic encounter, a compromise of unresolved ideological standpoints in particular historical moments of crisis, I will argue that *Il conformista* reflects exactly an experiment of this kind, its plot allowing the dialogization of two ways of envisioning and organizing the antifascist struggle. In between this fracture, in between Moravia, the author, and Rosselli, the hero-object of the novel, the pivotal figure of the protagonist, Marcello Clerici, is, instead, a fascist. Behind the stereotypical and caricaturesque features that we have by now seen as recurrent in many fascist characters — sexual deviance and innate fascination for violence, among others — the protagonist of *Il conformista* has the textual function to dialogize the contest between two opposing ideas of antifascism: on the one hand the liberal tradition of a bourgeoisie still rooted in the Risorgimento ideals of Mazzini, on the other a bourgeoisie adverse to idealism and more inclined to see the path to renewal not in an enlightened élite of intellectuals, but in the class struggle.

Florentine relatives. They appeared to him as «naïve and outmoded, illuded and 19th century like with a lot of generous but not so practical ideas in their minds,» he had a strange impression of them, as if they were «good and really honest people for this reason destined to end in tears.» Instinctively he perceives a contrast between past and modernity. «I was sixteen and politics did not interest me, however I always disliked fascism, and at the same time, in a contradictory way, I felt that antifascists were losers.» Compared to them he felt himself to be more cunning, endowed with a modern acumen that characterized also the fascists. [translation mine]

Moravia himself, more than in his famous interviews with Alain Elkann and Enzo Siciliano, writes a sort of indirect, precious analysis of the meaning behind *Il conformista* in a short introduction to *La famiglia Rosselli. Una tragedia italiana*. In speaking about his relationship with his cousins, Moravia briefly sketches his interpretation of Italian history from the Risorgimento to fascism and the postwar republic. The words he uses and the kind of political, ideological analysis he drafts show much more than the so often quoted biological hostility, which is reductive and, most importantly, infructuous for a refreshed critical insight on a novel locked up in in the same biographical criticism:

> Il Risorgimento era stato fatto da una borghesia che si illudeva di essere liberale ed era invece in realtà nazionalista. Il liberalismo, certo, c'era, ma era grande e privo di tradizioni ristretto in pochi gruppi familiari. Dopo l'unità e fino alla prima guerra mondiale, la borghesia martellò il popolo con una propaganda agiografica di tipo nazionalista delle più illiberali. Dunque: molto irredentismo, alcune guerre coloniali perdute o vinte, e la fissazione che l'Italia un giorno doveva diventare la nazione egemonica in Europa dopo la Francia, l'Inghilterra e la Germania.
> Cinquant'anni di nazionalismo fanno sì che quando esplode il fascismo, esso trova le masse perfettamente preparate a riceverlo, cioè del tutto impreparate sul piano politico. Bisogna vedere il fascismo come un fenomeno d'immaturità politica delle masse che per la prima volta si affacciavano, come si dice, alla ribalta della storia. Questo non toglie che Mussolini e i fascisti dicevano in piazza le stesse cose che per mezzo secolo la borghesia aveva detto nelle scuole o nei libri di storia patria.
> La famiglia Rosselli apparteneva alla minoranza sinceramente liberale. Era una famiglia con tradizioni risorgimentali (Mazzini era morto in casa Rosselli, a Pisa, sotto il nome di Mr. Brown) e il loro liberalismo aveva l'ingenuità politica che è propria di tutte le minoranze sprovviste di base popolare. Così quando venne il fascismo, essi non riconobbero in quella dittatura borghese che si serviva dell'esperienza socialista il frutto avvelenato dell'albero del nazionalismo risorgimentale. Ritennero di trovarsi di fronte a una tirannide. Avevano ragione: era una tirannide ma di carattere inedito, moderno, quella invocata e voluta dalle masse nel momento del loro apprendistato politico. Di qui la tragedia dei fratelli Rosselli, assassinati in Francia perché si erano opposti, in nome del liberalismo, alla demagogia fascista.[103]

---

103 Alberto Moravia, "Introduction" to Aldo Rosselli, *La famiglia Rosselli. Una tragedia italiana* (Milano: Bompiani, 1980), 1. «The Risorgimento was the product of a bourgeoisie that illuded itself to be liberal while actually being nationalist. Liberalism was, of course, there, but it was restricted to a few family groups. After

Moravia wrote this in 1980, and his ultra-leftist vision of Italian history had certainly changed from 1937, the year when the Rosselli brothers were assassinated. However, it seems that this interpretation might be detected, in its embryonic state, already at the time of *Il conformista*. In the above passage, he sees fascism from 'below,' from the perspective of the masses, whose political immaturity eased the spreading and good grip of the fascist political agenda and propaganda. It is a 'passive' envisioning of the subaltern, whose political inexperience derives not so much from their agency but rather from the wrong education, hagiographic and nationalist, imparted by fifty years of the 'fake' liberalism of the Italian bourgeoisie who believed itself to be liberal while being mainly nationalist. The Sartrean concept of bad faith clearly characterizes Moravia's description of the middle class, and Marcello Clerici himself is, as we will see, a perfect example of bad faith, only in reverse: he believed himself to be a fascist, while still an antifascist. This idea of immaturity also, I believe, indirectly somehow alludes to the famous split between spontaneity and organization that, as I will show in the next chapter, continued to be a matter of debate between *azionisti* and communists within the Resistance. The masses

---

the unity and until the First World War, the bourgeoise hammered the people with an agiographic, nationalist, illiberal propaganda. Therefore: a lot of *irredentismo*, some colonial wars lost or won, and the obsession that Italy would one day become the hegemonic nation in Europe after France, England and Germany. Fifty years of nationalism have the result that when fascism explodes it finds the masses perfectly ready to receive it, that is to say perfectly unprepared on the political level. Fascism needs to be seen as a phenomenon of political immaturity of the masses that were entering for the first time the stage of history. This does not erase the fact that Mussolini and the fascists were saying in the squares the same things that for half a century the bourgeoise had told in books of national history and in schools. The Rosselli family belonged to the honestly liberal minority. It was a family with Risorgimental traditions (Mazzini died at the Rosselli's place, in Pisa, under the name of Mr. Brown), and their liberalism had the political naivety which characterizes all those minorities which lack a base in the people. Thereby, when fascism came, they could not recognize that bourgeois dictatorship was using socialism as the poisonous fruit of the tree of Risorgimental nationalism. They thought they were facing a tyranny. They were right: it was a tyranny, but of a new type, modern, the tyranny invoked by the masses during their political apprenticeship. The tragedy of the Rosselli brothers stems from here and they were murdered in France because they had opposed, in the name of liberalism, fascism's demagogy.» [translation mine.]

are compared to an unprepared, immature youth whose spontaneity, i.e., lack of the right political education, facilitated the rooting and 'seduction' of the fascist credo. Later in the text, Moravia once again uses the term political apprenticeship, thus framing Italian history from unification up until the Second World War in a *bildungsroman* structure, in which the centrality of the political education and necessary 'correction' of spontaneity into organization, also resembles the master plot of the Soviet novel. In a way, it is as if the hero of Stendhal—like Julien Sorel, for example, who never really abandons his innermost true values and ideals but only conceals them, faking a double nature and a perfect adaptation and fitness to those of the bourgeoisie—perfectly exemplifies the result of the liberal, nationalist, idealist education of the Italian bourgeoisie that eventually paved the way to fascism. In contrast, the hero of Gorky, for example, embodies the correct framing of spontaneity and immaturity in political organizations that would straighten and filter the agency of the masses. The configuring of the interpretation of fascism as a problem of immaturity and apprenticeship translates formally into the novel *Il conformista,* in which the two parallel and conflicting models of antifascist education cohabitate in the experimental space of the plot.

Together with the political *bildungsroman*, the other literary genre that Moravia uses to define the experience of Carlo Rosselli and his family, and through him also more generally the experience of a certain liberal bourgeoisie of Risorgimental tradition, is a tragedy, a genre that in the next chapter I will associate with the historiographical accounts of the Resistance written by members of the Action Party. Why does Moravia call the parable of the Rosselli brothers a tragedy? It seems that there is more than a mere sentimental and 'pathetic' judgment of their destiny influenced mainly by the violent circumstances of their death. It is, on the contrary, a precise literary choice with specific ideological connotations that will, together with the *bildungsroman* and the Soviet novel, shape the form of *Il conformista*. The tragedy of the Rosselli brothers is the result of a misrecognition: they could not recognize in fascism and in its signs of an altogether new, modern form of 'tyranny,' the poisonous fruit of that very same tradition of Risorgimento nationalism in which their liberal, idealistic antifascism was also deeply rooted. They could not, in a way, recognize, anticipate, or foresee the consequences, the material realizations of their doctrine. The unity of thought and action, *pensiero e azione*, was one of the ideological standpoints that Carlo Rosselli inherited from Mazzini's philosophy, and *Il conformista* is structured exactly to split the two poles into irreconcilable dimensions, as the slingshot scene in the prologue adumbrates. Recognition is one of the three key generic characteristics of tragedy, according to Aristotle in his *Poetics*. In *Il conformista*, the separation, the severing of Marcello's *pensiero e azione* is realized exactly in a highly problematic and understudied recognition scene, after which the ideological castle Marcello builds in his head in order to justify his action collapses, leaving his acts without any moral necessity. Another inherently tragic aspect is the anti-modernity of Rosselli and his family, seen by Moravia as stuck in 19th-century tradition and incapable of truly understanding the masses and the Italian people from an up-to-date perspective. An anachronistic hero who recalls at once Stendhal's Julien Sorel, still at heart a devotee of Napoleon during the Bourbon Restoration, and the tragic hero torn by the archaic mythical set of values and the 'modern' law of the polis.

Il conformista came out in April 1951. Carlo Rosselli's widow, Marion Cave, his sons and relatives had since 1937 cut every tie with Moravia and the publication of the novel was also received with resentment and hatred. Professor Quadri, in fact, the character based upon Carlo Rosselli, is depicted as a deformed, naïve, snobbish and depraved idealist. However, Rosselli's mother, Amelia, wrote, after a silence of many years, a letter to Moravia in which she must have expressed her opinion on the novel about her two sons. That letter is lost, but it is possible to argue from Moravia's answer that her judgment must have been, surprisingly, not exclusively negative, as she particularly appreciated the page of the killing of the 'two' — her sons — in the woods. Together with the above introduction to Aldo Rosselli's memoir, this letter must be the inescapable starting point of an investigation of the novel that does not content itself with a purely negative judgment of the formal quality of the work and its ideological premises. Yes, *Il conformista* is an important testimony of an unapologetic criticism of one type of anti-fascism. However, what constitutes its unique status in postwar Italian literature is how that criticism takes its shape as a complex novelistic experiment and construction. There is more than its overt psychological meaning and oedipal undertones, and, in a way, it is a work that, by taking the same path as much more celebrated later works such as *Una questione privata,* had the even more ambitious project of framing ideology within the genre of the novel. This may be one of the reasons for its failure as a novel and one of the reasons why it represents an ideal case study of how the novelistic form, in Jamesonian terms, works as a non-genre and experimental field.

In the letter to his aunt Moravia alludes to other contemporary works on the fascism-antifascism couplet and to what he considers the higher stakes of his intentions. Only his aunt seems to have glimpsed the true sense of his attempt:

> Tu hai mostrato di capire il senso del libro e il suo intento, cosa molto più difficile per te che per i tanti critici che invece non hanno capito nulla. Soprattutto mi fa piacere che tu abbia apprezzato la pagina sui due, nel bosco. Io ho scritto quella pagina per i tuoi figli, soltanto quella pagina e lì ho espresso il profondo sentimento che aveva destato in me la vostra tragedia. Ma tutto il romanzo l'ho scritto per spiegare a me stesso e agli altri perché possano avvenire tali tragedie e in che modo. Sarebbe stato facile fare come tanti: mettere da una parte i cattivi e dall'altra i buoni. Ma la mia intenzione era più alta: volevo scrivere un libro che equivalesse ad una tragedia e nelle tragedie non ci sono né cattivi né buoni, ma soltanto personaggi dai diversi destini. Non so se ci sono riuscito ma tale insomma era la mia intenzione.[104]

---

[104] Simone Casini, edited by, *Alberto Moravia. Lettere ad Amelia Rosselli,* 293. «You showed that you understood the meaning of the book and its scope; and this was an even more difficult task for you than for the other critics that did not understand anything. I am especially pleased by the fact that you appreciated the passage about the two, in the forest. I wrote that page for your sons, just that page and there I expressed the deep feeling that your tragedy aroused in me. But I wrote the entire novel in order to explain to myself and to others why certain tragedies happen and how. It would have been easy doing as many do, i.e., putting on one side the villains and on the other side the good ones. However, my purpose was more ambitious: I wanted to write a book that could be read as tragedy and in tragedies there are not good nor evil ones, but only characters with different destinies. I don't know if I succeeded in doing so, but, nevertheless, this was my intention.» [translation mine].

Il conformista is a tragedy *and* a thesis novel whose thesis coincides exactly with its form as tragedy because the author tries to explain why the experience of the Rosselli family was a tragedy by enframing its characters in tragic destinies. This formal choice also has a precise ideological meaning. Moreover, Moravia demonstrates how Rosselli's *Weltanschauung* was itself a tragic perspective on Italian history and present events. It does so by contaminating and undermining the tragic foundations of the plot — prologue, *peripeteia, anagnorisis, deus ex-machina* — with patterns typical of a 19th century, Stendhalian, *bildungsroman* and of the Soviet novel, as hypocrisy and career within a political party, plus the existentialist bad faith. A thesis novel against the bourgeoisie conducted through one of the bourgeois genres *par excellence,* the *bildungsroman.*

Quadri-Rosselli is in *Il conformista* a modern tragic hero, as defined by Agostino Lombardo, a master who educates Marcello — the embodiment of the new generation — as the hero of a book by Stendhal, a subject who embodies an ambiguous compromise between ancient and modern, in whom old, outdated ideals, although still active, needs to be hidden and betrayed in order for him to conform to the modern social rule represented by fascism.

Hence, Moravia envisaged the very plot structure of *Il conformista* as a machinery to deconstruct — and demonstrate as fallacious and counterproductive — the cornerstones of Rosselli's bourgeois ideology: voluntarism, anti-determinism, idealism, humanism, moral individualism and, of course, liberalism. Marcello Clerici is a fascist, but his master Quadri is an exaggerated figure of Carlo Rosselli. The failure of Marcello's strategy of justification, his will to find a logical reason for his action, and his consequent tragic destiny are the direct result of Rosselli's anachronistic values, i.e., ideals that are old illusions that cannot be realized in the concrete historical present by the masses.

Nadia Urbinati, in her introduction to the English edition of *Liberal Socialism,* describes Rosselli's liberalism as a humanism imbued with voluntarism and Bergsonism. His political message was one of contingency over necessity, in which every step of the struggle has a value in itself and not in function of some other future goal and event:

> We will have not *a* goal but *many* goals, as many as are the spaces of our lives in which we succeed in recognizing that our lives perhaps are, or can be, better now than they were before. This time, our actions will have an *absolute* value, not an *instrumental* one. Every point of the space covered by our actions has its own importance, and the results of our deeds will count, even the negative ones, because a defeat can damage us much more now than when we cling to a vision of the final battle. In a permanent war of position, every individual, deed, and result is relevant. And for a liberal socialist there is no other war than a war of position.[105]

The final recognition scene in *Il conformista*, as we have seen, reveals how the first crime had an absolute meaning and not an instrumental value as justification for the second. Tragic necessity targets and annihilates the hero's freedom and voluntarism by revealing his actions to be heterogeneous contingencies and his thought only a universalism forced and imposed on events. In this sense, *Il conformista* is also an important case study to investigate the peculiarities of the Italian tradition and how socialism and Marxism were interpreted and readapted by such political thinkers as Gobetti and Gramsci:

> Both liberals and socialists were reaffirming the humanism of Italian political thought. In the country of Machiavelli and Vico, wrote Norberto Bobbio, it would have been hard to subordinate political action and historical creation to some abstract model or to ironclad laws. [...]
> Rosselli and Gramsci tried to overcome abstract internationalism by inscribing socialism in the Italian tradition, the latter by interpreting Marxism as a radical historicism (following the legacy of Antonio Labriola and Benedetto Croce), the former by activating a dialogue between liberalism and socialism (going back to the liberal-anarchic and the republican roots of the Risorgimento). Whereas Gramsci intended to create an alternative cultural and political hegemony, Rosselli assigned socialism the goal of extending democracy as much as possible and wherever possible. The former envisaged a preferably homogeneous and organic society, the latter a more antagonistic and conflictual one.[106]

There is, then, much more in *Il conformista* than a simple obscure and unnamable hatred towards the bourgeois and Risorgimento values of Rosselli. It is a dialogue and encounter between necessity and liberty, framed in a novel in which the genres of *bildungsroman*

---

105 Nadia Urbinati, "Introduction," in Carlo Rosselli, *Liberal Socialism*, edited by Nadia Urbinati and translated by William McCuag (Princeton: Princeton UP, 1994), LXIV.
106 Urbinati, "Introduction" to Carlo Rosselli, *Liberal Socialism*, XX, XLII.

and tragedy function as the narrative shape of this *quaestio*. Liberty of the bourgeois individual on the one hand, tragic necessity on the other. The fact that Moravia thought of *Il conformista* – and of the life of Carlo Rosselli himself, and of the trajectory of the Italian, bourgeois liberal tradition – as tragedy is of extreme importance to understand that Moravia does not oppose absolute determinism to Rosselli's spirit of liberty, but questions voluntarism through that tragic ambiguity that complicates any clear-cut distinction between good and evil. Of course, Urbinati's elegant, insightful interpretation of Rosselli's thought in relation to Gramsci was not that of Moravia, who, on the contrary, seemed to be more in line with Togliatti's vision of Carlo Rosselli and *Giustizia e Libertà* as a dangerous petit-bourgeois ideology serving capitalism. In a 1931 article published in *Potere Operaio* and titled *"Sul movimento Giustizia e Libertà,"* we can recognize many of the points made by Moravia in his introduction to Aldo Rosselli's memoir: the myth of the Risorgimento as a reactionary tool poisoning the masses, and the conservative, bourgeois and capitalistic nature of Rosselli's idealism, an anachronistic remnant of the previous century. Rosselli is portrayed as being like a protestant preacher enunciating the empty rhetoric of the scandalous gesture and trying to enframe the working class in the ironclad reactionary ideology and philosophical system of the bourgeoisie, a mere tool in the hands of capitalism. Togliatti names his thought, «Rossellismo», as a *poison*, in the same way Moravia will do fifty years later:

> Il piccolo-borghese che era stato sinceramente antifascista, tradito in tutte le sue aspettazioni, aspira al «gesto» come ad una liberazione. Il gesto lo «redime» dalla vergogna di essersi ingannato e di essersi lasciato ingannare, di essere stato, ancora una volta, strumento di una politica che si è conclusa in modo contrario alle sue aspirazioni. [107]

---

[107] Palmiro Togliatti, "Sul movimento Giustizia e Libertà," in *Lo stato operaio*, 5, No. 9 (September 1931) now in Ernesto Ragionieri, ed. by, *Opere*, vol. III (Roma: Editori Riuniti, 1967-1979), 412. «The petit-bourgeois that had been sincerely antifascist, and that saw all his expectations to be betrayed, now aspires to the "gesture" as to a liberation. The gesture redeems him from the shame of having deceived himself, and having let the others deceive him, that is to say, of having

This short passage might as well be the synopsis of *Il conformista*, with the search for a redeeming 'gesture' and an action that ends up contradicting its aspirations. Marcello, then, is a fascist who acts following the lesson of his antifascist master, whose ideals and education produced the contrary of what they intended: a fascist and not an antifascist, a fascist who, actually, will assassinate an antifascist. The boundaries between fascism and a certain antifascism are blurred, and the distinction between the two seems to evaporate altogether since Rosselli's critique of fascism is, according to Togliatti, *still* the fascism it tries to fight:

> La sua critica è quella del pensiero reazionario di cinquanta o sessanta anni fa, è la critica del sistema «che sopprime ogni funzione della volontà umana,» la critica del sistema che vuole «abbattere» ma non può costruire (e il piano dei cinque anni?), è l'affermazione che il proletariato non ha «la capacità» di ricostruire, è la esaltazione dei «valori eterni dello spirito» (sic!) in opposizione al «materialismo» dagli orizzonti limitati, è la protesta perché il marxismo trova una «gioia particolare a spegnere in germe le velleità idealiste,» e così via. Ma che cosa è questa critica del marxismo se non una critica *fascista*? [...] Partito alla scoperta di una sua nuova e originale concezione del socialismo, questo intellettuale democratico non riesce ad altro che ad aggiungere un anello — fragile anello, peraltro! — alla catena con la quale in tutto il mondo le classi dominanti si sforzano di tenere ideologicamente schiave le classi lavoratrici.[108]

The myth of the Risorgimento seems to be the evident proof of *Giustizia e Libertà*'s mirroring of its enemy, fascism. Already in the thirties, before the war, the patriotic component of antifascism

---

been, one more time, an instrument of a political strategy that ended in the opposite way of its aspirations.» [translation mine.]

108 Idem., 416. «His critique is the same one of the reactionary thought of fifty years ago, it is the critique of the system "that suppresses every function of the human will," the critique of the system that wants to destroy but does not desire to build, it affirms that the proletariat is not capable to rebuild, it is the exaltation of the "eternal values of the spirit" (sic!) in contrast to the "materialism" of limited horizons, it is a protest against "Marxism" which finds a "particular joy in erasing the vain ambitions of idealism." However, how this critique can be defined if not as a *fascist* critique? Started off with a new and original conception of socialism, this democratic intellectual [Carlo Rosselli] cannot but adding a ring — a fragile ring moreover — to the chain that the dominant classes of the world uses to keep ideologically enslaved the working classes.» [translation mine.]

created those frictions in the lefts that will reemerge in the heterogeneous nature of the Resistance:

> La dissoluzione del mito del «Risorgimento» nazionale è uno dei risultati cui era già arrivata la critica storica più spregiudicata. Nella propaganda di Giustizia e Libertà il mito viene restaurato in pieno, e nella sua forma più pacchiana, nella stessa forma del resto, in cui lo si trova, col marchio di dottrina ufficiale, nei «libri di Stato» del fascismo per le scuole elementari. Il «Risorgimento» è per il piccolo-borghese italiano, come la fanfara militare per gli sfaccendati. Fascista o democratico egli ha bisogno di sentirsela squillare agli orecchi, per credersi un eroe. [...] Il Risorgimento è stato l'avvento di una classe borghese economicamente debole, non omogenea, interiormente disorganizzata. [...] Perciò il Risorgimento ebbe un carattere stentato, una impronta reazionaria, mancò del tutto dello slancio di altre rivoluzioni borghesi. Ma appunto perciò è assurdo pensare che vi sia un «Risorgimento» da riprendere, da finire, da fare di nuovo, e che questo sia il compito dell'antifascismo democratico. [...] La tradizione del Risorgimento vive quindi nel fascismo, ed è stata da esso sviluppata sino all'estremo. Mazzini, se fosse vivo, plaudirebbe alle dottrine corporative né ripudierebbe i discorsi di Mussolini su «la funzione dell'Italia nel mondo».[109]

From the poisonous fruit of the myth of the Risorgimento to the myth of the republic born out of the Resistance, from one generation to the next, the critical discourse on 'democratic,' bourgeois antifascism keeps certain recurrent patterns, as, still in 1970, the backbone of *Il conformista* will be reused by a young Marxist intellectual, Bernardo Bertolucci, as the ideal text with which, once again, to experiment on similar ideological knots.

---

109 Idem., 418-419. «The dissolution of the myth of the national Risorgimento is one of the results reached by the most unbiased historiographical critique. The propaganda of Giustizia e Libertà renovates this myth in its most tacky form, in the same form that moreover the myth also has in the history books of fascism for elementary schools. The Risorgimento is for the Italian petit-bourgeois what the military fanfare is for the idle ones. Fascist or democratic he needs to hear it in his ears, in order to believe himself a hero. The Risorgimento was the advent of a bourgeoise economically weak, not homogenous, disorganized. Thereby the Risorgimento had a labored character, a reactionary mark, and it completely lacked the impulse that other bourgeois revolutions had. But exactly for this reason it is absurd to thinlk that it exists a Risorgimento that needs to be restored and completed, to be done once again, and that this must be the task of Italian democratic antifascism. The tradition of Risorgimento relives, then, with fascism and it was developed by fascism until its extremes. Mazzini, if he was alive he would have applauded at the corporative doctrines and at Mussolini's speeches about "Italy's function in the world".» [translation mine.]

Il conformista is, then, a palimpsest that, far from being a text merely *against* liberal bourgeois antifascism, deals more, both in its 1951 and 1970 versions, with the question of continuity between the Italian pre-fascist liberal tradition, fascism, antifascism, the Resistance and post-fascist Italy. Two bourgeois authors such as Moravia and Bertolucci, both close to the Italian Communist Party, identify themselves in Marcello Clerici, their hero educated as an antifascist and, eventually turned, on the contrary, into a fascist. His conduct, though, is still inspired by the ideals of his master. Both authors lived the continuity with their past and their belonging to the bourgeoisie with ambivalence. More than a sense of guilt, *Il conformista* – in different ways, of course as a novel and as a film – signals the recognition of an inevitable ongoing presence of fascism in Italian history as an underground, latent, constant. They both explicitly identified themselves with a hero similar to that of Stendhal, while the older generation took the shape of the tragic hero, neither good nor evil, who committed a crime while unaware of doing it and whose aspirations and thoughts resulted in an action with a opposite outcome. Both novel and film were criticized, if not overtly despised, from a political standpoint because of the negative representation of an antifascist martyr such as Carlo Rosselli and also because they targeted and demystified antifascism instead of dealing with the difficult memory of fascism. *Il conformista* is, by some, taken as an example of how Italy avoided the recognition of its past role of evil and guilt, of its responsibilities in the tragedy of the war.

I believe, on the contrary, that if one starts by considering *Il conformista* in its two versions not as a mere 'attack' on Rosselli but as a precisely designed critical tackling of his thought, the palimpsest of *Il conformista* will demonstrate a far more nuanced recognition of the contradictions shared by both fascism and antifascism and an attempt to go beyond that dichotomy. Vittorio Foa, a member of GL and later of the Action Party, in his autobiography, offers a lucid analysis and self-criticism of what those two political movements and realities were trying to achieve, what they did wrong and what, on the contrary, should have been pursued with more tenacity:

> Fascismo e antifascismo, come cemento «esterno» della sinistra, furono un fattore di debolezza; quanto più facile la mobilitazione tanto più difficile l'elaborazione. La più sacrificata della «riduzione» antifascista fu l'elaborazione di un socialismo nutrito di libertà. Qualsiasi tentativo di elaborazione libertaria, negli anni della guerra e anche in quelli successivi, appariva difficile. Resta da capire perché quell'ipoteca è durata così forte e così a lungo in un mondo in rapido cambiamento. È il fenomeno che spiega anche l'anomalia della politica italiana, quella di un partito comunista forte e filosovietico e al tempo stesso sostenitore convinto della democrazia e dei valori nazionali.[110]

Not only is *Il conformista* a sort of *quaestio* on the problem of human liberty and determinism, masked and softened as a tragic necessity, but it is also a novel on projectability, a reflection on how a plan realizes itself as continuity and why, on the contrary, projects might fail, resulting in fractures or in outcomes that contradict their premises and their original aspirations:

> In che misura il postfascismo ha restaurato il prefascismo oppure ha continuato il fascismo? Quale è stato il rapporto fra i valori della Resistenza e il postfascismo che essa ha contribuito a creare? Certo, l'anno 1945 è stato vissuto dai contemporanei come una data di rottura, se non altro perché era finita la guerra e il fascismo non c'era più. [...] Vorrei invece fermarmi un momento sul mutamento nel tempo delle stesse categorie analitiche di continuità oppure di rottura. Penso al mutamento dei giudizi nel tempo. Quello che *prima* si presenta come rottura *poi* si rivela come continuità. La dimensione temporale potrebbe essere il fondamento della vichiana eterogenesi dei fini, secondo la quale i progetti *non si realizzano* nel modo atteso o desiderato ma si *realizzano* sia pure in modo diverso. In carcere ero stato un appassionato lettore della *Scienza Nuova seconda* di Vico e mi sembrava di avere in parte recepito la comprensione della relatività dei processi storici. La storia italiana postrisorgimentale, delle cui letture ero allora assiduo, mi offriva tanti esempi di progetti realizzati in modo imprevisto, magari con espliciti ribaltamenti. La Sinistra storica era stata sconfitta nel processo

---

110 Vittorio Foa, *La mossa del cavallo* (Einaudi: Torino, 1991), 161. «Fascism and antifascism were a factor of weakness if considered to be the external concrete unifying the left; when the mobilization is easy, the elaboration becomes more difficult. The most sacrificed by the antifascit reduction was the elaboration of a socialism fed by freedom. Every other attempt of libertarian elaboration, both during the war and also in the immediate postwar years, seemed hard. It is yet to be understood why such a difficulty lastes for so long in a rapidly changing world. This i salso the phenomenon explaining the Italian political anomaly, i.e., the anomaly of a strong and filosoviet communist party that at the same time is a strong supporter of democracy and national values.» [translation mine.]

unitario e poi occupava il potere con la rivoluzione parlamentare del 1876; l'eredità mazziniana sulla libertà delle nazioni si realizzava ribaltandosi nei nazionalismi oppressivi; più in generale le istanze liberatrici e libertarie della cultura del primo Novecento offrivano il quadro teorico al nuovo assolutismo. Non può essere successa una cosa analoga al postfascismo? E poi ancora per il movimento del 1968?
Ecco allora due domande: perché i progetti falliscono? E come invece si realizzano diversamente, per esempio nel caso specifico del postfascismo? Perché ogni progetto fallisce? Solo perché non se ne possono prevedere tutte le variabili?[111]

Foa's words might as well serve as a critical commentary on Italian postwar literature. A striking number of plots, in fact, are centered upon the question of continuity and break, and, most importantly, on projects and crimes that have gone wrong and on effects that contradict the causes that originated them, on arrows missing their targets and hitting a different one. Rationality and logic are perverted when they face the enigma of fascism. *Il conformista* is only the most exemplary manifestation of this scheme.

---

111 Idem., 161-162. «In what measure postfascism restored prefascism or it continued, on the contrary, fascism? What has been the relationship between the values of the Resistance and the postfascism that the Resistance contributed to create? For sure, 1945 was lived by contemporary people as a date of fracture, at least because the war was over and fascism was not there anymore. I would like, instead, to focus on how the very same categories of fracture and continuity change over time. I think about the change of the judgments about Time. What at first appears as a break *then* reveals itself to be continuity. The temporal dimension could be the foundation of the Vichian heterogeneity of the ends, according to which projects do not realize themselves in the expected or desired way but get realized, regardless, in some other way. In jail I had been a passionate reader of Vico's *Scienza Nuova Seconda* and I thought I partly understood the concept of the relativity of historical processes. Italian post-risorgimental history provided me with many examples of projects realized in an unexpected way, sometimes even with explicit overturns. The *sinistra storica* (historical left) was defeated along the process of unification and then it came in a position of power after the parliamentary revolution of 1876; the heritage of the Mazzinian concept of "the freedom of the nations" was realized, but only by being overturned in oppressive nationalisms; more generally the liberating and libertarian instances of the culture of the beginning of the 20th century provided the theoretical frame of new absolutisms. Could not have happened something similar with postfascism? And then once again with the 1968 protests? Two questions: why projects fail? And how, instead they have a different outcome, for example, as it is the case of postfascism? Why every project fails? Only because it is impossible to foresee all the variables?» [translation mine]

Moreover, Foa's mention of Mazzini echoes Moravia's analysis of Risorgimento nationalism as the unintended cause of fascism and, more broadly, all the libertarian ideals characterizing the beginning of the 20th century, which turned out to constitute the theoretical framework of new forms of absolutism. In the same way, Quadri-Rosselli's ideals of liberty and bourgeois antifascism ended up educating the fascist secret agent who would murder him. A project gone wrong and a theoretical frame linking two crimes — one as the logical, necessary continuation of the other — reveals itself to be an illusionary ideal of continuity covering up a material break, a disruption of meaning and a lack of finalization. The reference to Machiavelli's simile of the archer in the prologue of *Il conformista* exactly alludes to a tradition that will lead to Vico's heterogeneity of ends. In between *thought* and *action,* both Moravia and Bertolucci perceive a break: the unity of the two is an illusion, a chimera of idealism. The awareness of the rupture between ideas and their material realization is the focal point that grounds the narrative and visual organization of *Il conformista.*

1.7 Against Godard?
Bertolucci's *Il conformista* as the formal resolution of two contrasting ideas of cinema: the idealist and the materialist one.

Bertolucci's 1970 adaptation of the novel is now considered one of his finest films, having been both a critical and commercial success. Also, critics read *Il conformista* as a sort of watershed in the career of the young director, whose five previous works — *La commare secca, Prima della rivoluzione, Partner, Agonia, Strategia del ragno* — were highly influenced by the Nouvelle Vague stylistic codes and they were low-budget, alternative films. *Il conformista* was, on the contrary, the first of his works to be produced by a big studio, Paramount, and also the first one starring, in the main role, an international icon of bourgeois, mainstream cinema of the time: Jean-Louis Trintignant. The film, then, was rejected by the most intransigent, leftist critics as a conversion to the mainstream, capitalist production system and distribution circuits, an explicit turning the shoulders to Jean-Luc Godard and to an *engagé* type of cinema that until that point had seemed to inspire Bertolucci's filmmaking practice and philosophy. *Il conformista* represents or better, was perceived as, in fact, also a break from the Nouvelle Vague aesthetics and idea of cinema, a kind of reading corroborated by one, by now notorious, detail: Professor Quadri's address and phone number were Godard's real ones at the time the film was shot and released.

From this detail—that, moreover, Bertolucci defined first as a joke, then, only retrospectively, as perhaps a sign revealing he was actually making fascist films, while Godard's were communist ones—the critical scholarship on *Il conformista* has based the majority of its readings of the film, and of its meaning, on one analytical key, acting both at the formal and at the content level: the Oedipal motive. Through *Il conformista*, Bertolucci kills his 'spiritual' father, Godard, by separating himself from his 'essayistic,' too cerebral style, and at the same time, he 'kills' the generation of his actual father, the poet Attilio Bertolucci, the political fathers of a certain branch of the Resistance, that very same liberal antifascism exemplified by Rosselli, because, by embracing in this way the same Marxist reading of Moravia, Bertolucci sees fascism and the antifascism of the Parisian expatriates, of *Giustizia e Libertà*, as the two sides of the same coin: bourgeois capitalism.

The oedipal, psychoanalytical reading of the film, I think, occluded every other attempt to venture into new, original takes on *Il conformista*, resulting in a sort of critical dead calm, with investigations on the film that have always been following the same, well tested and in part undeniably valid, pathways: Bertolucci rejects Godard, Bertolucci demystifies the Resistance as the founding myth of the First Republic, Bertolucci reveals the continuity between pre-fascist and post-fascist Italy. All these are certainly true points; nevertheless, I am going to demonstrate how they also contributed to, say, 'simplify' *Il conformista* as film, in the end not adding much more than was not already there in Moravia's text.

Bertolucci did not try to kill Godard with *Il conformista*, and, at the same time, his accusation against bourgeois antifascism, old and new, is much more nuanced and ambiguous than it might have seemed. *Il conformista* is, on the contrary, a work of compromise, the site in which the ambiguity of the author, as both filmmaker in between Renoir and Godard, and as Marxist, bourgeois, intellectual, is accepted as the constitutive part of the self. The ideological contradictions and troubles of the young Fabrizio in *Prima della rivoluzione,* again a hero of Stendhal who still lived his belonging to aristocracy with existential angst and a sense of guilt, are now accepted by the author's consciousness: the impossibility of making the revolution is not perceived as guilt but as a fundamental part of the author's own identity and class. Living before the revolution is not perceived any more as a condemnation—as the protagonist of the 1964 film famously stated—but as the opportunity, first, to get rid of a certain kind of idealist remnant and illusion of participating, as bourgeois, in the class struggle, and, second, to do everything is possible within the timeframe of that before, until the revolution will be made by those who are historically 'designed' to actually make it. Films do not, in fact, make the revolution, Bertolucci will state.

The film is, then, more the experiment of a possible coexistence of opposites than the resolute, determined removal of historical and filmic masters. It is a coexistence that also manifests itself at the formal level through a highly complex stylistic ambivalence and generic ambiguity. *Il conformista* is a political film because of its lyricism, its consequences and its completely autobiographical, subjective and self-referential nature. Although this last point has already been noticed by David Forgacs in his audio commentary on the Arrow Films edition of the film—i.e., that the film neither intends to nor does offer a realistic representation of fascism—*Il conformista* has often been read as portraying fascist Italy, and its bourgeois-capitalist continuation after the war, as regimes of shadows and illusions, as societies blinding citizens through the allure of a rhetorical and fictional façade hiding and making up for an ideological emptiness. This interpretation of fascism, as we will see in the next chapter, was a familiar and recurrent one both among liberal socialists and Marxists. In 1970, though, and in Bertolucci's film in particular, this discourse cannot be considered in isolation from the discourse on cinema itself and representation *tout court*. Here,

Godard comes back into play, and his symbolic presence as Professor Quadri—whom we will see is a highly dynamic character embodying at once Godard, Rosselli, Bertolucci himself and his actual father Attilio—turns *Il conformista* not into an oedipal figurative crime but rather into a compromise, a dialogue between different conceptions of film language and the consequent acceptance of the radical ambiguity of the cinematic image. In this sense, the dialogic encounter of idealism and materialism, active as we have seen in the novel, is still present in the cinematic version of the text, this time in the form of a compromise between two distinct notions of cinema, an idealist and a materialist one.

During the years of the shooting and distribution of *Il conformista*, the debate on the essence, meaning and ultimate function of cinema reached its peak, especially in the aftermath of the May 1968 student revolt in Paris, coinciding with the contemporary diffusion of Althusser's works on ideology and apparatus, and, more in general, of post-structuralism. In film theory, this translated into the editorial and critical projects of *Cahiers du cinéma* and the *Cinéthique* group, which, between 1968 and the early 1970s, hosted on their pages a famous debate on the nature and goal of cinema on its history and its relationship and role towards reality. I think it might be useful and fruitful to read *Il conformista* as Bertolucci's contribution to that debate, as an attempt to conjugate a political and a metalinguistic discourse on film and on the acts of both making and watching a film. The highly stylized, metaphorical form through which *Il conformista* continuously refers to voyeurism—to different scenarios of seeing, in a word, to itself as a medium—beyond being a reference to fascism and 1960s bourgeois capitalist society, as empty rhetorical spectacles, are also an attempt to save cinema from a merely ideological reading by reflecting on and accepting its core ambiguity as dreamlike spectacle and as a political tool. In 1970, in that specific theoretical context and moment in the history of film theory, the allusion to Godard is not, then, the declaration of war of the rebellious son in search of an autonomous identity from his father, but, rather, the deictic indication of the addressees of Bertolucci's alternative discourse: the critics of *Cahiers*, of *Cinétique* and, more generally, the French and Parisian cultural milieu of those years, imbued with Althusser's, rather than Gramsci's, interpretations of Marxism.

Bernardo Bertolucci saw one after the other *Deux ou trois choses que je sais d'elle* and *Made in U.S.A.* at Godard's apartment in Rue Saint Jacques in 1966, right after the sound mixing of the two films was simultaneously completed. When asked to pick his favorite by Godard, Bertolucci chose *Deux ou trois choses,* explaining his choice with the help of Roland Barthes' distinction between the *fait divers* and a political murder:

> Mentre *Deux ou trois choses* ha all'origine un fatto di cronaca, *Made in USA* è ispirato a un omicidio politico. Chiamiamo in nostro aiuto Roland Barthes, che ci chiarisce la differenza tra i due termini del problema: l'assassinio politico è sempre, per definizione, un'informazione parziale che rinvia necessariamente a una situazione che incombe all'esterno, prima di esso e intorno ad esso, ovvero «la politica». Il fatto di cronaca, al contrario, è un tipo di informazione totale, o, più esattamente, è un'informazione immanente. Esso non rinvia formalmente a nient'altro che a sé stesso. Ma ecco che Godard rovescia in maniera scandalosa la regola: *Made in Usa* conserva una struttura tragicamente chiusa, mentre il fatto di cronaca di *Deux ou trois choses,* che avrebbe dovuto conservare intatti la sua bellezza e il suo senso—in quanto entità immanenti destinate a risolversi al suo interno—si apre come uno di quei fiori strani e ineffabili che vediamo nei sogni. [...]
> Ora, in *Made in USA,* film politico, traditore della politica, paralizzato nella sua grande libertà dal conformismo ideologico, i colori svaniscono nella magnificenza stessa dei loro smalti—i rossi, i blu, i verdi non sono mai stati al cinema così rossi, così blu, così verdi—e tutto sembra molto simile ad Atlantic City, come *Alphaville* avrebbe dovuto assomigliare a Parigi e al contrario si avvicina troppo ad Atlantic City.[112]

---

112 Bernardo Bertolucci, "Versus Godard," in Bernardo Bertolucci, *La mia magnifica ossessione. Scritti, ricordi, interventi (1962-2010),* ed. by Fabio Francione e Piero Spila (Milano: Garzanti 2010), 141-142. «While *Deux ou trois choses* was inspired by a *fait divers, Made in USA* was inspired by a political murder. Roland Barthes may help us clarify the difference between the two cases: the political murder is always, by definition, a partial information that necessarily refers to an external situation, happening before and around it, i.e., politics. The *fait divers* is a type of information that is complete in itself, or more precisely, an immanent kind of information. It only refers back to itself. Now, Godard reverses in a scandalous way the rule: *Made in Usa* keeps a tragically closed structure, while the *fait divers* of *Deux ou trois choses* that should have kept intact its beauty and meaning—as immanent entities bound to be resolved inside it—opens itself like those strange and ineffable flowers we see in dreams. Now, in *Made is Usa,* a political film that betrays politics, paralized in its freedom by ideological conformism, the colours vanish in the brightness of its tones—the reds, blues,

This article was published in 1967 in issue 186 of *Cahiers* with the title, significant for our purposes, "Versus Godard." The 'pupil' was, hence, already going against his master, but by rejecting only one aspect of one of the two films. He was not convinced by *Made in USA*'s closure and self-referential mechanisms, which eventually turned a film that was thought to be political into its opposite, a betrayal of politics. *Made in USA*, in fact, obsessively refers back to itself rather than opening its discourse to people, to everyone, to a reality closer and familiar to the spectator. *Deux ou trois choses*, instead, avoids self-referentiality to become the carrier of a discourse that regards us all.

1.8 *Cahiers du Cinéma* and *Cinéthique*: The Debate on Cinema in France between 1968 and 1969. Perspective, Depth of Field, Spectatorship.

Starting from the immediate post-1968 years, Jean-Louis Comolli — one of the editors of *Cahiers* and among the most influential figures in French film culture at that time — published in the journal a series of writings — one editorial in 1969 and his key, extensive and wide-ranging work "Technique et idéologie" appeared serially in 1971–1972 — dealing with two main themes of film theory: an interrogation of the realist claims of cinema and an emphasis on spectatorship as necessarily interconnected with ideology, and activity and not as a passive submission to an illusion.

During the late 1960s and early 1970s, Marxism represented the inescapable theoretical framework of film theory in France. The *Cahiers* explicitly turned to Marxism in 1969 and officially aligned itself with the PCF in 1970, only to move toward Maoism in 1971. The key theoretical mentor of the journal's path was, of course, Louis Althusser, and it is through the optic of the Althusserian reinterpretation of the Marxist concept of ideology that the debate, or

---

greens have never been in cinema so red, blue and green — and everything looks very similar to Atlantic City, like Alphaville should have looked like Paris and on the contrary it was similar to Atlantic City.» [translation mine]

better, dialogue, between *Cahiers*, *Cinéthique*, and other figures of French film culture, takes shape.

Through cinema's mechanism and practice — and by means of the impression of reality they offer to the spectator — films contribute to naturalizing "bourgeois ideology" and crystalizing its tenets. The spectator, then, seems to be passively duped, or better, lured, so that they misrecognize the very nature of the impression of reality offered by the camera as an ideological construction. Comolli and Narboni rejected this vision of a passive spectator. They underlined, instead, ideology's interpellation of the individual and the spectator's consequent active participation in the *recognition* of the inadequacies of cinema to transparently transmit reality. In a 1969 editorial titled "Cinema/Ideology/Criticism," they proposed a classification of films into seven categories according to their different degrees of complicity and/or levels of militant intervention toward ideology:

> A) Those films which are thoroughly bathed in ideology, which express it, carry it forward without any gaps or distortions; B) Those films which operate a double action on their ideological insertion. Firstly: a direct political action, at the level of the "signifieds," through the treatment of some kind of explicitly political subject. [...] In order to have any effectiveness, this political act must be linked to a critical deconstruction of the system of representation. [...] C) Another category comprises those films in which the signified is not *explicitly* political, but, in some way, "becomes;" [...]; D) Fourth case: those films which have an explicit political "content" [...], but which in fact do not operate any veritable critique of the ideological system in which they are captured, as they adopt its language and modes of figuration without question. [...] E) Those films which are apparently representative of the ideological chains to which they appear subjected, but in which, through the truthful work through and in the film, there is installed a discrepancy, a distortion, a rupture between the conditions of its appearance [...] and the end product. [...] F) Films pertaining to the direct cinema, first group: those which are constituted by political (social) events or reflections, but which do not truly differentiate themselves from non-political cinema. [...] G) Films of the direct cinema [...] which concentrate on the problem of the representation in making the filmic material function.[113]

---

113 Jean-Louis Comolli and Jean Narboni, "Cinema/Ideology/Criticism (I)," in Jean-Louis Comolli, *Cinema Against Spectacle*, edited and translated by Daniel Fairfax, (Amsterdam: Amsterdam UP, 2015), 252-258.

At first, the above classification seems to be based on an absolute dichotomy, on the opposition between a film practice as a transparent impression of reality or as a conscious, self-reflexive exposure of the impossibility and faults of a transparent impression of reality. In reality, the writers at *Cahiers* tried to go beyond the mere binary opposition, promoting areas of compromise and intersection between the different categories and between the dichotomies of cinema's transparency and self-reflexivity themselves. In this sense *Cahiers'* supposedly oedipal rejection of their master and spiritual father, André Bazin, needs to be considered as a cliché. The Bazinian heritage of the journal is evident, and it represents the crucial, radical difference between *Cahiers* and *Cinéthique*. Bazin's intuition that the fundamental essence of cinema is its relationship with the real was never rejected by *Cahiers,* and, on the contrary, it always inspired and oriented the journal's critical effort to investigate the auteurist canon in search of fractures, distortions, anomalies in their figurative and productive mechanisms, rather than unquestionably dismissing them as the *Cinéthique* group did.

In 1971 Jean-Patrick Lebel wrote for *La Nouvelle Critique* a series of articles—later collated and published by Éditions sociales, the official publishing organ of the PCF—titled "Cinéma et Idéologie," in which he undermined the reading of cinema's "base apparatus" as fully, only, directly determined by ideology, while stressing, on the contrary, the prominence of the *scientific* and *technical* independent nature of cinema and its machinery. In reaction to this *revisionist* text, in *Cinéthique* no.3, Marcelin Pleynet, one of the editors of *Tel Quel,* insisted on a definition of the cinematic apparatus as an entirely ideological instrument diffusing bourgeois ideology. As a consequence, the only viable alternative filmmaking practice left would be one of radical self-reflexivity and "mutism." *Cahiers* never endorsed *Cinéthique*'s dogmatism, proclaiming, instead, that reality itself is "entirely ideological" to begin with:

> It is known that cinema "reproduces" reality "totally naturally," because cameras and film stock are made in view of this very goal (*and within the ideology that imposes this goal*). But it is clear that this reality—susceptible to being reproduced faithfully, reflected by instruments and techniques which otherwise form a part of it—is entirely ideological. In this sense, the theory of transparency (cinematic classicism) is eminently reactionary [...]. Thus, the cinema is burdened from the very beginning, from the very first meter

of film processed, by the inevitability of reproducing things not as they are in their concrete reality, but as they are when refracted through ideology. [...] This is how ideology re-presents itself through the cinema. It shows itself, speaks to itself, teaches itself in this very representation. The most important task of the cinema, once we know that it is the nature of this system to turn it into an instrument of ideology, is therefore to question the system of representation itself: to question itself as cinema, in order to provoke a discrepancy or a rupture with its ideological function.[114]

Bazin and his 'ontological realism' — his conception of cinema as a transparent 'window' on the real, his faith in the camera's ability to capture reality as it is, in its ambiguity and continuity of movement — is, then, questioned, alongside Bazin's idealist history of cinema as the concretization of one of the most ancient dreams of humanity: the myth of reproducing reality and thus of reproducing himself. Bazin's idealism consisted of humanizing the invention of cinema by re-inscribing it within the ancestral space of mythical archetypes while simultaneously denouncing the secondary role played by technology and sciences compared to the magical, dreamlike desire of capturing and representing life itself.

In the framework of his attempt to construct a materialist history of cinema that would go beyond Bazin's ontological realism and the scientific/technological position of Lebel and *Cinétique's* dogmatic self-reflexivity, Comolli, nevertheless, recognizes the importance of Bazin's insistence on cinema as the realization of "an ancient dream of humanity" because, in the end, it correctly, fundamentally places cinema in the area it belongs to that of signifying processes which produce meaning and ideology. Comolli even quotes Lenin's *Philosophical Notebooks* and his admission that "intelligent idealism is more intelligent than stupid materialism." Also, Narboni claims, in his review of *Othon,* that idealism and materialism are separated by an "essential almost *nothing.*"

Comolli's argument in *Technique and Ideology* turns around three main points: perspective, depth of field and the birth of cinema. Bazin's idea of cinema as a transparent "window opened onto the world" is a reference to Leon Battista Alberti's idea of *prospectiva* in his 1435 treatise *De pictura.* Bazin envisages quattrocento's

---

114 Idem., 254.

perspective as the first step leading toward the realization of a faithful capturing of the living world. Thanks to the introduction of the perspectival technique into painting, for Bazin, artists were able to reproduce reality as it was captured by the human eye. According to Bazin's reading of Alberti, perspective was a neutral device, not interfering at all with the objects received and captured, and thus able to imprint reality with transparency. From this system derived the 'birth of cinema' with the invention of the *Camera obscura,* which exactly accomplished what painters had demanded of the *prospectiva artificialis.*

Cahiers and *cinéthique* rejected this idea of perspective, stressing the ideological nature of the scientific discovery, thus conceiving the *prospectiva* — and its rational, mathematic specular code of vision — as the technical tool through which Renaissance humanism and society started to submit Western visual arts to its ideological demand. In conclusion, the camera is an ideological apparatus because its ancestor, the *prospectiva artificialis,* was already an ideological apparatus contributing to regulating all *mimesis* around the singular, unique, central, mathematically established point of view of the human eye. The prominence of the eye and its vision was, then, founded. This conception of perspective as the concretization in the field of the figurative arts of the Renaissance humanistic ideology derives from Pierre Francastel's 1952 work on perspective in *Peinture et societé* and, more directly, from his 1967 *La Figure et le lieu: l'ordre visuel du Quattrocento.* In both treatises, Francastel sees in the Italian painting of the quattrocento the birth of a system of three-dimensional organization of space that satisfied for the next four hundred years the figurative needs of Western civilization. Agreeing with Warburg and Panofsky, he sees the Renaissance perspective, first, as a subjective adaptation of space to the human eye rather than an objective mirror of reality and, second, as a structure, as a quality of the work of art and not as an external cause:

> Une œuvre d'art quelconque n'est pas une représentation, une transposition figurative ou symbolique d'une réalité. L'œuvre et l'artiste ne sont pas extérieurs au monde sensible et au monde sociale où ils s'agissent. Tout cet ouvrage est écrit pour défendre l'idée de la valeur non pas symbolique mais significative de l'œuvre d'art. La perspective n'est pas une cause extérieure,

une recette ou un moyen, elle est un attribut de l'œuvre et de l'activité créatrice, une structure.[115]

The code of monocular perspective also regulates the camera work. Through the use of deep-focus lenses, the space in front of the camera eye duplicates the space as it was organized by the *perspectiva artificialis* in the quattrocento. An apparent depth is given to an otherwise two-dimensional surface thanks to a distribution of objects according to their varying sizes, depending on their relative distance from the fixed, unique point of view of a single spectator. Bazin's special interest in depth of field can thus be explained by the 'reality effects,' by the 'surplus of realism' that deep-focus lenses accorded to the filmic image. Depth of field, according to Bazin, realizes the "realist vocation" of cinema by enabling the cinematic image to capture the ambiguity of the real. Ambiguity means that depth of field is able to frame reality in its continuous unfragmented physical unity, and at the same time, it allows the spectator's gaze to move freely on the surface of the image, from object to object, from foreground to marginal, unfocused detail in the background. The natural unity of objects is not broken—as happens with montage, for example—and the relationship between viewer and image replicates the actual relationship the viewer has with reality itself.

According to Comolli, Gérard Leblanc, writing in *Cinéthique*, aligns himself with Bazin as far as the realist vocation of depth of field is concerned. The camera, by means of long takes and deep focal lenses, works as a *camera obscura* and as a reinforcement of the *prospectiva artificialis*, and, thus, it actually does offer a vision of space comparable to that of the human eye. While criticizing the idealism of Bazin's premises and conclusions, and in particular, as we have seen, his notion of the camera as a neutral, transparent window onto the world, Leblanc, nevertheless, uses Bazin's definition of depth of field as a realist device as proof of the direct dependency of primitive cinema on the *prospectiva artificialis* of the quattrocento and, finally, on its ideological demands. Comolli, instead, claims that depth of field is not a technical instrument that

---

115 Pierre Francastel, *Peinture et societé* (Paris, Lyon: Audin, 1984) 357-358.

offers an unproblematic augmentation of realism «precisely because the depth of field inscribes the representative code of linear perspective better than any other procedure for recording images.»[116] The surplus of realism that perspectival optics is supposed to grant to the filmic image becomes, in Comolli's vision, its opposite: distortion, emphasis on that realistic code for signifying, and not mimetic, strategies. The perspective is, then, not a surplus of realism but an excess of realism, resulting in theatrical, dramatic deformation of space. Comolli can, in this way, highlight the specific, historical meaning of a figurative process—the depth of field—which changes through time and the different styles of different authors. If primitive depth of field might have been misrecognized as realism, it was because reality itself was already organized according to the regulations of monocular perspective. Through a materialist, anti-teleological history of cinema, it is possible, instead, to see how that very perspectival code of vision turns, at some point after the primitive phase of early cinema, into a device with the opposite function of organizing reality in a word, into a signifying practice: «the emphasis on the perspectival code denaturalizes the scene, the code presents itself as something to be read, it functions as a form of reading, and not as "nature," (as was the case in the early cinema.)»[117] Thus, a figurative process that was considered the clearest example of both an idealist and a too-dogmatic ideological categorization of film techniques—as a device fixed, unchangeable throughout the history of cinema, and one that authors could return to and use in the same way, without much difference—becomes, in Comolli's investigation, a historicized phenomenon which might end up signifying the opposite of its original meaning and function. This conclusion allowed the *Cahiers* to revise a lot of Hollywood classics without rejecting them completely in search of those ruptures and anomalies within the formal code of the ideological apparatus. Lebel and Pleynet, by substituting the camera for the cinematic apparatus as a whole, precluded the possibility of considering separately different aspects of film practice

---

116 Idem, 181.
117 Idem, 213.

and its signifying strategies (for example, sound or light or color grading). The camera is then burdened by this identification with a historically specific, determined ideology, which greatly limits the possibility of scrutinizing and analyzing film language and camera work in a specialized fashion, assigning to different practices monolithic fixed labels. In a famous critique of *Cinétique,* published in *Cinéthique* itself, Julia Kristeva argued that the metonymical substitution of the camera for the cinematic apparatus, i.e., the substitution of ideology for the signifier, is a theoretical mistake that leads one to sabotage any specific analytical work on cinema, which thereby gets inevitably obscured by discourses on ideological functions. As Daniel Fairfax precisely puts it:

> What may appear as a contradictory argument can perhaps be clarified with recourse to two Althusserian concepts. The first is the distinction between ideologies in the specific, historically determinate sense, and ideology more generally, as that which "human societies secrete [...] as the very element and atmosphere indispensable to their historical respiration and life." The second is Althusser's concept of overdetermination: that is, the fact that any given situation is "complexly-structurally-unevenly determined" by the structural totality". Reading Comolli in the light of Althusser, then, the cinema is historically *overdetermined* by bourgeois ideology, but this by no means entails that film is by its very nature an idealist phenomenon unwaveringly diffusing this selfsame ideology.[118]

In reinterpreting, years later, Alberti's passages on *prospectiva* in order to undermine Bazin's idea of transparency and window onto the world, Comolli focuses on the ambiguity of the device. Perspective, far from neutrally capturing life as it is, lures the spectator, veiling as much as unveiling reality:

> The veil is, of course, transparent; its transparency, however, is not immaterial. It thus evokes a *screen,* so much so that the scene which is visible on it resembles a mental projection, without the projection ceasing to be a material *dispositive.* The veil serves to distance us from the world. There is a distancing, a gap in the creative gesture. [...] Such a *mise en perspective* can be given the name *"mise en scène."* The practical and moral distance which is interposed between the desire of the artist and the object of this desire appears as the condition of the very possibility of the artistic gesture.[119]

---

118 Daniel Fairfax, "Introduction" to Jean-Louis Comolli, *Cinema against Spectacle,* 10.
119 Comolli, *Cinema against spectacle,* 63.

Cinema shares with painting the necessity of hiding its two-dimensional form with the lure of depth. Depth of field is, then, the quintessential cinematic lure, the masking-unmasking of a flat surface as depth. World and the filmic image are conjugated only on the basis of their uncomplicated 'ideal' correspondence, but because of the perception of a gap, there is a lacuna between them. The material incidence of the human and the camera work cannot be effaced, and it is at once revealed and hidden by the cinema's signifying process. Rather than continuity and transparency, a *cut* stands in between representation and reality, and cinema's vocation is the suture of this lack, of the distance in between:

> When filmed, the world goes missing: from now on, the cinema takes its place, by representing it — in both senses of the word. "The represented is not the real," as Roland Barthes said. Nor is representation. Representation signals the vacancy, the lacuna and the malfunction which makes it possible and maybe even necessary; it notes the lack as real; it joins the edges up, it sutures the cut: it creates matches. Thus, the cinema is above all the art of the match, of montage; and montage is first of all composition, articulation. Whereas the world allows its cuts, interruptions, breaches, fractures, jerks, jolts and elisions to be seen, the cinema intervenes to keep the machinery fastened and secure. This is why the world invented by the cinema is more cyclical than the world of our daily experience. It starts over with every film, every screening. There is a beginning, and an end. In the cinema, we are taken into this repetitive temporality, which is to say that we are far from the eternity of Paradise. So let us here leave all transparency behind.[120]

Alongside perspective and the illusion of depth, montage and its work of cut-suture on the material recorded by the camera becomes the other favorite object of debate between the idealist and materialist conception of cinema. Montage, according to Bazin, disrupts the realism of cinema, destroying the continuity and unity of the real as captured by the camera-window. The *Cahiers* group, on the contrary, rescued the 1920s' avant-garde works of Russian Formalism on cinema and Sergei Eisenstein's theory of montage, seeing in montage a dynamic creative process made of breaks, traces, and ellipsis as long as matches. Montage becomes the re-writing of a preexisting text, an embroilment of a sequence of different texts, thereby showing the referential and not transparent nature of

---

120 Idem, 62.

cinema. While the depth of field might be considered an example of a 'reactionary' cinematic practice because it submits the spectator to one predetermined fixed point of view, montage is 'progressive' because it continuously moves from *estrangement* to *estrangement*, thus provoking 'thought' in the spectator who is not duped and numbed by beguilement and illusion, but, on the contrary, is solicited to maintain a reflexive stance towards the screen.

In an article titled "Montage," published in the March 1969 issue of *Cahiers,* Jean Narboni, Sylvie Pierre, and Jacques Rivette discuss the meaning and function of montage, taking as case studies a series of contemporary films and classic examples from the auteurist canon. A history of montage is then outlined by Rivette, who perfectly puts into practice the idea of an anti-teleological, Marxist approach to cinema:

> So one might, very schematically, distinguish four moments: the *invention* of montage (Griffith, Eisenstein), its deviation (Pudovkin-Hollywood: elaboration of the techniques of propaganda cinema), the rejection of propaganda (a rejection loosely or closely allied to long takes, direct sound, amateur or auxiliary actors, non-linear narrative, heterogeneity of genres, elements or techniques etc.), and finally what we have been observing over the last ten years, in other words the attempt to 'salvage,' to re-inject into contemporary methods the spirit and the theory of the first period, though without rejecting the contribution made by the third, but rather trying to cultivate one through the other, to dialectize them, and, in a sense, to *edit* them.[121]

One of the films that attempt to realize this last principle—together with *Méditerranée* by Jean-Daniel Pollet (1968–)—is Godard's *Made in U.S.A*, released in 1966. Shot in a hurry, in two weeks, during the breaks from the shooting of *Deux ou trois choses que je sais d'elle, Made in U.S.A.* is a hyper-experimental, almost plot-less project loosely inspired by the mysterious disappearance of the Moroccan leader of the National Union of Popular Forces—and of the revolutionary movements of the Third World and the Tricontinental Conference—Mehdi Ben Barka, which occurred in Paris in 1965 in circumstances that have never been clarified. The film appears as a fragmented, disjointed and shredded 'collage,' a visual riddle whose

---

[121] Jean Narboni, Sylvie Pierre and Jacques Rivette, "Montage," in *Cahiers du Cinema 1968-1972. The Politics of Representation,* ed. by Nick Brownie and John Hillier (Cambridge: Harvard UP, 1992), 32-33.

pieces, if correctly re-ordered together, would re-compose the narrative of a *film noir* reminiscent of the great Hollywood *noir* tradition and full of references to the Ben Barka case. Anna Karina plays Paula Nelson, who has come to the imaginary town of *Atlantic-Cité* to find traces of her lost husband. After she murders an informant who is similarly sketchily described, she soon gets caught up in an inexplicable, mysterious political intrigue with two tough guys/secret police officers (played by the two *Nouvelle Vague* regulars Jean-Pierre Léaud and Lásló Szabó, the former bringing with his character a sort of slapstick, comic relief to the film), who follow her moves and the series of deaths that she encounters along her quest. The film was inspired by Howard Hawks' *The Big Sleep* – and by its famously incoherent plot – and it is an open polemic against the cultural, figurative imperialism of the visual and economic imaginary of the USA (in a famous line Karina's character – dressed in a trench-coat as Humphrey Bogart – defines advertising as a form of *fascism*). Godard described the film as political, yet it is shot as a Disney cartoon. Rivette's remarks on the role and use of montage made by Godard in this film insist on one point in particular: the all-compassing referentiality of a film that seems, actually, to be born out of the editing, stitching together of two distinct texts, a visible and an invisible one, lacking one which nevertheless preexisted it:

> With him [Godard] one feels there was (or used to be) an earlier state of the film, an inference the others do not permit. In *Made in U.S.A.* Godard leaves the impression of an earlier film, rejected, contested, defaced, torn to shreds, destroyed as such, but still subjacent. The film only functions in relation to simultaneous referents, more or less tacit but proliferating, encroaching on each other so that they themselves ravel up and weave the entire filmic texture, since ultimately one can feel that there is nothing, no phrase, shot or movement, that is not a more or less 'pure' citation or referent: the important thing being, during the course of the film, not to try to identify all the referents, which would be both impossible and pointless, but to realize that everything is referential, though the referents are set with traps, dissembled, deconsecrated, by an operation that is literally 'terrorist.'
> The initial impulse of the film [...] is in fact a montage idea: what happens if one edits together, if someone combines some lousy *série noire* novel with the Ben Barka affair: not of course the reality of the affair, which I don't know, which escapes me, but as I might have read it about in the papers, as

> I might reconstruct it, *image* it, from a collage of newspapers cuttings; hence a montage of two texts (but also shredding of the pre-texts.)[122]

This passage is an example of how French film criticism of the time began to reflect the critical trends and tendencies of contemporary literary criticism, semiotics and linguistics, as promoted by journals like *Tel Quel*. The focus of criticism ceases to be the 'signified' content and message of a film. It is the signifier now in the foreground, i.e., the analysis of montage and *mise en scène*.

By 1969, Godard had already, in a way, turned his back on *Cahiers* – which he labeled as revisionist – and had chosen to collaborate more closely with *Cinéthique,* founded in February 1969. After having seen an ad in *Tribune socialiste* for a film series on post-1968 cinema organized by two future editors of *Cinéthique,* Jean-Paul Fargier and Jean Puyod, he invited them to a private screening of his last film, *Un film comme les autres*, and decided to give the reel to them so the film could be part of their film series. Narboni, editor at *Cahiers,* attended the event and could not believe *Cinéthique* had been able to get their hands on Godard's last work. Since then, Godard and *Cinéthique* started a close collaboration – the journal was always the first to see his movies – and this might be the reason for the initial distance between the two journals.

Over time, the theoretical positions of *Cinéthique* and *Cahiers du cinéma* varied, getting the journals now in agreement, now in total polemics with each other, following changes in their political views – their alignment with the PCF or their Maoist turn – and also reenacting in film theory the turbulent and complex relationship between the critical rival 'schools' of *Tel Quel* and *La Nouvelle Critique*. It is not my aim to provide here a thorough, in depth analysis of the complicated connections between the journals and their critical and political shifts. With the above overview, I intended to give an idea of the current status of film theory in the years when *Il conformista* was thought, written, shot and edited (also considering it was partly shot in Paris.) Moreover, Bertolucci always considered himself as more belonging to the French 'school' than to the Italian film tradition, as his privileged relation with Godard and his direct

---

122 Idem, 25-26.

collaboration with *Cahiers* show he wrote several articles for them after they had 'adopted' him after a screening of *Prima della rivoluzione* (1964) in Venice. The 'inside joke' and covert reference to Godard in *Il conformista* – Professor Quadri's address and phone number were Godard's at that time – has so far, in my opinion, misled the critical studies on the film toward an Oedipal reading at the formal level – the student kills his master, thus becoming an 'adult' moving beyond his *Nouvelle Vague* youth – with which to confirm both the overall psychoanalytical undertones of the film – the son kills his father – and its political message – the new generation of post-'68 Marxists getting rid of the bourgeois antifascist myths and idealism of the older generation. The result is, somehow, that of a dog chasing its tail, constraining, in most cases, the readings of the filmic text to the cyclical return to the same clichés. One critical key to access the text gets used for every level of interpretation: formal, lyrical and political. I believe that the reference to Godard might be used, instead, as the indication of a will to participate directly in the cultural, critical and theoretical turmoil of those years, with a work that would address, in practice, all the main topics and points of the current debate among film theorists. *Il conformista* is, in this sense, a very Godardian 'film essay,' through which Bertolucci positioned himself in relation to the fundamental discourses on the essence and history of cinema, and thus on perspective, montage, *mise en scène* and spectatorship. The coeval studies of all these themes in *Cahiers* and the other contemporary French journals are all indirectly present and alluded to in *Il conformista*, a film in which perspective and depth of field, montage and their relation to the spectator are all major concerns for Bertolucci, who structures his film around them, as a study on them, on their history as signifying processes and specific film practices, and on their place and function in contemporary cinema. It is a discourse on gaze, then, and, more broadly, on spectatorship and the type of involvement and relationship that the film image activates triggers in the cinematic audience. In shooting *Il conformista*, Bertolucci intended to give his contribution to a reassessment of the history of cinema itself, starting from a reflection that goes as far back as to the mythical or scientific origins of cinema to the primitive relations that the camera's apparatus establishes between itself, reality and the spectator **(Fig. 36-40)**. Bertolucci's wide, constant use of quattrocento perspective testifies to his reflection on the nature of the cinematic apparatus as 'technical' rather than as a transparent gaze. While on the Trocadéro, Giulia even directly refers to the tricks of perspective, and Bertolucci seems to answer her by playing with the constant perspectival resizing of the figures of Marcello and Giulia, now larger, now smaller than the Eiffel Tower in the background **(Fig. 41-43)**. The Trocadéro is an example of a perspectival organization of the urban space, in much the same way as the Renaissance ideal city of Tara was in *Strategia del ragno*. It is not by chance that Bertolucci, between 1968 and 1970, decided to shoot on location, to film on a reality already framed in perspective before being framed by the camera. As Comolli thought, it is not that cinema is ideological; reality is itself, since the beginning, marked by ideology.

As we have seen already in Moravia's novel, the conflict between idealism and materialism — and their corresponding, alternative ways of framing and interpreting both fascism and antifascism itself — was the philosophical as well as the formal premise and structuring pivot of the entire work. Carlo Rosselli's thought is not only targeted but, more importantly, also addressed and rhetorically challenged by Moravia, who metonymically takes his cousin as the representative of an entire class and specific politico-philosophical tradition. It seems that the film, too, stages a similar encounter between an idealist and materialist side. However, this time, the encounter takes place at the level of concurrent ideas on the nature of cinema, i.e., the idealist 'ontological realism' of Bazin and his belief in the transparency of filmic practice on the one hand and, on the other, the deconstruction of realism in cinema as one signifying practice among others and the materialist notion of cinema as an 'opaque' apparatus diffusing the dominant bourgeois ideology.

However, just as Moravia did not completely turn his back on Rosselli and *Cahiers* did not absolutely reject their spiritual father, Bazin, so did Bertolucci when it comes to finding an independent position on contrasting ideas about 'making' cinema. I will show how *Il conformista* attempts a compromise between the two poles, favoring and accepting ambiguity over a dogmatic, radical Manichean choice, implied, instead, by the widespread oedipal reading. Bertolucci, in fact, in superimposing the images of Quadri-Rosselli-Attilio Bertolucci (his actual father and famous poet) to that of Godard, is actually staging a parallel conflict taking place within himself, with one idea of cinema—a Bazinian one, rooted in the French cinema of the 1930s—still latent and able to coexist with a new idea of cinema as, in part, theorized by the contemporary French film theory. Thus, Bertolucci 'kills' Godard by savaging what could actually still be saved of the cinema of Godard's 'fathers'—Bazin, Renoir, and others—aligning himself more toward the *Cahiers'* history of cinema and Comolli's recuperation of certain film practices of Hollywood's golden age and the European auteurist canon, rather than the dogmatic and radical rejection of all idealism-realism realized by *Cinéthique* and by the Godard of the late sixties. The paradox is that, while Bertolucci, in my reading, seemed to base *Il conformista* on Comolli's anti-teleological history of cinema by recuperating the 'grandfathers' over the 'fathers' and by making them coexist, film historians have framed *Il conformista* in a teleological narrative by reading it as Bertolucci's rupture with the past and as his stylistic 'coming of age.' In the same way as the very function of the teleological plot structure of Moravia's novel was exactly that of being finally negated and revealed as an illusion through the final recognition scene with Lino, the 'montage' of *Il conformista* is essentially anti-teleological and disruptive of narrative linear progression.

Marcello Clerici, the hero of both the novel and its adaptation, is a fascist character, one of the few examples in Italian literature and cinema (but doubtless the most famous case) of a plot with a fascist as protagonist and not a minor figure or villain. He, in some measure, ambiguously embodies both authors, Moravia and Bertolucci, who do not enframe and emplot their hero as the mere other, as the fascist-bourgeois enemy to absolutely condemn. Marcello Clerici represents their common, inescapable bourgeois upbringing and roots, recognized with a mix of guilt, resignation and awareness, and in fact, they emplotted him within a tragic discourse and a psychoanalytical one, thus explaining his life as a product either of tragic fate or of subconscious forces that escape his will. Both authors assign to their hero the function of relativizing and questioning a certain kind of bourgeois, liberal and idealist antifascism. Marcello Clerici is an enigma, the ambiguous figure in which the opposites mirror each other and abnormality and normality, fascism and antifascism, villain and hero, idealism and materialism, coexist. In the novel, the recognition scene is the textual place that unveils the enigmatic structure of the representation, turning the two crimes into the two nonmatching parts of a metaphor. In the film, it is the *mise en scène* itself and, especially, the editing that inscribes an enigmatic 'logic' by turning every shot of the film into the pieces of a riddled, oneiric structure, continuously suggesting a meaning only to deny it later, by trying to superimpose in every scene difference, rupture, dissymmetry and incoherence at the level of film practices and choices. The carnivalesque, dynamic relativity and ambiguity of the hero are reflected in the aesthetic form that enframes him.

The relationship between *Made in U.S.A.* and *Il conformista* cannot go unnoticed, given the extremely similar political-murder plot (even though studies on Bertolucci have always preferred *Le Petit soldat* as the main Godardian referent because, anachronistically, in my opinion, the signified has been preferred over the signifier). Bertolucci takes Godard's film as the starting point of his formal operation, which is both similar and opposite to his master's **(Fig. 1-6)**. While in *Made in U.S.A.*, as we have read in *Cahiers'* article, the spectator has the impression of a disrupted, shredded urtext preexisting the actual film — which appears then as an editing of two films, a *noir* and a Disney-pop version of it — in *Il conformista* the cinema of the 1930s of Renoir, Ophüls, Von Sternberg and Welles is used as a historical reconstruction of that epoch, the story being set in 1938. Bertolucci, who did not directly live and see those years, gives cinema the status of reality: «pensare il cinema degli anni 30 come se fosse la realtà degli anni 30.» There is no stitching together of two films that might activate a process of estrangement in the spectator, constantly made aware of the existence of a multiplicity of independent texts and thus of a reality that exists only as pure referentiality. Bertolucci uses citation to recreate the illusion of reality, of a specific time and place in the past, in a way rescuing the Bazinian vocation of cinema as reality itself, or at least as the only viable substitute for a lost past reality never directly witnessed. Thereby, there is in *Il conformista* a different idea and function of referentiality and quotation, which are used by Bertolucci not to denounce them as a closed process with no ultimate access to the real, to the 'signified,' but, on the contrary, to recreate a past world that to the eyes of Bertolucci, i.e., to the eyes of someone who never witnessed it, has actually only been existing in cinematic form. Referentiality is lost here, too, but this loss has an altogether different meaning and connotation than in *Made in U.S.A.* The author and the spectator occupy the same point of view as voyeurs and cinephiles.

1.9 Theory in Practice: 'Inside the Gaze' of *Il conformista*.

Il conformista seems to be more interested in 'seeing' practices and in structuring itself around the gaze of spectators rather than deviating their look onto the nature of the film as the text of a text. In this sense, I will propose an analysis of selected sequences of the film, those in which perspective and depth of field, montage and subjective shots play with the spectator's gaze by simultaneously questioning the nature of the camera's eye itself and by addressing, alluding to, the history of the different ideas of cinema and its relationship to the real. *Il conformista* always seems to hide the point of view from which the scene is seen. It simultaneously includes in the sequence multiple possible coexisting perspectives, which seem to negate each other reciprocally. The subject of the gaze is constantly questioned, and so is their apparently safe point of view on the events taking place. The identification of the onlooker's gaze with one of those perspectives is troubled by a series of visual lures, hints and expectations punctually betrayed. The act of looking is left without a fixed, secured subject and origin. It is an enigma in which the camera's and the spectator's eye give, at times, the illusion that they coincide, allowing transparent access to the world, and at other times, the opposite, estranged recognition of their irreconcilable difference and then of the camera's opaque materiality. The ambiguity between idealism and materialism, between a Marxist and a liberal antifascism, between fascism itself and antifascism tout-court, and between a Bazinian and an ideological conception of cinema surfaces also at the level of the formal strategies through which Bertolucci inscribes in the film his and the bystander's gazes.

After having left the Hôtel d'Orsay and having been picked up by the OVRA agent Manganiello, Marcello sits in the back of Manganiello's car. While the two drive across a gloomy, blue Paris — with an objective shot of the car crossing a bridge and being overtaken by a moving train — the sequence is organized as a series of four close-ups of Marcello seen through the windshield, his face obliquely cut by the wiper, interlaced with a series of three subjective tracking shots of Paris buildings from Marcello's point of view in the back seat on the right **(Fig. 7-8)**, or at least they seem to be subjective shots. In fact, in none of these close-ups does Marcello look outside the car window on his right. Instead, in all four shots, his gaze is lost straight in front of him. So, who is looking outside? Whose gaze is that? The four shots with the camera in movement on the car are, in fact, "falsely subjective" because each close-up shot that introduces them suggests the typical, apparently linear shot/reverse-shot — subject looking/object looked at — construction of the subjective shot. The sequence could work as a subjective configuration if only the subject and object were disposed along the same visual axis, but they are not. Francesco Casetti, in his *Dentro lo sguardo,* defines the "falsely subjective configuration" of a shot as an unkept promise, a lure as theorized by Roland Barthes. [123]

Hence, while in the subjective configuration, the bystander's look coincides with the diegetic gaze of a character, thus being dragged to look from the inside of the filmic text, in the falsely subjective configuration, there is a sort of tension between the will to be and the being of facts, the vocation, promptly masked, revoked, of getting the spectator in direct contact with the character's stance towards the reality in front of them. In *Il conformista* the "falsely

---

[123] Francesco Casetti, *Dentro lo sguardo. Il film e il suo spettatore* (Milano: Bompiani, 1986), 85-86. [Francesco Casetti, *Inside the Gaze. The Fiction Film and Its Spectator,* translated by Nell Andrew with Charles O'Brien (Bloomington: Indiana UP, 1998), 67-68.]

subjective configuration" is a recurrent syntactic construction that says a lot about what is meant by the positioning of the spectator. After the 'terrorist' stance toward the audience of Godard and of the early Bertolucci, the frequent use of this kind of construction in *Il conformista* certainly signals a change, but, once again, it is an ambiguous one because the false subjective winks to the role of the onlooker but it does so by means of rupture, dissymmetry and a break in the expected, linear syntactical order.

The tracking shot of the Paris buildings has at least three main meanings: first, it defines Marcello in the position of an ambiguous viewer, as he seems to be the subject in charge of the gaze and then refuses the role; second, it suggests to the onlooker that what they see on the screen is shown by the camera, thanks to the author's gaze and not because Marcello is looking at it for diegetic reasons related to the story; third, it inscribes the author's discourse on cinema itself, as a reflection on its nature as 'reality' of the illusion. In fact, right after an objective shot of a train taken from the same angle as Lumière's *L'Arrivée d'un train en gare de La Ciotat* (1896), the 'artisanal' tracking shot from the car in movement is, I believe, if not a direct reference, an allusion to the same estrangement effect and illusion of movement that the first tracking shot in the history of cinema provoked in the audience. Alexander Promio, who was Lumière's most famous cameraman, while on a boat with his camera, started to film Venice's palaces facing the Grand Canal as they passed by. Promio was worried: would spectators think that the palaces were weirdly, unnaturally moving, all by themselves, along the canal? He thought the illusion of movement might have generated a reaction similar to the locomotive coming out of the screen at the *Grand Café* in Paris. The shot of the palaces—a view that Marcello ignores because lost, as we will see, in his reveries—is part of the author's and the camera's own gaze, thereby activating a dialogue with the spectator on the birth of cinema and a reflection on the primitive illusions triggered by the apparatus. The onlooker is brought back to its original innocent relationship with cinema. Is it the world within the frame that is moving, or is it the other way around, the frame that moves, and the world is fixed? In order to believe in the illusionary movement of things, the spectator needs to forget and overlook the frame, thereby allowing that transparency of the apparatus as imagined by Bazin; the frame is, then, an opened window onto the world. The homologous relationship between window and frame is underlined as one of the main objects of reflection throughout the film, especially in the sequence coming right after this one and taking place in the EIAR, the radio broadcasting studios, or in the famous scene when Marcello and Giulia are in the train cabin, while behind them, through the window, the spectator can see highly overdramatized scenarios passing by. The look out of the train window and the spectacle of early cinema are once again superimposed: «The train is above all a place where the immobile traveler is seated and watches a framed 'spectacle' pass by.»[124] Bertolucci keeps the ambiguity between window and frame open, on the one hand, by making camera movements evident, thus attracting the attention of the bystanders in the frame and negating the Bazinian "window open onto the world," on the other hand, by bringing back to the spectator a configuration frame/window/movement allusive to the illusion of that transparency given by early cinema, Bertolucci reclaims the illusion of reality, transparency as artifice, as cinema's essence. Many critical readings of the film — including Christopher Wagstaff's still fundamental formal analysis — assign to Bertolucci's meta-discursive practices and the recurrent presence of cinema-within-cinema constructions the meaning of a critique of fascist and bourgeois ideological propaganda built on the contraction of a fictive, illusionary world of shadows (hence the reference to Plato's Cave). This is partly true; however, it seems that as far as the discourse on the nature of cinema is concerned, Bertolucci goes in the opposite direction by recognizing the mythical, idealist 'dreamlike' vocation at the core of filmic practice, namely to make shadows be misrecognized as images of the real. Cinema is not merely an ideological apparatus, and the cinematic lure, far from being a technique to diffuse the bourgeois dominant ideology indiscriminately, is a pleasure that cinema has offered, by its very nature, to the spectator since its mythical 'birth.'

The next sequence takes place at the radio studio of the EIAR. The middle horizontal third of the frame is filled with another

---

124 Jean-Louis Leutrat, "Les chemins de fer," in Leutrat, *Le Cinéma en perspective: une histoire* (Paris: Nathan, 1992).

frame, or more exactly, a window, through which Marcello is watching what is going on behind the screen: a small orchestra and a choir of three ladies recording a song. Marcello has his back turned to the camera, but then he suddenly turns towards it and the person he is talking to, Italo. Christopher Wagstaff describes the beginning of this sequence as a classic reverse-angle sequence carrying the dialogue between Marcello and Italo about the former's desire to achieve normality through marriage. In what seems to be a classic subjective configuration, we first see Marcello from Italo's point of view and then Italo from Marcello's perspective. Nevertheless, this is, in a way, falsely subjective if we consider that Italo is blind and thus, the spectator's gaze cannot find its diegetic anchor in Italo's gaze. Who is looking at Marcello while he is looking at the spectacle behind the glass? The blindness of Italo turns the subjective configuration into an "unreal objective view," further marked by the horizontal movement of the camera that apparently follows Marcello as he moves horizontally along the window while telling the anecdote about Hitler: the author is showing the spectator that what they are seeing is thanks to him, to his *mise en scène*, and not because an identification with a character's point of view is possible. The attention is directed towards the camera and towards the movement of the frame, which follows, as a shadow, the main character. If we look more closely at the movements in the scene, we can notice a third horizontal oscillation taking place simultaneously with Marcello's and the camera's tracking shot that seems to mirror it. Behind the window, in fact, the singing trio starts a little choreographed dance, oscillating their bodies and arms now to the right and now to the left, in coordination with the music, Marcello and the camera. Who is following whom? Is the camera following Marcello's movement or the parallel movement taking place behind the window, or is every move paced by sound? Both David Forgacs and Christopher Wagstaff agree in seeing in this scene a reiteration of Plato's cave and a representation of the fascist regime as a show, a display of empty rhetoric and illusion:

> The life he is trying to establish with Giulia has the same status as the show that is going on behind him. The girls are *choreographing* their song to nonexistent viewers (a microphone cannot pick up a visual message). The brightness of the light and the dancing of the girls contrast with the darkness

and immobility of Marcello, and the effect is to endow the world beyond the pane of glass with greater intensity as an object of desire, corresponding to Marcello's heaven. But it is in fact, a show, an illusion, and the pane of glass 'says' that. [...] Bertolucci wishes to suggest that the radio broadcast is bourgeois capitalism's way of 'selling' an ideology to the masses.[125]

The show going on behind the glass pane is interpreted, then, mainly negatively as an illusion sold by capitalism to the masses/audience. David Forgacs in his audio commentary to the film, does underline Bertolucci's cinephilia as one of the main themes of the scene at the radio studio. I would try to expand the textual consequences in the syntactical configuration of this scene. In fact, in my opinion, the framed show behind the window — as Forgacs notices a screen within a screen — does not metaphorically allude only to the negative illusion of both capitalism and fascism (as framed by a Marxist interpretation of both as bourgeois ideology's products), but also to the positive 'idealist' myth of transparency of the cinematic apparatus. The camera, by replicating the dance of the singing trio through the tracking shot, betrays its involvement in the show and the pleasure of watching it. Marcello, once again, is not the object of the gaze, or better, not directly, at least. He cannot see what is happening behind the glass pane. What he does see is the camera movement in front of him: the character mirrors the tracking shot while the author confesses his pleasure in looking at a nostalgic illusion. The reality of the camera is made evident, and the transparency of the window is revealed as artifice while, at the same time, the camera apparatus gets fascinated by the show taking place in the screen within the screen. Cinema mirrors cinema. Bertolucci turns the self-reflexivity of cinema into the methodological principle of the scene's *mise en scène* and makes it a pleasurable spectacle rather than a 'terrorist' practice toward the viewer. The Bazinian window onto the world is both a transparent and reflective surface. Wagstaff further comments that Bertolucci does not maintain a coherent formal and political discourse throughout the film. In his discourse, he explains:

---

125 Christopher Wagstaff, *Il conformista* (London: BFI / Palgrave McMillan, 2012), 32.

many say lots of things without ultimately saying any one overall thing. And in this it breaks away from political cinema of the time, where discourse, and a coherent 'position', were critical. This can help us to understand Bertolucci when he says that he moved from demanding penance from his viewers to wanting a dialogue, to penetrate directly to their emotions to give pleasure to his audiences.[126]

More than a dialogue, *Il conformista* represents a compromise between 'penance' and pleasure. As we have seen, the positions of 'political' film criticism of the time were not at all coherent, and they were shifting from journal to journal and from editor to editor. Bertolucci, with *Il conformista*, attempted to turn *Cinéthique*'s discourse on cinema — and more generally the ideological 'apparatus' conception of cinema — into a spectacle, into *Cahiers*'s idealist take on the original essence of cinema. Godard's 'terrorism' toward the viewer is reconfigured as *mise en scène* that is a pleasure for the viewer.

There is another shot in the sequence that Wagstaff does not notice or decides to skip. After Marcello delivers the punchline ("It was Hitler") of his speech, and the singing trio has finished the song and left the studio — parading in front of Marcello, who faces the window but cannot be seen by them — Marcello suddenly turns toward the camera again, which cuts towards a profile image of Italo who tries to get into the recording studio through a door **(Fig. 9)**. This is another falsely subjective configuration. The reverse-angle sequence of shots of Marcello looking at Italo standing up and of Italo, as seen from the point of view next to the glass pane, of Marcello suggests that we viewers are looking at the scene with Marcello from his visual angle. The onlooker is given a position from inside the frame; they see, know and believe as Marcello does. The will to be and the being are once again severed. The camera follows, in an indecisive, slightly trembling movement very reminiscent of a human eye, Italo, as he moves from the door to the window **(Fig. 10-11)**. Once he gets to the glass pane, Marcello unexpectedly appears behind him, in the field in the background of the frame **(Fig. 12)**. What we supposed to be the subject of the camera's gaze is revealed to be another object of that very same gaze. A subjective shot is unmasked as an unreal objective that, instead of bringing the

---

126 Idem, 36.

bystander inside the frame, keeps their gaze outside of it. The author's gaze is, then, the protagonist of the scene, having dispossessed by means of *decoupage* and *mise en scène* both character and spectator of their chances to be subjects of the look. As Marcello is kept outside the window of the radio studio (but inside the frame of the shot), so it is the audience of the film whose gaze is first let inside the frame through the identification with a diegetic point of view and then left outside the 'window', which is at once transparent and opaque.

There are three more scenes in which the unkept promise of the falsely subjective configuration is charged with the author's reflection on the different acts of looking and framing put in motion by the cinema apparatus. The first two cases I am going to investigate are both set in Paris and have Marcello and Anna Quadri as protagonists. After the reenactment of Plato's myth of the cave in Quadri's studio, Marcello crosses a long corridor (the shot makes wide use of perspective and depth of field to frame Marcello in a clearly defined geometrical space—something I will discuss shortly) and then stops on the threshold of a room, looking at Anna Quadri and Giulia, his wife, while they listen to a record and the professor's wife declaims a poem by Apollinaire. First, we see a close-up of Giulia, then a low-angle shot of Marcello stopping on the threshold of the room, where in the distance, we can glimpse the two women, and third, a medium-long shot of Anna and Giulia in the room **(Fig. 13-14)**. Presumably this last frame is Marcello's subjective, what he sees as captured from his point of view right on the threshold of the room. When Anna acknowledges his presence by looking directly into the camera, Bertolucci does not show what she is looking at because it is obvious it is Marcello. However, with a tracking shot to the left, the camera follows Anna entering an adjacent room and inviting Marcello to follow her so they can talk in private **(Fig. 15)**. The camera seems to be Marcello moving on the left to follow the parallel movement of Anna while keeping an eye on her. However, then—in much the same way as the scene described earlier in the EIAR studio—Marcello appears on the threshold of the other room **(Fig. 16)**, with his back to the camera and already looking at Anna. He closes the door and then Bertolucci cuts inside the room, with Marcello once again shot from behind while he still holds the handle of the door, as seen from Anna's point of view from within the room. The falsely subjective construction of the first part of the sequence is, once again, a lure that leaves the gaze as if suspended and floating without a subject for the duration of the tracking shot. The end of the camera movement reveals that the character we thought was the subject of looking is also an object of that same look. As Marcello is always represented on thresholds, the bystander is constantly kept in the uncertain position of recognizing their gaze in a diegetic point of view and then realizing they have been 'tricked' and left out, as literally happens in this scene when Marcello shuts the door in front of the camera. There is also an interesting use of the depth of field and perspective that frame Marcello before one of his acts of voyeurism, placing him at the center of a well-organized, rational, and controlled space. Then, the object of his gaze, Anna, in this case, seems to deconstruct the perspectival, mathematical laws that organize the profilmic space around one fixed point of view. Depth of field, considered by Bazin the foundation of cinema's 'ontological realism,' of its quality of transparent window opened onto the real world, is paired with a tracking shot. This minimal horizontal camera movement undermines every 'geometrical' humanist certainty built by perspectival vision and a mathematically determined point of view.

The sequence inside the adjacent room—while Giulia is left alone in the other room still listening to the gramophone—indicates Marcello's lack of control and inability to dominate the object of his gaze, Anna, always by means of a configuration of different gazes at play and subjective, semi-subjective shots. In Anna Quadri, Marcello recognizes his abnormality. In fact, the protagonist of the scene is a mirrored armoire **(Fig. 17)**. Bertolucci uses the mirror to place Anna and two versions of Marcello along a transversal axis that crosses the frame. We see Marcello's reflection looking at Anna's from behind (thus unseen), then Anna looking at the real Marcello out of frame. Bertolucci manages with this frame to superimpose an unreal objective on a semi-subjective shot, signifying Marcello's absence as an actual viewer and his simultaneous presence as framed reflection and object of Anna's gaze.

Moreover, while Marcello is enframed in a mirror, Anna is framed by a window. Cinema as transparent opened window onto the world, and cinema as a reflection of reality is inscribed in the décor of the set. The theatrical *mise en scène* brings the off-screen space into the frame, once more attracting the onlooker's attention to the artificiality of cinema as a reflection of reality. Nevertheless, the negation of transparency and the simultaneous lure that unmasks the illusionary nature of the filmic image do not aim at a reaction of estrangement in the audience but, on the contrary, are carried on by a *mise en scène* that transforms the ideological standpoint into spectacle, into pure cinema. Bertolucci's discourse on cinema as illusion and as an ideological apparatus does not only have a *pars destruens*; it also has a *pars construens* consisting of finding a space for the illusion of cinema's transparency within the signifying practices of what the *Cahiers* defined as militant cinema.

It has already been widely noted how the film is constructed as a series of repetitions and variations of motives, also thanks to the editing by Franco "Kim" Arcalli. His technique of montage is fast-paced and based on allusive, diegetic references between frame and frame, collapsing scenes together as if moving through 'layers' of a Bergsonian memory. The link between shots favors metaphor over metonymy, free association over contiguity, but is always symbolically motivated by the psychology of the main character, Marcello, and the work of his subconscious. The result is a montage that dismantles a previous narrative told in chronological order and redisposes its fragments in an ambiguously anti-teleological and cyclical structure. It is ambiguous because, however disjointed, *Il conformista* works more or less as a tale within a tale, with a framing narrative – the car ride, a classic device – and the story of the events that led to that point in time. The joint between two narratives – the chronological one and its anti-teleological redisposition – very literally puts into practice the distinction of *fabula* and *syuzhet*, also considering that Arcalli's editing is heavily influenced by Eisenstein's theoretical work on montage. Those were exactly the years when Russian Formalism started to be rediscovered in French literary circles, and their works on early cinema, as well as Eisenstein's theories on montage began to be published in *Cahiers* right between

1968 and 1970. If we consider Godard's *Made in U.S.A.* as the antimodel of *Il conformista*, the latter's ambiguous formal strategy might appear more clearly compared to the 'radical' and 'terrorist' take of the former on the matter: the meaning of the fragmented preexisting text is not lost, but, on the contrary, it represents the solution to the *enigma* of the framing text, Marcello's journey to the assassination of the Quadris, his complex psychological motives. Referentiality between the jointed texts is thwarted, but citation, reference, allusion and free association are the very formal devices that montage uses to both destroy *and* reconstruct a narrative. Also, at the level of montage, we might notice a 'materialist' technique — Eisenstein's montage, and montage in general, was considered by Bazin as the number one enemy of cinema's ontological realism — guided by an idealist, Bergsonian, conception of time. Spontaneity and organization, free will and determinism are the opposite poles within which this further narrative of the ambiguity between fascism and liberal, idealist antifascism oscillates.

The parallel scene to the 'mirror' one described above takes place at the Hôtel d'Orsay, where Marcello and Giulia are staying. After having passed through a mass of upper-class guests of the hotel — he is getting out of the elevator while they try to flock inside it — Marcello is framed in a long shot that places him at the end of the corridor, further framed by a mirror, exactly at the vanishing point of a quattrocento like perspective **(Fig. 18)**. Bertolucci uses a highly stylized depth of field for purely dramatic and rhetorical reasons: Marcello's isolation and lack of conformity, also signified by the group of upper bourgeois individuals going in the opposite direction to his, as will happen again in the farandole scene and at the end. However, as we have seen, the deformation of space according to the mathematical, rational scheme of the *prospectiva* also refers to a system of domination of the profilmic space thanks to a gaze well secured in a fixed, unique and anthropocentric point of view. By way of the perspectival organization of the profilmic space and of depth of field, Bertolucci introduces a voyeuristic scene — the witnessing of the 'primal scene' — that will shake Marcello's conformism to the dominant ideology, reminding him of his tendency to perversion (and I have already noticed how both in *Cahiers* and

Cinéthique the quattrocento perspective has an important role in the function of the camera as ideological apparatus.) Fascist Rome and antifascist Paris are antithetical spaces famously dramatized by opposite décor and lighting. They have one thing in common, though: the use of quattrocento-style perspective to frame Marcello at exactly the vanishing point of the camera's gaze. Perspective and depth of field become, in a way, a quality of the character rather than of the space surrounding him, a quality that Bertolucci assigns to his character by means of an interaction with the camera's gaze and the spectator's.

When Marcello enters his hotel room, the voices of Anna and Giulia having an allusive, erotic conversation in the bedroom can already be heard. We see the two women through a total subjective shot from the point of view of Marcello, who is spying on them hidden behind the half-closed door of the bedroom, with the door frame also included at the margins of the shot. Anna is trying to seduce Giulia. The 'deviant' sexual attraction of the professor's wife for Marcello's 'normal' wife also stands for Bertolucci's interpretation of Anna's and Quadri's antifascism. Their, and the antifascist bourgeoisie's, interest in the masses—embodied by the naïve Giulia—their "liberal-socialism" is inspired by sexual desire rather than actual political collaboration, a desire that, furthermore, seduces and corrupts, instilling in the other, the proletariat, a deviant desire to become someone else, a bourgeois. They are desires that mirror each other, generating a perverse inversion of roles or role plays (Giulia mocks Anna's desire to dress her, funnily commenting, "How strange you are. You want to be my *maid* now?") It is nothing more than an abnormal, deviant desire for an object that can never be fully attained. The condemnation of the bourgeois intellectual to exist always out of time before the revolution without being able to participate in it—one of the main autobiographical themes of Bertolucci's career—finds here another configuration.

When Giulia and Anna's discourse indirectly alludes to Marcello without naming him—"you have to understand married to whom"—Anna suddenly looks toward Marcello. A reverse-angle shot shows as her subjective, but through the half-closed door, Marcello cannot be seen since the half space between the door and wall is covered in darkness. The angles of the shots clearly show how Marcello's objects of attention slightly shift according to the action happening on and around the bed. We can perceive his gaze moving freely around the profilmic space, now looking below at Anna, now looking up at Giulia (in the first case, the phone is included in the frame, while in the second, it is cut out.) Then, after Giulia asks Anna to turn around and not look at her while she tries on a dress, Anna looks straight into the camera **(Fig. 20)**, which reacts to the direct 'interpellation,' as if it were scared by having been caught spying, with a zoom out that ends including in the frame the profile of Marcello's head **(Fig. 21)**. The camera movement simultaneously translates Marcello's reaction of stepping back after his unauthorized gaze has been intercepted and captures Marcello while he is still looking. This last zoom-out changes the meaning of the entire sequence: what was a subjective configuration is, in reality, a semi-subjective, that includes in the same shot both the subject looking and the object looking at. According to Francesco Casetti, in his analysis of Antonioni's *Cronaca di un amore*, semi-subjective shots mean the inability of the subject to dominate and enframe the object of their gaze:

> Spesso le sue soggettive sono più propriamente delle semisoggettive, e cioè delle inquadrature che partono dall'oggetto visto per arrivare a includere nel quadro, senza soluzione di continuità, anche il soggetto vedente; L'effetto cui porta lo star troppo addosso alle cose è allora di non dominarle più. [...] Il ricorso alla semisoggettiva esemplifica l'idea di un personaggio vedente talmente compromesso con l'oggetto visto da non riuscire a dominarlo.[127]

Il conformista insists on this incapacity of the subject to put the object at a distance, in a word, to put it *in perspective*. In this case, Marcello fails to dominate Anna, who also symbolizes his abnormal drives, and recognizes they both belong to the same universe. The initial

---

[127] Casetti, *Dentro lo sguardo*, 115-117. «the subjective shots which involve him are usually semi-subjective, beginning with the object seen and ending by including the seeing subject within the frame, without a solution of continuity. In this kind of construction, the observer is no longer opposed to the observed [...] a semi-subjective configuration best expresses the idea that characters can be so taken by what they see as to be unable to understand it fully.» [Casetti, *Inside the Gaze*, 102.]

well-framed quattrocento perspective of Marcello in the corridor gets denied by the zoom-out and the final semi-subjective shot that ends the sequence. It also testifies to the author's idea of the incapacity of the cinema apparatus to put reality itself in perspective, to objectivize and then submit reality to the unique, dominating point of view of the human eye. Bertolucci does not merely negate and criticize cinema's vocation to an objective, transparent view of the real. He maintains it as an innate characteristic of the cinema apparatus, which having lost its claims of capturing reality as it is, remains as a signifying practice through which the author can construct their discourse on reality. In this sense, with *Il conformista* and with the discourse on the perspective that is inscribed in it, Bertolucci aligns himself with Comolli's argument on the subject: cinema is an ideological apparatus, but this does not mean that films indiscriminately project bourgeois ideology. The political ambiguity of Marcello, Anna and Professor Quadri, the ambiguity between fascism and antifascism, is also the ambiguity of the cinematic apparatus itself, as investigated by film theory of the late 1960s and early 70s. *Il conformista* would, then, classify as a category "E" film on Comolli's spectrum of militant cinema:

> The ideology not being directly transposed from the intentions of the author to the film itself, but encountering obstacles, making detours and short cuts, seeing itself exhibited, shown up, denounced by the filmic framework in which it is captured and which *acts against it*, allowing us to see its limits but at the same time what transgresses them.[emphasis mine][128]

Falsely subjective configurations and semi-subjectives exemplify an attempt and a failure to put at a distance, objectivize and enframe the other, signifying the ambiguity of one who occupies a position in between, both inside and outside the frame, on the threshold. These shots are connected with the coexistence of two opposite and simultaneous tendencies: the fear of a dangerous involvement that a point of view from the inside would entail and the pleasure of dominating from the outside the situation. In Casetti's reading, the falsely subjective shot is a compromise solution, a precious

---

[128] Comolli, "Cinema/Ideology/Criticism (I)," in *Cinema Against Spectacle*, 257.

indication of how to represent an object as it is seen both from the outside and the *inside*.

There are only two cases throughout *Il conformista* of total subjective shots, the first one during the flashback about Marcello's first encounter with Lino, doubly framed — as in a Chinese boxes system — within the car drive and the confession scene. After Lino has picked up the young Marcello with his car in the park — saving him from a flock of boys that were bullying him — he drives him to a villa on Monte Mario, presumably owned by the family that employed him as a chauffeur. The stunning view of Rome is taken from almost the same angle as the last frame of Rossellini's *Roma città aperta* (1945) **(Fig. 22)**, and the unreal objective that follows the car literally replicates the camera movement that follows the group of boys going downhill at the end of Rossellini's film. Citation here has a clear dramatic and political function, suggesting a connection between those boys and this one, the former symbolizing the neo-realist hope in the future generations for the material and moral reconstruction of Italy, the latter ironically situating in that same scenario the 'primal scene' that will determine all Marcello's future action, his corruption and eventual becoming a fascist. With the same unreal objective shot, Bertolucci follows the two, chasing each other until they enter the mansion. The first image of the young Marcello inside the sumptuous house is a reference to Godard's *Bande à part* (1964), the famous run through the Louvre's rooms and corridors: Marcello, while running, slides on the wooden floor, imitating Sami Frey's slide on the parquet of the museum. It is a signal that we are entering oedipal territory: after Rossellini here it is Godard. Moreover, the trio of *Bande à part* decides to defeat the record of the shortest visit to the Louvre — held by an American who supposedly visited it in 9:45 min — in order "to kill time" before a heist, "in the manner of low-brow American *noir* films." The scene of Lino's apparent murder, perpetrated by Marcello, has a lot to do with time, memory and repression-killing of past trauma.

After a long chase, when Lino stops in front of his bedroom and is about to open the door, Marcello tries to run away through a sort of labyrinth made of layers of hanging white sheets **(Fig. 24)**. The run lasts a few seconds before Lino catches Marcello and throws him on his bed. The duration of the run coincides with a total subjective shot of Marcello's point of view in the middle of the sheets, the hand-held camera being a prolepsis of another chase filmed as a total subjective shot with a hand-held camera: Anna's run and execution in the woods. While in this shot, we have a total subjective of the temporary victim—Marcello is the one being chased at the moment—in the latter, the total subjective will be that one of the killer. Only the *mise en scène* indirectly suggests Marcello's guilt and responsibility in the slaughtering of the Quadri's, and it does so, once again, through a subjective configuration, the only real, total point of view shot of the protagonist, of the entire film. The total subjective shot signifies Marcello's incapacity to dominate his childhood trauma and his abnormal homosexual desire, and the entire film will be a representation of his attempt and apparent success in dominating his real and lost object of desire. The world of shadows he decides to live in is a totally and successfully objectified and enframed reality, i.e., the illusion of a perfectly imitated reality as provided by the cinema apparatus that realizes, through the perfection of the *camera obscura* and quattrocento perspective, the ancestral dream of humanity. Marcello's point of view shot is the highly perspectival view of a corridor whose walls are made of white sheets. Bertolucci superimposes in the same shots the two rival 'techniques:' the perspective and the signifying practice that he has been using throughout the film to question it, the subjective configuration, which, as Casetti explains, entails a weakening of the gesture highlighted, i.e., the act of looking itself. The human eye's primacy and the relationship of dominance it establishes with the real are shown to be false myths by *Il conformista*, which nevertheless, by renouncing an intention to 'instruct' the audience to be directly political and 'militant'—since cinema is only a shadow, an illusion—has only one option left: to provide pleasure to the viewer.

Bertolucci's cinephilia, as underlined by David Forgacs, is one of the constructive principles of the work and not a mere self-referentiality. As we have seen, the system of quotations has precise dramatic meanings and also a role in revisiting and defining an anti-teleological history of cinema. Bypassing, in a way, Godard,

Bertolucci stresses his debt to the generation of the 'grandfathers' Renoir, Ophüls, Welles, and von Sternberg. However, there is one fundamental reference to a source that has never been mentioned, and if *Made in U.S.A.* was the anti-model, it actually represents, I believe, the closest model for *Il conformista*. I am alluding to *Ashes and Diamonds* (1958) by Andrzej Wajda, an adaptation of the 1948 novel written by Jerzy Andrejewszy (perhaps a source of Moravia's text, too?) The plot and its political meaning are strikingly similar to *Il conformista*. In a small town in postwar Poland, after Germany has surrendered to the Red Army, Maciek is a disbanded soldier of the Polish army who, having fought the Germans in a patriotic group of the Resistance, has been now assigned the task to assassinate a communist political Commissar Szczuka. After having failed the first time, he is given a second chance during a feast and banquet in a hotel where the Commissar is staying for a night. However, once at the hotel, Maciek falls in love with Krystyna, the bartender, and starts to question his mission and to think about a future with her that seems possible only if he will actually renounce his political duty of killing the Commissar. After having been convinced by his accomplice and superior Andrzej, he decides to leave Krystyna forever and to accomplish his mission. He will die, killed by the Soviet soldiers in a runaway attempt along a labyrinth of hanging white sheets, his blood coloring the white fabric red. Besides various literal, direct references, too many not to have a precise meaning (the chase and death amidst white blankets; children selling violets outside of the hotel; the light coming from a street-level window; the scene in the toilets of the hotel, when Maciek tries to escape his duties in front of Andrzej; the dancing scene before the murder; the oedipal motive: the son of the communist commissar is a 'nationalist' partisan [**Fig. 23-35**]), *Il conformista* and *Ashes and Diamonds* share a similar political meaning. They represent a fracture within the left, between its nationalist and communist sides, as much as Rosselli in Moravia was antagonized because of his patriotic Risorgimento ideals. They are also both obstacles to the private destiny of the individual with the universal trajectory of history and the role the subject is unwillingly called to play in it. Finally, both Bertolucci and Wajda represent a blind and unconscious society unable, or unwilling, to face the reality of things, thereby using the image of the dance party as a metaphor for the desire for shadow and illusion rather than light and objectivity.

List of Figures

Figure 1   Godard, *Made in U.S.A.* (1966) — Canted shot of secret police agent following Anna Karina.

Figure 2   Godard, *Made in U.S.A.* (1966) — Canted shot of Anna Karina being followed.

Figure 3 Bertolucci, *Il conformista* (1970) — Canted shot of Manganiello chasing Marcello.

Figure 4 Bertolucci, *Il conformista* (1970) — Canted shot of Marcello being chased.

Figure 5 Bertolucci, *Il conformista* (1970) — Falsely Subjective 1.

Figure 6 Bertolucci, *Il conformista* (1970) — Falsely Subjective 2.

142 THE FASCIST CHARACTER AS ENIGMA

Figure 7 Bertolucci, *Il conformista* (1970) — Falsely Subjective 1.

Figure 8 Bertolucci, *Il conformista* (1970) — Falsely Subjective 2.

THE PALIMPSEST OF *IL CONFORMISTA* 143

Figure 9   Bertolucci, *Il conformista* (1970) – Falsely Subjective 3.

Figure 10   Bertolucci, *Il conformista* (1970) – Falsely Subjective 4.

144 THE FASCIST CHARACTER AS ENIGMA

Figure 11 Bertolucci, *Il conformista* (1970) — Marcello perfectly framed in perspective before spying on Anna and Giulia.

Figure 12 Bertolucci, *Il conformista* (1970) — False POV shot of Marcello.

THE PALIMPSEST OF *IL CONFORMISTA* 145

Figure 13 Bertolucci, *Il conformista* (1970) — Anna sees Marcello looking at them and moves to the adjacent room.

Figure 14 Bertolucci, *Il conformista* (1970) — This shot reveals the previous one as falsely subjective.

146 THE FASCIST CHARACTER AS ENIGMA

Figure 15 Bertolucci, *Il conformista* (1970).

Figure 16 Bertolucci, *Il conformista* (1970) — Marcello perfectly framed in perspective before spying on Giulia and Anna.

Figure 17 Bertolucci, *Il conformista* (1970) – Anna POV shot, Marcello looking from the darkness.

Figure 18 Bertolucci, *Il conformista* (1970) – Marcello POV shot.

Figure 19 Bertolucci, *Il conformista* (1970) – Zoom out and semi-subjective shot.

Figure 20 Bertolucci, *Il conformista* (1970) – Lino drives Marello to the villa. View of Rome replicating the same angle as the last frame of *Roma città aperta*.

THE PALIMPSEST OF *IL CONFORMISTA* 149

Figure 21 Bertolucci, *Il conformista* (1970) — Total POV of Marcello running away.

Figure 22 Bertolucci, *Il conformista* (1970) — White sheets labyrinth.

Figure 23 Wajda, *Ashes and Diamonds* (1958).

Figure 24 Wajda, *Ashes and Diamonds* (1958) Andrzej buying a violet outside of the hotel.

THE PALIMPSEST OF *IL CONFORMISTA* 151

Figure 25 Bertolucci, *Il conformista* (1970) — Marcello buying a violet outside the hotel.

Figure 28 Wajda, *Ashes and Diamonds* (1958) — Maciek in the restroom of the restaurant, hiding from Andrzej.

152 THE FASCIST CHARACTER AS ENIGMA

Figure 29 Bertolucci, *Il conformista* (1970) — Marcello in the restroom of the Chinese restaurant, hiding from Manganiello.

Figure 30 Wajda, *Ashes and Diamonds* (1958).

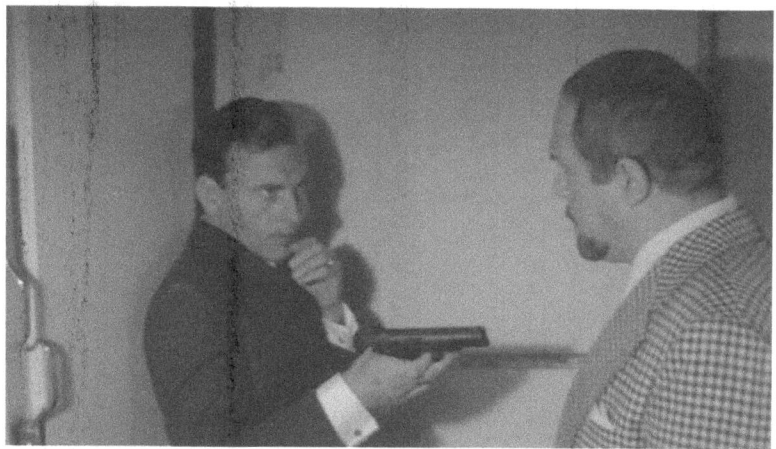

Figure 31 Bertolucci, *Il conformista* (1970).

Figure 32 Wajda, *Ashes and Diamonds* (1958) — Light coming through the basement window.

154 THE FASCIST CHARACTER AS ENIGMA

Figure 33 Wajda, *Ashes and Diamonds* (1958) — Legs of people walking by can be seen in the background.

Figure 34 Bertolucci, *Il conformista* (1970) — Light coming through the basement window.

Figure 35 Bertolucci, *Il conformista* (1970) — Legs of people walking by can be seen in the background.

Figure 36 Bertolucci, *Il conformista* (1970) — Perspective and depth of field.

Figure 37 Bertolucci, *Il conformista* (1970) — Perspective and depth of field.

Figure 38 Bertolucci, *Il conformista* (1970) — Perspective and depth of field.

THE PALIMPSEST OF *IL CONFORMISTA* 157

Figure 39 Bertolucci, *Il conformista* (1970) — Perspective and depth of field.

Figure 40 Bertolucci, *Il conformista* (1970) — Perspective and depth of field.

Figure 41 Bertolucci, *Il conformista* (1970) — Perspective and depth of field at the Trocadéro. Giulia comments on the perspectival illusion and trick. The Eiffel Tower in the background changes size at every shot.

Figure 42 Bertolucci, *Il conformista* (1970) — Perspective and depth of field at the Trocadéro. Giulia comments on the perspectival illusion and trick.

THE PALIMPSEST OF *IL CONFORMISTA* 159

Figure 43 Bertolucci, *Il conformista* (1970) — Perspective and depth of field at the Trocadéro. Giulia comments on the perspectival illusion and trick.

CHAPTER 2
The *Bildungsroman* of Italian Antifascism. Spontaneity and Organization as Narrative Motifs in Antifascist Historiography on the Resistance

2.1 A Sacred Story

In 1985, Luciano Canfora, in the preface to his work *La Sentenza – Concetto Marchesi e Giovanni Gentile*, writes:

> La riduzione a pupi, dei quali è rigidamente previsto ogni gesto e ogni battuta, tanto da suscitare, al cospetto di grandi e remote epopee, l'impazienza del pubblico, ansioso della rasserenante conclusione, è l'esito estremo, e caricaturale, di ogni storia divenuta «sacra.»[129]

By his passionate, attentive reconstruction of the events that led to the assassination of the official ideologist of the fascist regime Giovanni Gentile, perpetrated by members of the Florentine *GAP* in 1944, the eminent classical philologist is, in reality, simultaneously aiming to the further, wider objective of deconstructing another, bigger, tale. In fact, the story that has by now become holy, as he beautifully puts it in the above passage, is the history of the Resistance, and those puppets forced within the fixed limits of mechanically predetermined lines and gestures are the rival protagonists of that story of national liberation and civil war: fascists and antifascists. In this particular case study, the fascist is obviously Gentile himself, and the antifascist is the Latinist scholar Concetto Marchesi, both intellectuals being widely considered and remembered as some sort of sacred, untouchable icons of their opposite political sides. One, Marchesi, became a national hero, while the

---

[129] Luciano Canfora, *La sentenza. Concetto Marchesi e Giovanni Gentile* (Palermo: Sellerio, 1985), 11: «Every sacred story ends up reducing its protagonists to caricatures, to Sicilian puppets whose gestures and words are highly predictable. The audience, having in mind great and remote epics, become even more impatient to know the appeasing and cheering ending».

other, Gentile, was condemned to oblivion and silence. While attenuating and problematizing the fascism of the former and the communism of the latter, offering a less monumental portrayal of them, grounded in a more dynamic relation to the historical context in which they were both politically involved, Canfora suggests, never explicitly, always obliquely as in the preface, that a similar demystifying operation has been somehow lacking in the historical accounts and the official, subsequent memory of those final months of the war in Italy, i.e., from the destitution of Mussolini (July 25th 1943) to the final liberation (April 25th 1945.) His intention, as he explains at the end of the preface, was to subtract those characters from the «fissità manichea dell'Istoria di Gano e dei Paladini di Francia,»[130] from the uncomplicated classification of good and evil typical of the *chanson de geste*.[131] While recognizing that historical figures and events are destined to turn into caricatures and puppets of sacred stories, epic poems and romances, somehow pushed in that direction by the expectations of an impatient audience, Canfora decides to free them from the restrictions of a too-linear, schematic plot, by moving those same characters into a plot of a different kind, with hopefully less stereotypical, predictable development and roles. As the title, *La sentenza*, already suggests, Canfora's work reads as a perfect *giallo* and as a suspenseful detective and spy story. Certainly, the object chosen, a political murder, presupposes, in a way, the form of the crime fiction; however, the choice of a topic of this kind as a new, supposedly less biased point of view from which to attain a more truthful and impartial take on the difficult memory of the civil war, is indicative of, first, the inescapability of emplotment in historical reconstructions, second, of the fact that each genre of emplotment triggers a different interpretation and assignation of meaning. In *La sentenza*, events that were previously narrated as a romance are displaced in a mystery tale, in which the philological and archival research of the author closely resembles the enquiry of a detective. The truth about the civil war is hidden

---

130 Idem, 12.
131 Here Canfora more specifically is referring to the chivalric romance *Storia dei paladini di Francia* by the Sicilian puppeteer Giuseppe Leggio, published in Palermo in 1860, and since then a sort of *vademecum* for all the *pupari* of the island.

behind a hard-to-read palimpsest, a puzzle difficult to decipher: the exact opposite of the reassuring linearity of romance evoked in the preface.

In this chapter, I will investigate precisely the various forms of emplotment that have shaped the historical reconstructions of the civil war and, more generally, the historiography of the Resistance, from the immediate postwar years to Claudio Pavone's pivotal 1991 work *Una guerra civile – saggio storico sulla moralità nella Resistenza*. In particular, I will analyze the multiple ways in which the various interpretations of fascism each time modify the *genre* of the emplotment framing the events. The final goal of this essay is to identify the main, most recurrent narrative genres dominating the figurative strategies of the historical accounts taken into account. In other words, what type of emplotment has shown to be most apt to enframe fascism within the history of Italy after 1943? Which genre provided the formal characteristics for a less Manichean and clearcut distinction between fascism and antifascism, making possible a closer reading of their reciprocities?

I chose to start my enquiry with that passage from Canfora because I believe that even puppets and caricatures have a lot more to tell than what the audience might expect and because the 'inaugural motif' of his historical narration — of the one episode that he takes as a symbol of the entire Resistance — is the killing of a fascist, a mystery. In *La sentenza* the sacred history of the Resistance, then, of the encounter face to face between fascism and antifascism during the years of civil war, is first of all an enigma, a riddle that has somehow defied an agreed, univocal definition, veiling itself behind a patina of inexpressibility. Moreover, it brings to the foreground the moral question of violence and terrorism exactly by reversing the problem of responsibility, which here becomes the problem of the lack of a subject: the directive to kill Gentile came directly from the party's leaders, *dall'alto*, or was the free initiative of a single individual, *dal basso*?

Cosa fu la Resistenza and *Cosa fu il Fascismo* are the always recurrent questions in memoirs, pamphlets, essays, and historical works, suggesting an impulse to explain, to reach an exactness of closure that would finally grant the possibility to untie what appears to be the Gordian knot of the Italian 20th century. In order to solve this knot, to decipher its truth, resistance and fascism have been enframed in what has been so far, generally, and rather vaguely, defined as myths and legends, narrative schemata allowing historical explanation and an interpretative finalization. Following Hayden White's lesson, I will, first, identify the different myths and narrative strains of which the myth of the Resistance is composed, and, second, I will try to identify which master plots and genres of emplotment contribute to creating a more troubling, problematic closeness and continuity, rather than an irreconcilable fracture, between antifascism and fascism, good and evil, heroes and villains, paladins and Saracens.

2.2 The Desire to Know

First, then, there is the necessity to understand a phenomenon that seems to escape definition. An impulse that is shared by the two most active souls of the Resistance: the *Partito d'Azione* and the Italian Communist Party. In 1945, in front of the criminal court in Rome, Pietro Calamandrei, a member of *Giustizia e Libertà* first and then *azionista*, remembering Carlo and Nello Rosselli and the group of antifascists organized around the *circolo di cultura* in Florence, describes their common stance in front of fascism in terms of a will to know as the moral premise of any revolutionary act:

> E allora ai Rosselli, mentre quelli bastonavano e assassinavano impunemente e la gran massa inerte li lasciava fare, si presentò in termini angosciosi il problema morale dell' Italia. Perché accadeva questo generale sfaldamento di tutta una struttura nazionale? Perché questo crollo? Perché questa indifferenza? Prima di agire, bisognava poter rispondere a queste domande tormentose: *bisognava capire*.[emphasis mine][132]

---

132 Piero Calamandrei, *Uomini e città della Resistenza* (Milano: Linea d'ombra, 1994), 32. «While the great majority of people let them [fascists] beat and kill undisturbed and unpunished, the Rosellis realized with anxiety that Italy's main issue was of a moral nature. Why this indifference? Why this fall and deterioration of the nation's structure? Before taking action they wanted to answer these haunting questions: they needed to understand.»

Another member of GL and *azionista* like Vittorio Foa expresses the same necessity to observe and to understand the enemy, without reducing fascism to a stereotypical doctrine. Fundamental is, according to him, to:

> chiedersi a quali reali esigenze risponde l'opera dei loro avversari, quale è la loro volontà, il loro reale pensiero al di sopra delle loro stereotipe dottrine: come si fa a combattere un nemico che non si conosce?[133]

Years later, Carlo Ginzburg, the son of one of the most charismatic leaders of GL, Leone Ginzburg, debating with Foa around the real essence of anti-moralism, defines it, once more, as the need to learn from the enemy:

> Per me l'antimoralismo è stato ed è che bisogna imparare dal nemico. [...] Io credo che questo sia un chiodo essenziale perché è l'unico fondamento anti-ideologico. Ed è la cosa che ho imparato dal Gramsci dei *Quaderni dal carcere*, e cioè: siamo stati sconfitti dai fascisti, però i fascisti rispondevano a delle domande reali e quindi è alle domande che dobbiamo guardare e non solo alle risposte che non condividiamo. Secondo me la distinzione fra domande e risposte è quella cruciale. La domanda reale rimane anche se la risposta non ci piace. Questo è l'antimoralismo per me.[134]

This drive to investigate the rival, looking past its apparent irrationalism and absurdity, is, according to Marco Bresciani, the most enduring lesson that Rosselli and GL left. Besides the practical inflexibility face to face with the enemy, there is also a theoretical and pedagogical moment that sees the difference with the other in an educational dimension: «I giellisti combinarono le due mosse, l'una in funzione dell'altra: l'indispensabile necessità di far fronte al

---

133 Vittorio Foa, *Il cavallo e la torre* (Torino: Einauidi, 1991), 33. «To ask ourselves what motivates the actions of our enemies, what is their real belief beyond their stereotypical doctrines: how can someone fight an unknown enemy?».

134 Aldo Colonello and Andrea Del Col, ed., *Uno storico, un mugnaio, un libro. Carlo Ginzburg, il formaggio e i vermi (1976-2002)* (Trieste: Edizioni Università di Trieste, 2003), 97. «In my opinion, antimoralism meant and means to learn from the enemy. [...] I learned this while reading Gramsci's *Prison Notebooks*: Fascists won and defeated us, they were finding answers to real questions and, then, we need to look at those questions and stop inquiring about the answers we don't like. This distinction between answers and questions is the crucial one. The actual question remains even if we did not like the answer. In my opinion this is what antimoralism means».

nemico e la sorprendente disponibilità a muoversi obliquamente, per proiettarsi oltre di esso.»[135]

Giorgio Amendola, partisan and deputy of the *PCI*, highlights too the same need to comprehend what exactly fascism was:

> Anzitutto: "che cosa era il fascismo." Perché, sembrerà strano, noi eravamo già da anni sotto il peso della dittatura fascista, questo disastro era da anni caduto sul popolo italiano, e ancora noi andavamo discutendo per sapere che cosa era accaduto. Come chi abbia ricevuto una tegola in testa e vada barcollando e si domandi di che materia è fatta questa tegola.[136]

The aporia of fascism and the consequent will to uncover its mystery is a key starting point for the comprehension of the modalities regulating the composition and process of transfiguration of the historical data, not only into the founding myth of postwar democratic Italy, i.e., of the 'Republic born out of the Resistance,' but also into the other concurrent narratives each time assigning to the Resistance different meanings. It is time to look more closely at, first, how the diverse spectrum of antifascism resulted in multiple interpretations of fascism and, second, to analyze the different historical frames within which the experience of the Resistance has been translated into national collective memory. The two questions, I believe, spin around two pivotal concepts: those of continuity and break. Both fascism and Resistance are, in fact, alternatively considered either in continuity with Italian history or as breaking moments of the rational linearity of what is recognized as the Italian historical trajectory. The study of emplotment and narrative genres, then, as the reduction of the data of reality in a coherent whole and meaningful succession of beginning-middle-end, reveals once more to be a good access point to the historiography on that period, given

---

135 Marco Bresciani, *Quale antifascismo?* (Roma: Carocci, 2017), 287. «GL members combined the two moves, one in function of the other: the indispensable necessity to oppose the enemy and the surprising availability to move obliquely in order to surpass and go beyond the enemy».

136 Giorgio Amendola, "Il tribunale speciale e l'antifascismo all'interno," in *Fascismo e antifascismo (1918-1936) Lezioni e testimonianze* (Milano: Feltrinelli, 1962), 230. «First, what exactly was Fascism? Because we were still discussing about what had actually happened many years after the dictatorship started. Like someone who just got a brick on their head and starts asking about the material the brick was made of».

the fact that studies on the interpretation on Fascism and the historical accounts of the Resistance are already countless and still comprehensive. What, in my opinion, is lacking is the attempt to problematize the notion of myth and legend by specifying and differentiating the different emplotments and genres otherwise too loosely comprehended in the wider category of myth.

2.3 The Interpretations of Fascism: Parenthesis, Autobiography or Counterrevolution?

There are three main interpretations of fascism. The first one, widely the most successful during the immediate postwar years until 1960, was conceived by Benedetto Croce in a speech given in Bari in 1944, *La libertà italiana nella libertà nel mondo*,[137] and it famously envisages fascism as a parenthesis and as a moral disease. Fascism, then, is seen as a deviation from and an interruption of the positive liberal, pre-fascist Italy born out of the Risorgimento:

> Croce fu colui che per primo formulò l'interpretazione della «malattia morale», chiarendone i due punti più importanti, quello che il fascismo «non fu escogitato né voluto da alcuna singola classe sociale, né da una singola di queste sostenuto», ma «fu uno smarrimento di coscienza, una depressione civile e una ubriacatura, prodotta dalla guerra;» e «una parentesi» di abbassamento «nella coscienza della libertà.»[138]

The second one, on the contrary, frames fascism in continuity with Giolitti's *Italietta*. According to the pessimistic reading made by Giustino Fortunato, Fascism is the revelation of the true, purely negative, Italian essence, not an accident but the necessary degeneration of an actual reactionary spirit until then hidden underneath

---

[137] Benedetto Croce, *Scritti e discorsi politici* (1943-1947), (Napoli: Bibliopolis, 2010), 54- 62.
[138] Renzo De Felice, *Il Fascismo – le interpretazioni dei contemporanei e degli storici* (Bari: Editori Laterza, 1970), 391. «Croce was the first one to come up with the formula of «moral illness», and clarifying two major points: «Fascism wasn't prepared and willfully provoked by one specific social class» but «was a sort of bewilderment, a civil depression and an intoxication caused by war» and a «parenthetical, temporary lapse in the consciousness of freedom».

a 'thin layer of liberal paint' as Lelio Basso phrases it[139]. Piero Gobetti proposed a variation of Fortunato's insight. For the young radical, liberal antifascist, Fascism was the autobiography of the nation, as he wrote in 1922:

> L'*attualismo,* il garibaldinismo, il fascismo sono espedienti attraverso cui l'inguaribile fiducia ottimistica dell'infanzia ama contemplare il mondo semplificato secondo le proprie misure. [...] Il fascismo in Italia è un'indicazione di infanzia perché segna il trionfo della facilità, della fiducia, dell'entusiasmo. Si può ragionare del ministero Mussolini: come di un fatto d'ordinaria amministrazione. Ma il fascismo è stato qualcosa di più; è stato l'autobiografia della nazione. [...] Mussolini non è dunque nulla di nuovo: ma con Mussolini ci si offre la prova sperimentale dell'unanimità, ci si attesta l'inesistenza di minoranze eroiche, la fine provvisoria delle eresie. Certe ore di ebbrezza valgono per confessioni e la palingenesi fascista ci ha attestato inesorabilmente l'impudenza della nostra impotenza. A un popolo di dannunziani non si può chiedere spirito di sacrificio . [...] C'è stato in noi, nel nostro opporsi fermo, qualcosa di donchisciottesco.[140]

Gobetti wrote in the aftermath of the 1919–1920 'civil war' (*biennio rosso*), and he praises those years of violent political fights as the exception to the rule, as a rare moment of mass participation and awakening political consciousness in a people otherwise naturally more inclined to the passive, unproblematic acceptance of authority. Fascism is, then, seen in continuity with an ideal Italian essence. More than an interpretation of fascism, Gobetti provided us with a

---

139 Lelio Basso, "Le origini del fascismo," in *Fascismo e antifascismo (1918-1936). Lezioni e testimonianze* (Milano: Feltrinelli, 1962), 10.
140 Piero Gobetti, "Elogio della ghigliottina," in *La Rivoluzione Liberale. Saggio sulla lotta politica in Italia* (Torino: Einaudi, 1964), 164-166. «*Actualism, Garibaldianism, and Fascism are expedients by which infancy, with its incurable trusting optimism, loves to contemplate a world simplified to its own dimensions. [...] Fascism in Italy is a sign of infancy because it signals the triumph of the facile, of trust, of enthusiasm. We could analyze Mussolini's cabinet as though it were just another governing ministry. But fascism has been something more: it has been the autobiography of the nation. [...] So Mussolini is nothing new; but Mussolini offers us experimental proof of that unanimity; he attests to the nonexistence of heroic minorities, the provisional end of heresies. Certain spells of drunkenness are as good as confessions, and the fascist palingenesis has inexorably confirmed the impudence of our impotence. You can't ask for the spirit of sacrifice from a people of D'Annunzians. [...] In us, in our firm opposition, there has been something quixotic*» [Translated in English by W. McCuaig, in P. Gobetti, *On Liberal Revolution*, ed. By N. Urbinati, New Haven & London: Yale University Press, 2000, pp. 212-215].

character study, reducing the fascist, and as a consequence, the Italian, to a supposedly ideal 'type' with latent, fixed traits. The fascist stance on the world is the naive, imaginative, optimistic one of childhood, while antifascism conceives life pessimistically as a tragedy. The former is nothing more than an imitation of D'Annunzio, while the latter is a Don Quixote. Hence, this interpretation enframes fascism in a teleological and deterministic emplotment as the finalized autobiography of the specific type of the *cortigiano*. *Ebbrezza* and *malattia* are keywords that will come back also in Croce's parenthesis definition (as *ubriacatura* and *morbo*), which is also based on a supposedly ideal and eternal national 'type,' whose essence is contaminated and corrupted by the contingent infectious accident of the fascist *ventennio*. In this way, considering Fascism as an exogenous disruption, Croce was able to tie back Italian history to the uncontaminated thread of its 'innocent' and radiant past. This emplotment was a necessary, vital operation to free newborn democratic Italy from the too-heavy burden of responsibility and guilt. As Pier Giorgio Zunino explains:

> In effetti, il retorico interrogarsi di Croce su che cosa mai fosse «nella nostra storia una parentesi di venti anni» a cos'altro conduceva, potremmo chiederci a nostra volta, se non a mettere l'arco di volta a una vera e propria costruzione mitica? E si potrebbe aggiungere, in che cosa consisteva questo mito se non nell'affermare, e propriamente inventare, una tradizione di libertà di cui nelle patrie cronache si era invece persa traccia?[141]

The myth of fascism as a moral intoxication and temporary interruption of ideal progress will have an enormous influence not only in historiography but also in the figurative representations of the fascist, both literary and cinematic. The fascist as a deviated and deformed character driven by immoral, abnormal sexual desire is a direct displacement in fiction of the Crocean model.

---

141 Pier Giorgio Zunino, *La Repubblica e il suo passato* (Bologna: Il Mulino, 2003), 284-285, 286-287. «To what led Croce's rhetorical question about what might have meant «for our history a parethesis of twenty years» if not to the completion of the encompassing arch of a mythical construction? And we could add of what consisted this myth if not in the affirmation and, more properly in the invention, of a tradition of liberty that was nowhere to be found in the national chronicles?»

Carlo Rosselli, founder and leader of *GL* and ideologist of Liberal Socialism, followed Gobetti and assigned to fascism the same meaning as autobiography of the nation, stressing once more the moral divide between a morally lazy people and a heroic minority of paladins of all the moral virtues. The *Italiano medio*, according to Rosselli, is a byproduct of catholic education, of the lack of a protestant reform, of the failure of the Risorgimento as a truly European Bourgeois revolution and, finally, of a long series of paternalistic governments. In his view, the autobiography reads as a process, a development, of the tendency of the individual to passively renounce freedom altogether:

> Gli italiani sono moralmente pigri. C'è in loro un fondo di scetticismo e di opportunismo che li porta facilmente a contaminare, disprezzandoli, tutti i valori, e a trasformare in commedie le più oscure tragedie. [...]
> Il fascismo è stato, in certa misura, l'autobiografia di una nazione che rinuncia alla lotta politica, che ha il culto dell'unanimità, che rifugge dall'eresia, che sogna il trionfo della facilità, della fiducia e dell'entusiasmo.[142]

Both in Gobetti and Rosselli, the fascist corresponds to the typical Italian personality, which naturally prefers to read the world through the infantile lens of comedy rather than embracing the more perilous path of a tragic vision of life, following the example of the heretic and heroic antifascist minority. In both cases, fascism, enframed as autobiography, reads as the final stage and revelation of the development and *bildung* of a typical personality.

The other main, classic interpretation of the enigma of fascism, after the liberal and socialist liberal ones, is the Marxist reading: Fascism is an anti-proletarian, authoritarian reaction. The official interpretation of the *Internazionale* was that fascism embodied the decline of capitalism, its terminal phase of decomposition. Fascism

---

142 Carlo Rosselli, *Socialismo liberale* (Roma-Firenze-Milano: Edizioni U, 1945), 110, 116. «Italians are morally lazy. There is an underlying skepticism and a low-grade Machiavellianism in them that induces them to contaminate all values with ridicule and to transform the darkest tragedies into comedy. [...] Fascism has in some sense been the autobiography of a nation that shrugs at the political contest, that worship unanimity and shrinks from heresy, that dreams of the triumph of facility, trust and enthusiasm.» [English translation by W. McCuaig, in C. Rosselli, *Liberal Socialism*, ed. by N. Urbinati, (Princeton: Princeton University Press, 1994, pp. 104,108].

became, then, the extralegal, armed branch of the weakened, decadent capitalist bourgeoisie, both urban and agrarian, unable to contain otherwise the rise and revolution of the subaltern classes. A sort of compromise between the idealist vision of fascism as revelation and the emplotment within the historical materialist master plot as violent counterrevolution was reached after the Congress of Lyon in 1936, and also thanks to the analysis of fascism made by Antonio Gramsci in his *Quaderni dal carcere,* as Amendola summarizes:

> Il fascismo veniva spiegato non soltanto colla sua base di classe, che essenzialmente era capitalistica, ma anche col carattere della borghesia italiana, con lo sviluppo del capitalismo italiano, coi modi dell'accumulazione capitalistica in Italia. Si risaliva così alle premesse create dalla storia d'Italia secondo un filone della critica storica italiana che andava da Cattaneo, a Oriani, a Salvemini, a Gramsci, a Gobetti—e cito non a caso nomi che indicano correnti diverse e anche contrastanti, che tutte si mossero tuttavia nel promuovere una critica del Risorgimento.[143]

The social base of fascism is identified with the urban middle class, the petite bourgeoisie of the city, composed mainly of small professionals and employers of the state bureaucratic apparatus. The Great War is constantly seen as the true turning point and the main cause that directly activates the social turmoil that will eventually originate the fascist phenomenon. In this sense, the spirit of adventure inspiring the *interventisti* and a widely spread sentiment of *antigiolittismo* inform the 'type' of the fascist of the first hour. The economic misery and delusions of the First World War veterans are another factor triggering and favoring the ascent of Mussolini as *deus ex machina,* as he is defined by both Gobetti and Rosselli, capable of consigning the Italian middle class in the hands of the

---

143 Amendola, "Il tribunale speciale e l'antifascismo all'interno," 231-232. «Fascism was not explained only as a class phenomenon within capitalism, but also in relation to the character of Italian bourgeoisie, to the development of Italian capitalism, to the ways of capitalist accumulation in Italy. It was possible, then, to trace it back to those premises created by Italian history according to a thread in Italian historical criticism which included Cattaeo, Oriani, Salvemini, Gramsci and Gobett, and I am quoting here, and not by chance, only names belonging to different and diverging currents which, nevertheless, all shared a critique of the Risorgimento».

industrial and agrarian capital. Key, deeply interdependent concepts are, then, those of consensus and violence. The problem was to determine and understand whether fascism was passively accepted by the masses or if it was mainly imposed by capital through the violent repression of a 'police' state on the middle and working classes. As Quazza writes:

> È la natura stessa della programmazione degli strumenti per ottenere il consenso e il carattere dell'uso quotidiano di questi strumenti, comunque la si esamini, a denunciare l'alto grado di coercizione, al quale corrisponde, non si dice certo una diffusa resistenza, ma una passiva e spesso rassegnata accettazione. Non c'è vero consenso, dunque, perché non c'è partecipazione, ed è grave confondere termini sostanzialmente diversi.[144]

This short excerpt clearly shows how all three interpretations somehow are in exchange with one another and merge without permanently negating each other. The passivity of the consensus alludes to the typological analysis of the *Italiano medio* in Rosselli and Gobetti. At the same time, the use of violence has, in my opinion, all the traits of an external imposition: fascism is fetishized as a tool, the *manganello* of the blackshirts, being in this way exteriorized from the subject, that does not act but is acted upon instead, their political consciousness abruptly struck and sedated in a dizziness of the will. This element is not in strong opposition with the parenthetic, idealist reading of Croce which apparently favors break over *bildung*.

The three classic interpretations of fascism, as autobiography, as parenthesis and as counterrevolutionary tool, will, in time, intertwine and coexist, moving towards a mutual attenuation and compromise. Among others, the socialist Lelio Basso stresses the necessity to integrate elements of continuity and those of novelty and disruption in a dynamic reading that would in this way avoid uncomplicated categorizations and fixed moral abstractions:

---

[144] Guido Quazza, *Resistenza e storia d'Italia* (Milano: Feltrinelli, 1976), 70. «The very nature of the programming of the tools to be used to obtain consensus and the character of the everyday use of these same instruments, however we look at them, denounce the high degree of coercion and its correspondent passive acceptance. There is not true consensus, thus, because there is not participation, and the two terms are not to be mixed up».

> nella società contemporanea coesistono forze contrastanti, alcune cariche di una spinta democratica e altre di una spinta eversiva della democrazia, e che dal conflitto permanente di queste forze nasca un equilibrio che sarà tendenzialmente democratico o antidemocratico a seconda del prevalere delle une o delle altre, ma sarà in linea di massima un equilibrio instabile, un equilibrio in movimento, o per meglio dire una successione di equilibri che si distruggono e si ricompongono permanentemente. Ma anche là dove, pur fra alti e bassi, permane un equilibrio fondamentalmente democratico, elementi di fascismo sono presenti perché essi sono coessenziali al tipo di società industriale moderna, ne costituiscono anzi in un certo senso la tendenza di fondo.[145]

Fascism appears as a constant, immanent menace, a latent, hidden possibility of darkness behind the thin, bright layer of democracy.

The historiography on the Resistance has exactly this structural tendency to emplot fascism and antifascism as the melodramatic clash of darkness and light embodied by precise types, paladins and Saracens enframed, as puppets, in the predetermined motives of a specific narrative genre. The three interpretations, quickly observed above, shape and highly influence the myth of the Resistance. Its occurrence is now seen either as a foundation of a new state, a revolution and break from the fascist past, or as a failed revolution, a parenthesis between fascism and a state that hides behind a democratic mask, a latent, permanent fascist core.

2.4 The Myths of the Resistance: History as Romance, Tragedy and Comedy.

The myth of the Resistance is, in reality, composed of a variety of myths interlaced with one another. There are several sub-myths that concur to form a larger, all-encompassing master plot. The interpretations of the Resistance might be traced back to mainly three

---

145 Basso, "Le origini del fascismo.", 11-12. «In contemporary society contrasting forces coexist, some charged with democratic thrust, some other with a subversive stance towards democracy. From the permanent conflict between these two forces stems a certain equilibrium, now more democratic, now more antidemocratic. It will be, then, a precarious balance, one in becoming, or better, a succession of different types of equilibrium which break and recompose permanently. However, even where, with ups and downs, democracy is stable, elements of fascism are still there, present because they are intrinsic to modern industrial society, and they actually represent its core tendency.»

sources, corresponding to the three parties that had a major role within the CLN (Council of National Liberation) and in the battleground, in the *lotta armata:* The Italian Communist Party (PCI), the *Partito d'Azione* (P. d'A.) and the Christian Democracy (DC). The historiography of the Resistance is profoundly faulted by the political roots and provenience of its authors, and that is why I believe analyzing and rearranging their works following a formalist and morphological method might be a more fruitful and unpredictable approach in a field of study already so widely and exhaustively frequented by historians and cultural historians specializing in the Italian 20th century. The myth of the Resistance as a particular genre of emplotment of fascism has not, in fact, yet been taken into consideration, given the prominence always granted to a mainly political and socio-economic interpretation. After a short introduction and summary of the three major interpretations, I will proceed to a detailed analysis of a few examples for each different myth, investigating how the different genres of emplotment are modified by a corresponding interpretation of fascism, resulting in a diverse and dynamic framing of the fascist as historical agent.

The official myth is the foundational narrative of the new democratic republic born out of the Resistance. In this version, the liberation movement is washed out of all its political contrasting different souls. The Christian Democrats, in power after the elections of 1948, were interested in transmitting a less radical image of the Resistance, negating all sorts of hierarchy among the political parties that formed it, in particular fighting against the hegemony of the Communist Party in the CLN. The political and class connotation of the movement is omitted in favor of a neutral image of the Resistance as moral and ethical, with religious undertones, a battle won by a resurgent Italian nation against the German invaders. The war of liberation is a repetition of the Risorgimento, the redemptive and liberating patriotic win of a country all reunited to fight for a common, shared ideal and cause.

The myth of the Resistance as a 'second Risorgimento' obliquely returns in many historical reconstructions, regardless of the political ideals of the author. Nevertheless, the Risorgimento of the *azionisti* is different both from that of the Marxist historians and from the Christian democratic ones. Only the latter has a totally positive value. At the same time, in the other cases Risorgimento has a more ambiguous meaning according to an interpretation that reads it also as a missed opportunity and as a territorial conquest of the crown. Other recurrent patterns are the Resistance as *union sacrée*, as a unique and compact bloc of Italian antifascism, without the supremacy of any specific party; the mass participation, besides the working class, of the peasantry; the Resistance as *rivoluzione mancata* or *tradita* (mostly a myth of the *azionisti*); the Resistance as a successful revolution resulting in the promotion of the Italian proletariat as *classe dirigente,* as leading class (an early myth, obviously of the PCI).

The *azionisti,* the PCI and the DC all tell a specific type of story of the Resistance and its encounter with fascism, mainly with the fascism of Salò. Each story-myth coincides with a different genre of emplotment, which, in turn, provides an alternative meaning and classification of the historical data. As Hayden White famously theorized, applying Frye's categorization and terminology to the historiographical field:

> Providing the "meaning" of a story by identifying the *kind of story* that has been told is called explanation by emplotment. If, in the course of narrating his story, the historian provides it with the plot structure of a Tragedy, he has "explained" it in one way; if he has structured it as a Comedy, he has "explained" it in another way. Emplotment is the way by which a sequence of events fashioned into a story is gradually revealed to be a story of a particular kind. Following the line indicated by Northrop Frye in his *Anatomy of Criticism*, I identify at least four different modes of emplotment: Romance, Tragedy, Comedy, and Satire. There may be others, such as the Epic, and a given historical account is likely to contain stories cast in one mode as aspects or phases of the whole set of stories making up his narrative in one comprehensive or archetypal story form.[146]

By using White's methodology, I am going to propose a classification of the various *mythoi* of postwar Italian historiography on the Civil War. The Christian democratic tradition is more inclined towards an emplotment of history as Romance, as a redemptive Christian tale of salvation. The historians belonging to the tradition of *Giustizia e Libertà* and the *Partito d'Azione* generally tend to emplot their fight against fascism and Nazism, both before and during

---

146 Hayden White, *Metahistory* (Baltimore: Johns Hopkins University Press, 2014), 7.

the Resistance, as Tragedy; on the contrary, Marxism emplots history in a comic frame:

> The Romance is fundamentally a drama of self-identification symbolized by the hero's transcendence of the world of experience, his victory over it, and his final liberation from it—the sort of drama associated with the Grail legend or the story of the resurrection of Christ in Christian mythology. It is a drama of the triumph of good over evil, of virtue over vice, of light over darkness, and of the ultimate transcendence of man over the world in which he was imprisoned by the Fall. The archetypal theme of Satire is the precise opposite of this Romantic drama of redemption: it is, in fact, a drama of redemption, a drama dominated by the apprehension that man is ultimately a captive of the world rather than its master. [...]
> Comedy and Tragedy, however, suggest the possibility of at least partial liberation from the condition of the Fall and provisional release from the divided state in which men find themselves in this world. But these provisional victories are conceived differently in the mythic archetypes of which the plot structures of Comedy and Tragedy are sublimated forms. In Comedy, hope is held out for the temporary triumph of man over his world by the prospect of occasional *reconciliations* of the forces at play in the social and natural worlds. Such reconciliations are symbolized in the festive occasions which the Comic writer traditionally uses to terminate his dramatic accounts of change and transformation. In Tragedy there are no festive occasions, except false or illusory ones; rather, there are intimations of states of division among men more terrible than that which incited the tragic agon at the beginning of the drama.[147]

The encounter with the necessity to include fascism, and Nazism, in the frame, as I have already briefly sketched, provokes a disruption of the tragic and comic emplotments with the romantic and melodramatic, Manichean ones: the fascist and the partisan opposing, then, each other as unproblematic embodiments of good and evil, light and darkness. However, through a comparative, morphological study of the different emplotments at stake—originating in contrasting, far from each other, political and ideological premises—and of their dynamic contamination, I think that it is possible to recognize an alternative emplotment of fascism which, by challenging the melodramatic one, would also result in a more nuanced, ambivalent, perhaps more instructive and less reassuring, one. There are, in fact, recurrent motifs and patterns recognizable in all the different emplotments suggested above that trigger a sort of estrangement, an interruption in the automatic reading of the

---

[147] Idem, 8-9.

fascist-pure evil/antifascist-good hero equation, thus allowing the reader to recognize a more dynamic, carnivalesque reciprocity between fascism and antifascism, and those characters that 'singularize' them in the plot. While appearing as undeniably framed as the rival protagonists of an uncomplicated schematization, the good and the wrong sides of history famously set in stone by Italo Calvino, when the reader recognizes the simultaneous presence of alternative morphological themes and motifs, the fascist and the partisan, fascism and resistance, suddenly appear as characters of a different, less redemptive, kind of story: an alternative emplotment that does not finalize them into a fixed definition and closed meaning, but that, on the contrary, conceive them as ambiguous, reciprocal entities lacking closure by activating grotesque relativity of values instead. I think that all three kinds of stories are all simultaneously readable as a *bildungsroman,* a genre of emplotment in which the conflict between the self's inner ideals and the laws ruling society resolves not in resignation or victory, but in compromise, in an equivocal instability of values. There are a series of key themes structuring the historiographical debate on fascism and resistance that seem to belong to a plot of that kind perfectly. Such as the famous, omnipresent question of whether the Resistance was the consequence of a spontaneous outburst of antifascism or the organization of the antifascist parties' clandestine work, and then, the related dilemma of the generational gap between the old antifascism of the *ventennio* and the new one of a younger generation born under fascism and that never saw an Italy without it.

2.5 Resistance as Comedy in the Epic Frame of Roberto Battaglia's *Storia della resistenza italiana.*

Perhaps the most influential historian of the Italian Resistance is Roberto Battaglia, who took part in the resistance with the *Partito d'Azione* and who, later on, after the war, joined the PCI. Since its publication in 1953, his *Storia della Resistenza Italiana* has been the inevitable point of reference for every scholar approaching the field and the undeniable master plot of the Resistance as a grand national epic made possible primarily by the mass revolt of the working classes. Battaglia's tale of the Resistance is an «epica popolare»[148] accompanied by the rhythm of «squilli impetuosi»[149] and that hurries towards victory as a «tumulto epico.»[150]

The *Storia* frames the parable of the Resistance also as a slow evolution and gradual ripening: a process of *bildung*, that starts from a condition of spontaneity and still uneducated, instinctive spirit of rebellion and hate against fascism and Nazism, and reaches, through the successive steps of the fight, a complete political and ideal maturity thanks to the *organizzazione*, and moral education, provided by the party: «c'è subito e innanzitutto "l'organizzazione" cioè lo strumento di lotta con cui la classe dei poveri e degli sfruttati, il proletariato, vince le sue battaglie.»[151] The old *quadri* of the PCI emplot the spontaneous, unbridled impulse of the younger partisans in the wider scheme of the Marxist vision of history as class struggle. Even the chapters' division signals the emplotment in a *bildungsroman*, with direct references to Dickens' *Great Expectations*, as chapter XIV is titled "Grandi Speranze. Terribili lutti," and a process of education (Chapter XI is "La maturità della Resistenza.") Battaglia often uses a figurative strategy consisting of natural metaphors that transfigure the Resistance into the sublime spectacles of nature: now a «procella,»[152] now a «fenomeno della natura[153]» and «incendio,»[154] «vulcano.»[155] At some point, the Tuscan landscape seems to join the partisans in their fight:

> La saldezza d'un movimento popolare che ha lo stesso respiro vigoroso delle cose della natura, sembra insorgere contro il nemico lo stesso paesaggio toscano, così colto ed elaborato dall'uomo, simbolo di civiltà di fronte alla barbarie scatenata.[156]

---

148 Roberto Battaglia, *Storia della Resistenza Italiana* (Torino: Einaudi, 1964), 357. «Epic story of the people».
149 Ibidem. «impetuous blares»
150 Idem, 112. «epic uproar».
151 Idem, 198. «First of all there is organization, that is to say the fighting tool which helps the poor and exploited class, the proletariat, to win its battles».
152 Idem, 49. «storm».
153 Idem, 122. «natural phenomenon».
154 Idem, 125. «fire».
155 Idem, 368.
156 Idem, 357. «The strength of a working-class movement that shares the same breath of natural things, that seems to rise against the enemy united with Tuscan landscape, symbol of civilization facing unbridled barbarity».

This figuration as 'natural evolution' and unstoppable force of nature is widely used for the preliminary, spontaneous outbursts of the Resistance, such as the great but immature revolt in Naples, only to be later gradually replaced by the vocabulary of organization, political consciousness and discipline, obedience to the party's directives.

Workers and strikes unmistakably play in Battaglia's history the key, hegemonic role. The coup of July 25th becomes, then, a direct consequence of the strikes of March 1943, and, more generally, the working class is the real guide of the insurrection:

> Nel momento più difficile della Resistenza come al suo esordio e a ogni sua tappa principale, spetta alla classe operaia gettare il suo peso sulla bilancia, far valere le sue qualità di compattezza, di disciplina, di spirito di sacrificio.[157]

In Pietro Secchia and Luigi Longo — the 'historians' of the party — the hegemony of the Communist Party and the proletariat is, naturally, even more stressed. In *Sulla via dell'insurrezione nazionale*, Longo identifies in the participation of the urban masses the peculiar element of the Italian Resistance, a force capable of guiding the rest of the Italian people to national redemption, as a sort of imitation of the October revolution:

> Noi subito indicammo che la Resistenza, che la lotta partigiana non doveva essere vista solo come lotta armata, di formazioni militari, ma anche come lotta, resistenza delle grandi masse lavoratrici sul luogo stesso del lavoro, e come combinazione e fusione di queste varie forme di azione antitedesca e antifascista in un solo e grande movimento popolare di liberazione nazionale.[158]

The preliminary role given to this one aspect of the Resistance also had the function of demystifying the official and concurrent myth,

---

[157] Idem, 542. «During the most difficult times of the Resistance, at the beginning and at each new step, the working-class undertake the task of throwing its weight on the scale and make count of its qualities of discipline, sacrifice and compactness».

[158] Luigi Longo, *Sulla via dell'insurrezione nazionale* (Roma: Editori Riuniti, 1971), 14. «We right away understood that the Resistance, the partisan fight had to be seen not only as an armed fight involving military formations, but also as struggle and resistance of the working-class masses on their workplace, and as combination and fusion of these various anti-German and anti-fascist forces within a widespread people's movement of national liberation».

coming from the DC area, of a Resistance supported in equal measure by all Italians. In this sense, the opposition between spontaneity and organization becomes the distinction between two myths of the Resistance: the spontaneous character being the dominant factor in liberal and Christian democratic accounts, while the organization being the discriminant element stressing the hegemony of the PCI both within the CLN and in the armed revolution. Pietro Secchia is more 'Manichean' than Battaglia, who started as *azionista*, in decisively favoring the organization of the party as the true, almost exclusive, force of the insurrection:

> Vi sono oggi due teorie che più delle altre cercano di farsi strada. L'una è quella dei responsabili del fascismo i quali per cancellare i loro tradimenti e le loro responsabilità sostengono che bisogna dimenticare il passato, che non bisogna più parlare di fascismo, né di Resistenza, che tutti, fascisti ed antifascisti, hanno le stesse colpe e gli stessi meriti e così via. Chi ha avuto ha avuto, chi ha dato ha dato, ecc. L'altra teoria è quella di coloro che avversarono quasi sempre il fascismo, ma che non mossero dito per combatterlo, ed attesero l'undicesima ora per uscire dalla loro inerzia, dalla loro passività e dalla loro prudenza. Costoro tentano oggi di creare la leggenda che tutti gli italiani furono per la Resistenza, che il movimento partigiano non venne organizzato da nessuno ma fu un fenomeno spontaneo. Ognuno sentì, dicono costoro, dal profondo dell'animo una voce: qualcuno la chiama la voce della patria, altri la voce della coscienza ed altri infine la voce di Dio. Questa comoda teoria, sostenuta dai ceti borghesi […] fa parte anch'essa dell'azione delle forze conservatrici per avvilire o svalutare quest'epica lotta del nostro popolo.[159]

---

159 Pietro Secchia, *I comunisti e l'insurrezione* (Roma: Edizioni di Cultura Sociale, 1954), IX. «There are two major theories now trying to prevail. One belongs to those accountable for Fascism who, in order to erase their betrayal and guilt claim that it is necessary to forget the past and stop talking about Fascism and Resistance altogether, and that everyone has the same faults and credits. The other theory belongs to those who almost always opposed Fascism but that didn't take action to fight back, and waited the eleventh hour to abandon their inertia, their passivity and carefulness. These last ones are trying to create the legend that all Italians supported the Resistance, that the partisan uprising was not organized by anyone, being instead a spontaneous one. They say that everyone heard growing from the bottom of their soul a voice: some calls it the voice of fatherland, some the voice of consciousness, finally other called it the voice of God. This convenient theory, supported by the middle classes […] belongs to those conservative forces which try to underestimate and sadden the epic fight of our people».

Through the gradual emplotment of spontaneity within the ranks of the party, through its work of political education and organization of the subaltern masses, the great tale of the Resistance reads as a comedy ending with the Italian working class achieving the mature role of governing and directing political force of the new democratic life of the country.

The dilemma of spontaneity and organization is tightly bound to the myth of the Resistance as a *secondo Risorgimento*. Historians belonging to the communist area had an ambivalent stance regarding this concept. In fact, if, on the one hand, they were ready to deny an identity and juxtaposition between the Risorgimento and Resistenza, mainly on the grounds of the bourgeois character of the first and the proletarian supremacy of the second, on the other, the communist partisans were called *garibaldini,* suggesting how the patriotic aspect of the revolution was never overlooked or disregarded. It was a secondary but present aspect of the Marxist emplotment of the Resistance, capable of giving to the people's insurrection that national, unifying character necessary to aspire to a hegemonic role in the future government. First, the famous polemics between Togliatti and Rosselli about the concept in the 1920s — the leader of the PCI affirming the hegemony of the Marxist reading and rejecting the attempt of bourgeois correction offered by Rosselli — and second, the redirection represented by the 1926 Lyon congress — without counting the thesis of Gramsci on the topic — demonstrate the long-lasting ambiguity and partiality surrounding the different interpretations of the first Risorgimento: a fractured memory that will reemerge during the war as one of the multiple myths emplotting the Resistance. Battaglia, in reviewing an essay by Claudio Pavone on the different ideological and party appropriations of the first and second Risorgimento, claims the anti-rhetorical use of the Risorgimento made by the communist party. According to him, Risorgimento has, within the discourse of Italian Marxism, a national-popular and strategic meaning allowing the communist party to align and root itself in the Italian national *tradition*:

> Rievocando la lotta per l'indipendenza e per la libertà d'Italia, assumendo il nome di «secondo Risorgimento»—che è il nome infatti che ricorre più abitualmente nei suoi atti o nei suoi documenti—il movimento partigiano intese dare una precisa definizione di sé stesso, rivendicare in modo esplicito il carattere «nazionale» della guerra che conduceva riprendendo d'istinto e allargando i termini della vecchia polemica antifascista.[160]

Then, the emplotment of the first and second Risorgimento as mirroring events should not be a symptom of the spontaneity of the Resistance, of the younger antifascists joining the Resistance after the armistice of September 8th, as Pavone seems to suggest. However, it is a *topos* primarily rooted in the old antifascist tradition. Once again, the crucial riddle of the historiography on the resistance seems to lie in this problematic continuity and filiation between the old antifascism and the new two generations divided by their diverse experience of the fascist regime. It is both a generational and a 'narrative' issue, the riddle consisting in the necessity to conjoin in one coherent whole two discrete parts because the interpretations of fascism of the two generations were not precisely matching, the missing piece thwarting the teleological continuity of the *bildungsroman* of Italian antifascism. Stressing the prominence of the older generation, trained in the clandestine antifascism of the *ventennio*, i.e., the antifascism of conspiracy, of exile, of confinement, of expatriates and prisoners, meant to emplot the Resistance mainly as an ideological war between fascism and antifascism. Leo Valiani, a former communist who fought with the Resistance as *azionista*, in defining what exactly was the Resistance in Milan, writes: «E se mi chiedete cos'era la Resistenza, a Milano, dirò che era una simbiosi, anzi una sintesi, di vent'anni di cospirazione antifascista e delle forze nuove, scevre di passato politico, e che talvolta

---

160 Roberto Battaglia, *Risorgimento e Resistenza* (Roma: Editori Riuniti, 1964), 29-30. «By evoking the fight for the independence and liberty of Italy, by claiming the name of «second Risorgimento»—this is in fact the most frequently used name in its documents and acts—the partisan movement proposed a precise self-definition and explicitly reclaimed the national character of the war it was conducting, taking inspiration from and broadening old antifascist terms».

avevano debuttato nelle organizzazioni giovanili fasciste, che il 1943 aveva destato.»[161]

Valiani fought in Spain and, maybe, the pivotal moment of education, both political and military, the true rehearsal of the Resistance was exactly the Spanish Civil War, which Aldo Garosci, another *azionista* historian, defined as an «enigma.»[162] Communists, socialists and liberal socialists framed the two events in their political *Bildungsroman*, of the development from spontaneity to organization. The Civil War prepares and forms an entire class of antifascists that, by passing over to the younger generation what they learned in Guadalajara and on the Ebro, will compact and organize the Resistance.

In the autobiographical novel *Il voltagabbana*, Davide Lajolo locates Spain as the crucial turning point of his life. The encounter with the 'other side' while fighting as a soldier of the Italian army — and as a member of the Italian Fascist Party (PNF) — makes him fully aware of the contradictions and betrayals of the regime, which sent an unprepared, badly equipped army to fight a war that revealed to be worth fighting only for the blackshirts. The young Lajolo matures, then, the ideological premises that will eventually lead him to a political, radical conversion to switch sides. The story of his life is interlaced with that one of Francesco Scotti — signaled by the use of *italics* — an antifascist who fought in Spain with the international brigades. After a short, indirect contact in Spain, the two will cross and join their paths a second time during the Resistance, this time fighting on the same side, both for the right cause. Lajolo is one of those *giovani del passo romano* who grew up under fascism, who joined it because: «il fascismo era davvero l'unica via per un giovane, per sentirsi vivo, per fare, per agitarsi, per combattere affinché le cose potessero cambiare. A ma piaceva essere attivo,

---

[161] Leo Valiani, "Il Partito d'Azione nel Comitato di Liberazione Nazionale per l'Alta Italia." In *Fascismo e antifascismo,* 588-594, 592. «And if you ask me what the Resistance was in Milan, I would say that it was a symbiosis or rather a synthesis of twenty years of antifascist conspiracy with those new forces awaken by 1943 and which lacked political past and had at first even joined Fascist youth organizations».

[162] Aldo Garosci, *Gli intellettuali e la guerra di Spagna* (Torino: Einaudi, 1947), 33.

muovermi, vivere ogni giorno qualcosa di diverso. Il fascismo era eccitante.»[163] Scotti, when he welcomed Lajolo in the Resistance — also taking advantage of his military training — justified in front of the most intransigent partisans his problematic choice and the ex-fascist's possible future role in the communist party, as follows:

> È giusto, tu hai fatto il tuo dovere, ma non devi considerare la partecipazione alla guerra partigiana come un atto di riparazione. La lotta di liberazione è qualcosa di più per te e per tutti. Il Partito ti vuole nelle sue file attive anche per il bagaglio amaro di esperienze che tu puoi portare. Molti di noi sono vissuti in galera o fuori d'Italia in tutti questi anni; se vogliamo comprendere a fondo la situazione abbiamo bisogno soprattutto di voi. Bisogna parlare alle generazioni giovani che il fascismo ha travolto un linguaggio che siano in grado di intendere, ridare loro fiducia per cercare la strada della libertà. Per questo tu non puoi rifiutare l'invito del Partito. [164]

The inclusion within the antifascist organization of the younger generation compromised with fascism will help the party to understand the enemy, leaving a sectarian dogmatism aside, and to acquire, to learn, a new language in order to more effectively communicate with a generation educated in the triumph of empty rhetoric. The encounter of fascism and antifascism of the party with the ex-fascist youth culminates in a mutual, reciprocal education pushing forward the plot of that national, political *bildung* that will eventually recompose, in peaceful compromise, a nation fractured by still acute ideological factions.

Antifascism was a school, and its work of education will continue among the *Brigate Garibaldi*, thanks to the role of the political *commissario* who realized a process of politicization of the new, younger and mainly apolitical, if non-ex-fascist, recruit:

---

163 Davide Lajolo, *Il voltagabbana* (Milano: Il Saggiatore, 1963), 25. «Fascism really was the only path for a youth to feel alive, to do something, to stir himself, to live everyday something different. Fascism was exciting».

164 Idem, 291. «It is right, you have been dutiful, but do not consider the participation in the partisan war as an act of compensation. The fight for freedom is something more for you and for everyone. The Party wants you among its active members also in reason of your bitter experiences. Many of us have lived in prison or outside of Italy during all these years; if we want to fully grasp the situation we need you more than anything. We need to speak to the young generations crushed by fascism in a language they can understand, we need to restore in them the trust necessary in their search for freedom. For this reason you cannot reject the invitation to join the Party».

> Al processo di "militarizzazione" corrisponde infatti, necessariamente, quello di "politicizzazione," di presa di coscienza degli obiettivi della guerra di liberazione, di trasformazione d'ogni ribelle in "patriota." [...] Sintomo più evidente di questo processo di "auto-educazione" è l'istituzione, prima nelle brigate Garibaldi e poi in quasi tutte le altre formazioni, del "commissario politico," derivata anch'essa dalla guerra di Spagna, ma radicata nell'esperienza stessa dell'antifascismo che mai aveva rinunciato al dibattito, allo studio, all'approfondimento dei motivi della lotta; tanto da trasformare anche le carceri in "scuole," da reagire alla terribile inerzia della prigione con lo studio e con la discussione ideologico-politica.[165]

The presence of a political leader will be strongly contested and not always seen in a good light, as the works of Fenoglio testify. There were, in fact, some partisan brigades which escaped ideological and political indoctrination, stating their mostly military scope and nature, as their leader, Enrico Martini "Mauri," explain: «La Resistenza checché se ne dica non è stata il monopolio di una o più corrente specifica e l'esigenza della guerra contro il tedesco e il fascista non è stata sentita soltanto dai reduci dal confino, dall'esilio, o dalla Spagna rossa, ma anche da coloro che la guerra fascista l'avevano combattuta e combattuta bene.»[166] In fact, another fracture within the Resistance is the distinction and sheer rivalry in many cases between 'military' and 'political' formations, which I will discuss later on more extensively. For now, it is enough to highlight how the question of continuity and education between opposite political and ideological beliefs and the generational gap dividing them are the true moments of truth, of cohesion or

---

[165] Battaglia, "La resistenza italiana: lo sviluppo dell'intervento armato fino all'insurrezione." In *Fascismo e antifascismo*, 472-498, 487. «To a process of militarization corresponds a process of political education making aware of the goals of the Liberation war and turning every rebel into a patriot. [...] Most evident symbol of this process of self-education is the institution, first among the Garibaldi brigades, later among all the other formations, of the political commissary, a practice derived from the Spanish Civil war but rooted in an antifascism which never renounced to debate, to study, to examine the motives behind the fight so that even prisons were turned into schools in order to react to the inertia of prison with study and ideological-political discussions.»
[166] Enrico Martini, "Le formazioni Mauri," *Mercurio*, (May 1945): 169. «The resistance wa not under the monopoly of one or more specific side, and the need of the war against the German and the fascist was not felt only by those returning from political confinement, from exile or from Comunist Spain, but also by those who had faught, and well, the fascist war».

possible disruption of that *bildungsroman*-like emplotment in which spontaneity and organization needed to coexist.

Marxist historiography largely considered, at least until the 1960s, the evolution-development of the Resistance as a comedy ending positively, the final resolution resulting in a consistent victory of the subaltern masses after a tragic and dark beginning with the 8th of September and the first merely spontaneous sparks of insurrection: «tragico e oscuro il suo inizio,»[167] «prevalgono i sentimenti elementari e immediati che scaturiscono dalla grande tragedia nazionale,»[168] «indubbiamente spontanea è l'insurrezione di Napoli,»[169] «spontaneo è l'episodio di Cefalonia.»[170] On the occasion of the first decennial of the Liberation, Togliatti writes that the outcome was the ascent of the working class as *classe dirigente* of the country, i.e., a completed *bildung*, because the true objective of the Resistance never was an immediate revolution, in the model of the Russian one, but a step further towards 'progressive democracy.' The resistance was a maturation from Tragedy to Comedy.

What risks disrupting Comedy with tragic undertones is the encounter with fascism, that, as we have seen, is deeply related also to the generational and educational question troubling the antifascist organization paradigm and emplotment. Learning from the enemy and comprehending its essence must be the essential prerequisite of any historiographical reconstruction of the Resistance, as Roberto Battaglia explains:

> Ormai non sarà più possibile fornire una propria interpretazione del movimento di liberazione senza, al tempo stesso, rendere più o meno esplicita l'interpretazione del fascismo nelle sue varie accezioni. L'improvvisa «malattia morale» di crociana memoria o la dittatura violenta dei gruppi più reazionari e più sciovinisti della grande borghesia, o la «involuzione democratica» della classe dirigente italiana, costituiscono ormai tanti obbligatori punti di riferimento anche per chi scrive la storia della resistenza nell'ultima sue fase; e non sempre si mantengono rigorosamente distinti, ma tendono spesso a integrarsi vicendevolmente. Si fa comunque sempre più viva l'esigenza di questo più vasto inquadramento, di questo allineamento della

---

167 Battaglia, *Risorgimento e Resistenza*, 478. «tragic and obscure beginning»
168 Ibidem. «The immediate and elementary sentiments generated by the great national tragedy are the prevailing feelings».
169 Ibid. «The uprising in Naples is undoubtedly spontaneous».
170 Ibid. «The episode of Cefalonia is spontaneous».

storia della Resistenza con la storia più generale dell'Italia contemporanea.[171]

The interpretation of fascism within the frame of historiographical reconstructions of the Epic of the Resistance also connects with the problem of violence. The equation fascism-violence is a direct result of one of the classic, most recurrent meanings of fascism as the repressive tool in the hands of authoritarian capital. Even in historiography, then, the fascist keeps disrupting the documentarian, realistic account of events with a heavily caricature-like, morally charged vocabulary. The figurative transfiguration of the fascist — from the historical data to the textual space — always ends in a melodramatic and grotesque portrayal. Battaglia refers to fascism as a Hydra, a many-headed monster difficult to interpret because of continuous movement and metamorphosis. If the Resistance is a natural evolution, Fascism is a disturbing, uncanny deformation of anthropomorphic traits with animal forms. One seems to be reading a medieval bestiary. Mussolini is often referred to as a Satyr in the *Storia*, while the *banda d'avventurieri* of Fascism is composed of a mixture of hybrid forms: «donna-iena,»[172] «vermi,»[173] «vespe,»[174] Kesserling watches Rome resembling a dark eagle «annidato nelle caverne del Soratte.»[175] The *topos* of the *belva fascista* are traceable almost everywhere in the historiographical tradition of the

---

171 Idem, 217. «By now it will be impossible to provide an interpretation of the Liberation movement without, at the same time, making more or less explicit the interpretation of Fascism in its various senses. The sudden «moral illness» or the violent dictatorship of the most reactionary and chauvinist groups of the bourgeoise, or the «democratic regression» of the Italian ruling class, all constitute fundamental reference points for the writing of the history of the Resistance in its last phase; and it is not always possible to distinguish one point from the other since they often tend to complete each other. Such wider framework, such juncture between history of the Resistance and history of contemporary Italy become day after day more urgent».
172 Battaglia, *Storia della Resistenza,* 238. «woman-hyena»
173 Idem, 302. «worms»
174 Mario Argenton, "L'esercito partigiano," *Mercurio,* (May: 1945): 94. «wasps»
175 Idem, 237. «nestled in Soratte's caves».

Resistance: «groviglio di vipere»[176] and «cani sanguinari.»[177] As Calamandrei writes: «il fascismo fu un'invasione che veniva dal di dentro, un prevalere temporaneo di qualche cosa di bestiale che si era annidato o si era ridestato dentro di noi: e la liberazione fu veramente la crisi acuta di un morbo che finalmente si spezzava dentro al nostro petto, come lo strappo risoluto con cui il popolo italiano riuscì con le sue stesse mani a svellare dal suo cuore un groviglio di serpi, che per vent'anni l'aveva soffocato.»[178] Croce's parenthesis and moral poisoning explanation of the fascist mystery emerges as a rhetorical figurative strategy in almost every postwar historiographical work, regardless of the political faith of its author. In listing a series of notorious local fascists, Bocca includes the 'vain' type of fascist and the fascist of 'character'. Both kinds have motives for their absurd adhesion to the regime first and to Salò later, which is a matter of psychology rather than politics. Among them there is even one affected by elephantiasis syndrome: «agiscono, probabilmente, i complessi psichici imprevedibili, di inferiorità, di vanità.»[179]

The hybrid inhuman shape, a disrupted unity of animal and human, has a formal variation when the object is Nazism: the human nature is contaminated this time by mechanical forms, turning the Nazi soldier into an *automa*: «un fantoccio, un automa così imponente visto dal di fuori e, dentro, così privo di cervello e astuzia!».[180] This hybridity also results, on the morphological level, in an iteration of the modes of tragedy and melodrama in association

---

176 Giorgio Bocca, *La Repubblica di Mussolini* (Bari: Laterza, 1977), 192. «a tangle of vipers»
177 Elio Vittorini, "Eugenio Curiel," *Mercurio*, (May: 1945): 149. «Bloodthirsty dogs»
178 Calamandrei, *Uomini e città della Resistenza*, 56. «Fascism was like an invasion that came from within, the temporary prevailing of something wild and beastly that had settled and reawaken inside us: the liberation really was the acute crisis of a disease finally bursting out of our chest, like the strong resolution with which the Italian people decided to pull out from its heart, with its own hands, that tangle of snakes which once had suffocated it».
179 Giorgio Bocca, *Storia dell'Italia partigiana* (Bari: Laterza, 1966), 48-49. «Unpredictable psychic complexes of inferiority and vanity are in action».
180 Battaglia, *Storia della Resistenza*, 387. «such an imposing puppet and automaton seen from the outside and so lacking brain and cunning inside».

with fascism. The fascist is a «fantasma tragico e grottesco,»[181] while fascism is a «clownesca tragedia.»[182] As an embodiment of evil deviance and moral deformity, the fascist symbolizes an ambiguous being condemned to exist in between human and inhuman, reality and fiction, decadence and modernity. Spies, collaborationists and torturers are the incarnation of sadism, and the mark of evil laughter is the evidence of their incongruence with the present:

> Ad un certo punto, in un risucchio di gente, vidi due omerottoli, due spie, cacciati avanti con le canne dei moschetti. Uno era cupo, grigio in volto; l'altro aveva gli occhi deliranti e rideva. [...] I neo-fascisti venivano accoppiati uno ad uno: il gerarca insieme alla spia, lo sgherro con l'aguzzino, l'antico bastonatore del '21 assieme al giovinetto pallido e sadico del '43. [183]

Fascists are reduced to the subhuman form of «pigmei malevoli,»[184] the evil antagonists of 19th-century melodramatic tradition, sick carriers of moral debauchery and vices, often poisoned by the troubling corruption of the feminine. «Cori di ubriachi e risa femminili»[185] comes from restaurants frequented by fascists, while sadistic laughter is their unnatural response to murder:

> L'ultimo volto che vedo, abbandonando la piazza, è quello di un repubblichino, che ride istericamente. Quel riso indica l'infinita distanza che ci separa. [...] Loro ridono. Hanno appena ucciso 15 uomini e si sentono allegri. Contro quel riso osceno noi combattiamo. Esso taglia nettamente il mondo: da un lato la barbarie, dall'altro la civiltà. I cordoni di repubblichini sono sempre fitti. Ad ogni passaggio, ad ogni posto di blocco, mi imbatto nella loro insolenza, nella loro spavalda vigliaccheria: mitra ostentati, bombe a mano al cinturone, facce feroci, lugubri camicie nere. Ancora una volta,

---

181 Idem, 298. «tragic and grotesque ghost».
182 Nino Valeri, "La marcia su Roma." In *Fascismo e Antifascismo*, 105-119, 105. «Clownish tragedy».
183 Pietro Bianchi, "La morte sulla via Emilia," *Mercurio*, (May,1945): 87-89. «At some point, in the crowd, I saw two creeps, two spies, pushed forward by the musket's barrels. One had a grey and gloomy face, the other laughed and was delirious. [...] Neofascist were killed one by one: the *gerarca* together with the spy, the pig with the jailer, the old thug from '21 together with the pale and sadistic kid of '43».
184 Ferruccio Parri, "Introduzione," *Mercurio*, (May, 1945): 18. «malevolent pygmies».
185 Gaetano Pesce, *Senza tregua – la guerra dei GAP* (Milano: Feltrinelli, 1967), 81. «the sound of women laughing and the noise of a drunken chorus».

come in Spagna di fronte alla spietata ferocia degli ufficialetti nazisti, si rivelano i due mondi in antitesi, i due modi opposti di concepire la vita.[186]

If the epic of the Resistance can count on a Tuscan environment that joins the fight against the fascist and Nazi enemy, the headquarters of the paramilitary, fascist *banda Carità* is the irrational space of materialized nightmare and vice. In the chronicles of the Resistance war in Florence by Carlo Francovich, literary motifs intervene to distort the realistic account of those months:

> Il 24 novembre, gli sgherri di Carità piombarono nel negozio di Pretini e lo arrestarono, insieme a diversi suoi compagni di lavoro e di cospirazione. Furono portati in via Ugo Foscolo, nella villa citata, dove gli ospiti vivevano in un'atmosfera di delirio e d'incubo kafkiano. [187]

The men of Carità are «avvinazzati aguzzini»[188] and, among his spies appear the «ributtanti figure»[189] of two defrocked priests, don Ildefonso and don Gregorio, the former being famous for his habit to play Neapolitan *canzonette,* or Shubert's *Incompiuta*, while tortures were happening in the next room. Florence, then, is a city invaded by all the different manifestations of vice, invaded by prostitutes and *meridionali*: «Firenze pullula di puttane pervenute da vari centri d'Italia: ristoranti di lusso notturni, orchestrine,

---

186 Idem, 204. «The last face I see leaving the square belongs to a *repubblichino*, who laughs hysterically. That laughter indicates the infinite distance separating us. [...] They laugh. They have just killed 15 men and they feel happy. We fight against that obscene laughter which deeply cuts the world in two: on one side brutality, on the other civilization. The cordons of *repubblichini* are always dense. At every corner, at every checkpoint I bump into their insolence and cowardice: machine gun well on display, grenades on their gun belt, ferocious faces, grim black shirts. Once again like in Spain, in front of the unforgiving brutality of Nazi officers, two antithetical worlds reveal themselves as the two opposite ways of conceiving life».
187 Carlo Francovich, *La resistenza a Firenze* (Firenze: La Nuova Italia, 1962), 93. «On the 24th of November, the pigs of Carità stormed inside Pretini's store and arrested him together with his work and conspiracy companions. They were brought to via Ugo Foscolo in the afore mentioned villa, where guests lived in the delirious atmosphere of a Kafkian nightmare».
188 Idem, 95. «drunken jailors»
189 Idem, 97. «disgusting figures»

automobili requisite, orge.»[190] New Fascists are a «stortura patologica»[191] and, generally, they can all be framed by the same definition:

> i nuovi elementi furono quindi in buona parte teppisti di vecchia data, reclutati fra il *lumpenproletariat* fiorentino, nonché alcuni individui che, nutrendo istinti pervertiti e tenuti fino allora nascosti sotto l'involucro della educazione e delle consuetudini borghesi, vedevano finalmente presentarsi il momento di dare sfogo a quegli istinti con il ladroneccio e la strage dei propri simili. [...] Il Fascio repubblicano tornò ad essere quello che era stato il vecchio partito fascista: un'accolita di violenti, che adesso più che mai avevano mano libera per dare sfogo ai loro istinti brutali.»[192]

History and romance mix in a transfiguration of the historical figures of fascists into Don Rodrigo's «bravi,»[193] a similitude that, as Battaglia highlights, has something to do with the equation fascist/beast. Manzoni in fact famously compared the *bravi* to a pack of bloodhounds: «si pensa—siamo in clima lombardo—al ritorno dei bravi di Don Rodrigo "come un branco di segugi, dopo aver inseguita invano una lepre, tornano mortificati verso il padrone, co' musi bassi e con le code ciondoloni..."»[194]. Partisans, on the contrary, in facing Nazis, remind Battaglia of Fra Cristoforo's manners,[195] while Salvatore Satta, in his *De Profundis,* mainly following Gobetti's lesson, identifies the typical Italian with Don Abbondio.[196] A reversed spontaneity characterizes fascist figures even in historical

---

190 Idem, 56. «Florence is crammed with whores from all sides of Italy: expensive night restaurants, little orchestras, confiscated cars, orgies.»
191 Idem, 48. «pathological twistedness».
192 Idem, 49. «The new elements were mostly old times thugs, recruited from the Florentine *lumpenproletariat,* in addition to certain types who, feeding perverted instincts kept hidden under the veil of education and bourgeois customs, finally saw the opportunity to unload those instincts through robbing and slaughtering their counterparts. [...] Republican fascism became again what the old fascist party was: a pack of brutes now freer than ever to satisfy their most violent instincts.»
193 Bocca, *Storia dell'Italia partigiana,* 47. «thugs»
194 Battaglia, *Storia della Resistenza,* 569. «We think of, and afterall we are in a Lombarian setting, Don Rodrigo's thugs who "like a pack of bloodhounds after having followed a lare's track in vane, return to their master mortified, lowered faces and their tails dangling».
195 Idem, 493.
196 An important role in this constant parallel with Manzon's characters might have been played by Lukács reading of *I promessi sposi* in his Historical Novel, published in 1937.

and autobiographical semi-historical accounts of the war, as if that same spontaneity that the organization of the Resistance was able to frame within the discipline and rectitude of the party in view of a common goal went on the contrary, astray, uncontrolled, infected. The fascist looks like a young boy who, freed from the restrictions of bourgeois education, can satisfy, finally unrestrained, his most inhuman, beast-like, violent and sexual instincts without the frame of measure and limit.

According to Claudio Pavone in *Una guerra civile – saggio sulla moralità della resistenza,* a work that will later conclude my analysis, the experience of the republican fascism of Salò has to be considered the main cause of this semantic excess of the epithet "fascist":

> È probabilmente proprio durante la guerra civile che la parola fascista si caricò con particolare intensità di un significato che andava al di là della concreta e specifica esperienza storica del fascismo, finendo col designare un tipo umano negativamente connotato sotto tutti i profili pubblici e privati. [...] Il persistente uso di «fascista» quale epiteto ingiurioso, globale e riassuntivo delle ignominie capaci di installarsi in un essere umano, può considerarsi un'estrema conseguenza di questa dilatazione, cui la RSI diede un conclusivo contributo, del contenuto semantico della parola oltre i limiti storicamente verificabili.[197]

A semantic excess that simultaneously pairs with a perversion of the teleology of the historical account and of 'natural' time, as republican fascism seems to be a grotesque resurrection of the old, already dead fascism, in a way, as Lino will resurrect from the dead in *Il conformista:*

---

[197] Claudio Pavone, *Una guerra civile. Saggio sulla moralità della resistenza* (Torino: Bollati Boringhieri, 1991), 260. « "Probably, it is precisely during the civil war that the word 'Fascist' acquired, with particular intensity, a meaning that went beyond the concrete and specific historical experience of Fascism, eventually coming to denote a kind of human being with negative connotations from every public and private point of view. [...] The persistent use of fascista as an epithet that was insulting, global, and expressive of all the ignomity that could reside in a human being may be regarded as the extreme consequence of this expansion, to which the RSI gave a decisive contribution, of the semantic content of the word beyond historically verifiable limits.» English translation by P. Levy with the assistance of David Broder, in Pavone, *A Civil War: a History of the Italian Resistance,* Verso Books: New York, 2013, pp. 313-314]

> Un sentimento sicuramente molto diffuso, e che alimentò la repulsione subito manifestatasi verso i fascisti repubblicani, sta nel carattere che quelli assunsero di lugubri ma sfacciati *revenants*. [...] Ora i fascisti resuscitati sembrava facessero, contro natura, scorrere il tempo a ritroso. Erano appena usciti dal sepolcro e subito davano ordini.[198]

The reading of the Resistance and the war of liberation as a civil war, at the center of Pavone's reinterpretation of those events outside of a merely teleological reconstruction from spontaneity to organization, exactly breaks and disrupts that comic emplotment we have seen characterizing Battaglia's epic history of the Resistance and, more generally, the Marxist interpretation of the fascism and antifascism struggle. Thus, starting from Salò and the consequent semantic expansion of the word "fascist," the traditional emplotment is substituted by the civil war one, more apt to combine fascism and antifascism in a dynamic relation of reciprocity. Comedy mixes with Tragedy in a master plot in which the motifs of violence and moral choice are the key thematic areas in which ambiguity and carnivalesque relativity serve to demystify and problematize that Manichean divide into good and evil puppets. Pavone's pivotal work is the outcome of fifty years of historiography on the subject, profoundly redirected and influenced by the multiple heterogeneous seasons and changes in Italian political history. As the surveys on the matter by both Quazza and Battaglia perfectly demonstrate, during the 1970s, mainly as a consequence of the 1968 student protests, the reading of the resistance as a successful revolution, i.e., as Comedy, that the party historiography of the PCI strongly promoted, as we have seen, was attacked and discussed. The policy of the PCI was criticized and accused of having been too submissive to the evident reactionary nature of the DC governments, now seen as continuity with the past fascist regime. From the compromise of the *svolta di Salerno* in 1944 to the *compromesso storico* of 1975, the younger generation of antifascism, also disillusioned by the

---

[198] Idem, 253. «A sentiment that was certainly widespread, and which stoked the loathing that was immediately manifested for the republican fascists, lies in the way the latter assumed the character of dismal but brazen *revenants*. [...] Now the resuscitated Fascists seemed, against nature, to be making time flow backwards.» [Ibidem, p. 306]

revelation of the true nature of the Soviet regime, criticized the PCI for passively following the directives coming from Moscow. From the victorious revolution of the Italian working classes, the Resistance came to be read as a betrayed revolution, as a missed opportunity deeply weakened by the internal fractures of the lefts within the CLN. As Quazza notes in 1972, both elegantly and neatly, historicizing an always evolving process:

> La direzione stessa dell'attacco—contro i partiti rivoluzionari ache avrebbero sostanzialmente tradito la classe rivoluzionaria e la Resistenza, da rivoluzione convertendola o lasciandola convertire in restaurazione—ha colto, pur nella sbrigativa semplificazione, se non la soluzione, i termini centrali del problema. Termini che stanno essenzialmente nella natura complessa, diciamo pure dialettica, del rapporto tra resistenza e fascismo, nei caratteri di interdipendenza e reciprocità, non di pura contrapposizione, che fin dal suo sorgere il rapporto riveste, immerso com'è in tutto il quadro delle relazioni fra società e stato.[199]

Once again, the crucial aporia of the Resistance and the relationship between fascism and antifascism is the narrative problem of the difficult emplotment of spontaneity and organization, in which the motifs of education and generational gap play a decisive role, as the second contrast between different, successive generations of antifascism in the 1960s and 70s confirms. Quazza continues:

> Il significato politico non rispecchia la lotta armata perché i rapporti tra le forze costitutive della Resistenza sono condizionati dal processo di formazione della Resistenza stessa, nel quale l'antifascismo «organizzato» del ventennio è una parte soltanto e non la più forte, perché molto vi pesano sia il nuovo antifascismo «spontaneo» dei giovani nato dalla guerra e dal disastro dell'8 settembre, sia quello di comodo di tanti ex-alleati o promotori del fascismo.[200]

---

199 Guido Quazza, "Storia della Resistenza e storia d'Italia—Ipotesi di lavoro," *Rivista di storia contemporanea* (Jan 1, 1972): 50. «The target itself of the attack—against those revolutionary parties that had betrayed the revolutionary class and the Resistance by basically turning revolution into restauration—hit the key terms of the issue, i.e., the complex and dialectical relationship between Resistance and fascism, in their reciprocal characters of reciprocity and interdependence, not of pure contrast, that could be traced back to the wider framework of society- state relations.»
200 Idem, 51«The political meaning does not mirror the armed fight because the relationships between the constitutive forces of the Resistance are influenced

The solution to the *impasse* for Quazza was to ground the historiographical approach to the Resistance on the prospective of the continuity between the pre-fascist and post-fascist Italy, of the parallel processes of formation and development of the organized, old antifascism into the new, spontaneous one, and of the latent persistence of the old fascist regime under the democratic veil of the postwar republic. Enigma and *bildungsroman*, the emplotments of the coming-of-age novel and the detective, whodunnit, story. These new tendencies in the historiography of the Resistance, noticed by Quazza in 1972 in response to specific contemporary political upheavals, are, in my opinion, as I have tried to show so far, already active before their recognition and canonization, even though still in a confused preliminary phase, in the historiographical accounts of the immediate postwar years and the 1950s. Behind the mask of the fascist stereotype already hides the more dynamic, reciprocal rendition expressed by Quazza that is found in Pavone's account: a more nuanced, anti-teleological and less Manichean analysis.

2.6 Resistance as Tragedy:
the 'Betrayed Revolution' of the *Azionisti*.
The 'Civil War' Thread from Massimo Salvadori's
Storia della resistenza italiana,
to Claudio Pavone's *Una guerra civile*.

The definition of the war of liberation as a civil war and of the Resistance as a betrayed revolution are pivotal points of the historiographical accounts coming from previous members of the *Partito d'Azione*, the antifascist intellectuals whose political education traces back to Rosselli's *Giustizia e Libertà*: among others, Leone Ginzburg, Norberto Bobbio, Vittorio Foa, Nicola Chiaromonte, Umberto Calosso, Andrea Caffi, Carlo Levi. Quazza himself was a

---

by the process of *bildung* of the Resistance itself, in which the organized antifascism active during the *ventennio* is just one and not the strongest part of it, because of the role played by the new antifascism of the youth born out of the war and of September 8, and by the antifascism conveniently embraced by ex-allied and promoters of fascism.»

historian of *azionista* inspiration, and Pavone too was highly influenced in his development of the idea of the Resistance as a compound of three simultaneous wars — patriotic, classist, civil — by the *giellista* Norberto Bobbio. It was during the crisis opened by the Tambroni government in 1960 and culminated in the 1968 student protest and the *anni di piombo* — the years of red and black terrorism — that the younger generation of antifascism will recognize itself in the kind of story told by the *giellisti* and *azionisti* in the immediate postwar years:

> La loro posizione trovò piuttosto parziali convergenze con il mito della Resistenza «tradita» o «incompiuta» che tra anni Sessanta e Settanta rispose alla parola d'ordine di riprendere la «rivoluzione», laddove era stata interrotta nel 1945. Questo mito puntava a spezzare la gelida crosta del dopoguerra, facendo riaffiorare una preesistente tensione rivoluzionaria, sopita ma non del tutto spenta. Fu soprattutto la grave crisi politica dell'estate 1960 a restituire all'antifascismo una patente radicale in virtù di una nuova spinta che emergeva al di fuori dei partiti tradizionali. Carlo Levi parlò di «nuova Resistenza» durante una cerimonia pubblica cui partecipò, insieme a Vittorio Foa, nello sperduto paesino abruzzese dove era stato confinato Leone Ginzburg.[201]

The Action Party, following the path opened by *Giustizia e Libertà*, aimed at a total renewal of the Italian State institutions. The Resistance, then, was not only conceived as the mere occasion for a radical change, but it represented the very necessary condition for its realization, the first, true revolution in a country that, having not witnessed anything like other great European revolutions — protestant and bourgeois, and whose unity was the result of the crown's initiative — could have been awakened and deeply transformed itself only thanks to a national uprising of the people, both

---

201 Bresciani, *Quale antifascismo?*, 283. «Their stance aligned itself with the myth of a betrayed and uncomplete Resistance that in the 60s and 70s answered the call to resume the revolution interrupted in 1945. This myth aimed at breaking through the thick shell covering the post-war years, letting out a persistent revolutionary strain, not yet completely extinguished. The 1970 serious political crisis returned antifascism the old radical spirit thanks to the pressure of non-traditional parties. Carlo Levi spoke of a new Resistance, during a public ceremony together with Vittorio Foa, in a remote village in Abruzzo where Leone Ginzburg was confined.»

patriotic and moral. This is how Bobbio defines the Action Party's ideology:

> Negare il fascismo che era stato negazione di liberalismo e di socialismo, voleva dire affermare contemporaneamente entrambi. [...] Il rinnovamento totale non poteva venire che da un'ideologia antifascista totale. Poiché il rinnovamento totale comportava una trasformazione rivoluzionaria, la nuova ideologia si contrapponeva a ogni forma di restaurazione del passato prefascista che stava a cuore ai liberali, ma insieme a ogni tentativo rivoluzionario che ripetesse pedissequamente gli schemi di una rivoluzione già esaurita nella capacità di creazione di una nuova società, quale la rivoluzione sovietica.[202]

The antifascism of the GL first and of the Action Party during the Resistance later—whose partisan brigades were named GL as a sign of continuity with the tradition of Rosselli's clandestine movement—was, then, profoundly different from the Marxist kind and, it inevitably translated into an alternative emplotment of fascism and the Resistance, a more ambiguous and for many aspects highly influenced by a more reciprocal relationship with fascism—liberal-socialists, were, after all, called *social-fascisti* by the more intransigent representatives of Italian Marxism—and by a contradictory stance on Stalinism and Marxism. Born in the same anti-political and *interventista* climate of the First World War and of its immediate aftermath and developing, in the 1930s, a less negative and intransigent view of Marxism, the movement *Giustizia e libertà* embodied in a dynamic, in between mix of all the different souls of its components, a varied spectrum of political and ideological positions often in open contradiction with each other. Their interpretation of fascism first and of the Resistance later had, nevertheless, some recurrent patterns and unavoidable premises. First, the tendency to emplot fascism in a wider European context, as the most

---

[202] Norberto Bobbio, *Profilo ideologico del Novecento italiano* (Torino: Einaudi, 1986), 155-156. «Denying Fascism, which had been a denial of both liberalism and socialism, meant affirming them both [...]. Total renewal could only come from a "total" antifascist ideology. Since total renewal implied revolutionary transformation, the new ideology opposed all forms of restoration of the prefascist past that the Liberals held dear, but it also rejected any attempt at revolution that slavishly imitated the Soviet revolution, which had already exhausted its capacities for the creation of a new society.» [English translation by L.G. Cochrane, in N. Bobbio, *Ideological profile of Twentieth-Century Italy*, Princeton University Press: Princeton, 1995) p. 147.

degenerative symptom of a moral crisis of civilization investing European society *tout court*, of which totalitarian regimes—the soviet one included—were the unmistakable symbol. Second, the necessity of a 'religious' war against fascism, not only a political battle but mainly a moral clash of opposite ideas of civilization, one depriving people of freedom, the other one founding itself on the freedom of individuals as the first unalienable value, in the tradition of Croce. Their antifascism tended, in fact, to be of an existentialist kind, moral before being political. Third, the stress on the guiding role of a restricted *élite* of intellectuals—the notion of *minorité agissante* inherited by Sorel and Herzen—another heroic and virtuous Italy that would have saved from the crisis the other Italy—an autobiography of a nation—naturally forever receding in the opposite direction, towards vice and opportunism. There is, then, in the new élite, a pedagogical tendency to educate the nation in order to trigger, first, an awakening in the people's moral and political consciousness and, second, the concrete, radical revolutionary act. GL was exactly a compromise between morality and will, thought and action, in the tradition of the Risorgimento's hero Giuseppe Mazzini. The moment of choice will acquire in the historical emplotments of the Resistance a prominent role: the 8th of September as the moment of truth, as a dramatic crisis and tragic choice between a multiple universe of destinies, as in Pavone's 1991 reconstruction. The 'symbolic' date of the armistice was intended as the opportunity for a new humanism capable of resurrecting Europe from a spiritual, universal decadence, thanks to the political, educational and exemplary morality of figures such as Leone Ginzburg, true inheritor of Piero Gobetti's antifascist moral intransigence:

> Infine, gobettiana fu l'intransigenza antifascista, la resistenza al fascismo come fatto morale prima che politico, come valore culturale oltre che politico. [...] Era un antifascismo fatto di disdegno, di fierezza d'essere dalla parte giusta [...] nutrito di quella cultura storica, umana e umanistica che permetteva di distinguere, senza possibilità di sbagliarsi, la civiltà dalla barbarie, i germi di progresso da quelli di decadenza, la durevole conquista dall'avventura, il pensiero dalla retorica. [203]

---

[203] Norberto Bobbio, introduction to *Leone Ginzburg—Scritti* (Torino: Einaudi, 1964), xxvii-xxviii. «Finally, inspired by Gobetti was the consideration of antifascist intransigence, of antifascist resistance as a primarily moral fact and not

Gobetti's *Rivoluzione Liberale, GL* and the *Partito d'azione* recapitulate the parable of that very same tradition of antifascism, which framed fascism as revelation and autobiography of the nation, of its true essence. This kind of emplotment helped to solve the riddle of the enemy, to understand the deep reasons for its development and its grip on Italian society. Moreover, it did not imply an absolute negation of it as Marxism did, but it did allow the subject to surpass the enemy, to move further and not only against it, because there was the recognition that fascism was born too as the anti-political, *antigiolittiano, interventista* response to a universal crisis:

> Rosselli e compagni cercavano di comprendere il nemico, di imparare da esso, per meglio combatterlo. I comunisti miravano soprattutto a contrapporsi al nemico – un nemico che era di volta in volta definito sulla base degli orientamenti della politica estera sovietica.[204]

Hence, the first lesson to be learned from the enemy should have been a linguistic one in order to better the educational strategy and drag into the antifascist field the younger generation that the language of fascism had seduced and conquered. GL needed to imitate somehow that same rhetoric made of a mythological, irrational, symbolic repertory more apt to shake and captivate the masses. The appeal to Mazzini, to the rhetoric of Risorgimento, became, then, an urgent, strategic need to combine with a Manzonian 'religious' horizon:

> Rosselli privilegiava ormai il conflitto ideologico tra fascismo e antifascismo quale chiave interpretativa dell'Europa post-bellica; ma, al tempo stesso, rinverdiva i suoi legami con l'eredità dell'interventismo e con la più lunga tradizione del nazionalismo democratico. Innestando su un tronco essenzialmente mazziniano la prospettiva delineata da Lenin durante la Grande guerra, sosteneva che questa rivoluzione sarebbe stata il prodotto di una

---

just as a political one, in view of its cultural more than political value. This antifascism was made of disdain, of the pride to be on the right side [...] this antifascism was nurtured by that historical, humanistic and humanitarian culture that helped distinguishing with absolute certainty civilization from brutality, the seeds of progress from those of decadence, the lasting conquest from adventure, thought from rhetorics».

204 Bresciani, *Quale antifascismo?*, 187. «Rosselli and his companions tried to understand the enemy, to learn from him, in order to better fight him who was constantly reinterpreted according to the positionings of soviet foreign policy».

trasformazione della prossima guerra tra Stati in una guerra civile. La sua accezione di «guerra civile europea», che opponeva «un partito europeo, socialista» contro «partiti nazionali, fascisti, nazionalisti», legittimava il conflitto totale tra due concezioni dell'individuo, della società e della civiltà, che attraversava i confini nazionali e sovvertiva le sovranità statali.[205]

Fascism and antifascism in GL, first, and Pd'A, later, were historical perspectives—influenced by 1919s *combattentismo* and by Gobetti's Liberal Revolution—that tended to emplot the historical season ended by the Resistance as Tragedy, as the dramatic collision between two opposite ideals of civilizations. Tragic also was the emplotment of the political fight against fascism as the moral task of the single, elected hero repository of the long-gone values of a past golden age of European society, now supplanted by the modern culture of the masses that made totalitarian regimes possible. The «fermezza tragica»[206] of antifascists amongst a world in ruins translates as strong mythopoeic temptation in historical accounts full of monumental portrayals of the partisan hero as both moral educator, virtuous example and fighter. Education was key, then, also within the antifascism of the Pd'A. However, it was different from the education as an organization that we have seen characterizing Marxist historiography. While in both cases, it is exactly through this pedagogical necessity that a more comprehensive interpretation of fascism, the clandestine antifascism of the 1920s and the new antifascism of the 1940s, could be framed together in a *long durée*, the education theorized first by GL and then by the Action Party does not completely negate the spontaneity of new antifascism born during the war years, an antifascism also made of the fragments of a dismembered army. While the education organization of the PCI

---

205 Idem, 166. «Rosselli favored by now the ideological conflict between fascism and antifascism as the best interpretative framework for post-war Europe; nevertheless, at the same time, he revived its ties with the legacy of interventionism and with the longer tradition of democratic nationalism. He juxtaposed the Mazzinian roots to the prospective Lenin outlined during World War I, claiming that this revolution would have been the direct outcome of the next civil war between states. His definition of the probable next war as European civil war, which entailed the contrast between a European socialist party and national, nationalistic fascist parties, validated the total conflict between two opposite ideas of the individual, of society and of civilization, which exceeded national borders and overturned statal sovereignties».
206 Bobbio, *Leone Ginzburg – Scritti*, xxix. «tragic resoluteness»

was a straightening of the individual's spontaneous yet apolitical antifascism that had the final goal to unproblematically frame it within the 'plot' dictated by the party and by its strictly deterministic view of history, the education of the GL brigades left some room for spontaneity to survive, as proof of the latency in Italian people of those moral values and irrational drives to act heroically that initiated the Risorgimento. It was not a lesson to be imposed, but, rather, the maieutic activity triggering the spontaneous recognition of latent, inner resources that would ease the choice between the good alternative over the evil one. The tragic choice was, then, left to the individual who was now free to pick sides and to assign to the war their private meaning. The inclusion of spontaneity as a factor with positive undertones results in a less Manichean and more carnivalesque reciprocity between the characters at play; it disrupts the teleological, causal connection between the two periods either as degeneration or as maturation of one another, and it undermines the meaning of the Resistance as new foundation and redemption of the nation, or as progress of the subaltern classes, with the simultaneous definition as civil war.

In the historiographical reconstructions of the Resistance written by authors coming from the socialist-liberal tradition of GL, who, during the war of liberation, joined the *Partito d'Azione*, there is less fear in defining the war of liberation as a civil war:

> I 300 partigiani morti combattendo per le strade di Firenze nell'agosto 1944 concludevano, vincendo, la Resistenza che datava non dal settembre dell'anno precedente, ma dal 1925, quando, con il gruppo riunitosi intorno al *Non Mollare* di Salvemini, era stato formato il primo movimento antifascista clandestino. Ci fu guerra civile – il risultato inevitabile della guerra civile iniziata dai fascisti venti anni prima, salutata allora con entusiasmo da tutti i fiancheggiatori. [207]

The clash between fascism and Resistance emplotted as civil war in Salvadori's work means first of all the joining together of old and

---

[207] Massimo Salvadori, *Storia della resistenza italiana* (Venezia: Neri Pozza, 1955), 145. «The 300 partisans who died fighting in the streets of Florence in August 1944 concluded with their victory that Resistance which started not in September 1943 but 25 years before, when the first clandestine antifascist organization, Salvemini's *Non mollare*, was formed. A civil war ensued, as the inevitable outcome of the previous civil war provoked by fascists twenty years before and welcomed by the many supporters with enthusiasm».

new antifascism in the coherent history of the *long* Resistance, as the story of the evolution of antifascism—that one of the veterans—into the concrete political action of an armed revolution: «le linee principali del movimento partigiano che della Resistenza fu il braccio, così come l'antifascismo ne era la mente e la coscienza.»[208] The partisan 'movement' realizes the theory—born in the various 'schools' of exile, confinement and prison—of the older generation of antifascists who really experienced what fascism meant and, most of all, what it was able to do, but that never had the historical occasion to fight against it with the same means. The resistance coincides with what Franco Moretti defined as 'moment of truth:' the hero of Tragedy reads reality as a series of moments of crisis, of decisive hours regulating their collision with the law of the gods: «questa è la volta buona, o mai più di compiere tutte le rivoluzioni, tanto necessarie quanto mancate dal 1862, cioè dalla morte di Cavour a oggi.»[209] Resistance and fascism are not framed within the deterministic boundaries and classifications of the class struggle, as there were partisans and fascists among all classes and social milieus: «già alla fine dell'autunno 1943, quindi, vi erano, nel movimento partigiano, uomini e donne di tutte le classi, di tutte le tendenze e di tutte le regioni.»[210]

The cohesive element of the Resistance is its antifascism, which in its essence was a moral resurrection of the dormant spirit of the Risorgimento, its quality as a religious war against the corruption of fascist vice and fanaticism. What counted was the base more than the organization, and, in this sense, the stress on spontaneity is the typical trait that distinguishes this kind of story from the other one told by the PCI:

---

208 Idem, 18. «The main traits of the partisan movement which was the armed branch of the Resistance, insomuch as antifascism was its mind and consciousness».
209 Sandro Contini Bonaccossi and Licia Racchianti Collobi, ed. by, *Una lotta nel suo corso* (Venezia: Neri Pozza, 1954), 38. «This is the right time to complete all those revolutions that are lacking since 1862, i.e., since Cavour's death up until today».
210 Idem, 84. «Men and women from every social class, region and tendency were already part of the Resistance since autumn 1943.»

> Come prima dell'inizio della seconda guerra mondiale, come dopo la vittoria del 1945, divideva i democratici dagli stalinisti il concetto di libertà, centrale per i democratici che mettono come base della struttura sociale la spontaneità dei cittadini [...] meno che secondario, addirittura insignificante per gli stalinisti i quali facevano proprio come base della struttura sociale il concetto dell'autorità dall'alto, erano insofferenti di qualsiasi opposizione ed eresia, esigevano l'uniformità e non potevano non essere autoritari e perciò contrari all'uguaglianza ed in favore della gerarchia. [211]

The deep fractures mining the unity of the Resistance are always brought to the foreground, explaining, retrospectively, why the Resistance, in the end, lost against the old *fiancheggiatori* of fascism: those who backed up the regime's take and hold of power (*in primis* the monarchy), those that opportunistically, passively, supported the Resistance and the *attendisti*, those who preferred to wait for the victory of the Allied forces opportunistically without taking sides. The political conduct of compromise with the reactionary catholic forces undergone by the Communist Party—inaugurated by the return of Togliatti to Italy in April 1944 and by the decision, in agreement with Stalin's new guidelines in foreign policy, to take part in the Badoglio's new government in the southern territory freed by the Allies—is, according to Salvadori, one of the main causes of the betrayal of the revolutionary spirit of the Resistance, and its inner contradictions:

> Quando i comunisti e i loro compagni di viaggio, che avevano costituito uno dei due elementi di maggior peso nell'antifascismo e nella Resistenza, decisero di ritornare alla tattica di una volta e di agire come se i democratici che avevano costituito l'altro elemento, fossero i peggiori nemici, la strada era aperta al ritorno degli ex-fiancheggiatori e di quanti trovavano il passato più soddisfacente del presente torbido e dell'avvenire incerto. [...] La frattura fra gli avversari del passato era esistita nel 1922; vi era un nemico comune, il fascismo; i democratici avevano preso una strada e per la libertà erano morti Don Minzoni, Piccinini, Matteotti, Pilati, Amendola e Gobetti, come più tardi morirono De Bosis, Carlo e Nello Rosselli; i comunisti avevano preso una strada diversa. Così avvenne dopo il 1945, a vantaggio questa

---

[211] Massimo Salvadori, *Breve storia della resistenza italiana* (Firenze: Vallecchi, 1974), 45. «Both before the war and after the victory of 1945, what really divided democrats from Stalinists was the idea of liberty, central for democrats who base society on people's spontaneity [...], of secondary importance for Stalinists who based society on an authority imposed from above. They were intolerant to every opposition and heresy, asked for uniformity and could not be anything else but authoritarians, thus against equality and for hierarchy».

volta degli ex-fiancheggiatori. La Resistenza aveva salvato l'anima della nazione; ma era un'anima divisa.[212]

By means of the emplotment as Tragedy, the Resistance appears less as a *union sacrée* and more as a heterogenous unity in which each faction was aware of the different final objectives of the others. The communists saw the Resistance as a progress towards the gradual realization of progressive democracy, bound to happen within the parliamentary institutions of the state, while the *azionisti* framed the resistance as a violent means to immediately trigger the total revolution of the pre-war and pre-fascist state. Two revolutions, two different temporalities and finalizations of the same historical event. Croce's reading of fascism as parenthesis and its vision of modernity as a moral crisis is still active in Salvadori's reconstruction, as in Gobetti's autobiography of the nation.

In the introduction to the special issue of the journal *Mercurio* in 1945, Ferruccio Parri writes that the Resistance was a long story and a long tragedy, the war fought by and for an entire people, regardless of their class of origin. In stressing the bourgeois character of the insurrection, Parri reads the Resistance as a second Risorgimento, made possible by a new generation of young martyrs repeating the mythical, archetypical Italian revolution of the first Risorgimento: «se quest'ora nasconde, come vogliamo, l'alba di un nuovo risorgimento, aggiungano gli storici di domani ai mille di Marsala, combattenti del primo risorgimento, i centomila della

---

[212] Salvadori, *Storia della resistenza italiana,* 180-181 «When the communists and their travel companions, who had constituted the two most influential elements of antifascism and of the Resistance, decided to restore the old strategy of acting as if democrats, who had constituted the other element, were their worst enemies, the path was laid open for the return of the old supporters of fascism and of those who favored the past over a murky present and an uncertain future. [...] The fracture among the past adversaries existed since 1922, there was a shared enemy, i.e., fascism, democrats had made a choice and Don Minzoni, Piccinini, Matteotti, Pilati, Amendola and Gobetti had died for freedom, as later did De Bosis, Carlo and Nello Rosselli. Communists made a different choice. The same thing happened in 1945, this time to the advantage of the past supporters of fascism. The Resistance had saved the nation's soul; albeit a divided one».

guerra partigiana, pionieri del secondo.»²¹³ The image that symbolizes the Resistance is the dead body of a young partisan hanged in Turin with a hook in his chin. Parri invites the future poet of the newborn literature on the Resistance to be like a father to him. He is once again drawing upon the imagery of the generational gap, transforming that image into the most symbolic myth of the Resistance, making it the emblem of its spontaneity (the son) before any specific organization (the father) could assign him distinctive character:

> Venga il poeta, ma sia un padre, e sappia dire il compianto per questi ragazzi assassinati che avevan ancora bisogno della carezza della mamma, per questi giovani massacrati di botte che non fiatarono, per quel biondino gentile come una signorina impiccato a Torino con un gancio al mento, per quegli operai, studenti, ingegneri, generali, per quei nostri compagni che sono andati al martirio ed alla fucilazione con l'animo dei martiri cristiani. Dica il compianto per le mogli e per le madri che non hanno una tomba su cui piangere.²¹⁴

This paragraph is a masterpiece in the art of compromise. Parri included all the different souls of the Resistance, regardless of their social class: workers, students, engineers, and generals. They were all described as martyr-like figures of comrades. Here, Parri's figurative strategy reunites the opposites of religious faith (dear to the DC) with the language of communism. The description of the sacrifice of a neutral symbol of youth – almost genderless and androgynous, as *biondino* and *signorina* further suggest—ends with reference to the repertoire of ancient myth: the tragedy of Antigone, the

---

213 Parri, "Introduzione," 19. «If this hour announces, as we believe, the dawn of a new risorgimento, future historians should add to the thousand fighters of Marsala, heroes of the first risorgimento, the hundred thousand partisans of the war, pioneers of the second risorgimento».

214 Idem, 18. «Oh poet, tell how a father would, the grief we felt for these boys who got killed although they were still in need of their mum's caresses, for these massacred boys who remain silent, for that blonde kid, kind as a young lady would be, who died hanged in Turin, a hook under his chin, and for those workers, students, engineers, generals, for our companions who sacrificed themselves and went to martyrdom and execution by firing squad with the same spirit of Christian martyrs. Oh poet, sing for mothers and wives who do not even have a tombstone where to cry».

dramatic experience of the exclusion of the dead son from the space of the community.

Parri also includes *generali* in the collective memorial myth of the slaughtered youth, the disoriented soldiers who, after the chaos of September 8th, after the dismemberment of the army, reacted by spontaneously joining the armed resistance. They are usually the obvious embodiment of that spontaneity that represents the true riddle of the historiography of the resistance. This recognition of the apolitical and mostly patriotic war of many military brigades of the Resistance severs the emplotment of the war of liberation from its *bildungsroman*-like structure, that progress and maturation of the spontaneous new antifascism which got gradually framed within the political, ideological, moral boundaries either of the communist party's maximalist, Marxist organization or the *Partito d'Azione*'s pedagogical, maieutic task as elected élite of masters. Soldiers and youth born and raised under fascism are the two overlapping categories that disrupt the taming of spontaneity in organization. Even collections of documents and letters are framed as a progressive formation and growth guided by the figure of the *commissario politico* in both the GL and Garibaldi brigades.

In the introduction to the collection of writings of Dante Livio Bianco, *giellista*, Franco Venturi writes: «negli articoli, nelle lettere di Livio Bianco, sentiamo come le cose stesse e l'opera maieutica del commissario politico trasformino le coscienze, come da «patriota», passando attraverso il «ribelle», nasca il «partigiano.»[215] The texts are organized chronologically, yet at the beginning of the collection, the editors place the necessity of a choice, first of all geographical, but more deeply ideological. Echoing Proust's alternative between the *Guermantes* and *Swann* ways, the partisan—active in Cuneo's area in this case, but, symbolically every partisan—faces the tragic dilemma between Boves and Paralup, between the military brigade and the political one:

---

215 Dante Livio Bianco, *Guerra partigiana* (Torino: Einaudi, 1954), xix. «In Livio Bianco's articles and letters we clearly perceive how the maieutical works of the political commissary can transform consciousness: how the partisan was born out of the patriot, passing through the intermediate status of rebel».

> Erano due mentalità, due «sistemi», due «stili» diversi. [...] La tesi, diremo bovesana era che le formazioni dovessero essere apolitiche.
> I fatti l'hanno poi dimostrato, dando ragione a coloro che vedevan la guerra di liberazione non come guerra fra stati, fra «nazioni» e «potenze» e «governi» in conflitto, ma come una vera guerra civile, una guerra ideologica e politica quant'altre mai, una guerra destinata non solo a scacciar gli invasori tedeschi e ad eliminare i traditori fascisti, ma a gettare le basi per un ordine nuovo politico e sociale. Niente di comune, dunque, fra partigiani ed esercito regio, ancora in mano a generali fascisti e a una dinastia fascista: niente apolicità delle formazioni, ma anzi, necessità assoluta di una coscienza politica, d'una consapevolezza delle ragioni profonde della lotta e degli obiettivi veri da raggiungere; ragioni ed obiettivi che si compendiavano, per noi, in due parole: rivoluzione democratica. [216]

It is worth noting here the particular meaning of civil war, the clash between two qualitatively different nations: the Italy of the continuity-identity between fascism and monarchy—Gobetti's autobiography paradigm—and the myth of the other Italy, a morally superior class still living out of the Risorgimento betrayed tradition. The archetype of the partisan of the military 'type,' of the Boves' *way*, absolutely refractory to every kind of political enframement, was Ignazio Vian.

La guerra dei poveri, the war journal of Nuto Revelli, exactly tells the story of his passage from the spontaneity of a purely patriotic cause to the organization of a more aware moral choice and political consciousness. The notes from his participation in the tragic, disastrous Russian campaign among the *alpini* are the necessary premise to the second part of the work consisting of the diary of the Resistance, his joining first of the *Boves* military brigade led by Vian, then of the GL brigade in which Dante Livio Bianco was

---

216 Idem, 21-22. «They were two different styles and systems [...] Boves' theory consisted in considering formations essentialy a-political. [...] Facts later agreed with those who saw the liberation war not as a conflict among states, nations, governments, powers, but as civil war, as the most political and ideological war ever, a war not limited to the expulsion of German invaders and to the elimination of fascist traitors, but a war on which a new political and social order could be founded. Partisans and the royal army did not have anything in common, since the latter was still in the hands of a fascist dynasty of fascist generals: no apolitical formations, but, rather, the absolute necessity of a political consciousness, an awareness of the profound reasons behind the fight and of the true goals to be reached; reasons and objectives that we summed up in two words: democratic revolution».

the political commissar. Hence, he is the perfect embodiment of the *bildungsroman* of the patriot turned rebel and partisan, as described by Franco Venturi. The retreat of the Italian army from Russia works, in Revelli's account, as a trigger for a radical conversion and awakening on the true, corrupted and illusionary nature of the fascist regime, in the same way the Spanish Civil War did, for example, in Lajolo's *Il voltagabbana*. The life trajectories of two militaries, Revelli and Lajolo, are the most vivid examples, first, of the merging of spontaneity into organization, and, second, they are the exemplary embodiments of a younger generation that, having been betrayed by fascism, found in the new education of antifascism the way back into the other, virtuous Italy:

> Senza la Russia, all'8 settembre mi sarei forse nascosto come un cane malato. Se nella notte del 25 luglio mi fossi fatto picchiare, oggi forse sarei dall'altra parte.
> Mi spaventano quelli che dicono di avere sempre capito tutto, che continuano a capire tutto. Capire l'8 settembre non era facile![217]

In front of the enigmatic, carnivalesque relativity of September 8th, Revelli recognizes the infinite array of solutions, the not-so-absurd possibility of making a different choice if it was not for his witnessing the tragedy of the Russian campaign. Even though his spontaneous antifascism will eventually join the master plot of the old antifascism of the *ventennio*, this recognition of the contingency of his choice, and then of the plausibility of the opposite alternatives, make the maturation of a political consciousness not a necessary progress, but a spontaneous, individual practice of freedom: «ho chiesto a Livio di far parte della banda "Italia libera": ho scelto. Ero incerto, non volevo piegarmi: non volevo riconoscere che i "politici" sono migliori dei "militari." Livio ha accolto con un sorriso aperto la mia confessione.»[218] The encounter with the 'master'

---

217 Nuto Revelli, *La guerra dei poveri* (Torino: Einaudi, 1962), 131. «Without Russia, on September 8 I would have probably hidden myself like a sick dock. If, on the night of July 25, I got beat up, maybe today I would be on the other side. Those who claim they have always understood everything and still do, scare me. It was not easy to understand September 8».

218 Idem, 151. «I asked Livio to join *Italia libera*: I made a choice. I was uncertain, I did not want to bend: I did not want to admit that political formations were

Bianco results in a mutual education between the two generations and between the anti-Germanic patriotism of Revelli and the political and moral one of Bianco. The former shares his experience in Russia, while the latter tells him about Rosselli and the Spanish Civil War. Even in a documentarian historical account that recognizes the contingency of destinies, the depiction of the fascist is always caricature-like and grotesque. The captured spy gets somehow deformed by the vocabulary used into a hybrid again, half human, half-dwarf, half older man and boy:

> Il primo fascista che è comparso era un nanetto pallido, goffo nella divisa troppo abbondante. Il nanetto si è guardato attorno, ha avuto un brivido di freddo, si è pisciato addosso. Adesso l'ho qui di fronte a me. È la «mascotte» della Muti di Borgo San Dalmazzo, un bambino di tredici anni, un bambino già vecchio.[219]

Other examples of fascists as uncanny figures are a nun-spy that smokes a cigar and another spy, Filiberto, half-fascist and the «*tipo del gigolò*.»[220] Revelli also notices, not without surprise, how American soldiers do not seem to hate the Germans: «nel tedesco vedono il soldato, non la bestia.»[221] The parable of the *Italia Libera* brigade narrated by Revelli mirrors a Resistance whose path is crossed and contaminated by a myriad of hybrid in-between figures such as spies, fascists dressed as partisans, partisans dressed as fascists, infiltrators and traitors, collaborationists and civil population, which, scared of the *rappresaglie*, looks at partisans with fear and suspicion. The Resistance itself is continuously fractured by inner endemic contrasts that will persist and survive the end of the conflict: «Sempre e ancora le vecchie questioni: politici e militari, gielle e apolitici.»[222]

---

better than the military one. Livio welcomed my confession with a broad smile».
219 Idem, 176. «The first fascist to appear was a pale little dwarf, who looked clumsy in his oversized clothing. He is now in front of me, he is the *mascotte* of the Muti in Borgo San Dalmazzo, a 13 yo kid, a kid already old».
220 Idem, 334. «the gigolò type».
221 Idem, 335. «they see in the German not the beast but the soldier».
222 Idem, 329. «Still the same old discussions: politicized and military formations, GL members and a-political recruits.»

Even in the Boves *way* the partisan falls somehow within a *bildungsroman* framework. His education will not be the political task of an antifascist commissioner, but it will be carried out by the environment itself. The partisan's voluntary ascent to the mountains becomes a new arcadia, the «*vita santa*»[223] of a mythical return to the teachings of nature in opposition to the urban degeneration of the fascist type, the *gigolò* way of life.

The challenging task of framing together spontaneity and organization is key to the moral problem of violence. It has already been observed how the fascism-perverse violence equation was one of the most recurrent patterns in interpreting the fascist phenomenon as the repressive tool of capitalism or as a sadistic, immoral deviation from 19th century's good values: «al terrore barbaro e indiscriminato degli oppressori si contrapponeva l'inarrestabile forza della giustizia popolare.»[224]

2.7 Education Through Terrorism: Enigma and Self-Evidence in Framing Violence.

In his pivotal 1991 work, Claudio Pavone—whose initial research on the Resistance focused on those areas in which fractures and contradictions were more manifest, i.e., the southern context and the myth of Risorgimento[225]—uses the 'grey areas' of the civil war, of violence and the military brigades in order to provide a historical reconstruction of the Resistance that would disrupt all the previous teleological emplotments and 'myths,' providing a scattered account in which the ambiguity, contingency and variety of the individual choice after September 8th would be the founding element and not *the* original sin, the problem to frame: «un momento di verità.»[226] The absurdity of the chaos following the armistice makes the choice that the Self faces problematic and clear at once, echoing, in certain aspects, that existential reading of antifascism dear to GL:

---

223 Italo Pietra, "Oltrepò, vita santa," *Mercurio,* (May, 1945), 120. «Saintly life»
224 Pesce, *Senza tregua. La guerra dei GAP,* 73.
225 As in the essay, reviewed by Battaglia, "Le idee della Resistenza: antifascismo e fascismo di fronte alla tradizione del Risorgimento," in *Passato e Presente,* no. 11-12, (1959): 1433-1444; and in his essay "I gruppi combattenti Italia," in *Fascismo e antifascismo* (Milano: Feltrinelli, 1962), 558-565.
226 Pavone *Una guerra civile* p. 37. « a moment of truth»

> All'interno del quadro fin qui tratteggiato si può cogliere una varietà di motivazioni individuali molto ampia: insopportabilità divenuto teatro di ferocia; ribellione contro i soprusi remoti e vicini, talvolta proprio come quelli «piccoli»; istinto di autodifesa; desiderio di vendicare un congiunto caduto; spirito di avventura; amore del rischio e insieme non piena cognizione di esso; tradizioni familiari; antifascismo di vecchia o di nuova data; amor di patria; odio di classe. Queste motivazioni, di diverso spessore culturale, si intrecciano spesso l'una con l'altra, e il loro dispiegarsi in conseguenti comportamenti lo si può cogliere solo tenendo presente l'intero arco dell'esperienza resistenziale. [227]

Antifascisms, old or new, are only one among many different motivations of the Resistance. Those who somehow escaped or refused the official 'organization' of typical antifascist framings of the war were to be equally considered part of the Resistance, which is now conceived as the totality of three wars: class, civil, and patriotic. The spontaneity of choice before an organized one is also the thematic key that Pavone uses to disrupt the usual Manichean split between good and useful violence (partisan) and bad violence intended as a desire to kill for the sake of it or as a natural inhuman tendency (fascist-Nazi). The problem of legitimizing and institutionalizing violence was extremely felt within the Resistance in order to avoid the slippage into the illegal violence of the outlaw. The autonomous brigades, such as that one of Boves, were since the beginning more in favor of adopting a military discipline, while in the political groups of GL and Garibaldi, the line of demarcation between bandits and partisans was thinner and more blurred:

> L'organizzazione della violenza quale strumento contro la sua degenerazione doveva fare i conti con la tradizione rivoluzionaria che non sempre tracciava un confine netto fra ribelli e banditi. [...] Nella dirigenza comunista e azionista è sempre tenuto ben presente il rischio che la fragilità

---

227 Ibid. p. 31. « Within the picture traced so far, a wider variety of individual motivations may be identified: the intolerableness of a world that had become a theatre of ferocity; rebellion against abuses of power coming from near and far, at times against the very smallest of abuses; a self-defensive instinct; the desire to avenge a dead relative; the spirit of adventure; love of risk together with a not fully conscious awareness of it; family traditions; long-standing or more recent antifascism; love of one's country; class hatred. These motivations, of differing cultural weight, often interweave, and we can only grasp how they unfolded in people's consequent behavior if we bear in mind.» [Ibid. p. 39]

dell'educazione politica faccia degradare i partigiani trasformandoli in «avventurieri...»[228]

The educative, pedagogical dimension of violence is the discriminant element also in the distinction between individualistic, spontaneous, revolutionary terrorism and organized 'mass' terrorism. The urban terrorism of the GAP had, according to one of its protagonists, Leo Valiani, the merit 'to galvanize the atmosphere of the city' by making manifest the presence of an underground army backing the masses in their revolt, especially during the strikes of 1944. The *gappista* Giovanni Pesce defines his autobiographical memoir *Senza tregua – la guerra dei GAP* as a 'teaching,' «un insegnamento»[229] both for future generations but also for the present state of a city that needed to be awakened from its endemic passivity. It was, once again, a distorted, problematic form of educating the more ambivalent and bourgeois world of the city about the needs of the partisan war, trying to combine urban and rural realities to dislocate the conflict where the indifference of *attendismo* was widespread. The exemplarity of the terrorist violence, as Pavone and Portelli, among others, have already shown, could have the opposite effect of reprobation and fear of a Nazi or fascist retaliation:

> La direzione che avrebbe preso la reazione popolare non era in realtà prevedibile con sicurezza; anzi, il timore che essa si volgesse contro i partigiani era presente e operante per la consapevolezza che le azioni più ardite potevano, come poi è stato scritto, suscitare «à la fois enthousiasme et réprobation.» [...] I costi umani andavano messi tutti sul conto del nemico. Era questo il punto che, in linea di principio, premeva soprattutto di ribadire, anche in seno allo stesso campo resistenziale, che non sempre lo accettava: i responsabili delle rappresaglie erano i nazifascisti che le attuavano, non i partigiani che compivano le azioni che le provocavano.[230]

---

228 Idem, 453-454. «The organisation of violence as an instrument against its own degeneration had to reckon with the revolutionary tradition which did not always draw a clear dividing-line between rebels and bandits. [...] The Communist and Actionist leadership were always well aware of the risk that the fragility of political education would degrade the partisans, turning them into 'adventurers'.» [Ibid., p. 541-542].
229 Pesce, *Senza tregua*, 9. «a teaching».
230 Pavone, *Una guerra civile*, 482-483. «One could by no means be certain what direction popular reaction would take; on the contrary, there was a real fear that

The violence of the *repubblichini* and the SS was often considered in historical accounts of the Resistance as objectively different, inhuman and brutal from the partisans' use of violence. In this sense, the way in which Battaglia enframes in his history the massacres perpetrated by the Nazis during their retreat in Italy is an exemplar of the negative theology adopted in the figurative strategy. Since no words are enough to describe what happened, Battaglia interrupts the telling of the Resistance epic to enunciate the list of the massacres in all their objectivity as a chronicle and not as mere history: «riteniamo impossibile cercare di descrivere con parole nostre le terribili imprese: possiamo soltanto raccogliere qualche testimonianza dei sopravvissuti alle stragi e su questa invitare a riflettere tutti coloro che non hanno conosciuto o hanno dimenticato troppo presto "che cosa fu il nazifascismo."»[231] The author suspends his task in front of the objective exemplarity and unambiguous evidence of the historical fact, while when the material is about the description of fascist or Nazi characters and their actions, the page generally overflows with a novelistic kind of narrative style in which the connotative mode of words prevails over the literal, denotative and objective one. The great quantity of eyewitnesses' accounts of the massacres, the evidence of their reports—of which Battaglia's examples are just one among many others—diverges somehow from what W.G. Sebald defined as the blindness of the German people in front of the spectacle of total devastation of their country perpetrated by the aerial bombings of the RAF. Sebald notices how the experience of humiliation without precedents in German history, directly lived by millions of people in the last years of

---

it would turn against the partisans, from awareness that the more hazardous actions might, as has been duly written, arouse 'both enthusiasm and reprobation'. [...] All the human costs — the tragic destiny of the 'unknown heroes' [47] — were to be put on the enemy's account. This was the point which, in principle, it was urgent to insist on, even within the bosom of the Resistance itself, which did not always accept it: those responsible for the reprisals were the Nazi-Fascists who carried them out, not the partisans who performed the actions that provoked them.» [Ibid., pp. 575-577].

231 Battaglia, *Storia della Resistenza italiana*, 504. «We believe it would be an impossible task to try and describe in our own words the terrible deeds: we can only gather the survivors' testimony and invite, all those who did not know or had forgotten too soon what *nazifascismo* was, to reflect upon it».

the war, could never find a way to be expressed in words. While Italy had many epic novels during the years of the Resistance, Germany is still waiting for its own grand war epic tale. Instead of a precise language, direct accounts of destruction tend in the opposite direction to the melodramatic mode of the 19th-century feuilleton:

> nei resoconti di chi non è riuscito a salvare nient'altro che la pelle è costantemente insito un carattere discontinuo, una peculiare qualità erratica, che è a tal punto inconciliabile con una normale istanza della memoria da assumere facilmente i tratti dell'invenzione e del romanzo d'appendice. Ma la patina di inautenticità che ricopre le testimonianze oculari dipende anche dalle espressioni stereotipe cui esse fanno ampio ricorso.[232]

In Italian epic novels and also in documentary data, memoirs, and historiographical reconstructions of the 1943–45 Civil War, violence and destruction seem to trigger the opposite figurative reaction. Fascism and Nazism, in different ways, escape objective language, being usually framed in the modes of melodrama, feuilleton and detective novels. The devastation they caused, on the contrary, is self-evident, straightforwardly expressed by the objective accounts of eyewitnesses. In striking contrast with the suspension and negative theology of the authorial voice in Battaglia, when the object is the reversed violence of the partisans against their enemies, the modes of the grotesque, of bodily abjection, prevail in the account:

> Si diceva che di là d'Arno, nel quartiere popolare di San Frediano, ci fosse un vecchio anarchico, il quale aveva conservato, ben tappata in una bottiglia di vetro, la sostanza che il suo intestino aveva emesso, dopo che dai fascisti gli era stata imposta una quasi mortale bevuta di olio di ricino. Egli conservava questo liquido semidenso, ripromettendosi di farlo ingerire proprio a quei fascisti che avevano partecipato alla impresa eroica e che egli da quel giorno non aveva perduto di vista.

---

[232] W.G Sebald, *Storia naturale della distruzione* (Milano: Adelphi, 2004), 35. «for the accounts of those who escaped with nothing but their lives do generally have something discontinuous about them, a curiously erratic quality so much at variance with authentic recollection that it easily suggests rumormongering and invention. However, the rather unreal effect of the eyewitness reports also derives from the clichés to which they often resorted.» [English translation by A. Bell in Sebald, *On the Natural History of Destruction*, Random House: New York, 2003) p. 32.]

> Ma nulla di simile avvenne. Circolarono voci; fra le quali quella che si riferiva a un certo Gambacciani, il ras di San Frediano, noto bastonatore, dalla corporatura enorme, accusato fra l'altro di avere ucciso a pugni un giovane antifascista in una notte dell'estate 1938 e di averne buttato il cadavere in Arno. Si diceva appunto che il Gambacciani fosse stato gettato ancora vivo in un forno, con una mela in bocca, come un tempo si arrostivano i maiali. Era un parto della fantasia popolare.[233]

While in Battaglia's report of eyewitness accounts, there is not a frame, here Francovich frames the legendary, rather creative acts of vengeance in a reported, indirect speech preceded by *si diceva,* or *circolarono voci* and ended by *era un parto della fantasia* in which the grotesque bodily imagery of the anecdote's content—fecal matter expelled and a product of the intestine—influences the bodily metaphor of the childbirth delivery. As violence against fascists escapes a realist account, an imaginative, fantastic, surreal, reported, and framed town's legend takes its place in the chronicle.

Hence, according to Sebald, stereotypes and melodramatic modes are clues of a lack, of a blindness in front of an overwhelming spectacle, and of an unwillingness, or incapacity, to uncover its true image. Sebald's indication allows us to recognize in the stereotypical and demonic shape of the fascist, the rhetorical trope of enigma or medieval *integumentum,* both being figures of speech that stimulate the drive to know by exactly thwarting it, by delaying the solution of the riddle, by turning the gnoseological process into a difficult operation. One of the recurrent interpretations of fascism was, as we have seen, that one of its ephemeral nature. Fascism, behind its façade of bombastic rhetoric, hid nothing else but a complete lack of ideology, i.e., the simultaneous combination of every

---

[233] Francovich, *La Resistenza a Firenze,* 18. «People said that across the Arno, in the neighborhood of San Frediano, there lived an anarchist who had kept stored in a well closed jar, the substance his intestines expelled after fascists had imposed upon him an almost deadly drink of castor oil. He saved this semi-dense liquid for those fascists who had participated in the old heroic expedition and that he never lost sight of. However, none of it ever happened. There was certain news circulating, one referred to some Gambacciani, the *ras* of San Frediano, a renowned thug with a huge body, who was believed to have killed an antifascist youth with his fists and to have later thrown his corpse in the river Arno. People said that Gambacciani had been thrown still alive in an oven, with an apple in his mouth, like people used to bake pigs. It was nothing but a product of people's imagination.»

ideology and, thus, the reciprocal negation of all of them. Togliatti defined it as 'malinteso,' Carlo Bo as «il regime dell'equivoco,»[234] while Vittorio Foa identifies as the main characteristic of the dictatorship «il divorzio tra la parola e il fatto.»[235] Such a thing as a fascist ideology did not exist; it was an absence, a mystery, and July 25th, 1943, revealed all its vacuity. The way the regime fell was *as if* it never existed:

> Al momento di dover fissare quella che è stata l'ideologia del fascismo, ci si accorge che non è mai esistita. [...] Non si tratta di un'idea ma di un insieme di idee parziali, rovesciate, che erano animate e coordinate esclusivamente da una ragione rettorica.
> La grande difficoltà dei suoi oppositori sta proprio nella mancanza di aggancio vero, sensibile: si poteva discutere con delle ombre, con dei programmi soltanto pratici e con funzioni meccaniche [...].
> La dottrina del fascismo non era che la veste, la maschera offerta nelle diverse occasioni per nascondere la reale situazione delle cose.[236]

The antifascist task is similar to a detective-like enquiry, a decipherment of shadows, a peering through the enigmatic smoke screen of empty words. Gadda will structure his *Eros e Priapo* as the at-once clinical and criminal research of «la causale del delitto.»[237] In this sense, the Marxist equation of fascism as an expression, however degenerative, of the middle class and as a bourgeois regime might explain the recurrent figurative strategy that frames fascism and the fascist as enigmas, as lacuna and as mystery tales. Paul Connerton notices how Marxism identifies capitalist society and its modes of production as based on oblivion and mystification. If certain aspects of social relations under capitalism appeared transparent,

---

234 Carlo Bo, "L'ideologia del regime," in *Fascismo e antifascismo*, 313. «The regime of misunderstanding».
235 Vittorio Foa, "Le strutture economiche e la politica economica del regime fascista," in *Fascismo e antifascismo*, 281. «The divorce of facts from words».
236 Bo, "L'ideologia del regime," 305. «When one is set to define what fascist ideology had been, we realize that it never actually existed. [...] It was not an idea but a series of partial and upside-down ideas which were coordinated only by a rhetorical reason. The great trouble experienced by its opposers laid exactly in this lack of a true, physical counterpart: one could discuss with shadows, about practical programs and merely mechanical functions».
237 Carlo Emilio Gadda, *Eros e Priapo* (Milano: Adelphi, 2016), 35. «The crime's motive».

some others are, on the contrary, opaque phenomena, such as the reification of the production process. According to Lukács, in fact:

> Il processo di produzione capitalista è *costituito dalla perdita della memoria* del processo stesso attraverso il quale essa si sviluppa. In quanto mistificazione strutturalmente organizzata, questo processo produttivo blocca l'accesso al ricordo dei processi passati che l'hanno costruito e che l'hanno mantenuto in vita. A partire dall'analisi di Marx, Lukács tentava dunque di strappare questo velo opaco e di individuare l'impronta lasciata sull'intera coscienza da ciò che viene generalmente chiamato «forma di merce», sostenendo fondamentalmente che i dettagli del processo strutturato della produzione delle merci vengono *dimenticati*. In altri termini, l'origine della forma di merce, l'operazione umana che crea i manufatti industriali all'interno di questa particolare formazione sociale, è vittima di un'amnesia culturale.[238]

Connerton continues and notes how Marx and others after him, when confronted by the analysis of social and cultural phenomena, often use a figurative language that draws upon the metaphorical repertoire deriving from the imagery of visual perception: «parlano di opacità, occlusione, oscurità, mancanza di trasparenza, difficoltà di decifrazione. [...] Così scrivono che le merci ci appaiono enigmatiche perché la gente dimentica come sono state prodotte.»[239] Then, it is not by chance that the classic detective novel reached its climatic moment of diffusion and success exactly in between 1890 and 1935: «in quanto genere può essere letto come sintomatico di quella condizione di crescente opacità che caratterizza le

---

[238] Paul Connerton, *Come le società dimenticano* (Torino: Einaudi, 2010), 53. «the capitalist process of production was constituted by the loss of its memory of the very process through which it is produced.4 As an organised structure of misrecognition, it blocked access to recollection of the past processes which erected it and maintained it in being. In trying to penetrate this veil of opacity, Lukács, building on the work of Marx, sought to decipher the 'imprint on the whole of consciousness of what is usually called the "commodity form"', his basic argument being that the precise details of the structured process of producing commodities gets forgotten. In other words, the genesis of the commodity form, the human agency that creates manufactured artefacts in this particular social formation, falls prey to a cultural amnesia.» [Connerton, *How Modernity Forgets*, Cambridge University Press: Cambridge, 2009, p. 43.]

[239] Idem, 63-64. « They speak of opacity, occlusion, obscurity, lack of transparency, difficulties in deciphering.[...] So they write that he commodity seems enigmatic because people forget how it was produced». [Ibid., 52]

formazioni sociali capitaliste.»[240] The interpretation of Fascism as an equivocal phenomenon, as misunderstanding, as absurdity, as empty signifier and lack of ideology might be read as a symptom of this aspect of Marxist readings of capitalist society, as much as the constant relapse to figurative and emplotment strategies drawing from the genre of the detective story in Italian postwar literature on fascism and antifascism. Moreover, in Fenoglio, Calvino, Pratolini or in films by Rossellini, Vancini, De Sanctis, and Bertolucci, fascist characters are often described as passionate *giallo* readers or moviegoers.

2.8 The Nexus Between Spontaneity and Organization as a Problem of Education: the Two Bildungsroman of Italian Antifascism.

The *topos* of fascism as an ephemeral and empty phenomenon is reinterpreted by Giacomo Noventa, who reads it as only the first phase of the antifascist interpretation of the regime. The poet, in fact, distinguishes between three different moments, or kinds, of antifascism. The first one, which, according to Noventa, the communists imposed on the non-communist factions of antifascism, was the belief that fascism was a non-thought, a colossus with a head of clay:

> Essi si erano tanto abituati a credere il fascismo un colosso dalla testa di argilla, da credere che una volta si fosse riusciti a farlo cadere, la testa dovesse andare in frantumi. Si erano abituati a crederlo un non-pensiero da credere che un non-pensiero bastasse a distruggerlo. Che impensierirsi del fascismo significasse, anzi, dargli vita e valore.[241]

---

240 Idem, 54. «since it can be read, as a genre, as symptomatic of that condition of increasing opacity which characterises capitalist social formations.» [Ibid. 44].
241 Giacomo Noventa, *Tre parole sulla resistenza* (Milano: All'insegna del pesce d'oro, 1965), 34. «They were so used to consider Fascism like a clay giant that they were convinced its head will have gone to pieces once they had succeeded in making it fall. They had become so used to considering it a non-thought that they were sure a non-thought would have been also enough to destroy it. To be worried by Fascism meant to assign it life and value.»

It is a moment characterized by the idea that since fascism lacks an ideology, then, no ideas are needed to destroy it, but only actions: it is the period of *biennio rosso,* the civil war 1919–1920. The second kind of antifascism started to mature the intuition of an opposite truth, that is to say, that fascism was not a colossus with a head of clay and an empty negativity of Italian culture and thought. However, no particular antifascist ideology could, alone, solve the riddle and problem of fascism: these are the years of the creation of GL and of other attempts to combine different ideologies into one, such as liberal socialism and Christian democracy. The third kind of antifascism was the Resistance:

> Nel segreto delle coscienze progrediva dunque il sospetto che il fascismo fosse propriamente la cultura ed il pensiero italiano. Che il fascismo fosse l'Italia. Che, per criticare il fascismo, fosse necessario criticare il pensiero italiano. Che, per lottare contro il fascismo, fosse necessario lottare contro l'Italia: contro se stessi. Nasceva così, diverso dal secondo e addirittura contrario al primo, il terzo antifascismo: la Resistenza.[242]

Noventa traces back the essential knot of Italian antifascism, the intimate reason for its failure and the consequent resurrection of fascism after 1945, to the absurd attempt to accord, to conform the antifascism of the Resistance with the first and second antifascism. While the communists interpreted the *long durée* of antifascism and the outcome of the Resistance as a gradual evolution within the frame of a 'progressive democracy,' those whom Noventa calls the improbable communists or leftist independents, the *giellisti* and *azionisti,* interpreted antifascism and the goal of the Resistance as revolution, in this sense being also *anti-communists,* against their policy of compromise with the Christian democrats:

> Ma combattendo il fascismo, come se il fascismo fosse tutta l'Italia o la punta estrema del pensiero della cultura e della storia d'Italia, secondo l'oscura affermazione rivoluzionaria della Resistenza, era particolarmente e

---

[242] Idem, 36-37. «In the secret of their consciousness they began to suspect that fascism actually represented Italian culture and thought. That fascism was Italy. That in order to criticize fascism it was necessary to criticize Italy itself. That in order to fight fascism, it was necessary to fight against Italy: against themselves. A third antifascism, the Resistance, was born in this way, different from the antifascism of the second kind and opposite to the antifascism of the first kind.»

> diabolicamente assurdo ridefinirlo e combatterlo, secondo le affermazioni del primo e del secondo antifascismo, come un colosso dalla testa di argilla, come un movimento assolutamente, o relativamente vuoto di cultura, di pensiero e di storia. Ciò significava aggravare l'errore dei primi e dei secondi antifascisti: sentirsi estranei alla cultura, al pensiero ed alla storia d'Italia, come essi si erano sentiti estranei al fascismo: non sentirsi corresponsabili degli errori e dei delitti dell'Italia come essi non si erano sentiti corresponsabili degli errori e dei delitti del fascismo italiano: lottare in Italia, come in una terra di nessuno: lottare contro l'Italia, non come contro se stessi, e per rinnovarne e continuarne le tradizioni, ma per sovvertirle e per distruggerle, e per inventarsi una Italia astrattamente nuova, o radicata se mai nelle tradizioni recenti di altre rivoluzioni e di altri paesi.[243]

The ideology of antifascism coincides, then, with a contradiction between an obscure revolutionary tendency—the recognition that identified fascism as the apex of Italian cultural tradition itself—and the old antifascist tenet of fascism as vacuous non-thought, of fascism as the *other* Italy and of antifascism as something different and external, escaping responsibility and guilt. Thus, the Resistance was founded on the absurd attempt to accord these two contradictory tendencies: revolution and evolution, fracture and continuity. The problematic emplotment of spontaneity within an organization is the conundrum of the *bildungsroman* that frames the history of fascism and antifascism in Italy. The ideological, absurd contradiction that Noventa highlights—and that we have seen is the central dilemma throughout the development of historiographical and autobiographical reconstructions of the resistance—mirrors, on a morphological level, the puzzling accord between two concurrent, contrasting, altogether different variations of the bildungsroman's form, stemming from two opposite ideological traditions. On the

---

[243] Idem, 39-41. «However, by fighting fascism as if fascism represented Italy or the evident extremity of Italian culture and History, as it was the case in the obscure revolutionary affirmation of the Resistance, it became particularly and diabolically absurd to fight and redefine it, going back to what the first and second antifascism did, as a clay headed colossus, as a movement relatively empty, devoid of any culture, thought and history whatsoever. This meant to aggravate the error of the first and second antifascists: feeling like foreigners to Italian culture, history and thought in the same way they had felt like foreigners to fascism, thus, not feeling responsible and guilty of Italy's crimes and mistakes. This meant also to fight against Italy, not in order to renew and continue its traditions, but to subvert and destroy them, in order to reinvent a completely new and abstract Italy, rooted in the recent revolutionary traditions of other countries».

one hand, the classic 19th century European *bildungsroman* and, on the other hand, the social realist *bildungsroman* of the 1920s soviet literature. The former frames the life of the hero in a development that ends in a compromise between spontaneity – the inner ideals of the individual – and organization – the expectations of the collective laws ruling society. The latter, emplotting the hero's destiny in the gradual maturation of political consciousness, thanks to the direct education that the guiding light of the communist party provides. The two bildungsromane end up promoting two slightly different systems of values, two unalike ways of envisioning the bond between the self and society and between thought, free will and action. While the classic, 19th-century realist bildungsroman is a genre in which neither of the two alternatives – ideals and laws – win over the other, resulting in a «universe of ambiguous values where nothing is ever stable or unequivocal,»[244] the Soviet social realist novel of education necessarily frames the individual in a preset constellation of values that the individual needs to recognize as the only valid truth and naturally conform to them. The first kind of plot overlaps with Greek tragedy as the accord between the human *daimon* and the divine *ethos*; the second kind of plot mirrors the Marxist deterministic idea of history as comedy. Revolution and evolution, spontaneity and organization are the opposites that the emplotment in the coherent whole of historical reconstruction needs to encompass, simultaneously coming to terms with the aporia of fascism, an enigma oscillating as well between the opposite poles of fracture and continuity, parenthesis and autobiography or class struggle. In this sense, the bildungsroman paradigm merges with the motifs of other genres stemming from the great European bourgeois literary tradition: the detective novel and melodrama. The emplotment as a *giallo* frames fascism either as a moral disease or as an enigmatic crisis without precedents in national history. In both cases, reality is an opaque screen that can be deciphered only through the 'semiotic' reading of symptoms and clues. As in Carlo Ginzburg's famous enquiry into this method crosscutting multiple disciplines: «solo osservando attentamente e registrando con estrema minuzia tutti i sintomi – affermavano gli

---

[244] Jean-Pierre Vernant and Pierre Vidal-Naquet, *Myth and Tragedy in Ancient Greece* (New York: Zone Books, 1990), 26.

ippocratici—è possibile elaborare "storie" precise delle singole malattie: la malattia è di per sé, inattingibile.»[245] The melodramatic mode coincides with a Manichean uncomplicated classification of moral values, a clear-cut distinction between good and evil, in a space that, nevertheless, seems to hide more than what it reveals, delaying the revelation of the ultimate truth until the very end of the story.

The emplotment of fascism and antifascism in Italian historiography is precisely the story of the mutual and reciprocal intertwining of all these various genres, each one being the symptom-clue of a particular ideological and political stance on the historical data. Recognizing this ambiguity of forms and tracing it back to works of the immediate and relatively immediate postwar years helps in understanding the more recent results of historiography, of which Pavone's is only the most accessible example, as the outcome of a process of 'natural selection' and evolution between genres of emplotments that is already active during those years still dominated by myths and legends, more or less 'official.' Then, it is also possible to identify those recurrent formal patterns that are shared both by the postwar historiography of the late 1940s and of the 1950s—surely still grounded on the figurative frame of a grand epic, teleological myth—and by the later generation of historians, such as Quazza and Pavone, that—on the wave of the 1960s and 1970s students' criticism of those reassuring, self-absolving myths—started to encompass fascism and antifascism in a more reciprocal and dynamic historical reconstruction, disruptive of the old myths and emplotments. There are genres of plots that already prefigure in themselves—in their themes, motifs, and characters—disruption, uncertainty and ambiguity of values. Some paradigms, such as Croce's parenthetic definition of fascism, were still active in the historical reconstructions of his most intransigent adversaries, exactly because his philosophy of history, in its favoring those more prosaic ages in between radical crisis and upheavals, already

---

245 Carlo Ginzburg, *Miti emblemi spie — morfologia e storia* (Torino: Einaudi, 1986), 169, 191. «The Hippocratic school maintained that only by attentively observing and recording all symptoms in great detail could one develop precise "histories" of individual diseases; disease, in itself, was out of reach.» [English translation by J. and A.C: Tedeschi, in Ginzburg, *Clues, Myths and the Historical Method*, Baltimore and London: The Johns Hopkins University Press, 1989, p. 105.

enframed the past in a *bildungsroman* structure, being this genre, according to Franco Moretti's reading, a celebration of a prosaic, bourgeois, middle way of life. Croce interpreted fascism as a parenthesis because, for him, all revolutions were parenthetic, temporary radical disruptions. Also, Croce's *Storia d'Italia* and *Storia d'Europa* were the most fundamental readings for the younger generation of GL, the generation of Leone Ginzburg, Norberto Bobbio, Vittorio Foa and Carlo Levi.

The persistence of the bildungsroman emplotment — in all its multiple variations and contaminations — is also confirmed and signaled by the recurrence of a pedagogical and oratorical orientation in postwar texts trying to address the generational gap that we have seen transversally crosscutting a number of historiographical and autobiographical accounts of the fascism-antifascism pair. The absurd emplotment of spontaneity and organization is also a generational question that in the postwar debates involves both the *Littorio* youth that vowed to the regime on the occasion of the 1933 decennial, and also the new spontaneous antifascism of the 1940s, that one of the disbanded army and of a generation that did not live the clandestine years of prison, exile and confinement.

Benedetto Croce in 1944 published an article titled "*La gioventù italiana.*" In sketching the portrayal of the younger generation that came of age under fascism, Croce describes the 'tragedy' experienced by this youth in terms of a good education interrupted by the evil education of fascism, i.e., the moral and intellectual work that educated and prepared pre-fascist Italy to win World War I being replaced by a work of seduction and corruption similar to the taming of an animal. Fascist education failed because it considered youth an actual force and not, as it should be, a potential one to let mature gradually through apprenticeship and experience. Thus, it excited and radicalized young souls, whereas the wise educator, as Croce writes, would have taken a different path:

> Laddove il buon educatore, tenendo ben diversa via, suol procurare di moderare la naturale esuberanza e baldanza della gioventù, di farla accorta delle

difficoltà, di amarla per esse, di inculcarle la modestia, d'innalzarla agli studi.[246]

The wise educator to whom Croce is alluding is liberalism, the balanced master of the generation that came out of the '*moto*' of the Risorgimento, noble exactly because it was capable of keeping itself out of the excess of every form of radicalism:

> S'era tenuta in guardia, tutta intenta a compiti particolari e determinati, poco sognando e poco ciarlando e molto lavorando, e così aveva portato il popolo italiano alla prosperità, alla civiltà e alla saldezza che gli permisero di dare alta prova di sé nella grande guerra.[247]

In the above passage, Croce's philosophy of history is translated into a pedagogical one, in which fascism's negativity lies in its excessive, disruptive nature, distracting an entire generation from the practice of everyday life and work, through a rhetoric that is «sconcia»[248] and «tumida,»[249] exciting the adolescent's soul in a way reminiscent of sexual desires and sudden passions. As Hayden White wrote, in a way that cannot but remind us of Moretti's definition of the classic bourgeois bildungsroman, Croce's histories:

> Are all transitions, low-keyed, gradualistic, low-mimetic, and do not have any inaugurations or resolutions to speak of. […] Croce's intention was to destroy the impression that any teleological process, such as those associated with the *mythoi* of Romance, Comedy and Tragedy, is at work. The effect was to render unimportant everything that "enthusiasm" thought important, and to elevate the drabber and more mundane aspects of everyday life to the status of genuine achievements, against whatever the irrationalists and intellectualists of the time might have thought of them.[250]

---

246 Benedetto Croce, "La gioventù italiana," in *La libertà*, no.1, (11 marzo 1944) now in *Scritti e discorsi politici* (Napoli: Bibliopolis, 2010), 45. «The good educator usually prefers to tone down and limit youth's natural exuberance and rashness, to make it aware of difficulties, to teach it modesty and promote studying».
247 Ibidem. «It stayed vigilant, focused on particular and precise tasks, working a lot and never dreaming or whining, in this way leading Italy's people to prosperity, civilization and firmness which were shown with great result during World War I».
248 Ibid. «indecent»
249 Ibid. «tumid»
250 White, *Metahistory*, 404.

Croce's article ends with a double, interesting and revelatory metaphor. First, the younger generation that comes out of fascism is compared to a son who, having left his homeland for a long time, returns only to find himself incapable of recognizing it. The task of the old ones is, then, to embrace him as fathers would do and to reteach him to recognize again and understand what he has missed during his absence:

> In coteste condizioni il caduto regime ci restituisce la gioventù italiana, che noi dobbiamo riabbracciare come figli che a noi ritornino, dopo lunga separazione, da lontano paese, e ai quali dobbiamo comunicare ciò che essi hanno ignorato delle cose di casa loro, e dei nostri affetti e dei nostri doveri, per metterli in grado di parteciparvi con noi e di lavorare con noi, riguadagnando il tempo perduto. La pianta italiana è un legno gentile, e presto rinverdirà e porterà i suoi fiori.[251]

This is a clear allusion to the parable of the prodigal 'extravagant' son who, after a time of deviance, intoxication and money waste, is welcomed back home as someone who was thought lost and is now regained. Croce, in this article, emplots Italian history as a perfect *bildungsroman* and hymn to the middle, bourgeois way of life, in which Italy's and its youth's paths of education are interrupted by the parable of the prodigal son: the Biblical story of redemption and forgiveness *par excellence*.

An example of the opposite kind of historical explanation through a different genre of *bildung* can be found in Palmiro Togliatti's speech given at the *Conferenza nazionale giovanile del Partito comunista italiano* in 1947, addressing the problem of which forms of organization were to be embraced by PCI's young members. According to Togliatti, the most fundamental point of the dramatic situation experienced by the youth coming out of the war only two years earlier was a certain feeling of nostalgia for fascism. He

---

[251] Croce, "La gioventù italiana," in *La libertà*, no.1, (11 marzo 1944) now in *Scritti e discorsi politici* (Napoli: Bibliopolis, 2010), 48. «The fallen regime gives us back the Italian youth in such conditions that we have to embrace them as sons returning to us after a long separation, from a far-away country. We have to communicate them those things from their home they had ignored, our feelings and our duties, in order to let them participate and work with us in reestablishing them, gaining back the lost time. Italy's plant is made of gentle wood and it will soon revive and blossom again.»

recognizes that fascism was able to understand and satisfy some of that youth's aspirations, only to reveal its ridiculous and deceptive nature later. The fact is that some of those aspirations were also shared by communism, and Togliatti expands his discourse, now especially addressing those young men and women who were, actively or passively, fascists, still believing in the possibility and in the necessity to recompose the old fracture between two generations. The party's organization needs to talk to them in order to frame them within the party's political line and objectives, finally making them aware that they were victims of a misunderstanding:

> La guerra di liberazione è quindi anche stata, lo sappiamo benissimo, la guerra tra italiani. Ma se nel corso della guerra vi era fra le due parti un abisso e scorse il sangue, questo non vuol dire che tra noi e una parte di coloro che combattevano contro di noi non esistesse quello che vorrei chiamare—se la parola non fosse inadeguata a un fatto politico e sociale così profondo—un «malinteso». Non ci eravamo intesi, con le generazioni che furono fasciste, sin dall'inizio, cioè sin dalla fine della precedente guerra, ma non è detto che non avremmo potuto intenderci, se non fossero intervenuti l'inganno e la violenza, che hanno falsato tutto il processo di sviluppo, rompendo l'unità delle forze nazionali. Il «malinteso» consisteva nel fatto che, quando una generazione di giovani aspirava alla grandezza della nazione italiana e alla felicità degli italiani che vivono di lavoro, aspirava alle stesse cose cui noi aspiriamo.[252]

The interpretation of fascism as *malinteso* and its alluded emplotment as a civil war is the prelude for a work of political education on the younger generation that saw its development suddenly interrupted and contaminated by the 'demagogy' of fascism. The scheme is not so different from Croce's one—with fascism

---

252 Palmiro Togliatti, *Opere, V 1944-1955* (Roma: Editori Riuniti, 1984), 300-301. «We are well aware that the war of liberation had also been a war between Italians. However, if during the war there had been an abyss dividing them and blood was spilled, this does not necessarily deny the fact that ourselves and a part of those who were fighting against us misunderstood each other. Us and the generations that had once been fascist did not understand each other since the very beginning, that is to say, since the previous war. We might even have understood each other had not violence and deceit interfered with and distorted the process of development, thus breaking the unity of all the national forces. The misunderstanding stemmed from the fact that both of us were aspiring to the same things: to the greatness of the Italian nation and to the happiness of those Italians who live out of their work».

representing a momentary lack of reason and fracture in the youth's education—except the fact that the father's role in the redemptive parable of the prodigal son is taken here by the organization offered by the party. Togliatti even directly refers to *Le rouge et le noir* when, while mentioning the works of literature that were capable of most vividly representing the inner anguish of youth, he adds: «e un romanzo famoso di Stendhal.»[253] Both Croce and Togliatti try to recompose the fracture with the generation that participated in fascism exactly by emplotting it as a *bildungsroman* – one through the realist kind, the other through the social realist kind—and the framing of the problem of that generation's innocent spontaneity within a pedagogical discourse on education allows for inclusion of the fascist other in the antifascist side, or at least for a compromise and blurring of differences; moreover, as in the case of Togliatti, it also allows for a redefinition of the war of liberation as civil war, i.e., outside of the usual classist scheme. An accord between fascism and antifascism can be found thanks to the older generation's enterprise of reeducation of youth, like a father who forgives a lost son, like a party's organization that breaks down a *malentendu*.

Ruggero Zangrandi, who converted to antifascism in the late 1930s after having been a militant of the fascist party, belonged to the generation both Togliatti and Croce were addressing. He identifies exactly in the pedagogical stance, in the will to reeducate, the fundamental mistake that antifascism made in attempting to recompose the fracture with the younger generations:

> La cosa che più mi colpì, in Italia, era il modo come i nuovi dirigenti, quasi tutti appartenenti alla vecchia classe prefascista, parlavano del fascismo ai giovani. E a quelli che tornavano dalla prigionia o dalla deportazione. Perché era lo stesso modo, di benevola condiscendenza, ma saccente e pedagogico, che avevano usato i soldati russi e americani con i prigionieri e i deportati italiani. Come, insomma, se il fascismo fosse stata colpa di costoro.
> Anche per i vecchi antifascisti, "ufficiali" sembrava che i giovani portassero la principale responsabilità del fascismo, almeno quella di averci creduto. E

---

253 Idem, 295. «a famous novel by Stendhal».

> perciò occorreva ammonirli, "rieducarli," con le buone maniere naturalmente. E spiegare loro che cosa era stato, realmente, il fascismo.[254]

The younger generation was not to be considered solely guilty of fascism because, Zangrandi explains, it was never really fascist; it only believed itself to be fascist, thus emplotting the long journey of that generation through fascism as an odyssey. The young fascist, in fact, as Ulysses, was seduced and deceived by the sirens' call of fascism, mistaking it for a «superamento del socialismo.»[255] This «abbaglio»[256] was a misreading of different nature compared to Togliatti's misunderstanding; it was, in fact, more of an «errore di precipitazione»[257] because it existed actually a sincere belief and faith in one aspect of fascism at least: its polemics against the forms of traditional democracy. It was the youthful mistake of a hasted judgment, not simply a *malinteso:* «ma il tratto saliente della nostra esperienza del fascismo rimane l'equivoco di averlo ritenuto una rivoluzione sociale. E di essersi trascinati, per anni, in questa illusione, favorita dalla eccezionale abilità con cui il regime fece credere ai giovani che fosse possibile svolgere un dibattito politico, impegnarsi in polemiche, assumere posizioni oltranziste e perfino eterodosse.»[258]

The illusion lasted until 1938–39, the moment of crisis and conversion. After Spain, the *Anschluss,* the straightening of the alliance

---

254 Ruggero Zangrandi, "I giovani e il fascismo" in *Fascismo e antifascismo,* 209. «The aspect that struck me the most, in Italy, was how new party leaders, for the vast majority belonging to the old prefascist class, were speaking about fascism to youths. And to those who were returning from prison or deportation. Because it was the same kind, but arrogant and pedagogical, condescendence which Russian soldiers had used with Italian prisoners and deported. As if Fascism had been their fault. Even according to the old, official antifascists it seemed that Fascism had mainly been their fault, even only for having believed in it. Then, it was necessary to warn them, reeducate them, naturally with kind methods. And, thus, teaching them what fascism had actually been».
255 Idem, 210. «Going beyond socialism»
256 Ibid. «Big mistake»
257 Idem, 211. «rushed conclusions»
258 Ibid. «The most important aspect of our experience of fascism is that we had mistook it for a social revolution. And that we had persisted in this illusion for many years, thanks to the regime's great ability in convincing the youths that political commitment and debate, extremist and heretical positionings, were still permitted».

with Germany, the racial laws, many passed to the other side, to antifascism, only to feel more alone than before, in a sort of no man's land, in between the blackmail of the *Patria* and the silence of the 'official' antifascism, without counting those 50 countries which officially recognized Mussolini's empire. An emblem of this loneliness due to the lack of a guide able to reveal what fascism really was is the story of Sigieri Minocchi, who, despite having understood the bitter truth behind fascism, preferred to still believe in it—*credo quia absurdum*—and fight, and eventually die, as a blackshirt in Libya.

Zangrandi's article is a *j'accuse* to the 'official' and old antifascism, guilty of having ignored and misinterpreted the tragic experiences, like the one above, of the "fascist generation":

> Probabilmente, i vecchi antifascisti non sapevano davvero cos'era accaduto, in Italia, durante quella che essi stessi definirono "la parentesi" del ventennio [...] sia che provenissero dall'esilio all'estero che dall'altro, vissuto in Patria. [...]
> Il guaio più serio, forse, fu che, quando costoro [...], vennero a contatto con la leva dei più giovani antifascisti indigeni—se così posso dire—si sentirono raccontare ciò che ad essi faceva piacere sentire: e cioè che gli italiani, i giovani soprattutto, erano stati purtroppo quasi tutti fascisti; e in gran parte lo erano ancora; sicché si poneva il problema di rieducarli, qualche volta di epurarli.
> Questo accadde—temo—per una sorta di nuovo conformismo, perché i giovani antifascisti che venivano a contatto con gli anziani attraverso l'esperienza del fascismo ritennero opportuno confortarne i giudizi o pregiudizi;[259]

The problem here is the encounter between the new and the old generations of antifascism and the filial conformism of the young one in confirming the predetermined schema—emplotments,

---

[259] Idem, 214. «Old antifascists probably never understood what happened in Italy during what they called the parenthesis of the *ventennio* [...] does not matter whether they experienced exile abroad or confinement here. [...] The most serious problem, perhaps, was that when they came into contact with the younger generations of 'indigenous' antifascists they were told what they liked to hear: that is to say that almost all Italians, especially young ones, had unfortunately been fascist, and that, since most of them still were, they had to be educated, and some of them ousted. I fear this was due to a kind of new conformism, because those new antifascists, who through the experience of fascism connected with the elders, thought right complying to their judgements and prejudices».

organizations—of the official antifascists. That is the main cause of the wrong education and explanation about what fascism really was and the consequent mis-emplotment of fascism as 'parenthesis' in Italian historiographies. Those who have actually been fascists could not recognize themselves in the portrayal of fascism framed in the antifascist official interpretation and *kind of story*:

> Certe prediche moralistiche risultarono davvero stonate. E lo stesso quadro della realtà fascista che veniva ora dipinto a chi l'aveva vissuta, tutto in nero, anche se ineccepibile dal punto di vista storico e scientifico, era un po' come sottoporre a un incompetente una radiografia, in luogo del ritratto di una persona nota, perché possa riconoscerla.
> E accadde infatti che molti non riconoscessero il fascismo in quelle descrizioni. Accadde, anche, che il disorientamento, anziché dissiparsi, si complicò.[260]

The education of antifascism resulted in a radiography of fascism, in a transparent demonstration that, despite the 'scientific' accuracy, actually made the recognition of fascism impossible; a portrait, instead, would have been more useful and effective. The conceptualization of the antifascist discourse as a precise yet useless radiography alludes to the original mistaken framing of fascism as an enigma, conceiving it as an opaque phenomenon. The necessity to conform to prefixed orders and organizations forced them to leave something behind for the sake of plot, coherence and teleology, forgetting and covering their own experience of the fascist past. The official emplotment of antifascism is, then, based on a fundamental miss-recognition, a failed tragic *anagnorisis* due to the excessive drive to see beyond reality, to interpret it as an opaque screen, the exact kind of hermeneutical frenzy that *enigmas* stimulate.

The solution to the problem lies in the substitution of that radiography with photography of fascism, the difference being that

---

[260] Ibid. «Some of those moralistic preaching sounded really out of tune. And the very same dark depiction of the experience of fascism which was now being presented to the eyes of those who had actually lived it, equated to let someone recognize a known person submitting to their attention a radiography rather than a portrait. Indeed many did not recognize fascism in those descriptions. Their disorientation did not dissolve, it got more complicated».

photography also enframes the surface, the face of things, making an immediate recognition possible:

> A questi giovani bisogna decidersi di dire tutto, di parlare chiaro, di spiegare anche le cose difficili o ingrate. Bisogna, con loro, spezzare gli schemi propagandistici convenzionali, di tutte le scuole. Insieme alla radiografia del fascismo—che spesso si riduce a una definizione—occorre consegnare loro tutte le fotografie possibili, di faccia e di profilo: anche quelle che, putacaso, lo facessero apparire più brutto di quel che fu.
> Altrimenti, essi non lo riconosceranno mai. E noi rischieremmo di aver educato le nuove generazioni a conoscere perfettamente, dal punto di vista scientifico, il male ma non saperlo individuare addosso a coloro che ne sono ancora affetti.[261]

Years later, Vittorio Foa, recalling in his autobiography the clandestine years of political engagement among the *giellisti*, defines antifascism's activity before the war years, in line, once again, with this 'paradigm of education' we have been tracing from Battaglia to Pavone, as a transversal interpretative key to access the master-plot of the fascism-antifascism fractures and continuities:

> Facevamo leggere e facevamo scrivere la gente, chiedevamo di estrarre dal proprio lavoro e dall'esperienza della loro vita il bisogno di libertà, il bisogno di giustizia, la fiducia nella possibilità di cambiare le cose. Visto da lontano negli anni quel nostro lavoro era un'opera di educazione: non dicevamo alla gente quello che doveva pensare, le chiedevamo di pensare essa stessa. Forse la politica come educazione è più pericolosa della politica come propaganda.[262]

---

261 Idem, 215. «We need to tell everything loud and clear to these youth, and teach them even the harshest and most ungrateful things. We need, together with them, to break once and for all with conventional propaganda schemes, with every school. Together with the radiography of fascism, which too often results in a definition, we need to deliver them every photograph, both face and profile ones: even those which make it appear worse than it was. Otherwise, we will never be able to recognize it. Our risk would be that we had educated new generations to perfectly recognize evil from a scientifical point of view, while leaving them unable to recognize it on those who are still affected by it»

262 Foa, *Il cavallo e la torre*, 41: «We made people read and write, we asked them to extract from their work and life experience the need for freedom, the need for justice, and faith in the possibility to change things. Seen many years later, the task we undertook had been a work of education: we were not saying people what they should think, we were just asking them to think. Perhaps, conceiving politics as education is more dangerous than conceiving it as propaganda».

Hence, antifascism was primarily a work of education because politics itself had, as its final goal, the maturation of the individual's consciousness, understanding of things, and ability to make conscious decisions and act in consequence. Carlo Levi, sketching Foa's alter ego's portrait in *L'orologio*, describes him as «un eroe di Stendhal.»[263] The *bildungsroman* was the genre that allowed the various contradictory factions of antifascism to emplot all the different phases of the encounter with fascism—clandestine years and resistance—in one frame, as the education, interpretation and dialogue between two generations. Filtered by Croce, the classic 19th-century *bildungsroman,* such as Stendhal's *Le Rouge et le noir,* frames the historical reconstructions of the 'socialist liberal' tradition of GL and Pd'A, while the post-revolutionary soviet realist novel of education is the preferred *genre* shaping the synthesis between spontaneity and organization in the more or less 'official' party historiography of the PCI.

---

[263] Carlo Levi, *L'orologio* (Milano: Mondadori, 1960), 236. «like an hero of Stendhal».

CHAPTER 3
Behind the Screen.
The Fascist Enframed:
Un eroe del nostro tempo and *Il prete bello*.

3.1 The Organization of Space in the *Bildungsroman* of Sandrino.

In reviewing *Le donne di Messina* by Elio Vittorini, and in particular writing about the character of the ex-fascist Ventura, Italo Calvino briefly comments on what he believes to be a common trend of postwar Italian literature:

> Forse per l'opinione che i «cattivi» nei romanzi «vengono meglio» dei «buoni», ecco che nella narrativa sul dopoguerra italiano i protagonisti preferiti pare siano personaggi di fascisti assassini. Pratolini in *Un eroe del nostro tempo* ci ha dato (pur in un debole romanzo) un preciso «carattere» di ragazzo neofascista.[264]

Under the appearance of a quick, not too precise, annotation, Calvino is hiding two straight-to-the-point analytic insights, not only regarding the Italian postwar novel but also about the theory of the novel in general. The somehow ironic tone of the first sentence suggests that Calvino does not share the common opinion that villain characters come off in a better aesthetic shape than the good heroes. Also, the *pare* of the second sentence indicates that fascist murderers were not his favorite characters either (nevertheless, *preferiti* might also have the second meaning of *most chosen* by Italian writers, that is to say, that fascist villains were invading the literature of the time). The third and last part of this short passage is an example supporting the above thesis, i.e., it is the particular that grounds the general statement. In this reference to Vasco Pratolini's least

---

264 Italo Calvino, "Le donne di Messina" in *Saggi*, Vol. I (Milano: Mondadori, 2007) p. 1265 «Perhaps because of the widespread belief that, in novels, *evil* characters are easier to write than *good* ones, postwar Italian literature seems to favor the character of the fascist assassin. Pratolini in *A Hero of our Times* gave us (even if in a weak novel) a precise type of neofascist adolescent.» [my translation]

appreciated novel, *Un eroe del nostro tempo,* Calvino gives the reader, again rather indirectly, a hint that the only good and consummated aspect of an otherwise "weak" novel is the characterization of the precise "type" of a young neofascist. Here, the keyword to keep in mind in order to completely grasp the sense of this apparently uncomplicated critical remark is the *pur* in brackets, which allows the reader to link the exactness of the representation of the type to the weakness of the novel (*debole* then needs to be taken as the opposite of precise, i.e., approximate, vague, obscure.) Hence, the precisely consummated form of the type corresponds to the unfinalized form of the novel, which enframes it.

In this chapter I will try to complicate the above insight from Calvino, unpacking the relationship between the form of the novel and that of its hero. If Calvino, on the one hand, is right in seeing a reciprocity between the imprecision of the former and the exactness of the latter, on the other, he fails to go further in relating the two forms in a dynamic process of mutual deformation. The fascist murderer, in my opinion, does not solely have the static, consummated aesthetic shape of the type, but it is also an open, mysterious and unfinalized figure. Then, the precision attributed by Calvino to its narrative form has to be read just as the initial attempt to enframe the character into the precise formal features of the type. Finally, the weakness of the novel is exactly the direct consequence of this failed creative process of finalization. So, the common opinion from which we started our discourse ends up being completely reversed: fascist villains did *not* come off as better finalized characters than the good heroes.

If in the first chapter, I highlighted the simultaneous nature of Marcello as both static type and dynamic hero, or more precisely, the shift-disruption from one form to the other in the recognition scene, in this chapter, I will show how the ambivalence type/hero, stasis/dynamism, plot/affect functions differently in two other novels also centered on fascist characters: *Un eroe del nostro tempo* and Goffredo Parise's *Il prete bello*. Moreover, if in my analysis of *Il conformista,* the focus was mainly on the disruption of the plot and of its teleology caused by the dynamism, formlessness and affect inherent in the fascist character, here I will investigate more closely another kind of formal disruption: that of space. In fact, both novels share, in addition to an extremely similar setting, an analogous disposition of the different characters in space.

Un eroe del nostro tempo tells the story of Sandrino, a sixteen-year-old neofascist who struggles to find his way in the immediate aftermath of the war. During the civil war, which followed the armistice of September 8th, 1943, he took the side of the Salò Republic, and his past as *repubblichino* did not ease a few years later—the novel was set in 1947—his inclusion into the newborn Italian Republic. Despite the attempts at redeeming him—made by a communist couple living next door and by a young lover whose father was killed in a concentration camp—Sandrino will never be completely reconciled with «the right side of history» and fully recognize his past guilt. His way to redemption will stop halfway, in the in-between 'grey zone' of ambivalence, on the threshold between good and evil.

> La narrativa italiana contemporanea è nata dunque sotto il segno d'una integrazione mancata: da una parte il protagonista-lirico-intellettuale-autobiografico; dall'altra, la realtà sociale popolare o borghese, metropolitana o agricolo-ancestrale. I tentativi di *Bildung-roman* politico, le storie dei noviziati cospiratori o partigiani d'un protagonista lirico-intellettuale a contatto col proletariato, che s'affollarono nei primi anni dopo la Liberazione, sembrarono la più naturale via per testimoniare sulla Resistenza, ma non riuscirono a rappresentare con accento di verità né il travaglio interiore dei protagonisti né quello epico e collettivo del popolo. [265]

Another 'negative' judgment from Calvino, and once again, Italian postwar literature is characterized as a failure, as a 'missed integration' between the lyrical 'I' and the epic 'we.' *Un eroe del nostro tempo* needs to be included among those attempts of political

---

265 Calvino, "Il midollo del leone" in *Una pietra sopra, Saggi,* Vol. I (Milano: Mondadori, 2007) p. 12. «Contemporary Italian literature was born under the sign of a missed unification: between, on one side, the lyrical-intellectual-autobiographical protagonist and, on the other, the bourgeois or proletarian, metropolitan or rural, social reality. The many attempts of political Bildungsroman, the various narratives of the lyrical-intellectual protagonist's conspiratorial or partisan apprenticeship that crowded the years immediately after the Liberation, seemed the most natural way to witness the Resistance. Nevertheless, these stories failed to represent with verisimilitude both the inner anguish of the protagonists and the epic and collective one of the people.» [Translation mine]

bildungsroman mentioned above by Calvino. The failure of the novel is, nevertheless, primarily formal: parallel to the attempted conversion and reconciliation of Sandrino with the 'winners'—the inner path of his spiritual and political redemption—there is the formal failure of the *bildungsroman* and of its teleological trajectory, which is sabotaged by the concurrent and non-realistic genres of melodrama and of the *roman à clef*. Sandrino will never reach the consummated and finalized shape of the hero of a *bildungsroman*, and the only true cause of this indefiniteness is another character, the veritable agent of melodrama and mystery in the novel: Virginia.

The first short chapter of the novel is a slow approach to her from the almost 'aerial' point of view of the omniscient narrator. She is the first to enter the scene even though she first appears as a mystery, as a person that nobody can directly see and know. People from the neighborhood refer to her without even naming her, instead using periphrasis and epithets such as «la signora del pollaio» and «la repubblichina.»[266] She is a widow, and she has to carry the burden of having married a fascist who was eventually shot dead during the Civil War. Since that moment, she has lived hidden in her bedroom, withdrawn from a society composed only of her enemies, the same ones that killed her husband. Virginia is the first enigma of the novel, both for us and for the characters themselves:

> Non sapevano altro di Virginia, se non che era vedova e che il marito glielo avevano fucilato i partigiani. Ella viveva sola, appartata: il suo ostentato cordoglio eccitava le immaginazioni. Era alta, bionda, col seno pieno e gli occhi chiari: bella per gli uomini, e superba per le donne.[267]

Nobody knows anything about her; she lives screened from the surrounding world, and here comes a paradox, an oxymoronic detail: despite her isolation and obscurity, her grief is on display, *ostentato*, she shows off her mourning, and this withdrawal excites the imagination of others, of those who cannot look at her from outside.

---

[266] Vasco Pratolini, *Un eroe del nostro tempo* (Milano: Rizzoli, 2013) p. 5 «All they knew about Virginia was that she was a widow, and that her husband had been shot by the partisans. She lived alone and apart. Her ostentatious grief stimulated people's imagination. She was tall and fair, with an ample bosom and light-colored eyes. Men thought her beautiful and women proud.» p.1

[267] Ibid.

Since the beginning and in these very first lines of the novel, Virginia, the widow of a fascist, is present in the text through her absence and lack of definition, though periphrasis and oxymoron: the opposite of that exactness which Calvino assigned to the portrayal of fascist murderers. As an *enigma*, Virginia is the first character to excite the imagination. That is to say, she is the one that functions as the trigger, the propulsive energy activating storytelling, the start of the *récit*. She is the site of what Roland Barthes defines as "the hermeneutic code," the code of the enigma, of that dilatory space between a question and its always delayed answer. If other characters do not have access to her and cannot see her, the narrator does, and the chapter continues with a description of her past life—her obsessive love for her father first and for her husband later—and briefly also of her character. In particular, the narrator warns us that «aveva tentazioni assurde, e più d'ogni altra, quella di recarsi al cinematografo,[268]» an apparently weird remark that nevertheless has the function of introducing a voyeuristic morbidity that somehow reverses the initial perspective of the novel: Virginia is an enigma for the others and the others are an enigma for her. She replies to the curious gazes that try to penetrate her *otherness* with her attempt to spy, to eavesdrop, to peer through doors and walls at what the other housemates are doing:

> Di ciascuno, origliando, ella aveva imparato le abitudini. [...] Nella camera accanto alla sua abitavano una madre e un figlio giovanetto. Virginia seguiva i loro colloqui attraverso la parete. Sapeva ormai tutto di essi; della loro povertà e dell'irrequietezza del figlio che la madre chiamava Sandrino. Il ragazzo era commesso in un negozio di tessuti. Virginia non lo aveva mai visto.[269]

They cannot know her, while *she knows everything about them*. She is, then, the only character who knows as much as the omniscient

---

268   Ibid., p. 6. «She was subject to the most absurd temptations, of which the strongest was to go to the movies.» p. 2
269   Ibid., p. 7. «She learned all their habits by eavesdropping. [...] The room next to hers was occupied by a mother and her son. Virginia listened to their talk through the wall. Very soon she knew all about them; about their poverty and the boy's restlessness. His mother called him Sandrino, and he worked for a haberdasher. Virginia had never seen him.» p. 3

narrator does. Sandrino, the protagonist of the novel, is introduced only now as the object of Virginia's special, lustful voyeurism:

> Se faceva rumore, il ragazzo! Ma era il rumore di un ragazzo, l'unico che non la costringesse a sussultare. Attraverso la parete Virginia lo seguiva ogni mattina, dal momento in cui si destava al suono della sveglia che la madre gli caricava uscendo: lo udiva lavarsi e cantare, frugare nei cassetti, spostare le sedie, percorrere il corridoio, e poi sbattere la porta sulle scale.[270]

Gradually, after the gazes of the neighbors on Virginia, after the eavesdropping of Virginia on Sandrino, we are introduced to the other fascist character of the novel, or better, to its true fascist hero. The main difference from the structure of *Il conformista* is exactly this simultaneous presence of two distinct fascist characters, one minor (Virginia) and one protagonist (Sandrino), as opposed to Marcello, who was only one hero split in type and protagonist within himself.

Like its spatial setting, *Un eroe del nostro tempo* is structured as a system of Chinese boxes, a space fragmented into mutually exclusive rooms in which all the characters live separated from each other and from the rest of the world by screens, walls, doors, lines, and borders. If, in fact, we observe more closely the realistic setting of the novel, it will be clear how this spatial organization into 'compartments' mirrors the narrative structure of the novel itself. The four main characters—Sandrino and his mother, Virginia, Faliero and Bruna (a partisan couple)—share the same apartment, and this is a sort of metaphor for the fractured and forced unity of postwar Italy: a failed and apparent harmony in which the divisions and conflicts of the war continued to survive unresolved. The only center that unites them all is Virginia, who excites the others' imagination and attracts like a magnet their secrets to her: «chiusa nella sua camera, i segreti della casa venivano a lei.»[271]

---

270 Ibid., p. 8 «Of course the boy made a noise when he got up! But it was a boy's noise, the only kind that didn't startle her. Every morning Virginia followed everything he did, from the moment when he was awakened by the alarm clock, which his mother wound for him before she left. Virginia heard him washing, singing, rummaging in the drawers, moving the chairs, rushing down the corridor and finally slamming the flat door behind him.» pp. 3-4.
271 Ibid., p. 11. «Without leaving her room, she learned all the secrets of the house.» p.7.

The structure of the novel as a *roman à clef* exactly mirrors the fragmentation of the apartment into rooms. The final solution to the enigma is delayed through a narrative strategy similar to that of Akira Kurosawa's *Rashomon*. Each chapter is only one version of the facts, as seen from the partial and limited point of view of one character. The main and true riddle of the story, though, is Sandrino and the secrets he is hiding. Faliero and Bruna will try to solve his riddle and integrate his difference into the newborn society, while Virginia is the opposing force that will thwart the solution and keep him as other, as an obscure unconsummated form separated from the world: an unperceivable enigma. The melodramatic, obsessive and almost incestuous desire she has for him will fragment and forestall the progress of Sandrino's redemptive political *bildungsroman*. Virginia is the fascist type that prevents Sandrino from acquiring the stereotypical shape of the fascist, thus becoming the hero of the novel.

The secret affair between the two begins the day Virginia turns 33. By now, she habitually spies on him through the keyhole and overhears his movements through the thin wall, especially after having heard one day the rhythmic creaking up and down of his mattress followed by a raucous, strangled sigh of joy. While she obsessively desires to hear Sandrino masturbating once again, nothing new happens until, one morning, something unexpected and different occurs: the alarm rings, but no sound of Sandrino waking up reaches Virginia's ears. She hurries to his room, opens the door, and he is there as if already waiting for her. When he suddenly welcomes her, she faints from surprise on the threshold. This falling before entering, her fainting in between his and her space, is of extreme importance, and we need to keep it in mind in view of the ending of the book. Virginia, in fact, will die in the same way, on a threshold, neither here nor there, as a perfect enactment of her being not only the in-between figure of the *repubblichina* but also the character that more than anyone else moves in between rooms and the riddles they hide.

Critics have always focused on the relationship between Sandrino and the two partisans, Faliero and Bruna, who, together with Elena — the girl Sandrino will fall in love with — will try to redeem and reconcile him with justice, society, and common sense. I think, on the contrary, that the relationship between Virginia and Sandrino is the interaction that structures the novel itself, making it collapse and eventually fail as a *bildungsroman*. Virginia is the true antagonist of Sandrino, and thus *Un eroe del nostro tempo* has a unique plot in Italian literature: a *repubblichino* against a *repubblichina*, a fascist against a fascist and ultimately a villain against a villain. This mirroring and duplicity are also testified by the somehow chiasmic redoubling of their names: Alessandro Vergesi and Virginia Aloisi. They are two sides of the same coin.

Furthermore, their relationship is characterized by a mutual desire for what they represent, not for what they really are. Like Marcello in *Il conformista*, they see another target behind the real, concrete one in front of them. Here, mourning deviates from desire's perspective. Behind Virginia, in fact, Sandrino sees, in the background, his father. Behind Sandrino, in turn, Virginia sees her husband. They both turn out to be, for each other, the symbolic tokens that would substitute their lost object of desire: the dead husband and the dead father, who are both past, dead, and mythical figures of fascist heroes. Their passion, then, is a work of mourning for, respectively, a father and a husband. Sandrino desires Virginia while he mourns his father because her husband was also a *repubblichino*, and by possessing her, he will, in a way, become like his lost father, finally identifying with him. In the same, only reverse way, for Virginia, being Sandrino's woman would mean overcoming a loss from which she never recovered. Both their desires are, then, actually a type of mourning for a past of fascism and guilt that still menaces to entrap or 'enframe' them as stereotypes, as in Calvino's words, '*precise* characters.' This time of mourning is the time of memory, pointing backward in the exact opposite direction of the teleology of the *bildungsroman,* which, on the contrary, would project Sandrino's life onto the future horizon of liberation and new form. She is a creature of the past who tries to keep Sandrino from changing, becoming other than the fixed, static mirror-image, repetitive stereotype of his fascist father: "Virginia era una creatura perpetuamente costretta a lasciarsi vivere ed a rimproverarsi un passato, astratto come un avvenire."[272]

Their passion lasts only 20 days, secretly from Sandrino's mother and, more importantly, from the compassionate gaze of Faliero and Bruna. One day, Sandrino disappears without notice, leaving Virginia in a state of desperate confusion. She decides then to confess her secret to Bruna, and it is now that we abandon Virginia's perspective on the story. We enter Bruna's point of view, only to find out that she has a secret to confess too, and the object is, of course, always the young neofascist. Together with Virginia, we find out that Sandrino tried violently, a few months ago, to kiss Bruna. Although she rejected him by not responding to his kiss, but somehow passively receiving it, Sandrino, since that day, started to blackmail her for money, keeping her under the menace of revealing the secret, unfaithful kiss to Faliero. One riddle is revealed, and immediately, a second, past one is unveiled, too. It is now clear that Sandrino is using Virginia in order to extort her money, the necessary sum to finance a desperate attempt at a neofascist 'counterrevolution.' Bruna's attempt to open Virginia's eyes, making her finally realize Sandrino's real intentions, fails as Virginia, in despair and in the grip of jealousy, disappears too from the scene.

The next part of the novel is the only one seen from the point of view of Sandrino, and it is not by chance that this shift of perspective coincides with the absence of Virginia and with his only true, concrete possibility to redeem and cancel his past. Once Sandrino is back, he meets Elena, a woman his age who lives in the apartment across the street and who used to spy on Sandrino from her window. Elena is then the nemesis of Virginia, the opposing gaze coming from outside the enclosed, claustrophobic microcosm of the apartment. Furthermore, if the past were the true bond tying Sandrino to Virginia, the past would be the only reason that would make the love between Elena and Sandrino impossible to fulfill. Her father, in fact, died in a concentration camp, so when Elena gets

---

[272] Ibid., p. 39 «Virginia was a being under a perpetual compulsion to accept life as she found it and to lament a past which was as remote from reality as the future which she contemplated.» p. 35

to know that Sandrino's father, on the other hand, was a fascist and that, moreover, Sandrino is *still* a fascist, she cannot but push him away, despite her love. Then, the past, or better, the creature from the past, assaults him again, all of a sudden at a street corner:

> Il passato lo aggredì d'improvviso, sull'angolo della strada in cui Sandrino abitava. Un'ombra di donna avanzò di un passo dalla parte opposta del marciapiede, lo chiamò con un tremore nella voce, poi più forte poiché egli procedeva senza averla udita, ripeté una terza volta il suo nome.
> «Sandrino, fermati» […]
> Subito egli si sentì incapace di rifiutarsi alla realtà quale gli appariva: la sua vita riprendeva il suo corso naturale dal punto in cui l'incontro con Elena l'aveva interrotta.[273]

Once again, as in *Il conformista,* the recognition scene marks the encounter of two different temporalities: the time of the winners (represented by Elena) and the time of the losers, the past embodied by Virginia. Actually, Virginia embodies something more nuanced than the mere past of guilt, loss and fascism. She expresses the break, the disruption and the negation of «the triumphant story of the future.»[274] Her reappearance on the scene rewinds the course of time. The recognition scene is the axial event that mixes the time of the romance with the time of the epic:

> The narrative time of epic is, we have said, the time of the project: it is in other words the time of the victors, and the temporality of their history and their worldview. […] "Romance" somehow expresses the experience of defeat, a shattering experience that annuls historical teleology.[275]

It is thanks to the character of Virginia that the plot of *Un eroe del nostro tempo* becomes a dialectic and Sandrino «an ambivalent simultaneity»[276] of positive and negative traits of success and failure.

---

273 Ibid., p. 201. «Suddenly the past assaulted him, at the corner of the street on which he lived. The shadow of a woman advanced a step towards him from the opposite pavement, called to him in a tremulous voice, the more loudly as he went on without hearing. Then she called out his name for the third time. "Sandrino, stop!" This time he heard and recognized her. […] He suddenly felt incapable of denying reality as it presented itself to him. His life was resuming its natural course a the point where Elena had interrupted it.» pp. 192-193.
274 Fredric Jameson, *Valences of the Dialectic* (London: Verso, 2010) p. 526.
275 Ibid., p.556
276 Ibid., p. 560.

The triumph of the victors is, in this way, undermined by the demonstration that postwar Italy was a failed attempt at unity, a still fragmented, fractured space in which screens and walls transform everyone into a riddle, an enigma impossible to perceive from the point of view of the *other* fully.

Sandrino, fermati. Even the words that Virginia pronounces three times with climatic intonation sound like an imposition to stasis, as if she and the stereotypical connotations she carries would deny him the possibility of moving on, both literally and symbolically. However, even moving on toward a future of redemption and inclusion would mean another kind of stasis and typicality. Once the *bildungsroman*'s teleological conversion plot had been completed, Sandrino would have become another finalized, consummated and completed character, static and not an «affective union of opposites.»[277] Virginia, writes Pratolini right before the epilogue, «con la sua presenza, aveva bloccato il tempo e doveva quindi volgerlo alla sua soluzione.»[278]

Sandrino and Virginia are walking alongside the park where they used to spend their dates when she tells him she is pregnant, with the prospect of being a family together becoming the only possible future. He pushes her against the park's pointed fence:

> Sandrino era piegato su di lei, attratto dal suo volto, dalla sua voce, col senso di precipitare assieme a lei in quell'oscurità senza fine; e ad ogni istante sempre più accresciuto della propria forza, come se fosse il pallore del volto di Virginia, il suono della sua voce a dargli un'energia sempre maggiore. Ed erano i suoi occhi, che adesso vedeva anche più bianchi del suo viso e della neve, rivolti in alto, ad attirarlo in un'intenzione animosa, di attimo in attimo sempre più intensa, a fargli nascere il desiderio improvviso, lancinante di schiacciarli, di cancellarli quegli occhi, con le proprie mani.
> Ella disse, e furono le sue ultime parole: «Se tu non mi lasciassi, potrei restare qui tutta la notte, a guardare le stelle come una bambina, infilata per la testa…»
> Le mani di Sandrino si serrarono sulle sbarre come draghe, con la stessa, graduale, implacabile intensità.
> E d'un tratto esse, le sue mani, sentì che gli esplodevano, agivano da sole, strinsero Virginia alle mandibole e cariche di tutta la loro forza, le

---

277 Ibid., p. 593.
278 Pratolini, *Un eroe del nostro tempo,* p. 217. «it was she who with her presence had blocked out time and was guiding him to the outcome.» p. 207.

riversarono la testa ancora più indietro, di colpo, da conficcarle la lancia della nuca.[279]

Virginia finally finds her cross, exchanging the roles with Sandrino, who, in the previous episode quoted earlier, she tried to call three times, echoing the triple denial of St. Peter. However, this violent, disturbing scene is noticeable because it, once again, makes explicit the interaction between the character of Virginia with the temporal and spatial dimensions of the text. In the first half of the scene, her pale face almost fades and merges with the whiteness of the background. She, in a way, is about to disappear, to dematerialize in front of Sandrino's eyes, who can hardly distinguish her anymore and cannot perceive her body against the background of the surrounding world. The synesthetic snow-pale face erases her otherness, denying Sandrino the possibility of finalizing her consummated identity. She dies in between the material threshold, on the border separating the park from the street, the inside from the outside, in the same way she fell on the door's threshold the first time she saw Sandrino. In the second part of the scene, before Virginia speaks, two prolepses disrupt the sequential temporality of the action, mixing up the objective time of the episode with an eternal indefinite present in which past and future are interchangeable poles. *She spoke, and those were her last words*: we know beforehand that those words will be her last, and also Virginia herself anticipates, maybe even suggests, to Sandrino the circumstances of her death: *I could stay here all night, staring at the stars like a child, pierced through the head.*

---

[279] Ibid., p. 220. «Sandrino was bending over her, attracted by her face and her voice, feeling that he was plunging with her into infinite darkness. He had a sensation of constantly gathering strength, as if he were deriving energy from Virginia's pallor and the sound of her voice. Her eyes, as she gazed upwards, now seemed to him to be wither/whiter? than her face and the snow; suddenly they roused him to a paroxysm of passion, filling him with an overwhelming desire to crush and destroy those eyes with his own hands. "If you stayed with me, I could stay here all night, gazing up at the stars like a child, with my head between the bars!" Those were Virginia's last words. Sandrino's hands were implacably gripping the bars behind her. He suddenly felt what was like an explosion in his hands, which seemed to act of their own accord. They seized Virginia's jaws and with all their strength started forcing her head backwards and downwards, driving the spike into the back of her head.» p. 209-210.

The tragic ineluctability of this ending and its brutal violence might easily be interpreted as a sign that fascism is an incurable disease. Nevertheless, this would still be an interpretation, a stereotypical reading of the fascist character as doomed by nature to be a villain, to murder and commit any sort of immoral violence. What, on the surface, characterizes the essence of both Sandrino and Virginia is, then, their inability to change, to move on, to redeem and convert, in a word, their incompatibility with the sequential, teleological narrative of the *bildungsroman*. Their melodrama is full of scenes that are typical of romance: the incestuous forbidden affair, murder, mystery, secrets, betrayals, disappearances, undesired pregnancy, conspiracy, and anagnorisis. They oppose this fractured, syncopated plot made of episodes and axial events, to the political *bildungsroman* in which, on the other hand, Bruna, Faliero and Elena, i.e., the 'good' characters, live and act in view of a better future of national unity and brotherhood. Virginia is the stereotype of the fascist woman: lascivious, weak, and corrupted by sick passion. She is a typical type of villain, a minor character usually to be found in a melodramatic plot. Sandrino, on the other hand, like Marcello in *Il conformista,* is both like Virginia, indeed the same as her — an inhuman beast-like creature driven by carnal desire and by a predisposition to kill — and at the same time, the potential hero of the political *Bildungsroman,* the positive protagonist of an exemplary, happy-ending parable. He is both Judas and Lazarus, both Iago and Fortinbras. Now, the emplotment of a hero that 'uncomplicatedly' is, or would become, a partisan has to be necessarily different than the emplotment of fascists or of in-between figures such as traitors, spies, and collaborators. The shift from type to hero, from the role of antagonists or evil 'messengers', to use Propp's terminology, is a totally, altogether 'special' process of aestheticization, a creative attempt to displace history into fiction complicated by the fact that the object is at the same time *other,* enemy, and a fellow compatriot. The result is an attempt to enframe, to finalize a character that floats without a static form, bringing to the text a dialectic of genres, of the dynamic simultaneity-flux of an unnamable otherness-identity. Novels such as *Un eroe del nostro tempo* and *Il conformista* are attempts to give the fascist a narrative shape displaced from history, and they exemplify the attempt to make the fascist the *other,* to enframe them, to confer it that otherness necessary to tell their story, to know and perceive their veritable essence. However, since the fascist is/produces a sort of 'concordant discordance,' authors such as Moravia and Pratolini could not completely observe the character from the outside, could not reach that detachedness and outsideness that is the preliminary requisite to perceive and know the world, and the *other.* Seeing requires a certain outsideness to what is seen, a certain stasis: «In the realm of culture, outsideness is the most powerful factor in understanding.»[280]

Instead, when trying to enframe a fascist, the author recognizes something of himself in the character, cannot perceive it as other than himself, and thus, the subject merges into the object, destroying the possibility of stepping back and occupying a transcendent point of view *outside* the object. Like Virginia, the author is stuck halfway between thresholds. The juxtaposition, then, of clashing and opposing narrative types, genres and temporalities denies irony to the author. On the one hand, the attempt to build a realistic narrative with a fascist as the protagonist—and not just as the stereotypical minor figure of the antagonist—estranges such a character from their usual genre and role in the plot, thus enabling a new, more complex and precise kind of perception, on the other, the estrangement activates a dialectic that complicates perception and makes it impossible to categorize and finalize the fascist as either villain or hero, as either totally good or totally evil.

Going back to the initial quotation from Calvino, villains usually come off in a better and more attractive, consumable aesthetic shape exactly because they are perceived as *others,* as enemies against the background of the world. However, fascists were not *just* enemies; they could never be enframed into the clear-cut lines of a 'precise character.' Authors needed to do so in order to create the illusory image of a unified Italy. The result was that their narratives lost realism and uniformity in the attempt to perceive the fascist truly and more objectively by way of generic aestheticization.

---

[280] Michael Holquist, *Dialogism* (New York: Routledge, 2002) p. 27.

In order to have consciousness of fascism, it was necessary to perceive it first as otherness. In my opinion, these novels are all about the problematic perception of the fascist and, consequently, of its *failed*, 'inexact' aestheticization into a realist narrative-plot. It is necessary to envisage and analyze the relationship between the author and the fascist character within the framework of Bakhtin's *dialogism* and its key concepts of otherness, simultaneity and outsideness.

> Dialogism, like relativity, takes it for granted that nothing can be perceived except against the perspective of something else: dialogism's master assumption is that there is no figure without a ground. The mind is structured so that the world is always perceived according to this contrast. More specifically, what sets a figure off from its dialogizing background is the opposition between a time and a space that one consciousness uses to model its own limits (the I-for-myself) and the quite different temporal and spatial categories employed by the same consciousness to model the limits of other persons and things (the not-I-in-me) — and (this is crucial) vice versa.[281]

The perceiver, the self, thinks in a time that is forever an open, unfinished projectuality and moves in a space that is always the center of perception, the still point that regulates the coordinates around which things arrange and obtain their meanings. On the contrary, the time in which we configure and consummate the other is closed and finished, and the space that surrounds it is the neutral, homogeneous world outside ourselves. From the point of view of the self, the other is out there, occupying a unique, meaningful, precise spot in the world. The meaning of the other is thus something completed, whereas the self is always in the process of creating its own: its essence is always a yet-to-be. The way the self perceives the world and assigns a meaning to things is the same as the way the author needs to enframe and finalize the hero within the clear-cut limits of a narrative whole: the beginning-middle-end causal structure of plot and the stereotypical, forever existing roles of characters. The self/other relation is an author/hero relation:

> The individual subject is conceived as similar to the artist who seeks to render what is *not* an artwork in itself (independent of the artist's activity) into

---

281 Ibid., p. 22.

something that *is* the kind of conceptual whole we can recognize as a painting or a text.[282]

The first fundamental premise of any aesthetic production is the position of the author outside the hero. In order to create form, a 'surplus of seeing' is needed, an author who sees and knows more than each hero of the novel. This excess of seeing enables the author to encompass with his consciousness the hero's world and consciousness by supplying what the hero, from its limited, particular and specific place in time and space, misses to see:

> Our concern is only with actions of contemplation—actions of contemplation, because contemplation is active and productive. These actions of contemplation do not go beyond the bounds of the other as a given; they merely unify and order that given. And it is these actions of contemplation, issuing from the excess of my outer and inner seeing of the other human being, that constitute the purely *aesthetic* actions. The excess of my seeing is the bud in which slumbers form, and whence form unfolds like a blossom.[283]

The beginning of *Un eroe del nostro tempo* is the perfect staging of a 'theater of vision' formed by a multiplicity of acts of contemplation that are either negated or granted by the author to its heroes. In the fragmented space of the apartments, every wall is a screen that veils and limits the point of view of characters and, then, the perception and knowledge they have of each other. They reciprocally perceive each other as riddles and otherness, i.e., the ideal formula from which the author can begin to create a consummated whole-aesthetic form. Virginia and Sandrino are the true objects of Pratolini's gaze, and they both are, at the beginning of the novel, closed off inside their rooms, hidden and separated from the surrounding background of the world. Initially, they both are perfectly enframed in the space of their rooms as much as they are finalized in the plot. Seen-not-seen from the outside by everyone, Sandrino and Virginia are the enigma that allows the story to begin and to capture the attention-voyeurism of the reader:

---

282 Holquist, "Introduction" in *Art and Answerability – Early Philosophical Essays by M.M Bakhtin* (University of Texas Press: Austin, 1990) p. xvi.
283 Bakhtin, Michail, "Author and Hero in Aesthetic Activity" in *Art and Answerability – Early Philosophical Essays by M.M Bakhtin* (University of Texas Press: Austin, 1990) p. 24.

> The general formula for the author's fundamental, aesthetically productive relationship to the hero [...] is a relationship in which the author occupies an intently maintained position *outside* the hero with respect to every constituent feature of the hero — a position *outside* the hero with respect to space, time, value, and meaning. And this being outside in relation to the hero enables the author (i) to collect and concentrate *all* of the hero, who, from within himself, is diffused and dispersed in the projected world of cognition and in the open event of ethical action; (2) to collect the hero and his life and to complete him to the point where he forms a *whole* by supplying all those moments which are inaccessible to the hero himself from within himself [...]; and (3) to justify and to consummate the hero independently of the meaning, the achievements, the outcome and success of the hero's own forward-directed life.[284]

To be initially placed outside their rooms allows us to perceive them as others, as identities that we both desire and can know. This initial placement enables what Roland Bathes defined as the 'hermeneutical code,' the posing of a question and the continuous, simultaneous delay and covering-uncovering of the answer. The text stays alive as a readable whole thanks to its static nature, built, we may add, on those static characters that are fixed, repetitive stereotypes:

> The dynamics of the text (since it implies a truth to be deciphered) is thus paradoxical: it is a static dynamics: the problem is to *maintain* the enigma in the initial void of its answer; whereas the sentences quicken the story's "unfolding" and cannot help but move the story along, the hermeneutic code performs an opposite action: it must set up *delays* (obstacles, stoppages, deviations) in the flow of the discourse; its structure is essentially reactive, since it opposes the ineluctable advance of language with an organized set of stoppages: between question and answer there is a whole dilatory area whose emblem might be named «reticence.»[285]

Also, the dynamic of the text works as a dialectic of two opposite temporalities: one that 'projects' meaning towards infinitude, as an everlasting yet-to-be, and one that, on the contrary, delays and antagonizes openness, exactly like Virginia who yearns to keep Sandrino as a riddle to others, and perceivable exclusively to herself. Since the beginning of the novel, Sandrino is characterized mainly by the fact that he is observed: he is more object than subject. The

---

284 Ibid., p. 14.
285 Roland Barthes, *S/Z* (Torino: Einaudi, 1970) p. 72.

author tries to enframe him within spatial and ideological limits-clichés, and, in this sense, his gaze superimposes to Virginia's gaze, who, in this first chapter, at least becomes the author's alter-ego, the two sharing a point of view outside Sandrino's bedroom. The aesthetic form of the novel, thus, depends on the externality of Virginia to Sandrino first and, second, on the complete outsideness of the author to Virginia, a character that is perceived by everyone—author, neighborhood, readers—as the true absolutely *other*: a deviate fascist widow.

As we have seen, the attempt of precisely enframing Sandrino into one stereotypical, consummated form fails insofar as the *bildungsroman* is unsettled by other narrative types—melodrama and *roman à clef*—and the protagonist is stuck in the dimension of a minor, typical character by his true antagonist-villain, Virginia. That is to say, the author loses, in the course of the plot, his position outside the hero, and Sandrino remains an undefined character, neither good nor evil, only on the threshold of becoming a new form. The novel, in fact, is open-ended; the only certainty that Pratolini gives us is Virginia's death, and Sandrino is left halfway in the middle of the street after having murdered Virginia. If, on the one hand, Pratolini spreads hints indicating that Sandrino will eventually end up in jail, convicted—two witnesses might have seen what happened—on the other hand, the last image of the novel is a redemptory and hopeful one: Elena is there, standing at the end of a long path, smiling at him. He is neither irremediably condemned nor completely freed from his past and guilt. The 'struggle' between author and hero is still open and undecided when the end comes:

> This relationship of the author to the hero [...] is deeply vital and dynamic: the author's position of being situated outside of the hero is gained by conquest, and the struggle for it is often a struggle for life, especially in the case where the hero is autobiographical, although not only there. For sometimes it is difficult to take up a stand outside one's partner as well as outside one's antagonist in the event of life; not only being *inside* the hero but also being axiologically *beside* him and *against* him distorts seeing and lacks features that can render him complete and consummate him. [...] A hero of this kind is not capable of being consummated: he surpasses within himself any comprehensive determination of himself from outside as inadequate to himself;

he experiences consummated wholeness as a limitation of himself and opposes to it an inexpressible inner mystery of some kind.[286]

After the initial position literally outside his room, which coincides with the intention to finally consider and look at the fascist as the other, the author, in the process of giving the fascist the coherent aesthetic form of the villain, finds himself at one and a same time inside, beside and against the hero. A dialectic of different genres of plots and characters — melodrama-*bildungsroman,* villain-hero — forestalls the finalization of both the novel and its fascist protagonist. Virginia and Sandrino both live in a time of mourning, and the temporality of the entire novel coincides with their uncompleted *trauerarbeit* for their husband-father. In conclusion, *Un eroe del nostro tempo* is many different things. It is a 'weak' novel, after all, as Calvino writes, and, in my opinion, it is weak because it tries, and fails, to give a 'precise' aesthetic form to a double mourning. Its heroes attempt without success to mourn their fathers, and its author tries to mourn, to close the circle around the inexpressible — because never completely *other* — figure of the fascist.

3.2 The Enigma of *don Gastone*: The Fascist Character as the Ineffable Object of 'Hysterical' Storytelling and *Voyeurism.*

Published in 1954, *Il prete bello* by Goffredo Parise was the first true Italian postwar bestseller, reaching a critical and mass acclaim that was denied to *Un eroe del nostro tempo*. Even though they differ in genre, tone and style — the former is much lighter, surreal and *picaresque*, the latter is rather dark, tense, and 'psychological' — the two novels share a similar, centripetal structure that rotates and arranges its parts, around a fascist, almost, protagonist. Nevertheless, the most striking and central similarity is, first of all, the space in which the action of the novel takes place. The initial setting is closely reminiscent of Virginia's fractured apartment. We have seen how, in *Un eroe del nostro tempo,* the 'acts of contemplation' of the

---

286 Ibid., p. 15

various characters point first at the mysterious fascist widow—and how she 'excites' the imagination of her neighbors—and second at Sandrino. In *Il prete bello,* too, the plot depends on the peculiar spatial construction of the setting.

The novel is set in Vicenza in the 1930s, in an old apartment block shared by people of various social classes and provenance. The building has three floors, and all the different apartments face inside, on a courtyard surrounded on its four sides by a portico:

> Oltre il portico si apriva un cortile e ai quattro lati del cortile muri, ballatoi e i sontuosi balconi barocchi della signorina Immacolata, la padrona di casa; era uno scenario sempre uguale e sempre mutevole a seconda delle ore, del riflesso del sole e degli umori dei numerosissimi inquilini. [...] In quel blocco di case attorno al cortile abitava una infinità di gente e io li conoscevo tutti.[287]

The owner of the tenement is Signorina Immacolata, a rich old lady who shares with Virginia not only a name with 'virginal' resonances but also an obsessive voyeurism that pushes her to spy on her tenants:

> Spesso la signorina Immacolata faceva il giro dell'intero edificio, con una lampada, ed esaminava i muri, i corrimano, l'interno delle stanze, le porte e le serrature. Saltellava da un angolo all'altro nella penombra e saliva la scala a chiocciola senza far oscillare le assi, senza scricchiolii, con l'austerità e il biancore di un gabbiano che battesse silenzioso le sue ali in direzione dell'uscita.[288]

---

[287] Goffredo Parise, *Il prete bello* (Milano: Adelphi, 2011) pp. 9-10. «Through the gateway a courtyard opened out with, on all four sides of it, walls, galleries, and the rich baroque balconies of Signorina Immacolata, who owned the place. It was a setting which was always the same and yet always changing according to the time of day, the reflected gleam of the sun, and the humors of the numerous tenants. [...] In that block of houses round the courtyard lived an infinite number of people, and I knew them all.» pp. 3-4.
[288] Ibid., pp. 10-11. «Often Signorina Immacolata went round the whole building with a lamp and examined the walls, the balustrades, the interiors of the rooms, the doors, and the locks. She hopped from one corner to another in the half-light and climbed the winding stairs without shaking the boards, without a creak of wood-austere and white, like a seagull silently flying toward the door with beating wings.» pp. 4-5.

However, the true target of her gaze and her forbidden desire is don Gastone Caoduro,[289] the handsome priest who every day comes to visit the families of the apartment block and, in particular, Immacolata, to whom, once a week, to her deep satisfaction, he brings his laundry. Once she has received the 'precious' bag full of his underwear, his thin black socks, and his vest, she examines every centimeter of it with her attentive, scrupulous gaze and «occhio di paradiso.»[290]

Thus, as in *Un eroe del nostro tempo,* the novel starts with the compulsive act of contemplation of a woman of dubious morality, and the fascist protagonist is, once again, introduced in the plot only indirectly as the mysterious object of this 'sick' gaze. Immacolata madly craves don Gastone, who had served as a military chaplain during the Spanish Civil War and who even wrote a book about his experience, in which «le atrocità e delitti dei rossi erano descritti in modo commovente.» [291] He is a true hero of the regime, a 'paradoxical' example of concordant dissonance, a champion of virtue and virility, a spiritual guide and a bodily temptation. It is worth quoting his caricatural portrait in its entirety:

> Praticava molti sport, era un uomo di azione e, col passare dei giorni, più virile che mai d'aspetto; sempre ben vestito, garbato, fumava sigarette con un bocchino d'oro e qualche volta un pipino inglese, di sambuco, ma quest'ultimo solo in privato. Sapeva tutti i buoni odori di questo mondo ma era privo di quello che gli sarebbe spettato per dote, quello cui la Provvidenza avrebbe dovuto fornirlo per prima cosa a custodia della sua illibatezza: l'odore del prete. Odore che non aveva; non un minimo d'incenso si attaccava al tessuto della sua tonaca, un sentorino di cera neppure quello, o quel selvatico che prendono i sacerdoti fin dagli anni del seminario. Don Gastone aveva indossato la veste dopo la laurea, e prima non si sapeva cosa mai avesse fatto, chi avesse frequentato, se era andato a ballare o aveva avuto una fidanzata. [...] Invece niente: sapeva di un buon profumo di sapone, di cuoi di capretto, di brillantina Arys, ma niente di prete. E un prete

---

289 It is curious that most fascists have names reminiscent of the male sexual organ. Like the Moravian Astarita (erected beam) in *La romana,* the name Caoduro, with the insertion of two zz in between the diphthong, would transform the name into, literally, 'hard dick.' But he is a priest, so he is in a way 'castrated' of the two zz, like *Sarrasine* in Barthes' reading of Balzac's story in *S/Z*.
290 Parise, *Il prete bello* p. 11. «with a look of bliss in her eyes.» p. 5
291 Ibid. «the crimes and atrocities of the Reds were described in a most moving way.» p. 5

di trentasei anni, bello, alto, che sapeva pilotare l'aeroplano, che andava alla palestra del ricreatorio e al cinema[292] quasi ogni giorno e per di più non sapeva di odor di prete, che prete era? [293]

This description is the perfect example of a stereotypical fascist, even though, if we look more attentively, Parise focuses on the most incidental and immaterial quality of his person: the odor. The focus is on his bodily and material strength, but the whole description is grounded on such a vague, unfixable sensation, a *sentorino*, a tiny scent. The result is an immediate contrast between the bodily features and the immaterial epithet and the subsequent deconstruction of the physical presence exactly by the absence of a specific, expected perfume.

Immacolata is not the only one to cast her desiring gaze on don Gastone. Literally, the whole tenement, for one reason or another, is fascinated by this walking paradox of a tall, handsome fascist hero who also happens to be a priest. The men admire him as an example of fascist dedication and bravery, and the communists are not indifferent to him because of their contempt. However, those who are more than anyone obsessively perturbed and attracted by his daily visits are the women of the building, who, moreover, are all old spinsters. Like a rooster in a henhouse, then, don Gastone is

---

[292] Again, after Virginia and Sandrino, another fascist who is characterized by his assiduous attendance at movie theaters.

[293] Ibid., p. 91. «He played a lot of games, was a man of action, and as time passed, became more virile-looking than ever. Always well dressed, well mannered, he smoked cigarettes in a golden cigarette-holder or sometimes-but only in private- an English brier pipe. He knew all the nice odors of this world, but he lacked the one you would have expected him to have acquired when he began his novitiate, the one with which Providence should have provided him in the first place to stand guard over his virginity: the smell of a priest. He had no smell. No trace of incense clung to the cloth of his gown, not even a whiff of wax nor yet that gamey smell which priests acquire during their years in the seminary. Don Gastone had assumed the gown after he had graduated, and there was no knowing what he had done before, what company he had kept-if he had gone dancing or had a fiancée. But after ten years spent going back and forth from one church to the vestry of another he really ought to have managed to absorb something, some faint odor of sanctity. But not at all-he smelled beautifully of soap, of kid leather, of brilliantine, but not like priest. What sort of a priest was he-thirty years old, handsome, tall, able to fly a plane, a priest who went to the gym and the cinema almost every day and did not smell like one? p. 88.

the object of the gazes and desires of the ladies, who try to interpret every movement and gesture he makes in order to understand who among them is his favorite, and mostly if there is an even remote chance to lead him into temptation:

> Alcune delle patronesse erano giunte a tale parossismo, che il desiderio di baci aveva mutato le loro labbra in becchi acuti, sempre volti in direzione di don Gastone. L'odore caldo, percorso da lievi zaffate di tabacco da fiuto, era diventato un'evaporazione di sensualità collettiva da cui don Gastone si sentiva visibilmente oppresso. [...]
> Esse saggiavano, domandavano, investigavano, supponevano a vuoto. [...] Ognuna vedeva affacciarsi, nella nebbia d'amore che offuscava la figura e i sentimenti di don Gastone, rivalità, indifferenza o addirittura antipatia. [...] La gelosia però covava, sicché una guardava l'altra ogni giorno con maggiore apprensione, e tutte insieme, alla sera puntavano gli occhi verso le vetrate del salotto giallo della signorina Immacolata dove lei e don Gastone si trovavano da solo a sola. Spiavano le ombre prodotte dai movimenti anche impercettibili; ogni interruzione di gesti, ogni pausa era una dolorosa fitta, pareva a loro, in quel momento, di morire.[294]

Their attention and jealousy focus on the shaded, glass windows of Immacolata's living room, where she and don Gastone meet daily. Their gazes try to penetrate, to see through those walls and finally know if something secret, sinful and forbidden is happening inside. However, the windows of the small room at the end of the vestibule are all not only closed but also screened with shields.

Don Gastone is, then, an enigma, a mystery both to the insider Immacolata, who cannot see what his intentions are under his tunic, and to the *outsiders*. His figure has since the day he entered the courtyard like «una farfalla incantata», an aura of «fatale

---

[294] Ibid., pp. 70, 82-83. «As for him, some of the ladies had got into such a state in their desire to kiss him that their lips had become sharp beaks turned perpetually toward him. [...] So they had been left with their thirst for information unquenched, half hysterical, upset, full of suspicion, doubt, and jealousy, all because of my replies. For since they could get nowhere, they saw looming through the mists of love which blurred the figure and sentiments of don Gastone, rivals, indifference or downright dislike. [...] So jealousy smoldered in their hearts. Daily each looked at the others with greater apprehension, and in the evening they all fixed their eyes greedily on the windows of the drawing-room where Signorina Immacolata and don Gastone sat alone. They watched the shadows produced by even the most imperceptible movements. Each time the gestures stopped, each pause, was a terrible pang and they felt they would die on the spot.» p. 78-79.

importanza.»²⁹⁵ Once again, the fascist, by 'exciting' the imaginations of the other characters, also excites the storytelling of the author, the curiosity of us readers and finally triggers the plot to start.

Hiding behind the 'opaque figure' of don Gastone lies a truth that none of the ladies can completely grasp. In order to know more than their other rivals, they 'hire' a messenger, a passe-partout, someone who has access to Immacolata's room and all the other houses, someone who can hear the confidences and secrets of everyone: Sergio, the child and narrator of the story. In fact, he spends much time with don Gastone and Immacolata because, under the initiative of the priest, he is asked to declaim a poem on the occasion of the imminent visit of Mussolini in town. The place of the rehearsals is Immacolata's living room, a stratagem maybe thought to delete any possibility of malicious suspicion.

Together with his friend Cena, he understands how to use his privileged point of view as an insider in order to get presents and food from Immacolata and the other *signorine*: he will 'buy' them by telling them what they want to hear, i.e., what is not actually happening in that room, sharing with them every gesture made and word pronounced by don Gastone. The narrator of the novel is then something in between an oracle and a pimp:

> In quei tempi [...] don Gastone Caoduro, fiore di serra, spuntò, crebbe e si abbellì in quel cortile in mezzo a noi, simile a un'orchidea in un cumulo di spazzatura. Forse era il destino a mandarlo. Dal momento che l'idolo più grande non bastava a tutti i caseggiati d'Italia, il cielo ce ne spedì in terra uno che fosse per nostra esclusiva adorazione, in via Corpus Domini numero 18, bello, a somiglianza di eroe ma, per un certo ordine e buon costume, in abiti da prete. ²⁹⁶

The 'bigger idol' is, of course, Mussolini himself, of whom don Gastone seems just a parody, a caricature, a stereotypical imitation, something like a hero, yet with only the appearance of a hero. Then,

---

295 Ibid., p. 18
296 Ibid., p. 78, 50 «Don Gastone Caoduro, that hothouse plant, grew and waxed beautiful in the courtyard, in our midst, like an orchid in a heap of sweepings. Perhaps it was fate that sent him. When the greatest idol of all no longer sufficed, heaven sent one down for our own exclusive adoration—sent him down to No.18, Via corpus Domini, as handsome as a hero, but clad, in the interests of decency and good order, in the robes of a priest.» p. 46.

as in Bakhtin, «the excess of my seeing is the bud in which slumbers form, and where form unfolds like a blossom,» it is from the excess of seeing guaranteed to Sergio and Cena that the form of the plot and its *almost* hero unfolds like 'an orchid amid a pile of trash.' The stories, lies, and gossip invented and spread by the two children will turn don Gastone into an enigma, a mysterious object of desire with an ever-changing, dynamic identity. The apartment block turns into an expressionist distorted space reminiscent of Kafka's *The Castle*, becoming a bodily creature with its own life. Every room and corridor smells *of* mystery, a labyrinth where truth is finally lost, where the gaze fails to reach its object:

> C'era in giro mistero [...] Stavano succedendo strani traffici; contenuti ma strani. Non avevo mai visto tanta animazione nello squallido cortile e dentro le finestre che erano buchi vuoti e oscuri circondati da un'aureola di muffa e da grondaie a brandelli; finestre e pertugi che davano nel nulla, in stanze mai aperte [...] Da qualche giorno alcune di quelle finestre avevano cominciato ad illuminarsi, si aprivano e si chiudevano, da esse uscivano brusii di voci distinte... [...] E diventavano degli scenari, nei quali, stando nel cortile, si vedevano muoversi le signorine con inconsueta allegria: ombre che attraversano la stanza saltellando, due volti apparivano di colpo...[...]
> E non era ancora tutto. Qualcosa si sentiva nell'aria e non si sarebbe potuto dire che cosa.[297]

The fascist excites imaginations. Every window, screen, and wall becomes a surface to be interpreted, and the tenement gets crowded with 'imprecise' shadows, half-seen silhouettes in half-light. Don Gastone is now a character with many changeable shapes, a flux of identities under the distorted gaze of the ladies. He is someone now

---

[297] Ibid., p. 24. «There was some sort of mystery afoot [...] Odd things were going on- subdued but odd. I had never seen so much animation in the drab courtyard or behind the windows, which were dark, empty holes ringed with a halo of mold and broken gutters-windows and openings onto nothing, onto never-opened rooms, onto corridors few people passed down, corridors which, with time, filled with sweepings, hens' feathers, and birds' nests, all of which fell from the roof. For a few days now some of these windows had begun to light up. They opened and closed; there came from them the hum of voices and an attempt at a song from some mad Catholic woman visiting her friends or returning their visit. [...] They became peepshows in which, if you stood in the courtyard, you saw the old maids moving to and fro with unusual cheerfulness-shadows crossing the room with a bobbing motion, two faces appearing suddenly on the sill.» p. 74, 18.

'a somiglianza d'eroe,' now «una figura di sogno, Robin Hood, San Luigi Gonzaga,»[298] now he plays simultaneously «la parte dell'eroe, del tentatore, di san Luigi Gonzaga e di Romeo insieme,»[299] now he is a «furbone, una vera volpe...un contrabbandiere d'amore...un peccatore...un uomo dai mille vizi.»[300] He is «un eroe di qualità»[301] who inspires *chansons de geste* and lyrical poems.[302] When Sergio and Cena fight and split, the truth becomes double, and they both start to exaggerate their messages to the point that the ladies do not know whose stories they can believe and trust: «tutto era eccessivo ...tutto un malinteso.»[303] The fascist character is the source of the plot and tale. These stories, though, are not unilateral and coherent narratives but distorted and partial as the obstructed gaze and point of view whence they originated. Don Gastone, the enigma, is the source then of *malinteso* and *equivoco* – misunderstanding and equivocal truth—as Fascism was itself defined by Togliatti as we have seen, or, for example, by Vittorini in his introduction to *Il garofano rosso*, as a *malinteso*, an 'innocent' misreading, a passive wrong interpretation and not an active, responsible, aware choice made by an entire country. It is important to mention that *la commedia degli equivoci* and, more generally, a plot structure based on exchanges of identities and on a language that deceives instead of communicating was widespread in Italian literature and cinema of the immediate postwar years. *Il vecchio con gli stivali* by Vitaliano

---

298 Ibid., p. 28 «a dream figure, a Robin Hood, San Luigi Gonzaga» p. 22.
299 Ibid., p. 90. «he played the part of a hero, of both St. Luigi Gonzaga and Romeo.» p. 87.
300 Ibid., p. 144. «and to the looker-on the portrait which emerged bore more resemblance to a great lover than to a sinner or a man with a thousand vices.» p. 142.
301 Ibid., p. 125. «And Cavaliere Esposito, who followed each development of the affair with interest and in great detail, enriching it with his Southern fantasy, had become a sort of minstrel. He did not merely tell stories or give information or say things in a whisper; he, too, had lost his head over don Gastone, so that for him the young priest was no longer merely the minister of God, but a real hero and a worthy representative of the race. Each day he dedicated real lyrical fragments, little poems-rather daring ones-to the old maids with a gallantry which perhaps went a little too far.» p. 122.
302 Ibid.
303 Ibid., p. 89. «Everything about the old maids was exaggerated [...] I assured Signorina Immacolata that there had been a misunderstanding.» p. 86.

Brancati has, for example, this kind of narrative device, moreover with a fascist character as protagonist and initiator of the misinterpretation. *Filumena Marturano* by Eduardo De Filippo is also based on the same stratagem.

The microcosm-community of the tenement will soon have to face two big crises. The first is the name of 'the countess *manina*,' an elegant lady infamous for her peculiar tendency-talent to masturbate men in church. It soon becomes clear to the other ladies that don Gastone and the countess are having an affair, and, full of suspicions and suppositions, they turn to the two young messengers-narrators for confirmation. One day in church, a priest surprises don Gastone and the countess together in the confessional. The scene generates turmoil that interrupts the ceremony and starts a scandalous chaos, coming and going of voices in the next days. Once again truth is hidden, veiled and inaccessible inside the walls of a secret room: everyone can imagine what happened behind the curtains, but nobody could really, fully see it.

> Una settimana più tardi si dava per certo che don Gastone era l'amante della Contessa. Dapprima nessuna notizia precisa, a conferma, solo mezze parole. «È una cosa tanto delicata» si diceva, ma ognuno sapeva già come si sarebbero concluse quelle frasi prudenti. Erano mezze parole che si agitavano nell'aria, non dicerie ma accuse, fatti gravi, perché da noi la diceria, la mezza parola, quella è la verità. Poi si seppe, ma non si seppe mai abbastanza. [...]
> Eppure in tutte queste frasi c'è un filo conduttore, parole non dette, serpeggiando in mezzo ad altre parole pronunciate, compongono un resoconto preciso, non privo di commenti, e il tutto della durata di pochi secondi.[304]

The novel's language, the language of the young narrator's messages, is disseminated of lacunae, blank spaces, elisions, ellipsis and

---

304 Ibid., pp.114-115. «A week later it was given out for certain that don Gastone was the Countess's lover. At first there was nothing definite to confirm the rumor-only odd hints. "its such a delicate matter," people said; but everyone knew what these prudent words were leading up to. Hints kept floating in the air-not mere gossip, but accusations; and they were serious because in our part of the world the real truth lies in half-finished sentences. Later we learned more, but never enough. [...] Now, through all these half-sentences there runs a thread; unspoken words, winding in and out of those spoken, make up a precise narrative, which contains its own comment. The whole thing is of a few seconds' duration.» pp. 112-113.

euphemisms.[305] It fails to categorize and fix who don Gastone really is, to consummate him into a unique, static form. The enigma generates nothing but rumors and half-truths, a disrupted thread-plot full of gaps and missing words that need to be completed with the help of the imagination. The fascist paradoxically avoids description even in a novel in which he appears as a highly stereotypical image: he generates only imprecise news, half-words and a truth that is always dynamic and unfinished, never enough. Language misleads meaning, disrupts the connection between signifier and signified, the sign and its referent, it delays the answer to the question and the solution of the riddle. Words about don Gastone have the same immateriality of his indefinable odor, the evanescence of a half-spoken murmur:

> Solo un veneto sa chiedere sottovoce: «Don Gastone ha l'amante?» in tono di affermazione e di rapimento insieme. Il bisbiglio, in questa curiosa regione dove stravaganti palazzi si ergono a formare una città al centro delle campagne, è antico, connaturato, raffinato dal tempo, postillato di una quantità di aggiunte non pronunciate ma che si esprimono con un doloroso giro dell'occhio, sì che la palpebra tremi e si afflosci sotto il peso di un peccato che non si vuol dire, con una piega della sopracciglia che, lenta, si dirige verso il basso, un tremolio del labbro e del mento [...] Assunto così a valore di linguaggio esso, mobile, terribile e serpentino, simile a una sottile e affilata lama invisibile, taglia i panni di dosso nel punto in cui questi panni si sostengono, recide il filo di quel bottone segreto e lascia di colpo nudi i peccatori, al ludibrio, con la sola mano in luogo della foglia. [306]

The aesthetic, narrative shape of the hero is then composed of words that are incapable of consummating a form. They are parts that do not become a meaningful system, the whole of a meaningful language. The message they compose is a mobile, erratic snake that cuts and disrupts any realistic consummation of truth. The murmur conveys its own indirect, unsaid and ambivalent truth, which, freed from reference, can finally be deformed into multiple tales and

---

305 Reminiscent of the famous «La sventurata rispose» in *The Betrothed*. The entire episode of *la Monaca di Monza* resonates in the novel.
306 Ibid., p. 115. Paragraph not translated.

fabula. The ladies talk about him with «voce atona,»[307] and their discourse is a «tacito messaggio.»[308]

Soon, the ladies will interpret don Gastone's relationship with the countess as a religious and redemptive narrative, and they forgive him, pretending, ironically, not to have seen enough: he is just trying to convert and purify her from sinful tendencies. He sacrifices himself in order to save her from carnal desire. Another different reading of his enigmatic personality will be that he is half a person, a man lacking virility. Otherwise, how come he has not surrendered to temptation yet? He is castrated, a *castrato* reminiscent of Balzac's *Sarrasine*:

> Non c'erano più dubbi, don Gastone non era un uomo per intero. [...] Dicevano che don Gastone era ammalato, che bisognava curarlo, e che, tutto sommato, era da amare ancor di più per quella sua grande e invisibile disgrazia, perché forse, proprio per questo ne aveva bisogno, di amore. Una disgrazia atroce, meglio gobbi piuttosto! Lui invece era bello, dritto, anche troppo, e il destino beffardo aveva *segnato quel corpo di una così amara mancanza*. [italics mine][309]

Don Gastone is not only narrated and described by false stories and distorted narratives; he embodies lack and invisibility; he is the object of desire-gaze that is unattainable from all the other characters' points of view. He is a fact «molto vago, che si capiva e non si capiva.»[310]

Don Gastone will fall sick for real at the end of the novel when his passion for the young, prosperous Fedora cannot be resisted and kept secret. He becomes, then, a positive, piteous character, ready to offer his support and consolation to Sergio when he is called to Cena's sickbed.

---

307 Ibid., p. 144. «So the words never got farther than the tips of their tongues» p. 142.
308 Ibidem. «colorless voice»
309 Ibid., p. 173. «Don Gastone was not a man in the full sense of the word [...] They said that Don Gastone was sick, that he must be made better, that, after all, he was to be loved all the more for his terrible, invisible misfortune. Because that was perhaps the very reason why he needed love. A terrible misfortune-it was almost better to be a deformed hunchback! But he was good-looking, held himself straight-perhaps too straight, and mocking fate had branded that body with a bitter defect.» p. 171-172.
310 Ibidem. «Something very vague, something they only half understood.»

The author has been shaping the ambivalent and mostly negative portrait of a fascist, vain, materialistic and 'false' priest; right before the ending, don Gastone reveals himself to be a positive figure, embodying, despite all appearances, all the good, old Christian-Catholic values. Hence, don Gastone has the multilayered form of a double deceit, a Chinese box again: despite his cassock and his appearance of being a priest, he is not a real priest but a Don Giovanni, and behind the false appearances of a non-priest, he is a virtuous, charitable man. From the initial enframed and stereotypical premises, the handsome fascist priest ends up being formless, an unfinished, open and serpentine presence that causes and initiates the mute speech of the novel. His presence deforms what was the static space of a realist setting and turns it into a dynamic, animated, obscure castle reminiscent of early expressionist cinema and literature. Meaning and truth are finally lost and untraceable behind the screens and dark corners of this magical labyrinth. The only possible gaze on things is, then, a refracted, indirect seeing through keyholes and slightly open curtains. We have already seen in the previous chapter how gaze is distorted in both ways, from *subject* to *object* and vice versa: the fascist is also characterized by a double-vision, by the deformation of the real target through the superimposition of a false, illusory one (Marcello). The fascist cannot be seen precisely and, in turn, cannot see clearly.

Sandrino and don Gastone are both 'precise characters,' stereotypes and repetitions of the usual image of the fascist as dominated by abnormal violent and sexual impulses. At the beginning of their respective novels, they appear as precisely enframed within the lines of a highly geometric enclosed space. They are observed objects, and the author can look at them from an outside point of view, which is, as we have seen, the preliminary requisite for the production of the consummated, meaningful aesthetic form of a hero at the same time, the static space that enframes the static character, delays and impedes its perception from the outside, thus triggering the plot to take its shape. Like Shklovsky's *Don Quixote*, the fascist as enigma-stereotype is a narrative device, a static formal element that enables the author to tell the story. However, the fascist's aesthetic form as mystery also has another consequence: it simultaneously thwarts and blocks the possibility of an uncomplicated, teleological, realist narrative. The enigma 'excites imagination' and a multiplicity of other, contrasting narrative genres blurs and disrupts a linear, undisturbed aestheticization of the fascist, which, in turn, remains an ambivalent figure in between the minor, stereotypical role it usually has in melodramas and crime stories, and the possible role as the hero-protagonist of a realist plot. This position is usually occupied by the positive, good figures of partisans. The stereotype at this point is broken, and behind the appearances of a repetitive, usual caricature, the fascist becomes an open, dynamic object that avoids uncomplicated categorization and disrupts that very same emplotment and enframing that, by being an enigma; it triggered and 'excited.' The fascist loses its precise name and meaning—and turns into an unnamable entity, simultaneously exceeding the initial spatial limitation-closure and the narrative closure of a clear-cut, realist emplotment. The initial formal enigma becomes affect: the fascist cannot allow the creation of an aesthetic finished, consummated, closed form because it cannot be finally recognized as merely other by the author.

CHAPTER 4
The Excess of Demarcation.
The Fascist Character and the Disruption of the Profilmic Space.

«We are separated from yesterday not by a rift, but by the changed position.»
Alexander Kluge, *Yesterday Girl*

4.1 Daniela/Lili Marleen: *femme fatale* and collaborator in *Caccia tragica*

In the previous chapters, we observed how fascist characters resist narrative emplotment and closure and how they exceed the precise boundaries of a framed space, thus escaping any uncomplicated categorization and attribution of meaning. Marcello, Sandrino, Virginia and don Gastone complicate the distinction between hero and minor character, protagonist and villain, disrupting the author's attempt to portray them objectively. The author's realist gaze on the hero is somehow distorted by the impossibility of really recognizing and defining their nature as completely *other*. The Fascist is not merely an enemy, and the author's detachment from the object of their aesthetic activity is put in danger by this ambiguity: an unwelcomed identification drags the author inside the hero, erasing the distance necessary to frame events, things, and characters into an objective, linear, coherent narrative. The fascist is hidden behind a screened, opaque reality, and the author tries to peer through the enigma from outside to spy through the keyhole.

In this chapter, I am going to investigate further the author's gaze on fascist characters, and I will extend my analysis to films, that is to say, to the author-director's actual strategies of looking at the fascist and to the attempts at enclosing them into the neat, clear-cut frame of a shot. If those novels failed to emplot the fascists, these movies fail to frame them. The fascist character is a complex, problematic presence that disrupts the formal and structural limits of the film, turning the sequence and the profilmic space into a visual enigma: the object that the camera wants to capture, seize and include within the frame of the shot, exceeds these limits, multiplies itself, duplicates its meanings. The profilmic becomes a riddled surface.

The fascist, the ex-fascist, the traitor or the spy-collaborationist reveal the world in front of the camera to be multilayered, many-sided: a riddle that subtracts its object from the process of interpretation. The truth is unreachable, and to know the truth is an "open," circular process that, without points of reference, continuously comes back to its starting point. End and beginning coincide, opposite characters identify with one another, and roles that we thought definitively assigned are known to be negotiated between characters once perceived as contraries.

Therefore, this chapter works as a visual counterpart to an intermission between the previous and following analysis of literary texts, continuing the discourse started with *Il conformista* in Chapter 1. From *Caccia tragica* (De Santis, 1947) to *Strategia del ragno* (Bertolucci, 1970), I will trace how—although the general portrayal changes across time, genres, and authors—the fascist always remains a dynamic character who defies the uncomplicated belief that the 'civil war' ended with liberation from German occupation. Every fascist character we are going to meet is a reminder to the viewer that deep fractures and misunderstandings continue to exist and undermine any idyllic representation of national unity after 1945.

Maurizio Zinni, in his comprehensive study on the filmic representation of fascists—entitled *Fascisti di celluloide. La memoria del ventennio nel cinema italiano (1945-2000)*—describes the common attitude of Italian cinema towards fascism and its protagonists as a mixture of, on the one hand, an in-depth historiographical approach and, on the other hand, a stereotypical, popular portrayal:

> A pochi elementi di effettivo approfondimento storico si accompagnano stereotipi, pregiudizi consolidati, semplificazioni unanimemente accettate e superstizioni fobiche.[311]

---

311 Maurizio Zinni, *Fascisti di celluloide — la memoria del ventennio nel cinema italiano (1945-2000)* (Roma: Marsilio, 2010), 4.

According to Zinni, the image of the fascist is the result of shared prejudices and clichés; that is to say, the fascist character is a perfect example of a particular type, the stereotypical villain, a 'mask' easily and readily recognizable by an audience used to looking at the fascist in a certain, typical, accepted way. Once again, the fascist character is seen only as a static character whose form and role within the plot never changes and evolves. The stereotypical form of the fascist is interpreted by Zinni as the final result of Italian political life. Then, the type is seen as the sign of closure, of the sedimentation of a fixed form representing the fascist. The status and form of stereotype are not problematized. While following the evolution of the fascist 'type' through the different phases and upheavals of Italian political history, Zinni does not consider the 'type' as a dynamic character in continuous change and evolution within and during the single film. If the fascist usually appears and acts and is recognized as a certain 'type' of character, it does not mean that this form, or status, lasts and resists throughout the different phases of the work. The fact that the author tries to enframe the fascist within the easily recognizable, clear-cut limits of a stereotype hides, in reality, a far more complex relation between the author and the hero-character, which is the object of their work. The 'type' is only the result of a process of enframing-typification, which might either succeed or fail. Given the traumatic and difficult memory that the fascist character necessarily evokes—both in the author and the audience—the aesthetic process of signification and closure of the fascist in a consummated, uncomplicated form, is more complex than others and most of the time ends in a dynamic formlessness opposite to the initial, ready-made cliché.

I am going to start my analysis with a movie not present in the 150 films investigated by Zinni. *Caccia tragica* is set in Emilia in 1945. The war is over, but a group of bandits steals a purse full of money destined for an agriculture cooperative. During the robbery—filmed in the style of contemporary Hollywood westerns and gangster movies—something goes wrong, and they are forced to take a young girl named Giovanna as hostage. The four 'outlaws'—the war survivor Alberto, the ex-collaborationist Daniela, a German soldier and a southern thief—start a desperate escape, chased by the ex-partisan workers of the cooperative. Michele—Giovanna's husband and a former prisoner in the same concentration camp as Alberto—leads the 'hunt' together with Giuseppe, the ex-partisan who guided the punitive, vengeful reprisal against Daniela right after the Liberation. In a short preface to one version of the treatment, De Santis writes:

> Questo soggetto propone ed affronta, in forma di spettacolo popolare e drammatico, il problema più scottante del nostro dopoguerra: il problema dei reduci. [...]
> La crudezza dell'impostazione, se serve a sottolineare le reali, dolorose condizioni del nostro paese ed a dare un'immagine veristica e non ipocrita di tutta la nostra esistenza di oggi, costituisce lo sfondo ed il contrappunto di una vicenda morale che trova il suo sbocco in un anelito alla rigenerazione ed alla liberazione dal male. [...]
> La trama del soggetto è lineare ma al tempo stesso assai ricca di motivi spettacolari e drammatici. [...]
> In questa parabola di fatti e di personaggi, se figurano come elementi di disgregazione e di disfacimento i residui di un'età passata, si pone in primo piano, come fattore di rigenerazione e di riscatto l'unica grande ricchezza di cui tutti gli uomini ed in particolare oggi gli italiani hanno diritto: il LAVORO.[312]

The film proposes 'in an entertaining and dramatic form," a 'raw' and 'veristic' parable of regeneration and liberation from evil. It is already clear, even at the early stages of writing and production, that *Caccia tragica* will be a mixture of different, contrasting genres: melodramatic and novelistic events—those 'spectacular and dramatic motives'—take place against a naturalistic background directly inspired by local news and social reality. The character who, without doubt, embodies all those 'elements of disintegration and decay residual of a bygone era' is Daniela, the ex-collaborationist and spy of the Germans, now the true leader of the gang. The different versions of the story and the treatment all have interesting descriptions of her character, and the portrayal of her evil is, in a way, darker, stronger and more exaggerated than her final image in the movie:

---

312 Soggetto di Beppe De Santis e Carlo Lizzani. [file **N 057236** at the Biblioteca Chiarini in Rome]

> Ed infine una donna, Daniela ex ausiliaria repubblichina, di cui il reduce traviato è succube e vittima. Daniela è il tipo di donna delinquente che questo nostro dopoguerra ci presenta spesso nelle sue tragiche cronache: è la giovane che ha visto nel fascismo l'espressione di un modo di vivere avventuroso quanto amorale, e che sfoga ora, dopo la sconfitta, i suoi istinti romantici in una isterica ed anarchica ribellione alla Legge ed alla Società.[313]

Despite the fact that she is said to be directly copied from the frequent 'tragic news' of the time, Daniela is already depicted in stereotypical terms. Her supposedly realistic portrayal is deformed by the vocabulary of tragedy, melodrama and adventure. As Sandrino was the exact 'type' of the *repubblichino*, she embodies a precise 'type' of 'female' villain, a hysterical, instinctive, romantic criminal whose conduct imitates the amoral and adventurous way of life of fascism. Despite the fact that she is only a minor character, the prey-villain — the hero being he who hunts, the character played by the rising star of postwar Italian cinema Massimo Girotti — the authors of the story outline dedicate more space to her portrayal than to that of the hero. She is the only one to be exactly framed, from the beginning, in a precise, static role and definition, as if she needed to be more fixed squared than the others. Let us read her description from another, later draft of the treatment, and let us observe how her final portrait gradually takes shape, or, better, how it loses a form:

> Alberto vive sotto il fascino malefico di Daniela, con la quale ha rapporti d'amore fin da prima della guerra.
> Ambiziosa ed intellettualmente malata, benché di buona famiglia, essa si era legata, negli anni precedenti, alle organizzazioni politiche fasciste, ed aveva finito per combattere con fanatismo, nelle file delle ausiliarie della repubblica sociale. Dopo la sconfitta, Daniela, anziché seguire la via del riscatto, ha preferito affondare ancor più nella sua stessa rovina morale, e il sentimento che più la rode è l'invidia verso la felicità e serenità altrui.
> Tra Karl e Daniela si è stabilita durante gli anni di lontananza di Alberto un rapporto di natura sessuale.
> Karl è del parere di uccidere la ragazza catturata ma è Daniela ad opporsi: vuole tenerla in vita, gustare la sofferenza dell'altra, compiacersi della sua angoscia.[314]

---

313 Ibidem.
314 Ibidem.

Hence, Daniela is a sort of *femme fatale*, a woman whose 'evil charm' and amorality distract the other characters from the good path of salvation and redemption. Her obsessive desire corrupts Alberto, while her sick jealousy and envy towards Giovanna hide something more. She desires to be like her, and the only way she can actually be her is by making her suffer as she suffered during the war. She does not kill Giovanna because she wants to torture her, as she was tortured during a partisan reprisal. Because of her past of guilt and suffering, Daniela cannot have a normal life and cannot marry as Giovanna just did. As she screams in the movie, «Non potrei sposarmi anch'io? Che ho io? Sono diversa da te? Che ho io di diverso?» she will be forever different, living at the margins, excluded from the postwar normality. She wants to see, sadistically, Giovanna suffering because she wants us to see how it feels to live like her, i.e., stranded without hope and a future. She loves Alberto because she is not allowed to love someone like Michele, the 'good' man that only women like Giovanna could aspire to. Conceived as a stereotypical villain, Daniela—thanks to her devious desires—turns all the other characters—including the hero—into satellites, into minor figures whose place and meaning in the movie are defined only according to their passive relation with Daniela. Her role 'grows' from the subject to the final version of the screenplay—while the roles of the others get smaller—and her scenes will be all saved while the scenes depicting the cooperative's subplot will be mostly cut, often with the margin notes of weak or too long. Daniela is the character that entertains the viewer, and she is necessary to convey the social message to the viewer even though she is simultaneously the very enemy of that same message.

For reality to be seen, it needs to be distorted and estranged into an 'entertaining and dramatic' form. If the naturalistic scenes flow slowly – they are too long—Daniela accelerates the time of the story, turning it into a series of crises, moments of truth and collision, into the decisive crisis typical of tragedy: «Daniela che vive dell'attimo e si compiace dell'avventura e di tutto ciò che è sensazionale ed emozione morbosa.»[315]

---

315 Ibidem.

Romance, adventure and tragedy are the genres that will shape Daniela's character because—as we read above in the subject—those were the 'genres' of living intrinsic to fascism itself. The time of Romance, of the 'tragic hunt'—a time which favors the instant over the sequence—disrupts the teleology of the redemption narrative centered on the 'veristic' background of the cooperative: the past conflicts are still alive in the present. Daniela not only 'lives the moment' but also diverts the present back to the unwelcomed memory of a traumatic past of reprisals and fratricidal conflicts.

The first sequence of the film shows the truck on its way to the cooperative. The two men in the front seats are in charge of the money, while, in the rear, they are also carrying Giovanna and Michele, who just married that same morning. Suddenly—interrupting the merry atmosphere of the truck—the drivers notice an ambulance stuck ahead in the middle of the street, blocking their way: the robbery has begun. This scene is mainly important for two details regarding Daniela, or, better, Lili Marleen. In fact, from the beginning, she appears as an enigma, avoiding the direct gaze of the camera. Her actual presence on the scene is anticipated by two indirect images. First, right before the driver sees the ambulance and has to stop the truck, we notice in the top left corner of the windscreen the face of a woman with a hat and dark sunglasses.

Fig. 1—De Santis, *Caccia tragica* (1947).

At this early point of the movie, we viewers cannot know who Lili Marleen is and, more importantly, what she would look like. Only the second-time viewer can retrospectively recognize who she is. This means that Lili Marleen can be looked at from two contrasting perspectives: one that proceeds along with the story and coincides with it, and one that looks at her only after the story has occurred, in retrospect. This mysterious picture anticipates what is going to happen: Lili Marleen is already there without actually being there, her presence being foreseen by the photo. As an allusion, the fascist character perverts the temporal order of the film and exceeds its spatial limits: she literally is in between, on the threshold surface of the windscreen, neither outside nor inside, in between inclusion and exclusion. The rectangular frame of the windscreen encloses nothing but her fictional reproduction, Lili Marleen: the actual en-framing of the real character, Daniela-Lili, will be, as we will see a much/very complex operation.

During the robbery, we do not see Lili Marleen, except, once again, only indirectly: the dark silhouette of a woman appears through the opaque side window of the ambulance.

Fig. 2 — De Santis, *Caccia tragica* (1947).

The red cross painted on the back and on the side of the ambulance is a sort of viewfinder that misses twice its target. Lili Marleen gradually materializes on the scene, now passing from being a photo to being a shadow. She turns the space of the frame into a mysterious, undecipherable image that anticipates a future yet to be known for the viewer at the moment of seeing it, and, on the contrary, recognizable by the viewer *a posteriori* exactly thanks to that knowledge of future events. Doubly observed and doubly framed: enframed in the wider limits of the shot and within the profilmic frame of the window. At the beginning of the film, her role and meaning are fixed and enclosed within the static characteristics of an exact 'type of woman.' However, it is a mere illusion because what they capture is, upon closer observation, only indirect simulacra: a photo and a dark profile.

There is a scene, in particular, which shows how Daniela-Lili Marleen disrupts the temporal structure and the spatial limits of the film. The gang has to load on the ambulance an injured worker who stepped on a minefield. While he is lying on the gurney, cutting the bottom half of the frame horizontally — Daniela is sitting next to him in front of his left side, facing us viewers — he starts to rant and rave about Germans coming, and, when he sees Daniela, he begins, first, to scream *infermiera!* and later, the name of Lucia clearly mistaking her for a nurse and his, probably dead, wife. With the injured body also, the past has entered the ambulance, materializing — in an emotional crescendo conveyed by the score and by accelerated editing — in front of Lili Marleen, her past of guilt, pain and vengeance. Karl, the German criminal of the gang, begins to whistle the song, *Lili Marleen*, underscoring the gradual climax of the hallucination until when, almost in a burst of fear, the wounded man grabs the woman's hair. In an attempt to take his hands off her head, Daniela loosens her blonde wig, revealing a brown, half-shaved head.

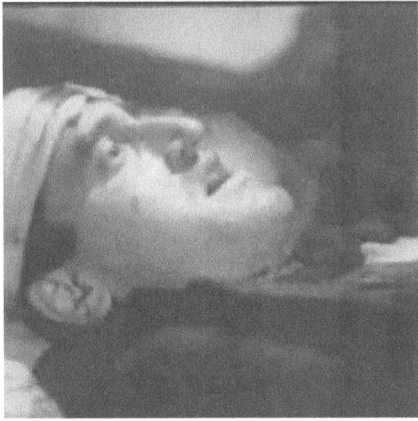

Fig. 3 — De Santis, *Caccia tragica* (1947).

The entire sequence is a continuous crossing and blurring of boundaries. The injured reliving a past trauma triggers Daniela's memory, who now literally lives suspended between past and present, her identity multiplying: she is the nurse, Lucia, Daniela and Lili Marleen at the same time. She simultaneously is the object of the other's hallucinated memory and the subject of her own, the scene being an intersection between these two opposing points of view: she is looked directly from the past — where the wounded man thinks he is — and she looks into her past.

Throughout the sequence, Daniela dominates the *other*, the injured man, from above. The fiction of the disguise — they are in an ambulance, after all — would assign to them, respectively, the roles of doctor and patient. The dreamlike ranting of the injured, though, disrupts the clear-cut demarcation between identities, between their past and present, fictional and actual shapes. In fact, during the war, she was the enemy of the ex-partisan here suffering in front of her, and now she appears as his torturer. We are witnessing, then, the reenactment of an old conflict: the traitor and the betrayed face-to-face. The hand surging from below symbolizes the crossing of the past beyond the limit of the present, the excess being activated when the injured half-sees Daniela in the ambulance. They are both dragged into an 'inverted' reality, to a time when he was the victim, and she was the executioner. Soon, though, the crosscutting dream vanishes. When the wig-mask is removed, the real roles of winner and loser are reestablished, triggering the hysterical reaction of Daniela, who brutally pushes away the gurney, with the injured man, off the van. The half-shaved head now reveals Daniela as the victim, her past of suffering, punishment and humiliation, which continuously undermines her current outer image of power, security and threat as a criminal leader.

The four outlaws find refuge in an old chalet. Here, Alberto and Daniela have time to find some rest, and once alone in a bedroom full of dolls, the two will be the protagonists of a scene that is the exact reenactment of the same trauma we saw recalled in the ambulance earlier. The point of view, though, is, once again, shifted. Many details connect the two scenes. First, the disposition of the bodies within the profilmic space; second, the *Lili Marleen* song, back then whistled by the German, now broadcast on the radio; third, the fact that Daniela is without her wig, suggesting that this scene is the continuation, and inversion, of the previous one.

Now Daniela is the one lying down, cutting the frame diagonally. She is about to vividly recall the night of the ex-partisan reprisal, when a group of *partigiani*, once the war was already over, broke into her house and shaved her head as vengeance as a punishment for her collaboration with the Nazis. She now occupies the position that the wounded ex-partisan previously had in the ambulance. If, in the former scene, she was the torturer, now she is the victim: she looks back at the same memory from an opposite, reversed point of view. By reliving the past trauma, she activates, once again, the same crossing of boundaries and redoubling of identities: the distinction between memory and present vacillates, and, in the same fashion, the difference between victim and torturer, hero and villain, subject and object is put into question, the two roles being dragged into a continuous vortex of exchange.

Moreover, the intertwining of boundaries, the redoubling of identities and the mixing-up of roles are underlined and suggested by the profilmic space itself. In fact, some details of the background wall—a woman's face, a devil's face on the poster of the vermouth "Pini"—are put into a mute dialogue with the characters and are used by De Santis to signify and make even more explicit the multiple overruns that are taking place. The scene, in fact, is a veritable, perfect visual chiasmus.

Fig. 4—De Santis, *Caccia tragica* (1947).

At first, Daniela's face covers and eclipses the woman's image behind her on the wall, while, on the top left of the frame, just above Alberto's head, a devil drinking a glass of vermouth is plainly visible. Then, in the movement that will lead her to lie down on Alberto's lap, she slightly bows, revealing a woman's face right above her own, perfectly aligned with the devil on the left. Now the four heads form a perfect cross: on the top left the devil, on the top right the woman, on the bottom right Daniela and the bottom left Alberto.

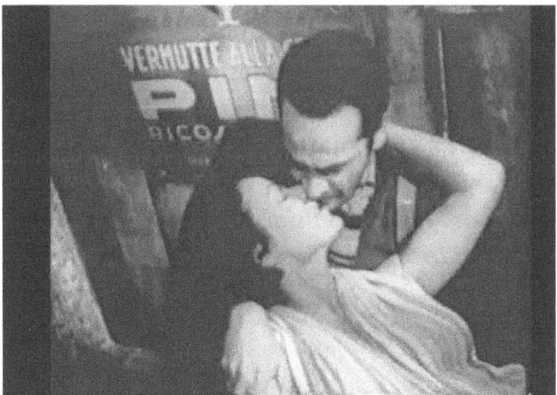

Fig. 5 – De Santis, *Caccia tragica* (1947).

The pairing has a striking meaning. As Daniela gradually lowers herself down in the recollection of the trauma, her face redoubles, signifying the splitting of past and present and, simultaneously, of her personality: the night she became Lili Marleen. Better, her face triplicates because the vertical doubling corresponds to the diagonal one with the devil's face: the gradual descent into memory means declining back towards an evil past of war and conflict and, most of all, towards the roots of her evil.

The ex-collaborationist and spy Daniela cannot be enframed and fixed into a static character with a precise, recognizable identity. The scene reveals her as a formless figure beyond any clear-cut, uncomplicated definition and role. The recollection of the past — of her private trauma and the collective one of civil war — revives an unnamable emotion, a memory of affect that disrupts and confuses easy categorizations, divisions and her very physical collocation in the profilmic space: the victim and the torturer coincide as an unwelcomed and unresolved past overruns the present illusory order of things.

This second scene repeats the same motives of the first outbreak of affect in the ambulance, only from inverted perspectives and with a twisted disposition of the characters: the past breaks in the temporal limits of the present and the extremes are shown to superimpose, and Daniela is revealed, literally, as a multifaced character.

Despite her presumed identity as a certain 'tragic type of woman,' directly known from the local news, Daniela-Lili Marleen exceeds boundaries and definitions and resists the director's gaze to enframe her in the consummated form of a villain. She is a dynamic, carnivalesque identity that sabotages any attempt to distinguish a good "we" of victors from a "them" of evil enemies, as everyone is revealed to wear a mask, simultaneously being also their opposite.

Fig. 6 – De Santis, *Caccia tragica* (1947).

The 'tragic carnival' and chaos that followed September 8th, 1943, did not end with the conclusion of the conflict: it continues to unmask roles and distinctions as relative fictions: «evviva il Carnevale!» — as shouted by Alberto's little brothers and sisters — sounds as a real warning to the ex-partisans Michele and Giuseppe who are convinced they are chasing their enemies, evil *others*.

4.2 Pinin the Spy: the Fascist Character and Reality Effect in *Il Cristo proibito*

In 1951, Curzio Malaparte — inspired by the directorial debut of André Malraux — wrote and directed his first and only film, *Il Cristo proibito*. Like *Caccia tragica*, the story is set in a rural community and takes place right after the war. A soldier comes back to his hometown, where, during his absence, his brother has been killed: a fellow partisan betrayed him, selling him to the Nazis. The portrayal of postwar Italy is not an idyllic fiction of untroubled unity and national cohesion set against a foreign enemy. The village where Bruno returns continues to be stirred by old, fratricidal conflicts and unfinished plots of revenge.

Moreover, reality appears to Bruno as a riddle, the assassination of his brother being an enigma that the entire village prevents him from solving in order to protect a precarious peace among its inhabitants. Even his mother and his ex-girlfriend — who, moreover, confesses to him she had an affair with his brother — hide from him the name of the assassin, of the traitor. Once again, a film mostly about the silenced civil war and fracture among Italians starts with a protagonist who finds between himself and the truth to which he aspires, the screen of an enigma, of a secret to be solved. The realist depiction of postwar Italy has, then, the shape of a melodramatic plot, with undertones typical, again, of the *roman à clef*, while *Caccia tragica* was mainly a Western or gangster film.

The fascist traitor-spy is unnamable, embodying, once again, affect, an unknowable truth that risks disrupting reality and the new order of things. The profilmic space of the village protects the spy — the town is curiously covered by posters of *Lancer spy*, a Hollywood movie with Peter Lorre and George Saunders from 1937, an intertextual reference that needs further investigation — transforming its surface into a mystery, triggering a 'genre' plot of melodramatic inquiry and vengeance. The traitor is, only apparently, enframed and literally emplotted too, in this case, as the object, the end, of a linear non-realist plot. Subject and object, hero and antagonist, are roles clearly assigned to Bruno and to a mysterious villain whose past guilt Bruno desires to unearth and resuscitate. There is a scene, though, that reveals how, as in *Caccia tragica*, the asymmetrical, opposite identities of subject and object, traitor and savior, villain and hero, conflate with one another, thus removing those static boundaries that made possible their uncomplicated naming and categorization. Seizing and enframing the collaborationist villain is more complicated than it might seem at first look.

It is the first night that Bruno is back, and the camera objectively follows him while he wanders across the 'regained' village. The scene does not have, apparently, any importance for the progression of the plot, appearing more as a 'veristic' portrayal of the ending of a working day in the rural community. It depicts, then, a contingent, unnecessary moment. This sequence appears as the classic realist filming of a *tranche de vie*, an avoidable moment of Bruno's first night in town, an excuse to show how a quiet evening in the village's streets looks. At one point, though, Bruno crosses on his way a stranger: an unknown man appears on the opposite end of the street, strolling towards him with two dogs beside him.

Fig. 7 — Malaparte, *Il Cristo proibito* (1951).

The profilmic space is, at the beginning of the sequence, very symmetrical: everything has a precise, fixed position within the limits of the frame. The four street lamps stretch the focus of the shot in all four directions: in-depth, at the center, in the foreground and on the right of the street. The viewers' attention is directed toward the entire surface of the screen then, and the four focal points signal the four positions that the characters will momentarily occupy in the temporal development of the sequence. Lighting is also meaningful: Bruno enters the frame as a silhouette, a shadow, while the stranger appears fully visible, well-lit at the center of the 'stage.'
Right before the two figures are about to pass in front of each other, that is to say, to cross their paths, Malaparte inserts an apparently meaningless detail: a cyclist enters the frame from below and steps in between them at the exact moment when the two were about to be face to face.

Fig. 8 – Malaparte, *Il Cristo proibito* (1951)

At first sight, the cyclist might appear like a stranger strolling with *two* dogs, as a realist detail added only to represent a 'typical' *tranche de vie*. He says hello to Bruno and disappears; nothing decisive for the future development of the story seems to happen. Bruno and the stranger, too – they did not say hello to each other, which is strange in a small town where notoriously everyone knows everyone – will exit the frame soon. The first to disappear is, curiously, Bruno; he takes the cross street on the right and leaves. The second is the stranger with his two dogs, who exits our gaze from the bottom side of the frame. Malaparte cuts the scene slightly too late when Bruno, the protagonist, has already left the frame a few seconds earlier. Thus, the sequence has an exceptional duration, a realist technique – typical of neorealism – usually used to include contingency and unnecessary details other than the actual object of the film – the hero, Bruno, in this case – in order to enframe the widest possible segment of the real.

If so, the cyclist and the unnecessary duration of the scene, which lasts beyond the actual presence of the protagonist, are, then, perfect examples of what Barthes defines as *l'effet de réel*: details that do not signify anything in particular – they do not have a precise referent in the real – and for this reason are perceived as reality themselves.

Fig. 9 — Malaparte, *Il Cristo proibito* (1951)

Nevertheless, despite its apparently 'naturalistic' value, the scene hides much more, and it contains in itself the entire future *dénouement* of the movie. The stranger whom Bruno is crossing without recognizing and greeting is, in fact, the spy he is looking for, Pinin, the traitor that denounced his brother to the Nazis. The scene, then, acquires a whole other importance and meaning: the two details of the cyclist and the excessive duration do not make the scene more realistic, but, on the contrary, they convey *enigma* and mystery. They both turn the profilmic space into a *riddled* surface that hides from the viewer's gaze, and Bruno's as well, the ultimate meaning and solution of the story. At the end of the plot, the truth Bruno will try to discover is already there in front of his and our eyes from the beginning.

The cyclist, by stepping between them at the right time and place, sabotages a recognition that would have made the rest of the film useless. The spy, Pinin, recognizes Bruno and stops for a second. Nevertheless, only an attentive spectator would notice it because there is the cyclist who, by passing between them, distracts both Bruno and the viewer, hiding with his presence Pinin from Bruno's sight and Pinin's act of recognition from our gaze. What looks like a realist detail is, in reality, an instrument of mystification placed by the director there, in between the two extremes, in order to separate them in order to avoid recognition, delay closure, and the detection of the plot. Thanks to that cyclist, the film gains its time and the duration of its plot.

Like the two scenes in *Caccia tragica*, this sequence is a visual chiasmus exemplifying how the presence of the ex-fascist turns the profilmic space, first, into a riddled surface, second, into a mutual crossing of boundaries, third, into an inversion of roles, fourth, into duplication and confusion of identities. The director's gaze, which, at first sight, perfectly succeeded in framing the villain into a realist, unproblematic and purely decorative shot, in reality, fails, being the enframing thwarted and disrupted by the formless, dynamic character of the spy, traitor, villain. He disrupts the profilmic space with his duplicity, perhaps indirectly alluded to also by the two dogs that walk on his sides.

Fig. 10 — Malaparte, *Il Cristo proibito* (1951).

At the end of the scene, the hero and minor character have exchanged their positions within the frame: the shadow in the foreground is now Pinin, the spy. The villain stands where the protagonist is, and the two have inverted their roles. Pinin is, then, the true hero of this scene, its main character, now appearing as a mysterious, dark silhouette. The spy turns this scene into an enigma because the viewer does not yet possess the means and the information necessary to solve it. From our point of view, nothing is happening, we cannot notice the missed recognition because we do not know yet who Pinin is. Like the photo on the windscreen in *Caccia tragica*, the fascist character appears prematurely, anticipates, unseen, an unrecognizable, formless identity, his actual materialization in the film. Time and space are perverted by a character which, as the scene suggests, merges with its opposite, with the hero and protagonist of the film. Pinin breaks the symmetrical frame of the profilmic space, exceeding and crossing the boundaries that keep distanced and differentiated villain and hero, traitor and good soldier. The mystery plot perverts realism. The enigma cannot be solved too soon and the cyclist has to sabotage and delay a recognition that would have happened before time. It is a *leurre* similar to the one we observed in *Il conformista*: Moravia makes us believe, despite all evidence, that Lino did not die after all, so the author keeps for himself a decisive piece of information that, if shared with the audience, would have brought the plot to its premature ending. In order for the story to keep, to preserve its linear shape or its spatial symmetry, the fascist character has to be outside of its limits, in between exclusion and inclusion. Like Pinin, a shadow without a name: he is present in the frame, but at the same time, he is hidden behind a riddled surface because we, viewers and Bruno cannot possibly recognize who he is. His presence can be conveyed only through a visual enigma, through his absence, which, nevertheless, already menaces the structure of the scene with a certain formlessness. When s\he is enframed in the shot, roles are inverted; identities are merged, and profilmic space and duration of the scene are deformed. The villain literally steals the scene from the hero, resisting the author's attempt to enframe them in a consummated, precise form.

Bruno will find out the truth, the real identity of the spy, too late, after he has already killed the wrong, innocent person. Once again, the fascist character activates an exchange of identity, a 'carnivalesque' misunderstanding and *quid pro quo*. Xavier Tilliette, in one of the few positive reviews of the film, describes it as «episodio della Resistenza, *equivoco* della colpevolezza.»[316] Through a reversal of Vittorini's definition of the Fascist years as a *malinteso*, I think Tilliette is right in considering the Resistance as the central theme

---

316 Xavier Tilliette, "Il Cristo di Malaparte," *Filmcritica*, n.18, (Nov, 1952): 170.

of the movie, despite the fact that it appears only as past, on the background, as the memory of a crime whose solution everyone knows, but that, at the same time, everyone covers. The film is aware that the postwar myth of the Resistance—around which the unproblematic image of a united nation was created—is founded on silence and oblivion, skating over a memory of the fratricidal conflict.

4.3 The Death of Tarcisio: *Era notte a Roma* as nemesis of *Roma città aperta*

During the fifties, the commercial industry steered away from the period almost entirely, with the exception of *Gli sbandati* (1955), directed by Francesco Maselli, from a story written by Eriprando Visconti, and a few other exceptions, consistently reducing the production of movies dealing with the difficult memories of war and civil war. In 1959 the situation changed, and cinemas were literally filled with films such as *Il Generale della Rovere* (Roberto Rossellini, 1959), *Era notte a Roma* (Rossellini, 1960), *La lunga notte del '43* (Florestano Vancini, 1960), *Tiro al piccione* (Giuliano Montaldo, 1961), *Il federale* (Luciano Salce, 1961), *Gli anni ruggenti* (Luigi Zampa, 1962), *All'armi siam fascisti* (Lino del Fra, Cecilia Mangini, Lino Miccichè, 1962) and *Il processo di Verona* (Carlo Lizzani, 1963). A decisive event that may have changed the trend might have been the passing of a new law in 1960, which extended to the Resistance and the War of Liberation, the teaching of history during the last year of high school. Films with this topic acquired, then, a new audience, a new pedagogic meaning and value. War and the experience of fascism were now part of history, ready to be turned into material objects of historical narratives. Maurizio Zinni rightly traces the cause of this revival back to the 1960 protests against the attempt to create a right-wing government guided by Tambroni:

> Nel 1960 la sconfitta del tentativo di realizzare un governo di centro-destra sostenuto dai voti del Msi a seguito di un governo di imponenti manifestazioni di piazza aprì la strada non solo alla creazione del primo esperimento di centro-sinistra sotto la guida di Fanfani nel 1962 (l'appoggio del Psi è ancora esterno), ma, ad un livello più simbolico, testimoniò come i valori della

Resistenza e dell'antifascismo, che erano stati alla base della nascente democrazia italiana, fossero ancora fortemente radicati nella popolazione.[317]

Era notte a Roma was conceived and immediately perceived as the reversal of *Roma città aperta*. Critics of the time mainly reproached Rossellini for having chosen a 'Catholic' production company owned by Cardinal Siri and by the Jesuit priest Arpa, which imposed a reduction of the role played by the communist fraction of the Resistance.[318] The communists, in fact, disappeared while they were represented by the engineer Manfredi in *Roma città aperta*. The movie was considered to be flawed also in its novelistic structure: «finisce con lo sfiorare e con l'attingere al "romanzesco" (e un "brutto" romanzesco.)»[319] Mino Argentieri too, in his review, writes about «un esemplare annegato in una costruzione a incastro, degno di un modello hollywoodiano perfettamente imitato.»[320] Compared to the higher realism and the stricter faith in documentary sources and memoirs of *Roma città aperta*, the last Rossellini is now guilty of deforming history through the lens of melodrama by enframing its story into the «intelaiatura di un romanzo cinematografico gremito di trabocchetti e di insufficienze narrative.»[321]

As my analysis of *Caccia tragica* and *Il Cristo proibito* has shown, the problematic memory of fascism was already challenging the realist vocation of cinema in those early postwar years. Neorealism appears as a coexistence of different genres, melodramatic characteristics mixing up with expressionist qualities and tragic overtones. The common trait is, once again, the presence of the in-between figure of the fascist traitor, of the ex-collaborationist or spy who, also in *Era notte a Roma*, enables a similar deformation of the profilmic space, of the temporal sequence and the same confusion-inversion of roles and identities. In this film, Rossellini tries to enframe two ambiguous characters: a minor one – the collaborationist Tarcisio – and a main one – the half-traitor Esperia. Another

---

317 Maurizio Zinni, "Uomini in nero: il Fascismo nel cinema italiano (1945-1962)" in *Cinema a passo romano* (Napoli: Liguori, 2012), 310.
318 L.p, "Era notte a Roma," *Cinema Nuovo*, n.149, (Jan-Feb, 1961): 56.
319 Ibidem.
320 Argentieri, Mino, "La notte di Rossellini," *Cinema 60*, n.3, (Set, 1960): 14.
321 Idem, 15.

constant is the absence of a real hero, their role being shared by various minor characters, among which, thanks to their melodramatic resonance, the two 'villains' outshine.

Brunello Rondi, one of the writers of the film, defines *Era notte a Roma* as a mystery, an abstraction of history.[322] Furthermore, literally, a true enigma will be staged in the scene that reveals Tarcisio's evil: when he unmasks – in a church and front of fascist authorities – a few partisans disguised as monks. All monks should know Latin, theology and metaphysics, and so Tarcisio, who is brought there because he knows Latin – he is, after all a defrocked priest – asks them two questions: first, «chi ha detto *quid autem amo cum te amo*?» quoting a sentence from Augustine's *Confessions*, second, «l'intelletto attivo fa parte dell'anima?» referring to a famous medieval debate about the immortality of the soul. Obviously, the partisans do not know the answers, and they are imprisoned. This sequence, I believe, is more problematic than it might seem at first because the way the partisans are caught reveals divisions still active among the partisan bloc fifteen years later. The Italian contemporary political situation is projected onto the past, where its roots can be traced. Then, it is not a mere Romanesque device that they are captured because they lack religious faith because of their unbelief in the immortality of the soul. Rossellini is looking back at the Resistance from the point of view of postwar fractures between communists and Catholics. The scene of their arrest does not only stimulate the usual empathy for the good heroes of the story, but it simultaneously looks at them with a critical, more aware eye, undermining the myth of an unproblematic, idyllic compactness of the victors. The enigma is, once again, a device that sabotages a linear, untroubled narrative, turning it into a more complex, problematic and dialectical form.

Tarcisio is «raffigurato *grottescamente* a somiglianza del Maligno, zoppo, butterato, lascivo…»[323] embodying the «bieca e *melodrammatica* figura dello spretato zoppo (o come taluni

---

322 Brunello Rondi, "Era notte a Roma," *Flimcritica*, n.95, (Mar, 1960): 23.
323 L.p, "Era notte a Roma" in *Cinema Nuovo*, n.149, (Jan-Feb, 1961): 56.

maliziosamente insinuano, dal piede forcuto.»³²⁴ Tarcisio, then, conforms to the usual stereotype of the fascist character, lascivious, physically and morally deformed; moreover, he is a defrocked priest like Lino in *The Conformist*. Maurizio Zinni, too, describes him, again, as a mere stereotype:

> La sua figura infatti si eleva dal piatto anonimato riservato ai fascisti in *Roma città aperta* solo per cadere nettamente nella caricatura di un personaggio assolutamente stereotipato in senso negativo. Tarcisio è uno spretato, con una malformazione congenita che lo rende zoppo, un individuo che raduna in sé tutte le caratteristiche del cattivo dei film di genere: è subdolo, è un delatore che tradisce anche i suoi stessi conoscenti e la cui malvagità si specchia in un viso tagliente e butterato, che ispira diffidenza. È fascista, più che per convinzione propria, per un disperato senso di rivalsa contro la vita e contro quanti, a differenza di lui, non vivono la loro esistenza come una colpa.³²⁵

In my opinion, Tarcisio enables the same disruption, formlessness and crossing of boundaries as Daniela and Pinin. He is a melodramatic and grotesque 'type' who will, nevertheless, subvert, with its carnivalesque dynamism, the spatial and temporal order of the film, together with the role and the meaning—and their position within the profilmic space—of the other characters. Zinni, on the contrary, sees in his stereotypical form a device that facilitates removal and oblivion by the spectator. Tarcisio is the sign that Rossellini wanted to consider fascism as a disease to expel and cure:

> Con la sua morte atroce l'autore sembra sancire definitivamente la scomparsa di una malattia che si era insediata nel paese ma che non aveva intaccato nelle fondamenta il suo spirito di resistenza e il senso di giustizia.³²⁶

According to Zinni, then, the sequence of his death is an expulsion of Tarcisio as the personification of evil, as the true scapegoat of Italian society.

Nevertheless, I think that this sequence shows, on the contrary, the very impossibility of enframing Tarcisio as someone who needs to be expelled and removed from memory. His death and disappearance from the scene are far from being a resolution and a closure. The scene is, rather, an opening. Tarcisio's character

---

324 Argentieri, "La notte di Rossellini," 15.
325 Zinni, *Fascisti di celluloide*, 110.
326 Idem, 111.

activates a similar formal disruption of space and mixing of roles as Daniela and Pinin did in the two previous scenes I analyzed from *Caccia tragica* and *Il Cristo proibito*. Let us look at the scene more closely.

The 'moment of truth' is set in Esperia's desolate apartment after Renato, her boyfriend, has been shot dead by the Germans. In a desperate attempt to save Renato, she denounced Pemberton and the American soldier to the Germans. Tarcisio tries to convince her to escape with him to Spain by saying that he, too, has tried to 'save' Renato, always dissuading him from joining the Resistance. However, as soon as he mentions the name of Renato, Esperia throws a pot of boiling water at his face, and Pemberton can easily strangle the now even-blinded Tarcisio in the next room. Esperia's unexpected, exaggerated outburst of violence is caused not only by her desire for revenge, but also by her sense of guilt, by her awareness of having betrayed Pemberton. She recognizes herself in Tarcisio; she is, after all, a spy like him.

Fig. 11 – Rossellini, *Era notte a Roma* (1960).

It is after his death, though — after he is actually excluded from the limits of the frame — that the body of Tarcisio, hidden behind a wall, activates that same crossing of boundaries and mixture of identities we have observed in the two other movies.

Fig. 12 — Rossellini, *Era notte a Roma* (1960).

Pemberton strangles Tarcisio off-screen while the frame is entirely occupied by a close-up of Esperia, and the atrocity of the 'reprisal' is only indirectly alluded to through her facial expressions. Now she understands that she is sharing with Pemberton the guilt of this crime and with Tarcisio the guilt of betrayal. The scene — with the help of a 'ghostly' score — conveys a highly problematic and 'unwelcome' meaning, and Rossellini fails to enframe its actual object: Tarcisio's body, which is present only as an absence. The dead body of the traitor, in fact, is the material, vivid testimony of truth and reality different from the official one, the crime unveiling a sharing of guilt and evil in everyone, even the supposedly good heroes of the story. This testimony of an unwelcome, traumatic truth disrupts any possibility of an unproblematic categorization of good and evil, heroes and villains, victims and perpetrators. The death of the villain thwarts the possibility of naming the hero of the story exactly, turning basically everyone into a multifaceted character resisting a clear-cut classification. The melodramatic 'type' of Tarcisio ends up being the one disrupting the Manichean uncomplicated categorization of good and evil, which, as we have seen in the first chapter, is one of the formal *clichés* of melodrama. What seemed to be a mere static character and narrative device to trigger a certain genre of plot now reveals itself to be a dynamic entity that puts everything in flux and the opposites in dialectic relation.

While lying off-screen in the other room, the dead body starts to redispose the bodies of the living, disarranging their positions in the profilmic space. Pemberton and Esperia start a 'chiasmic' dance around the chair previously occupied by Tarcisio, drawing an X and a circle within the frame. Tarcisio, the antagonist, a minor character, becomes now the subject, the true focus of the scene. It is precisely his absent body that is the only point of reference in this sequence, the axis of the profilmic space, according to which the others have to redispose in a circular, looping move which confuses their identities: they are now both guilty and their guilt paradoxically, retrospectively turns Tarcisio, their persecutor, into a victim. Identities and roles merge in a formlessness that thwarts interpretation and a precise assignation of meaning. Pemberton and Esperia appear alternatively in focus, revealing, in addition to the continuous crossing of their bodies, Rossellini's difficulty in framing characters in absolute definitions and fixed positions.

The linear eye of the camera is ignored, as Esperia is looking awry. Only at the end the linear gaze of the camera is recognized and acknowledged when Pemberton looks straight at us viewers through a close-up of his face. The gaze of the hero becomes aware of the gaze of the author, dragging it inside the scene: Rossellini loses his outside, transcendent point of view, and the frame, the form, loses its closure. In fact, the limits of the frame suddenly break, and through a cross dissolve, Pemberton's close-up overlaps with the next shot, a scene capturing the Nazis leaving Rome before the triumphal arrival of the allied forces. The presence of the enemy — of the other, the Nazis this time — again disrupts the image, literally tears it apart, the next scene overflowing the previous one from behind, which is anticipating its supposed time and accelerating the order of succession.

 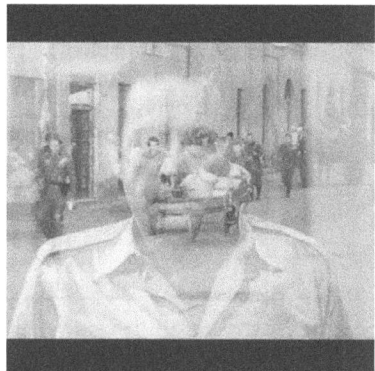

Fig. 13 — Rossellini, *Era notte a Roma* (1960)

In his fundamental article, *"L'antifascismo nel cinema italiano presente,"* Italian film theorist Gianni Rondolino does not even mention *Era notte a Roma*. In the long survey of movies about the Resistance and fascism, Rossellini is present only for his *Il generale della Rovere*, and the judgment is not positive. As a matter of fact, Rondolino reproaches the entire 'second wave' of so-called 'antifascist' cinema for being too Romanesque and overdramatizing historical events, while *Roma città aperta* and its contemporaries were closer to a documentary, objective rendition of facts. Postwar Italian neorealism is, then, idealized and seen as a sort of pure, truer first-hand representation of history, while basically everything that came after is considered as a deterioration from that supposedly honest and perfect form: «ma la prospettiva storica che distanziava gli anni di guerra impediva un contatto con la realtà secondo gli schemi neorealistici.»[327]

According to Rondolino, the reason was to be found in the longer distance from the war, from years that could not be seen anymore through the direct gaze of those who lived them. Thus, time opens up the space for historical narratives that typify events and characters:

> La resistenza non poteva più, per ovvie ragioni, *essere vista con gli occhi di coloro che la fecero nel momento in cui la fecero*: occorreva rappresentarla nel

---

[327] Rondolino, Gianni, "L'antifascismo nel cinema italiano recente", *Il nuovo spettatore cinematografico*, n.4, ago 1963, p. 8.

> suo svolgimento storico, secondo un'interpretazione dei fatti che solo lo storico, a distanza di tempo, può dare. Così fatti e personaggi, veri o falsi non importa, dovevano essere inseriti in una struttura narrativa che ne mettesse in rilievo il grado di tipicità nella situazione rappresentata, e tutto il discorso drammatico doveva confluire in una chiara e ordinata spiegazione di accadimenti.[emphasis mine][328]

Over time, historical accounts of the war deform into types and emblematic episodes of those same objects that neorealism represented directly. As I have demonstrated earlier on in my study, Romanesque, melodramatic, and mystery elements were already active in texts and films considered neorealist at the time, elements which were exactly enabled by the presence of fascist characters. Those kinds of figures were only apparently types—stereotypical representations of villains—being, in reality, charged with the disarranging and disrupting effect of trauma: the memory of still unresolved fratricidal conflicts and of guilt to be shared.

Romance, melodrama, and adventure are all ascribed by Rondolino to a cinema that uses history as a means to commercial success and as an escape from reality. These genres are forms of entertainment and nothing more, not worth being analyzed. In my opinion, as we have seen, they need to be seen as symptoms of a reaction imposed on the authors by the material itself of their aesthetic forms. On the contrary, Rondolino—and with him Italian film historians in general—see in the 'genre' an inevitable deformation of the real and not a process, a practice which can tell much more about the relationship between author and the material they are trying to enframe into a consummated aesthetic form. Then, in the 'antifascist' movies of the early sixties, war and fascism are narrated in the same way as other historical epochs, and the Nazi or the fascist is only one more embodiment of a 'type' of villain that always repeats itself, unchanged, in the course of history:

> Non molto diversamente che per altre epoche storiche, come il nostro risorgimento o l'antichità greca e romana (dove per altro il campo offerto alla fantasia e all'invenzione è molto più ampio), anche il fascismo e la resistenza sono entrati a far parte del repertorio del nostro cinema. Avventure d'amore e di morte, forti contrasti ideali, personaggi sanguigni, eroismi e basse

---

328 Ibidem pp. 9-10.

azioni, un tempo ottimo materiale da utilizzare sullo sfondo di epoche passate, sono oggi ambientati negli anni della guerra. [...] La vicinanza cronologica con gli avvenimenti descritti richiede questa maggiore esattezza storica e di costume; ma la sostanza del racconto non cambia: il contenuto è applicabile indifferentemente a ogni epoca. [...] Dato per scontato che in questi film il nemico è il tedesco, e non il Borbone o il francese, o, nel migliore dei casi, il fascista, e l'eroe è invece il partigiano o il popolo tutto, mi domando quale valore di critica del fascismo e del nazismo possa avere una vicenda che non molto si diversifica, se non per l'epoca storica e i personaggi, da qualsiasi altra vicenda della storia rivissuta in termini generali.[329]

Rondolino conceives the villain as a static narrative device and not as a formless, 'carnivalesque' and dynamic character who challenges and menaces the central, prominent position of the hero, then simultaneously disrupting the entire formal organization of the tale. He is basically considering fascist Italy as being like ancient Rome, paradoxically repeating in his criticism the basic comparison of fascist idealism and propaganda. The representation of an event can be mythical and dramatic even right after the event occurs: a representation that is more detached in time — less than 20 years in this case — does not automatically mean that it is inaccurate, and its increased romance or melodrama do not necessarily turn it into a less valuable document (or into a document only valuable to express negative judgments on the present time). Closer or distant, they both already deform the material they displace from life, and it is even more so for events carrying a traumatic charge — as a civil war, for example, clearly does — which inevitably escapes easy, unproblematic categorization.

The fascist character and, say, the Bourbon are not the same type of villain: they are different objects which enable altogether different formal patterns in the texts they are enframed in. Melodrama and romance are not mere ways to 'escape reality,' they are, on the contrary, precisely the site of *affect*, of a highly problematic, and still alive, testimony and memory. According to Rondolino, though, fascism and antifascism:

> non costituiscono più materia di scandalo, anzi possono essere fonte di guadagno. Svuotati del loro contenuto ideale, della loro polemica attiva, del

---

[329] Idem, 18.

> loro spirito critico, la resistenza e l'antifascismo sono entrati di diritto nella storia nazionale, accanto al risorgimento e all'epoca umbertina, senza contrasti, come in un libro di storia per le classi elementari. Fare oggi film sulla resistenza può essere un comodo mezzo *per fuggire la realtà*, per trasferire in *un passato ormai morto* i contrasti che ancora travagliano la nostra società, avendo cura di eliminare prima ogni possibile riferimento all'epoca presente. In altri casi addirittura, il film sulla resistenza può costituire *un nuovo genere cinematografico, come il western per gli americani*, ove la storia nazionale è solo più un debole stimolo allo scatenarsi delle *avventure più eccitanti*. [...] l'eventuale accusa contro il nemico nazista o i pochi repubblichini morti e sepolti non fa più paura a nessuno; anzi serve a scaricare su un obbiettivo ormai reso inutile, *su un falso scopo*, il latente spirito di rivolta del popolo italiano.[emphasis mine][330]

Caccia tragica was, indeed, an exciting adventure, *Il Cristo proibito* a crime story and *Era notte a Roma* a 'romance,' however, as we have seen, the fascist characters in them were far from being useless objects or 'false targets.'

Rondolino writes that *Il processo di Verona* by Carlo Lizzani perfectly exemplifies this degenerating tendency of recent 'antifascist' Italian cinema. He defines the film as a 'modern tragedy' that fails to propose—alongside the dramatization of a mostly forgotten historical event—a clear, direct moral punishment on Ciano, Edda and the *repubblichini*:

> Il giudizio sui fatti storici non è mai razionale e basato su una visione più ampia del problema storiografico, ma preferisce affidarsi alla commozione e al sentimento. [...] La pietà umana per i condannati, giusta e doverosa, ne assolve totalmente i delitti, d'altronde non detti nel corso del film; cosicché alla condanna morale e politica si sostituisce l'assoluzione, e il film, che doveva essere un'opera contro il fascismo, si trasforma tutt'al più in una invettiva contro taluni esponenti della repubblica di Salò e contro i soliti aguzzini nazisti.[331]

The key word in the above excerpt is *razionale,* the lack of a rational judgment of the narrated events. It indirectly confirms that fascist characters forestall the emplotment of historical events into a causal, rational sequence of beginning-middle-end, as, for example, happens in *Il conformista*. The fascist character, in fact, seems to enable a subversion of the relationship between History and the individuals acting in it. If, on the one hand, the partisan is the subject of

---

330 Idem, 24-25.
331 Idem, 20.

history because their war actively modifies its course, diverting it from decadence and loss towards liberation and victory; on the other hand, the fascist seems to embody an opposite kind of human type: he is the object of history, someone who is passively subjected to an ineffable destiny they are not in power to modify. A similar remark was made by Mino Argenteri negatively, reviewing *Era notte a Roma*:

> La storia è per Rossellini di *Era notte a Roma* ciò che stenta a ricevere una *classificazione razionale*: il nemico in definitiva, non lo si distingue né al di qua né al di là della barricata; il male, considerato come categoria astratta, si annida e riposa in ognuno ed è con lui che si è obbligati a fare i conti. […] Si ha cioè la sensazione che Rossellini, intenda ora porre l'accento su un *fato*, il quale, supremo rettore delle cose umane, renderebbe inutile ogni tentativo operato dagli uomini per realizzare i propri sogni e le proprie aspirazioni. […] Assistiamo al prevalere di un principio, in relazione al quale l'affannarsi dei personaggi condurrebbe appunto alla consapevolezza della propria incapacità e *impossibilità a resistere all'urto degli avvenimenti*, alla consapevolezza della propria fragilità, intesa come debolezza congenita ed eterna, stato immodificabile degli uomini, *metafisica* di una convivenza votata al dolore.[emphasis mine][332]

At stake is, then, an altogether different 'metaphysical' conception of humanity in relation to History. The fascist—as shown in *Il processo di Verona* and *Era notte a Roma*, according to Rondolino and Argentieri—enables the portrayal of human beings as impotent victims of fate, thus basically freeing them of any responsibility for their actions, absolving them of their sins. In *Il processo di Verona*, 'fate' is embodied by the Germans, and the film represents fascism as a subaltern of Nazism, as an object of the transcendent action of Hitler:

> In questa veste, *i pupazzi* che agiscono nel processo di Verona o intorno al processo sono *oggetti di imprese altrui*, non hanno neanche lontanamente una presenza tragica, non esprimono neanche lontanamente la storia come *protagonisti*.[emphasis mine][333]

As fascists, individuals are portrayed as 'puppets' as types, while as partisans, they are usually depicted as 'protagonists.' Therefore, Rossellini and Lizzani become, say, exponents of 'irrationalism',

---

332 Argentieri, "La notte di Rossellini," 12-13.
333 Pio Baldelli, "Il Processo di Verona e il problema dell'interpretazione cinematografica della storia contemporanea," *Cinema 60,* n.35, (May, 1963):16.

turning the fascist into an embodiment and emblem of the failure of human beings to dominate the world, to *emplot* and *enframe* it into rational, finite forms.[334] This confirms, on the historiographical level, the 'formalist' and Bakhtinian interpretation I proposed above and in the previous chapters: the hero of the plot loses his preeminence as the subject of the story, intertwining and merging with the minor character of the villain type. The fascist sabotages the closure of both history and story into a consummated, rational scheme.

4.4 The End of Ciano as Tragedy: History in *Il processo di Verona*.

In a famous article published in *La Stampa,* Paolo Monelli heavily attacked *Il processo di Verona*, criticizing its claim to *be* history. The film not only wanted to be considered equal to the works of writers, philosophers and historians but also to affirm itself as the sole instrument of knowledge and culture in those times of progress: «un film non vale la storia.»[335] Lizzani was also criticized by Edda Ciano, who officially asked the police commander of Rome to forbid the showing of the movie, unsatisfied by the inaccuracy of the historical account and of the portrayal of herself and her family, in particular of her husband, Galeazzo Ciano, as a man without dignity, intelligence and courage. She also reproaches the use of 'dreadful details' for the sequence of the final execution.[336]

Lizzani never intended to rob historians of their job; rather, his purpose was to create an epic tale:

> È degli ultimi mesi, in particolare, la ripresa impetuosa di quel grande filone epico che dovrebbe raggiungere un suo culmine – lo speriamo tutti – nel

---

334 Argentieri, "La notte di Rossellini," 16.
335 As quoted in Sacchi, Filippo, "Il dramma di Verona: un potente film storico," *Epoca* 24/03/1963 and in Baldelli, "Il Processo di Verona e il problema dell'interpretazione cinematografica della storia contemporanea."
336 Edda Ciano, "Questi i motivi della richiesta," *La Stampa*, 2, 03, 1963.

> *Gattopardo*. Anche *Il processo di Verona* vuol essere un tentativo in questa direzione. [337]

In the same article, he declares his skepticism regarding a certain 'mythology of the detail' which seems to have been guiding Italian cinema since the end of the war, his purpose being rather to regain a wider, *general* perspective in the inquiry into the real. Lizzani wants to *step back*, to observe events from a certain distance, from an altogether different point of view, not the partisan's one but the fascist's:

> Quante volte non sono ricorse sui nostri schermi certe date famose: 25 luglio, 8 settembre, 25 aprile eccetera? Le abbiamo sempre vissute dagli umili, dai resistenti, dai partigiani, dal popolo napoletano o dai pescatori delle valli di Comacchio, dagli operai e dai piccoli borghesi [...] Vogliamo provare a vederle, queste date, *tra le mura* di palazzo Venezia o del Quirinale, del Ministero della guerra o di un moderno Ministero degli Interni, *in casa* di Ciano o di Badoglio, al Comando di Kesselring o di Eisenhower o *alla corte* di Vittorio Emanuele III. [emphasis mine][338]

His goal is, then, a cinema of mostly interior spaces, with a broad, aerial, distant perspective on events that would allow him to create an epic. We recognize in his intentions that same tendency to peer into secret rooms, to violate from outside hidden truths and mysteries that we noticed regarding *Un eroe del nostro tempo* and *Il prete bello* in the previous chapter. Lizzani wants to enframe Ciano into a 'type' in order to create the character Ciano — *il personaggio Ciano* — the protagonist of an epic tale in a space, and through a perspective that is, however, typical of melodramas and other non-realist genres. In fact, melodramatic characters are often represented as trapped within a claustrophobic and prisonlike domestic space, in the same way, Lizzani wants to enframe his fascists: within the walls, in their houses, inside the corridors of political institutions. Dramatization means, in the case of *Il processo di Verona*, a displacement from outside to inside and an inversion of perspective, vertical over horizontal: a high, distant point of view instead of a lower one too focused on the detail. Then, when the fascist character is

---

337 Carlo Lizzani, "Il processo di Verona — dramma di corte," *Cinema nuovo*, no. 161, xii, (Feb, 1963): 30.
338 Idem, 31.

called to be the hero of an epic, melodramatic tale, they, once again, activate a deformation and disruption of both space and point of view. Compared to a narrative with a partisan hero, then, a very precise formal and focal change is necessary.

Carlo Lizzani was also one of the authors of *Caccia tragica,* and in *Il processo di Verona,* two protagonists of that film, Andrea Checchi and Vivi Gioi, appear as the two criminal 'leaders' in the 1948 movie. Then, they have had quite a symbolic career as villains because, in *Il processo di Verona,* Checchi plays the role of Dino Grandi, while Vivi Gioi is Rachele, the wife of Mussolini. I think this double recasting is very meaningful, and it creates an interesting intertextual connection between two movies and two different epochs. Dino Grandi was the fascist politician who — on July 24th 1943 — proposed the Fascist Grand Council to resume Mussolini's constitutional authority. The film begins with the *ordine del giorno Grandi,* initiating that chain of events that will lead to the trial in Verona and the condemnation and execution of Ciano, together with four other members of the council who voted in favor of Mussolini's removal. Andrea Checchi — the 'survivor' Alberto corrupted by the ex-collaborationist Daniela in *Caccia tragica* — again plays an ambivalent character, good or evil depending from which point of view we observe him: good as a half 'repentant' fascist, because he acted against Mussolini, but evil in the film because he somehow abandoned Ciano and the others that voted with him. Vivi Gioi is Donna Rachele, and in some scenes which place them face to face her past character seems to inspire and modify Edda, both her attire and her performance. That dark silhouette in the foreground on the left, with the collar staying up, could have been Lili Marleen-Daniela, who, now as Rachele, is facing her in the background.

Fig. 14 – Lizzani, *Il processo di Verona* (1962).

The overlapping with Daniela turns Edda into an ambiguous character, a *femme fatale* in between good and evil, and Daniela-Lili Marleen into a powerless old lady who, moreover, in the end, will tear up a photo of her husband, Mussolini. Still, after seventeen years, Lizzani did not change his view of fascism, rejecting again Manichean classifications between heroes and villains, victims and persecutors. *Il processo di Verona* is a highly problematic work that blurs distinctions and the usual 'frame' around historical characters: spectators are pushed to see villains and perpetrators as *victims* subjected to a tragic, unavoidable fate. The characters we see acting on screen are all objects of history, weighed down by a will that decides – from above – their destinies:

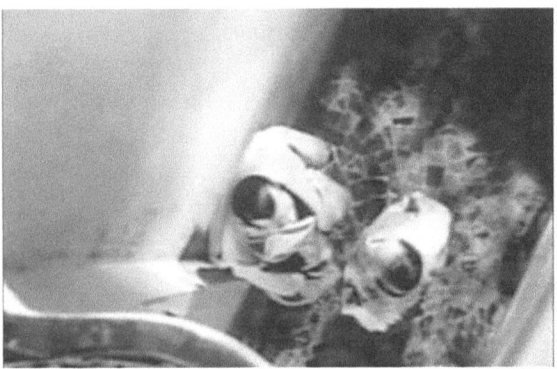

Fig. 14, 15, 16 — Lizzani, *Il processo di Verona* (1962).

These 'vertical' shots exemplify the use of space that enables Lizzani to convey his idea of the relation between history and hero, the latter positioned as a subjected object and powerless victim of a wider, general perspective. Those who used to look from above at common people—from higher, infamous balconies—are now lowered down to everyone's level and looked at. The roles are perverted. In almost every scene of the film, characters appear always enframed within the limits of windows, doors, columns, and architectural structures, conveying a sense of inescapability and entrapment in an already decided death sentence. The fascist is, once again, spied on and fixed within a delimited space by an outside and distant point of view.

Fig. 17, 18, 19, 20—Lizzani, *Il processo di Verona* (1962).

Then, not only is Ciano imprisoned, but symbolically, his inclusion exceeds the limits of his cell, and it drags inside with him all the other characters, his *aguzzini*, like Pavolini. The film problematizes and confuses the boundaries between prisoners and guards, indicted and judged, resulting in characters who resist their usual typification.

Ciano's cell, in particular, becomes a peculiar space, simultaneously a means for enframing and a site of openness. Little by little, Ciano's imprisonment—his being looked at and spied on from the small window of the cell door—turns into a condemnation *a posteriori* of his persecutors, the *repubblichini* and the Nazis. One sequence visually conveys this ambiguity of the profilmic space, at the point which becomes impossible to distinguish inside from outside Ciano's prison. The camera breaks the walls, ideally transferring everyone—the viewers from 1963 in particular—inside their limits. The character that triggers this overlapping and spatial disruption is, once again, a female spy, a German *femme fatale* who tries to put her hands on Ciano's diaries, full of potentially dangerous information for the Nazis.

The Excess of Demarcation 305

Fig. 21, 22, 23, 24, 25 – Lizzani, *Il processo di Verona* (1962).

At the beginning of the sequence Frau Lenz is waiting for Ciano inside his cell. The camera is placed in the impossible position exactly between outside and inside, precisely at their intersection, and the wall splits the frame in two, closing inside the cell a character that is not a prisoner. Once she is framed by the barred window of the door, she looks outside towards us viewers, but abruptly, something obscures the camera. The frame gets completely dark: Ciano's body has interposed itself between the camera and its object, basically erasing for an instant every distinction between outside and inside, obstructing the gaze of the camera, exceeding its spatial coordinates, thus avoiding and resisting the limited space of the frame. When he reappears he is already inside, once again enframed with the spy in his cell. At the end of the movie, Edda and Ciano switch positions, as Edda appears behind something that looks like a grid, the bars of a prison: again, a shot that confuses vertical and horizontal, inside and inside, leaving the character *floating* into an unreadable space lacking limits and points of reference. In fact, those are not the vertical bars of a cell but the horizontal grid of the bed base.

Fig. 26 — Lizzani, *Il processo di Verona* (1962).

Il processo di Verona is a film about a trial; however, its main purpose is to problematize the melodramatic Manichean split between good and evil, guilty and innocent, by disrupting the very same eye of the camera of its author. Lizzani disarranges and unsettles the profilmic space, turning it into a means to convey inclusion over exclusion instead of using it as a means of precise orientation or realistic accuracy. An unwelcomed silenced past and part of history is revived and displaced—from 'fascist' history—back inside Italian history by exposing to the audience fascist characters portrayed outside the exactness of their static 'type,' but, rather as a dynamic presence which exceeds a precise placement and classification. We are not looking at a trial against 'villains' getting the punishment they deserved, but at a film that tries to problematize its gaze, the way to look at and narrate a historical event through an epic tale rather than a documentary or realist account. Objectivity is reached exactly by this crossing and overlapping of boundaries, which triggers and enables a 'carnivalesque,' dynamic uncertainty of typical roles and meanings.

The final sequence of the film clearly shows how the act of filming historical material, of looking at them, is the true object at stake, what Lizzani cares about.

Fig. 27—Lizzani, *Il processo di Verona* (1962).

The event has been, all along, filmed from the beginning, simultaneously to its very happening. The gaze that the camera casts on its object already deforms it. In the last sequence, the one of the final execution, Lizzani follows the five prisoners with a long take, then expands the scene horizontally, while a deep focus shot shows the executioners already waiting for them in the background, widening further the frame. Both executed and executioners appear and disappear in between two walls, and they are visible to us only through openings and fractures in those barriers; that is to say, they are already present enframed in screens, in frames within the outer frame of the shot itself. Reality and history, when filmed, are already enclosed within the limits of a subjective, partial point of view within a closure. By showing this awareness, Lizzani enframes both executioners and executed, merging their roles, looking with his camera at those who are looking too, turning the subject who looks into the observed object of his gaze. The last shot includes Ciano's dead body and, beside him, the German cameraman, filming on his knees. In contrast, Lizzani's eye films them at a distance, from above, flattening both subject and object on the same horizontal level, both of them being 'dead' bodies-material of Lizzani's further, later filming: looking is always filtered, diverted by the perspective of another gaze.

Fig. 28, 29 — Lizzani, *Il processo di Verona* (1962).

4.5 'Rear Window' in Ferrara: Gaze and Space in *La lunga notte del '43*.

In *La lunga notte del '43* – the film debut of Florestano Vancini – once again, space and gaze are the focal elements of a plot taking place in Ferrara occupied by the *repubblichini*. The city space plays a decisive role in distributing the various problematic characters along different, gradual strata of ambiguity, evil and guilt. The initial, strictly geometric disposition and then classification of the heroes will little by little loosen up in the course of the plot and finally collapse into a confusing merging of opposites.

The character that triggers the story is Pino Barillari, a fascist who contracted syphilis in a brothel back in 1922 during the march on Rome. Sick and weakened by the disease, he spends his days withdrawn in his petit-bourgeois apartment, sitting in front of a window, half spying on the daily city life down on the street, half solving rebuses and crosswords in magazines. We recognize in him three typical and recurrent traits of the portrayal of the fascist: first, his disease, the result of immoral and unrestricted sexual conduct; second, the passion for enigmas and riddles, like Tarcisio in *Era notte a Roma*; third, the fact that he is a voyeur who spies from above on the others: like Virginia in *Un eroe del nostro tempo*, he is the one who knows more then the others do and, at the same time, he is also hidden from the other's gaze.

Fig. 30 — Vancini, *La lunga notte del '43* (1964).

The entire film will be a semi-subjective, point-of-view shot of Pino looking at the events taking place down in the street; that is to say, his sight line is the perspective of the film, and so we viewers will see what he sees through the frame of his window. The spectatorial gaze coincides with the character's. In this sense, a shot from below of the clock tower of the Este castle anticipates Pino's first appearance in the film. The shot of the clock is of extreme importance, because it is the only image of the actual castle, the entire set being recreated in the Cinecittà studios. Thus, the shot of the castle, of a real location, has an everyday quality in it which favors the identification of the viewer's line of sight with Pino's: anyone, any citizen living in Ferrara, now and back then, could have cast their gaze on the clock, in any day of their life. It is, then, a familiar, daily life image that lets the viewer perceive Pino's subjective view of the events that follow as their everyday subjective view. The perspective backward on a historical, past event superimposes and merges with a present, everyday perspective on the clock, which past and present share. A film founded on a character's look starts with a spectatorial, non-diegetic gaze, thus questioning, from the beginning, the authority and subjectivity of one of the film's main heroes and the quality of their testimony.

Fig. 31 – Vancini, *La lunga notte del '43* (1964).

The organization of the profilmic space — recreated entirely in Cinecittà — is imbued with a precise signification. Pino's apartment and the castle are the two extremes, two spaces developing in opposite directions: the castle enlarges the scene upwards, through the vertical body of its tower, occupying thereby a privileged position above everything, while Pino's apartment extends downwards, as a narrow stairwell connects it with his pharmacy downstairs. Between these two poles — the subjective gaze of an eyewitness and the objective gaze of the city itself, of history — there is the space of the street — not by chance called *via Roma* — which is, in addition, framed on the one side within a portico, above which Pino's apartment is located, and, on the other side by the water moat surrounding the castle.

This street is the space where the main object-event of the film will take place: during the night of November 14th 1943, eleven, mostly Jewish, anti-fascist personalities, were shot dead by a group of fanatical *repubblichini* as a reprisal ordered by the *gerarca* Carlo "Sciagura" Aretusi, in order to avenge the assassination of the town's fascist *console*. The street is, then, enframed by spatial 'wings' that turn it into a veritable theatrical stage: apartment and portico on the left, the street at the center, and the castle on the right. Despite the fact that the symmetrical disposition of the profilmic space turns the street into the site of perfect visibility—where everyone and everything is in the spotlight, at the center of an ideal quattrocento perspective, and under the voyeuristic eyes of Pino—the event taking place there will be, paradoxically, invisible, something that will defy visibility. The initial, ideal condition of evidence and perfect perceptibility will be disrupted by the traumatic value of the event, and the effect will, once again, resist static placement and exact definition. *La lunga notte del '43* is a film organized around the point of view of one eyewitness. It is a film about the failure of testimony, the limits of vision and the difficult memory of a past seen by everyone and forgotten by everyone almost instantly.

If the castle is the location of a historical landmark, thus symbolizing history itself and its extra-temporal stability, while the street is the stage of the main tragic event, the portico with the bar, the pharmacy and the cinema is the space of indifference and of the refusal to acknowledge the harshness of war. The colonnade is, in fact, filled with movie posters, behind which we see characters living their daily routine as if nothing terrible was happening, characters that refuse to act in history, preferring to be passive, untouched observers of the events. The portico is a screen that hides and protects everyone from the war, perceived to be happening in an absolute outside, on the street, somewhere else.

Fig. 32 — Vancini, *La lunga notte del '43* (1964).

The two main characters who hide behind the safe, enclosed space of the portico, thus embodying indifference and blindness, are Anna and Franco. She is Pino's much younger and good-looking wife who is running the pharmacy and who tries to escape her prison-like marriage by distracting herself with fiction: reading *fotoromanzi*, listening to *racconti sceneggiati* on the radio, and going to the movies. One day, at the cinema, she encounters Franco, a rich Jewish professor of Latin she used to date during high school before the war. Fiction and illusion literally screen them from reality, from historical events. That title, *Noi vivi*, on the poster behind which their first dialogue takes place, translates visually their actual thoughts and the only thing they seem to care about: being part of that privileged 'we' still alive.

Moreover, *Noi vivi* was a fascist propaganda movie by Goffredo Alessandrini, an adaptation of a bestselling novel by Ayn Rand, set in St Petersburg as the communists consolidate their power. Kira — the heroine at the center of the political intrigue — is a true *femme fatale* who makes everyone fall in love only in order to help Leo — her true love — pay for his cure for tuberculosis. The plot is, then, very similar to *La lunga notte del '43* because Anna will soon become Franco's mistress, with the hope of finally escaping from her claustrophobic life with the sick Pino. The only difference between the two stories is the context of political corruption that surrounds the characters: communists in the novel and the 1942 Italian adaptation, fascists in Vancini's rewriting. Fascist propaganda reversed itself, by the use of the same plotline. *La lunga notte del '43* is the last stage of a palimpsest, the adaptation of an adaptation that merges fascists and communists.

The romance subplot centered on Anna and Franco not only represents their guilty distraction and indifference towards history, but it also has the very target that *distracts* the spectator from the main event of the story. Their distraction *is* our distraction, thus conveying an identification between their guilty blindness and that of one of the 1961 spectators. An identification that, as we will see, will be made explicit only at the end of the movie, during a magnificent *coda* taking place exactly in 1961.

Parallel to the romance there is the crime story as seen by Pino's point of view. The political and spy story-like intrigue involve only fascists, represented, in particular, by Carlo Aretusi, known as *Sciagura* (Calamity) — the perfect 'type' of the *gerarca*, played by Gino Cervi, an actor who often played fascist characters — and by his lackey Vincenzi, who always wears dark sunglasses, a detail typical of genre gangster movies, which makes him an obvious object of suspicion. When the *console* is killed in an ambush, the guilt will obviously fall upon the resistance when, in reality, it was Carlo who commissioned the crime in order to take the lead of the fascist party in Ferrara.

Vancini gives us viewers a hint that Carlo is the real murderer before it is made evident in the film. The fascist, once again, disrupts the limits of the frame and perverts the temporal sequence of the editing, anticipating the pace of the movie of transitions between one scene and another. During a transition through a dissolve, the image of Carlo is superimposed for an instant on the head of the *console* while he is driving his car before Vincenzi stops and kills him on the road to Verona.

Fig. 33 — Vancini, *La lunga notte del '43* (1964).

This dissolve between the horizontal shot of the street, and the in-depth line of the country road is exactly enabled by Carlo, by his ambiguous role of a traitor among traitors. It is the only time that the symmetrical, 'flat' stage-like horizontal organization of the profilmic space has been deformed and the background 'wing' of the castle broken. The shot that closes and enframes the scene is, again, a dissolve that superimposes the now dead body of the console on the close-up of the back of Pino's neck while he is half-asleep, not looking, missing precisely what has just happened.

Fig. 34 — Vancini, *La lunga notte del '43* (1964).

The dissolve suggests an identification between murderer and eyewitness. In fact, Pino is the only one who will see and know the truth, the actual executor of this crime and its tragic consequence, but he will not do anything with this knowledge: he will not denounce him and, more importantly, he will not tell anyone, thus forestalling the future discourse of memory on that night.

As a reprisal, Carlo will order the execution of 11 well-known anti-fascist men of Ferrara, mostly bourgeois Jewish. They will be shot in the street, at night, against the low wall that separates the street from the water moat surrounding the castle right in front of Pino's window. Awakened by the screams and noises of the drunken *repubblichini,* he could witness, unseen, the cold-blooded massacre through the shutters of his closed window.

Fig. 35 — Vancini, *La lunga notte del '43* (1964).

The two shots above show how the profilmic space is used to convey and modify the actual meaning of the execution. What is taking place in front of our and of Pino's eyes is the disappearance of the victims, their dead bodies actually disappearing behind the low wall while falling on the street, that is on that in-between zone of apparent visibility, where everyone is the object of a geometrical, precise perspective. Those two frames have another important and unique characteristic: they are the only ones in the entire movie taken from the perspective of the castle, on the opposite side of the dominant point of view of Pino's window. If that crime and those dead bodies were fully visible to Pino, they are now invisible to the 1961 viewers, from their 'contemporary' point of view, coinciding with the castle. The reason for this invisibility is Pino himself, his silence and cowardice. By filming the death of the victims as a disappearance behind the hiding-delimiting space of the wall, Vancini is anticipating the fact that Pino will never denounce the true murderers, thus condemning those victims to oblivion, erasing them as objects of the gaze and of the memory of us viewers. Pino's seeing is revealed as blindness, as lack of testimony, which makes him a traitor, a villain, as the *gerarca* and murderer Carlo. The street, where history takes place, is the place of the only apparent visibility and ideal conditions for testimony. It is, however, revealed by Vancini to be, on the contrary, the simultaneous place of invisibility and oblivion. The identification and merging of identities between Pino and Carlo — between a sick and apparently powerless, innocent witness and the villain Carlo who, in addition to being a traitor from the point of view of the partisans, betrays the fascists too — is perfectly conveyed by the following shot, by that hand at first covering, and then gradually revealing the word 'traitors' painted on that same low wall in between street and castle.

Fig. 36 – Vancini, *La lunga notte del '43* (1964).

His observation of the writing is, in reality, a covering, a hiding exemplified by his hand that seems to obstruct his gaze. When he retracts the hand, thus making the 'traitors' fully visible, his eyes are closed: it will not be thanks to his seeing – finally revealed as, rather, spying – that traitors will be unmasked and the memory of what happened transmitted to future generations. When he appears to be looking at the writing on the wall, his gaze seems obstructed by his hand, while when his hand is not there anymore to block his vision, his eyes are closed.

The last sequence of the film is set in the 1960s, at the beginning of the economic boom. Franco comes back from Switzerland — where he escaped as a refugee after the assassination of his father — to Ferrara — and to that same via Roma, with his wife and his young son. Like *Il processo di Verona*, the film ends with a short reflection on the acts of looking at and filming history. The family arrives in a big car — a sign of the economic boom, together with a famous hit of the times playing in the background, *Il barattolo* by Gianni Meccia — and they get off right in front of the castle, opposite Pino's pharmacy. The son carries a camera around his neck, and the first question he asks *qu'est qu'il y a maintenant dans le château*? His father answers that now, there is actually nothing inside the castle: the historical landmark is, then empty, just a tourist attraction forgotten by the community: a highly visible monument seen and overlooked by the citizens. The memory of the tragic events that took place right there is not attached to that particular place any more. History, in the newborn Italy of economic splendor, is there, visible to everyone in its monumental presence and at the same time ignored and unseen by everyone; thus, memory and testimony failed, and the view of the monument does not activate their discourses. A few moments later, the son asks a second fundamental question: if he can take a picture of the castle. Franco says yes, because, he explains, now the castle is not a possible military target any longer. The son, then, takes, first, a quick shot of the castle and, right after, one of the two embarrassed parents. An equally unseeing look has taken, now in 1961, the place of Pino's impotent voyeurism and useless omniscience: the tourist gaze. It is clear by now that Franco came back to Ferrara not to transfer to his son the memory and testimony of the history he lived, but, rather, as a tourist who feels for the places of his youth only a distant nostalgia. The son's camera filters and makes indirect their gaze at history: their memory of the past is secondhand, from the detached point of view behind the viewfinder of a tourist camera, which protects their gaze from a too-close, too direct involvement with the past trauma. Right after the picture is taken, Franco notices on the wall a small commemorative plaque with the names of the 11 victims of the 1943 massacre. It will be once again the son who reads the inscription and recognizes the name of his grandfather, Attilio Villani. With a *tu vois, c'est le nom du grand-père,* he tries to stimulate his father's gaze and memory without success. As if testimony and memory had skipped a generation, Franco is shown to be unable to directly relate, witness and carry on the memory of what happened. Again, for a third time, insisting on vision, the son asks if he, back then, 'saw' the dead bodies of the 11 victims: *tu les a vus papa, c'est vrai?* The answer is, once again, negative, he did not actually 'see' them, only his sister did. The plaque—marking the exact spot of the execution—seems to be completely ignored by the daily life of Ferrara, by the contemporary citizen, being nothing but a list of names unable to incite any sense of history and remembrance in the viewer, empty as the castle behind it. After the plaque, they move to the other side of via Roma and sit at the bar under the portico. The tables are empty as everyone is standing inside the bar, watching a football match played by the Italian national team. Vancini represents everyone else in the act of looking, but their gaze is, once again, a non-gaze, a looking which rather signifies the unwillingness to look and to remember the past: it is more a refusal to look at, it is a diverting the attention from the traumatic object of memory to an empty form of low-brow entertainment. In fact, they are looking exactly in the opposite direction of via Roma, turning their backs on the stage of the past traumatic events, the street, and from the plaque now remembering them on the wall.

Fig. 37 — Vancini, *La lunga notte del '43* (1964).

The gaze on the street of Pino Barillari generated and resulted in a gaze away from the street, from the site of the tragedy. After a quick visit to the pharmacy — in search of the woman he abandoned — Franco sits at the table, turning his back to the street and the plaque, looking in the same direction as all the other men watching the game, while his wife looks up and his son down into a glass of soda. The site of memory and history is overlooked and avoided by everyone's gazes. We soon realize that one of those men standing in front of the bar is *Sciagura*, Carlo Aretusi, the fascist responsible for the massacre of 1943. He recognizes Franco and approaches the table saying hello to him and his family, as if nothing ever happened. The recognition scene reveals again Franco as incapable of seeing and recognizing history, his tragic past. In fact, he greets Sciagura without any sign of resentment or hate, unmistakably ignoring the fact that he is shaking the hand of his father's executioner. The incomplete recognition — the victim does not recognize the executioner — symbolizes the current state of Italian society in 1961: a unity founded on oblivion, on an ignored, silenced and forgotten memory that allows opposite factions to peacefully live together as if the events of the past never took place. Franco does not recognize Carlo as the assassin simply because he ignores what he actually did and not because «opportunisticamente egli sceglie di non riconoscere in lui il carnefice del padre.»[339] Franco did not choose to recognize the assassin of his father in Sciagura; rather, the answer is in the quality of his looking, of his testimony: he chose not to watch in 1943, he chose to escape to Switzerland, so he cannot know who Sciagura is, what role he exactly played that night. The true cause of his unawareness and this misrecognition is Pino's refusal to tell him what Sciagura did and who were the actual authors of the crime. A voice from the bar calls Carlo to come back and see what is going on in the match: «Carlo! Vieni a *vedere* e poi parlerai.» Another invitation to look, indirectly suggesting what really is at stake in the film and also highlighting the relation that links the act of seeing to the act of telling, of transmitting, thus keeping alive the memory of past historical events. When his wife asks him who that man is, Franco will annoyingly answer: «Era un gerarca di Ferrara. Nella Repubblica di Salò aveva ricoperto qualche carica importante. Un poveraccio, non credo che abbia mai fatto niente di male.» He cannot recognize it because he does not know the truth. He does not know the truth because he could not see and because someone refused to tell him what he saw.

The fascist character defies recognition and, in the end, escapes a fixed classification: he is the villain, but he is not seen and remembered as such by the subject. The act of looking at the fascist — and at his deeds — is problematized and shown to be qualitatively different. Despite the geometrical framing — Pino's window — the quattrocento perspective of Ferrara's streets, and the stratification of the set — the castle, the street, the portico — Sciagura sabotages the recognition because he is an object difficult to observe from a precise, unique perspective. If in the recognition scene of *Il conformista,* the victim and the assassin that recognize each other are no longer victim and assassin because the crime never took place, in *La lunga notte del '43,* the crime occurred. However, the victim and assassin do not recognize each other as such. The past crime

---

[339] Valeria Napolitano, "La repubblica sociale italiana nel cinema di Florestano Vancini" in P. Cavallo, L. Goglia, P. Iaccio (eds.), *Cinema a passo romano* (Napoli: Liguori, 2012) p. 326.

and trauma is either an illusion, a mistake or is forgotten: it is present, then, despite a perfect visibility that would normally ease testimony, only as lack. The fascist character enables exactly this oblivion and consequent confusion, instability of fixed roles and static identities. The past is a dynamic formlessness, an *affect* that challenges memory, recollection and the tale that is supposed to transmit those events as shared history.

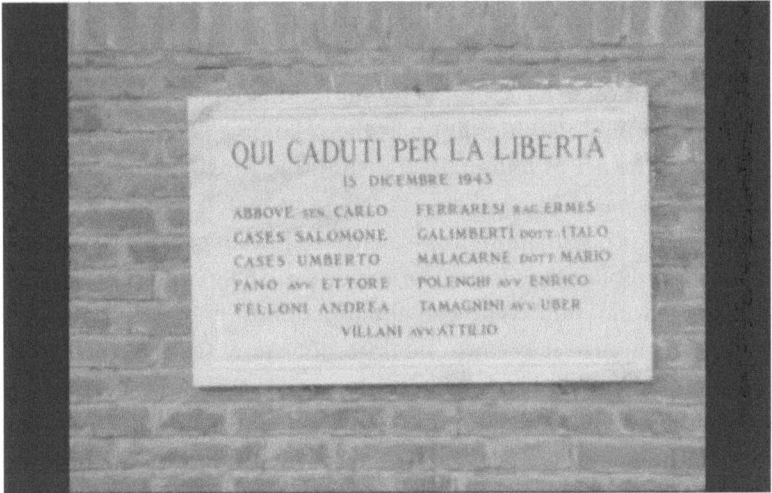

Fig. 38 — Vancini, *La lunga notte del '43* (1964).

The last image of the film is a close-up shot of the plaque. Who is looking now? Who's perspective is this? The point of view is too low to be that of an actual person, and it is not in a causal relation to the previous shot. A few frames earlier, we remember, the plaque was observed by Franco and his family: a semi-subjective shot included both viewers and the object they were looking at. The shot of the plaque would normally follow the shot of the subject who is looking, but, in this case, in between the semi-subjective shot, including subject and object and the subjective shot of the object, a space opens for the recognition scene, thus delaying the subjective shot of the plaque, the object seen by Franco's family. This delay favors oblivion: we viewers forget who was actually looking at the plaque; that is, we forget that this shot, this object, formally belongs to a subject and a particular perspective. The causal, narrative organization of the film's transitions and progress is altered and stopped in order to insert the recognition scene, i.e., a scene that exactly represents oblivion and blindness: a subject unable to see and recognize. The gaze on the plaque, a gaze that would allow the discourse of memory to start, does not belong to anyone: testimony is left without subject.

After watching the events of the film through the semi-subjective perspective of one character, Pino Barillari, now, the last gaze of the film is an impersonal and objective one, nobody's in particular and everyone's at the same time. The camera is located in an impossible place, thus disturbing at last the narrative and continuity of perspective of the film:

> «To the extent that the camera is located in an "impossible" place, the narration questions its origin, that is, suggests a shift in narration.» Impossible, of course, is here decided in respect of the possible positions of the observer moving about; the disturbance involved seen as a disjunction of the unity of narration and narrated, enunciation and enounced.[340]

Vancini chooses to end the movie with another act of looking, a direct, unmediated vision of where memory lies. Being left without a subject, the look on the plaque may now be left to the 1961 spectators: they are forced to be the actual subject of this final gaze. *La lunga notte del '43* is, then, an invitation to look, to remember and to tell the story of a past unseen and untold for too long. As the object of this looking, the plaque, despite its geometric, precise shape, complicates our vision. In fact, this is not the actual one—many different plaques were attached to the wall in remembrance of the different victims—but it was made exclusively for the movie, part of the set reconstructed in the Cinecittà studios. The choice to reunite the names of all the victims in just one plaque has, first of all, the meaning of promoting a sense of unity and of shared trauma rather than a private, individual one belonging to one particular family. Second, the name of Franco's father—*avv.* Attilio Villani—is the last one, as they are listed in alphabetical order. Something in the

---

340 Stephen Heath, *Questions of Cinema,* (Bloomington: Indiana University Press, 1981) p. 50

placement of that particular name in the list suddenly strikes the eye of the viewer, disturbing the numerical, symmetrical order of the framing since the name appears to be located in between the two columns as if it could not fit anywhere. The name of the father is difficult to place and to frame within the geometrical and numerical limits of the plaque and of the two columns of names, exactly because it is the object of a difficult, rejected and unwelcomed memory. Just as the shot of the plaque was misplaced with respect to what should have been its logical, causal placement, the name of the father is misplaced within the frame of the plaque. The name of the dead does not fit in the shared memory of postwar Italian society: it is placed, then, inside the plaque but simultaneously outside the columns and beyond the limits of the list. It exceeds the list; it does not fit the discourse of memory, i.e., a proper work of mourning did not start and could not be completed. The last name of the list does not find its right collocation, and it floats, unfixed in the middle, out of place, as *affect*. Supposed to be the end of the list, the name of the father fails to be that end and to provide the right, symmetrical closure to the discourse of memory and the subsequent work of mourning. The plaque symbolizes the flawed memory of a nation incapable of finding the right place for its dead. That is why Franco did not recognize Sciagura: all the protagonists of the past trauma, the victim and his executioner, are dynamic characters who disrupt discourse and plot, sabotaging memory, recognition and closure.

 The centrality of testimony and eye-witnessing in *La lunga notte del '43* is an evident reference to Neorealist cinema. Vancini belongs—together with Pasolini, Bertolucci, Bellocchio, and Montaldo—to that second generation of postwar Italian filmmakers that questioned the 'fathers' of Italian cinema and, namely, their ideas on *looking*, witnessing, and their use of bodily images to trigger a sense of charity and uncomplicated compassion. Karl Schoonover has argued that neorealism promoted looking as a form of political engagement and action. The image's structure of the point of view—the succession of angles, framing, and diegetic and non-diegetic perspectives—in depicting the imperiled, tortured body triggers, according to Schoonover, a form of seeing that challenges habitual modes of reception and asks for an outside, detached gaze transcending subjective differences: «by placing ocular witnessing at the center of their narratives, these films seek to transform seeing from a passive state of consumption into a powerful means of moral reckoning.»[341]

The second generation of Italian films he takes into account — from *Mamma Roma* to *Il Grido* and more — seems to frustrate exactly this moral and ethical value accorded to the act of looking by conveying the idea that being an eyewitness does not necessarily translate into political intervention and moral virtue. In these movies, the privilege of testimony might, on the contrary, «encourage false beliefs»[342] and afford the onlooker «little more than frustration and dystopia.»[343] According to Schoonover: «this next generation of neorealist films appear to disarticulate the corporeal means by which neorealism orients the spectator to the image as testimony. These films question using images of the body as uncomplicated evidence; hence, they critique attempts to represent the contingent or corporeal as substantiating the political potential of the cinematic image.»[344]

La lunga notte del '43 belongs to this second generation of neorealist films. In fact, it stages exactly this separation of seeing and testimony: the natural act of looking does not necessarily trigger the moral, ethical response of the eyewitness. Pino's refusal to denounce what he saw translates into the blindness of Franco, who, at the end of the film, cannot recognize the real identity of Sciagura — the exact role he played in the death of the father — thus allowing for continuity between the fascist years and the prosperous postwar Italy of the economic boom. Vancini, in my opinion, is saying that without the consequent act of storytelling, looking is a completely futile activity. This is a stark rejection of the postwar leitmotiv of Italian film critics such as Rondolino, who were attacking this second wave of antifascist films because they were narrating past

---

341 Karl Schoonover, *Brutal Vision – The Neorealist Body in Postwar Italian Cinema* (Minneapolis: University of Minnesota Press, 2012), 110.
342 Idem, 193
343 Ibidem.
344 Ibidem.

events from second-handed sources, and thus history «non poteva più, per ovvie ragioni, *essere vista con gli occhi di coloro che la fecero nel momento in cui la fecero.*»[345] The historical perspective was inevitably distorting the view on past events: 'epic' plot and narrative were, once again, considered as less true deformations" of the first-hand, documentary account of neorealism. Having been there and witnessed those events is not all, and, on the contrary, *La lunga notte del '43* even traces the source of the problem to the passive, outside looking of a bystander who, moreover, cannot act because of his crippled body.

The sequence that follows the execution on the street perfectly stages this alternation between diegetic and non-diegetic gazes, between a character's looking and the spectatorial one. After the disappearance of the dead bodies behind the wall, the film cuts to the interior of Pino's apartment, showing him turned away from the window in a state of visible distress. He slowly turns to the window behind him and closes it after having reopened the blinds. The categories of openness-closure are, then, blurred with the act of closing, which results in making vision again possible. He sits again in front of the window, now facing it, occupying the usual position he had all along the entire film. He casts his gaze down the street for a second, and, almost immediately after, he diverts his eyes back inside on the floor, thus stopping seeing, desperate; the camera suddenly moves forward towards the window with a tracking shot, leaving Pino out of the frame and then zooming in beyond the window, outside, on the eleven corpses lying on the street. As the shot of the memorial plaque during the final sequence, this sudden movement and zooming in of the camera disrupts the usual, logical sequence of semi-subjective and point of view shot, underlying the fact that Pino is not the subject of the subjective image of the corpses.

Furthermore, this is the only camera movement of the sequence and the only zoom of the entire film, and, thus, it contrasts not only with the fixity of Vancini's style but also with the disturbing stillness of the dead bodies, exposed as political spectacle, as a

---

[345] Rondolino, Gianni, "L'antifascismo nel cinema italiano recente," *Il nuovo spettatore cinematografico,* no. 4, (Aug, 1963): 8.

monument. Vancini draws a parallel between the already monumental display of the bodies by the fascists and the statuary plaque where the names of the victims are inscribed as names on a tombstone. The 'monumentalized' bodies have the function to trigger memory: in the former case, as a threat, in the latter as mourning. The bird's eye shot of the bodies from the window, while matching the character's line of sight, does not belong to him, as it comes from behind him. Furthermore, the zoom is exactly triggered by the sudden shutting of his eyes. Seeing and blindness are once again blurred, and an act of closure activates, paradoxically, an act of focusing. Looking at the massacred bodies is, then, an unclear, ambivalent synthesis, both diegetic—the vantage point is the same as Pino's—and spectatorial—Pino is not the one who is looking because we just saw his eyes closing. The eyewitness is, then, dispossessed of what could have been his gaze, and the object of his testimony is left without an on-screen, diegetic onlooker and subject. In fact, the following shot is a low-angle, side-street shot of the corpses lying outside, framed from an omniscient point of view. I believe that this particular shot is extremely important and problematic because it places the dead bodies against the background of a perfect quattrocento perspective view of Ferrara. The profilmic space in which the bodies are placed is not the typical ruined scenario of the "corpse city," as described by Noa Steimatsky, and it is also different from Sandro Bernardi's idea of the locations of Italian neorealism as "landscapes of death." The Ferrara rebuilt in studios is, on the contrary, a spectacle of geometrical, rationalized order that the war seemed not to have touched.

Fig. 39 — Vancini, *La lunga notte del '43* (1964).

The pairing of the disrupting contingency of the corpses and the perfect framing of the image according to the necessary, mathematical rules of perspective is a decisive moment of formal and authorial ambiguity that questions the subject-object and author-form aesthetic relationship.[346]

In his fundamental 1927 study *Perspective as Symbolic Form*, Erwin Panofsky conceives perspective as a highly ambiguous, double-faced, epistemological and pictorial tool that made it possible to construct a spatial structure of infinite extension where objects-

---

346 There is another important detail that makes this shot, and namely the placement of corpses within a space organized according to Quattrocento perspective, a decisive moment of the film: Pasolini was, in fact, one of the screenwriters. I believe that this shot evokes another later juxtaposition of dead bodies and perspective in *Accattone*, Pasolini's directorial debut of 1961 (then, only one year after *La lunga notte del '43*). The scene I am referring to is Accattone's dream: he imagines himself wandering on the edge of a bridge, when, suddenly, he sees the corpses of his friends half buried in the sand. As we know Pasolini was a student of the art historian Roberto Longhi, who extensively wrote about perspective in his essay on Piero della Francesca and about Ferrara in his study *Officina Ferrarese*.

volumes and the empty intervals between them could merge—following generally valid mathematical rules—into a coherent unity. Thus conceived, a perspective brought *infinity* from the divine to empirical reality, de-theologizing the vision of the universe and space. Perspectivism, then, meant relativism: it suggests that reality is always seen from a unique point of view, that an object is always framed from a particular vantage point. Panofsky argued that perspective institutes the perfect equilibrium between the claims of the object and the claims of the subject, allowing for both a more subjective representation of bodies in space as they appear from a particular point of view and, simultaneously, for a mathematical, generally valid, objective framing of reality:

> perspective is by nature a two edged sword: it creates room for bodies to expand plastically and more gesturally, and yet at the same time it enables light to spread out in space and in a painterly way dissolve the bodies. Perspective creates distance between human beings and things ("the first is the eye that sees, the second is the object seen, the third is the distance between them" says Durer after Piero della Francesca); but then it turns it abolishes the distance by, in a sense, drawing this world of things, an autonomous world confronting the individual, into the eye. Perspective subjects the artistic phenomenon to stable and even mathematic exact rules, but on the other hand, makes that phenomenon contingent upon human beings, indeed upon the individual: for these rules refer to the psychological and physical conditions of the visual impression, and the way they take effect is determined by the freely chosen position of a subjective "point of view." Thus the history of perspective may be understood with equal justice as a triumph of the distancing and objectifying sense of the real, and as a triumph of the distance-denying human struggle for control; it is as much a consolidation and systematization of the external world, as an extension of the domain of the self.[347]

In my opinion, the corpses visualized through perspective stress what Panofsky defines as «the objectification of the subjective.»[348] The rationalized vision of corporeal finitude disrupts, once more, the distance and demarcation between subject and object, simultaneously opening up and obstructing a space for a new vision from

---

347 Erwin Panofsky, *Perspective as a Symbolic Form* (New York: Zone Books, 2003), 67-68.
348 Ibidem.

outside, «a new protocol of vision removed from the diegesis.»[349] I believe that Panofsky's ideas on the ambiguity of perspective find a striking correspondence with the early Bakhtin of *Author and Hero in Aesthetic Activity,* who conceived the aesthetic experience as containing both "impressive" and "expressive" elements:

> All experience is mediated by the transcendental poles of *self* and *other*. The *self* names the mode of "intentional" comportment in the world that treats it as a horizon for action. It is spatially, temporally, and axiologically open to the surrounding world. It always projects: in space toward the object of its intentionality, in time toward goals that recede into a boundless future. […] The *other*'s relation to the world is one not of horizontal movement but of location within an environment. In space, the *other* is externalized as a bounded body among other physical objects. In time, the other exists as temporally bound by birth and death. […] For Bakhtin then, properly aesthetic experience contains both "impressive and "expressive" elements, involving as it does a double operation whereby the reader or viewer aligns herself with the "intentional" perspective of the hero and *simultaneously* recoils back into the totalizing outsideness of the author.[350]

The true object of the scene is not the bodies in themselves but, rather, the very vision of those bodies: the focus is on the looking at the corpses. The framing of the perspective turns them into monuments, absorbing them into the architectural surroundings of the Renaissance city, making them a version of that «umanità colonnare,» an expression used by the art critic Roberto Longhi to describe human figures as they are altered by perspectival relations with the surrounding space in Piero della Francesca's works. In a striking reversal of Bazin's conception of the body as the site of obscene contingency and brutal realism, in this image, the corpses reflect the constructed space of the frame: they divert the attention of the viewer to the very fact that the bodies are being looked at, are being framed into the rationalized form of the Renaissance city first, and into the neat limits of the camera angle: they allow the viewer to step back and eyewitness from outside their stillness, the stable, inevitable truth of their death. At the same time, though, the vision

---

349 Schoonover, *Brutal Vision,* 113.
350 Ilya Kliger, "Heroic Aesthetic and Modernist Critique: Extrapolations from Bakhtin's «Author and Hero in Aesthetic Activity,»" *Slavic Review,* Vol. 67, No. 3 (Fall, 2008): 555-556.

of those bodies is one of dangerous, disrupting contingency, the corpses being the object of an unmarked perspective, a vision floating without a subject capable of capturing and framing its traumatic meaning. The movement forward of the camera and the accelerated zooming have cut out the diegetic eyewitnesses from the frame. The bodies are not seen by Pino, as the close-up of the plaque is not the subjective of Franco's gaze. In the former case the camera accelerates the time of the subjective, skipping the semi-subjective shot, erasing one transition. In the latter case, the subjective is delayed; too much time has passed from the semi-subjective shot that would have related it to Franco's gaze. The filming of the victims of the fascist crime results in both a spatial and temporal perversion.

The memory of the fascist crime is a traumatic, disruptive object that brings to the foreground what Bakhtin called a "crisis of authorship" and, as we have seen, of testimony: the gaze that is finally cast on the corpses lacks, in fact, a subject. It is both a formal accident and an interruption of the filmic stylistic characterization and an image that the characters themselves refuse to see. The memory of fascism still endangers and fragments identity: a subjectivity that, in order to exist, it needs to hide and not look, and an aesthetic form which, in order to include, it needs to deform itself and alter its coherence.

4.6 The Plot of Athos Magnani: Perspectives and Frames in *Strategia del ragno*

I will close this chapter with an investigation of *Strategia del ragno*, directed by Bernardo Bertolucci in 1969. In this film, produced and broadcast by RAI in 1970, many of the 'typical' formal patterns we have seen active in the five examples analyzed earlier and in the novels of the previous chapters have evolved since the immediate post-war period and reappear now with even more evidence: the shape of the fascist character *is*, in fact, the true aesthetic problem at the center of *Strategia del ragno*. First, as in *Il conformista*, the rational construction of a coherent narrative plot plays a fundamental role in the plot. Second, as in *Il Cristo proibito*, the film has a crime story plot centered on the solution of an enigma: who really is

Athos Magnani? The fascist/partisan object of the enquiry is a riddle to be solved. Another aspect in common with Malaparte's film is the theme of the hero returning to his hometown in order to discover the authors of a crime: the space of the village and its inhabitants are obstacles more than clues to the investigations. Third, as in *La lunga notte del '43*, the film might be defined as a «veritable drama of vision,»[351] in which the difficult memory of fascism is dramatized as a complicated and problematic *looking* at the fascist character. Enframing and finalizing the ambivalent, traumatic hero is a complex formal operation that results in the disruption of the otherwise highly geometric, profilmic space and of the otherwise linear narrative plot. As I observed earlier about Vancini's film, also in *La Strategia,* the use of the quattrocento linear perspective has a decisive role in relating the author to its hero and the latter to its audience of onlookers: «the conception of the quattrocento system is that of a scenographic space, space set out as spectacle for the eye of a spectator. Eye and knowledge come together; subject, object and the distance of the steady observation that allows the one to master the other; the scene with its strength of geometry and optics.»[352]

Fig. 40 – Bertolucci, *Strategia del ragno* (1969).

---

351 Stephen Heath, "Narrative Space," *Narrative, Apparatus, Ideology. A Film Theory Reader* (Columbia UP: New York, 1986), 397.
352 Idem, 387.

Strategia was, in fact, shot on location almost entirely in the Renaissance town of Sabbioneta, in Emilia-Romagna. Founded by Vespasiano Gonzaga in the late 16th Century, it is one of the clearest and most accomplished examples of the Renaissance 'ideal city,' planned and built according to the mathematical principles of the linear perspective in order to obtain geometrical harmony and a rational disposition of spaces. As was the case with Renaissance Ferrara in *La lunga notte*, the linear perspective is not only an 'objective' code inherited by the medium cinema from the pictorial arts, but it is also an integral characteristic of the place of the movie, of the profilmic space itself. In other words, there is a formal framing of space that pre-exists the framing operations of the film, thus complicating the act of vision. The value and meaning of 'deep focus' and 'depth of field' in a film that is shot in such places that were precisely created to enhance a perspectival view of reality cannot be considered in the same way as in other films in which depth and perspective are only imposed, from the outside, by the camera. If the typical location of postwar Italian cinema was the 'exposed contingency' of the ruinous city and landscape[353], Bertolucci chooses the opposite: the 'exposed mathematical necessity' and harmonious space of a perfectly intact ideal city. Noa Steimatsky argues that «in the initial postwar moment, the ruinous landscape was itself an arena of confrontation between the imperatives of evidence and memory and the project of reconstruction [...] In a landscape of ruins, neo-realism was reconstruction.»[354] If, as Angela Dalle Vecche writes, *Strategia* is primarily a film against the «authority of the fathers,»[355] rather than a *reconstruction*, the film is a process of disruption both of the narrative plot and of the profilmic space that was built around the hero and martyr of the resistance: Athos Magnani. The perfect enframing into the perspectival and ideal space of Tara-Sabbioneta is there to be negated and exceeded by the character they were supposed to contain and to finalize the ideal into a consummated, aesthetic form.

---

353 Noa Steimatsky, *Italian Locations*, (Minneapolis: Minnesota UP, 2008), 42.
354 Idem, 44-45.
355 Angela Dalle Vacche, *The Body in the Mirror. Antifascism after May 1968* (Princeton: Princeton UP, 1992). p. 219.

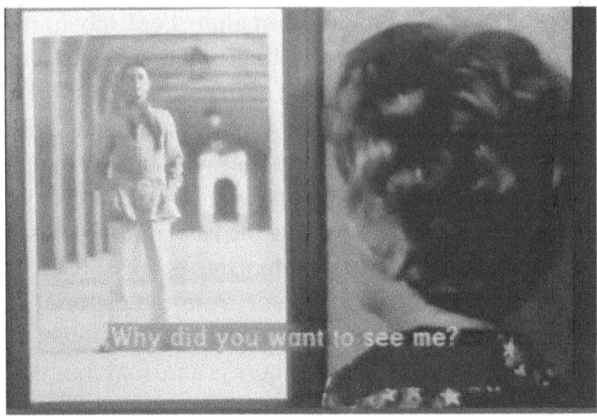

Fig. 41 — Bertolucci, *Strategia del ragno* (1969).

Athos is mysteriously asked to come to Tara by his father's mistress, Draifa. During his first visit to her house, Draifa and Athos look at some old photos of the father — portrayed in heroic postures under an arcade — while she recounts the circumstances of his death. She is the storyteller, and the account of the past story superimposes with images of a thrice framed Athos Magnani: well centered within the limits of the shot, inside the wooden frame of the photo and within the linear perspective of the arcade[356]. The

---

[356] Let's not forget that Athos' double, and father figure, in *Il conformista* will be named 'Quadri,' *cadres* in French, a possible reference to cinematic form itself

narrative plot that transmits the memory of Athos as a hero of the resistance killed by fascists coincides visually with the spatial enframing of his figure within highly demarcated formal boundaries. At the beginning of the movie his identity has a finalized shape with a precise meaning: Athos Magnani means hero and resistance.

In *Strategia*, then, 'place' does not have the disruptive value of pervasive contingency as in Bazin's interpretation of neorealism, but, rather, it is the symbolic form of the rational, teleological plot itself which enframes Athos as a mythical, epic hero. The perspectival view of Athos implies the presence of a «detached, untroubled eye, an eye free from the body, outside process, purely looking.»[357] Nevertheless, as David Forgacs mentions, «various defamiliarising techniques used in the film (reverse angle shots which fail to match, sudden changes of background, fades to black which do not mark any elapsed time, shots of empty squares and streets reminiscent of De Chirico's paintings) undermine the viewer's sense of being securely located in space and time.»[358] Bertolucci, in fact, constantly uses camera and editing to disrupt the profilmic space and to disorient the onlooker's secured positioning and well-centered point of view, thus progressively complicating that linear way to look at Athos, suggested by those photos, which also favored the narrativization of Athos Magnani's identity as a hero. The disruption of the mythical narrative corresponds to the formal disruption of the mathematical, ideal space of Tara-Sabbioneta operated by Bertolucci's camera.

In *Strategia*, then, the filming 'style' of the author brings contingency, while the real location, being conceived since its creation as 'ideal', stands, instead, as a 'monument' to formal necessity and rationalization. Tara-Sabbioneta is not merely the symbolic, surreal space of memory or the author's subconscious, as criticism of the movie constantly reminds us. However, it has a precise formal

---

and to its most basic act of *mise en cadre* or *cadrage*. Quadri is also considered to embody Godard.
357 Heath, "Narrative Space," 389.
358 David Forgacs, "Generations, History and Film in Italy," in *European Memories of the Second World War* ed. by Helmut Peitsch, Charles Burdett and Claire Gorrara (New York: Berghahn Book, 1999), 194.

function and value as an actual, real Renaissance 'ideal city,' a metonymic figure for that perfect aesthetic finalization which Bertolucci seeks to disrupt through his 'modernist' style: «non a caso esso [stile] produce sempre nuovi accostamenti tra le persone o tra un individuo e il suo ambiente: ciò che sottolinea (e ciò cui è finalizzato) è la costituzione di nuovi rapporti.»[359]

John David Rhodes and Elena Gorfinkel argue that place is not only a precondition of human subjectivity but also a constructive factor in the formation of the individual identity: «identity is constructed in and through place.»[360] In *Strategia*, Athos's identity as the hero is, at first, embodied, literally inscribed in it, by the urban space of Tara-Sabbioneta, only to be gradually disrupted in the course of the movie through a defamiliarising filmic style, which continuously undermines the spatial limits and clear cut measures of the profilmic field. Athos' identity, previously constructed in the past as the perfect space of the ideal city—which also dedicated a statue and a street to him—is now deformed in and through the formal disruption of that very same space.

The plot of the film is, then, the progressive undermining of the identity of Athos Magnani as the hero and the consequent revelation of his more ambiguous subjectivity. The diegesis of the film is the disclosure of history as diegesis, as the narrative plot itself. According to the myth that everyone in town is still telling his homonymous son, Athos Magnani was executed by fascists during an opera performance as a reprisal: he, together with three comrades, was 'plotting' to assassinate Mussolini during a performance of *Rigoletto*. Mussolini, in fact, was expected to attend that show as part of his visit to town, but a last-minute tip-off from a traitor unmasked the conspiracy plot, thus leading to Athos' killing. He then became the hero of a mythical narrative plot, which his son's investigation ends up undermining: the traitor who made the plot against Mussolini fails Athos himself. He was the spy who betrayed his comrades, who, in turn, killed him as a reprisal. Is this the final

---

359 Stefano Casetti, *Bertolucci* (Firenze: La nuova Italia, 1978), 65.
360 John David Rhodes and Elena Gorfinkel, *Taking Place. Location and the Moving Image* (Minneapolis: University of Minnesota Press, 2011), ix.

truth, the final solution of the enigma? Maybe. At this point, it is not clear if it was he who let them kill him in order to create a myth so that the resistance could exploit his legacy and memory for their cause or if they, having found out he was the spy, killed him without revealing his true nature as collaborationist in order to keep intact his memory as a hero, thus avoiding shocking in this way the entire community which so strongly identified him with the resistance. Is he the hero or the traitor? Or, as Athos Magnani himself says at the end of the film: *Qual è la vera trama di Athos Magnani?* Was the mythical plot imposed on him by the postwar anti-fascist simplified and reassuring vision of the past, or was he the author of a sort of master plot framing all the other subplots? In the end, Athos Magnani, like all the other characters I have investigated so far, is an enigma: his identity, at first well-centered and enframed as the static hero joining together the necessary, causal sequence of a narrative plot, gradually exceeds this very same well-consummated form, disrupting finalization, finally revealing itself as a dynamic character, no longer hero, whose identity is shuttered, uncertain and lacking the closure of a definitive meaning. Athos Magnani escapes a clear-cut, uncomplicated categorization, being neither the hero nor the traitor of the tale. The initial, well framed and centered 'point of view shot of a shot' of Athos under the arcade is no longer possible: Athos, in fact, is no longer the mere hero-object of the plot but, perhaps, also its possible author-subject. The demarcation between subject and object collapses, and, thus, also the possibility of finalizing the fascist character into the uncomplicated form of the type if, as it seems, the very author of the plot is the main hero of that same plot.

Moreover, I believe it is the very dynamic and disruptive nature of the fascist character that allows Bertolucci to use all those defamiliarising techniques mentioned above, enabling that contrast between the fixity and necessity of mostly perspectival space and the increasingly excessive, decentering identity of the collaborationist character. The film continuously mixes up interiors and exteriors, day and night, past and present, confounding the onlooker's ability to locate the events both in time and space safely and forcing them to dislocate their point of view, in this way, as

Karl Schoonover argues, stripping «the mask of the universal, monocentric perspective from which neorealists saw reality.»[361] However, I do not think, as Angela Dalle Vacche writes, «with Bertolucci, neorealism departs from documentary and turns into surrealism.»[362] Tara is not merely a surreal place; it is also the material reality that the film and its protagonist are there to distort.

The fascist character's identity is the plot of a classic tragedy with some elements of the spy-story genre. Like Marcello in *Il conformista*, Athos Magnani identifies with the coherent whole — with beginning, middle, and end — of a low-brow narrative plot, which later on will be, instead, revealed as fiction with no absolute value, leaving their identities without a fixed definition in between hero and villain, protagonist and minor character. They symbolize the negation of a transparent, uncomplicated representation of reality, and, on the contrary, they both 'lay bare the device,' as the formalists would say, by exposing the narrative ordering of the events as a teleological, causal plot obeying to typical generic patterns. They estrange this form as nothing but aesthetic form, from the reality it was supposed to mirror and refer to directly. The spectator is, then, made well aware of having been looking at a fiction, at a narrative construction and not at a documentary, an unfiltered historical account of past events.

Strategia has two Athoses: one well-enframed in a mathematically perfect teleological plot and linear perspective, another whom the author fails to emplot and to close into the spatial and temporal limits of a formal frame. The film might be considered a study in framing since all its spaces — both interiors and exteriors — are filled with frames, both picture frames and architectural lines. For example, juxtapose the various shots that portray Athos well-centered in a linear perspective or framed by doors or windows with the scene of the son's visit to Gaibazzi, one of Magnani's three friends and partners in crime. Gaibazzi and Athos are eating, facing each other while sitting at a small table. Behind the older man's back, hanging on the wall, there are many paintings and frames. He is talking

---

361 Schoonover, *Brutal Vision*, 200.
362 Dalle Vacche, *The Body in the Mirror*, 230.

about how, sometimes, a tiny, almost undetectable flaw in the wine might still be pleasing and even make it better. After a series of normal shot and reverse-shot transitions between Athos and Gaibazzi, Bertolucci literally disrupts the expected sequence of shots by interposing a completely displaced master shot of the room where the two are eating. The shot is taken from another, lower room so that the two men are barely distinguishable from afar. They are framed by the door, but the point of view is too low, too decentered. Compared to the previous framings of Athos, this one strikes the attention of the viewer for its unjustified and flawed nature.

Fig. 43 — Bertolucci, *Strategia del ragno* (1969).

Bertolucci chooses an unusual, inconvenient angle from which the surrounding profilmic space obstructs the viewer's gaze on the scene, obtaining the opposite result of that initial shot under the perfectly receding arcade. The flawed framing of Gaibazzi and Athos having lunch gives the spectator's eye nothing else to see but walls, stairs and, on the right, half of a half-opened framed window. As if Bertolucci himself agrees with Gaibazzi's praise of a flawed wine, he decides to instantly respond to his character by interposing, in a so far highly mannerist directing style, a flawed, unnecessary shot.

Another sequence that distorts the perfect spatial enframing of Athos as hero and monument is the often-quoted mutual looking between Athos and the statue of the father at the center of Tara-Sabbioneta's main square. Like Oedipus trying to peer through the enigma of the Sphinx, Athos walks around the half-bust of his father, of the hero. The first shot is a close-up of the statue. The camera movement around the father's face gives the optical illusion that the statue itself is moving, and is looking at something off-screen. The reverse shot is a close-up of Athos walking around the statue, thus revealing the subject who is looking: that movement belongs to Athos, to the subject looking and not to the object being looked at. The close-up of the statue was a subjective shot taken from the point of view of an onlooker always repositioning himself. And, until now, nothing too strange or flawed. The sight lines of the statue and Athos are matching, resulting in a perfect mirroring between father and son, subject and object. Nevertheless, this is only an optical illusion: the statue seems to move only as a consequence of Athos' moving in a circle around it; the shot of the statue only exists insofar as it is a subjective reverse shot showing us the object of the subject's gaze. Suddenly, though, Athos changes direction and starts to walk the opposite way. However, the following subjective shot of the statue does not change: the camera continues to film the statue as if Athos did not change direction. All the scene, then, needs to be reread in reverse: Athos has never been the subject who was looking, but the object of the statue's gaze. The hero/fascist Athos Magnani defies the inquirer's gaze; it disrupts the spatial coordinates of the camera movement and the expected horizontal flow of the shot, thus confounding the roles of subject and object and forestalling the fixed, secured placement of an ideal, detached observer.

Fig. 44 — Bertolucci, *Strategia del ragno* (1969).

This sequence is a veritable study of the possible interactions between looking and space and how the former depends on and is diverted by the latter. The horizontal, only apparently looping, circular camera movement is, in fact, dictated by the shape of the square where the scene takes place.

Another important detail intervenes now to disturb the mutual gazing of father and son, subject and object, enigma and enquirer: in the background, behind the statue, there suddenly appears an out-of-focus but very luminous and white silhouette of Draifa. The close-up and the in-depth shot mix each other up, also blurring the difference between foreground and background. Athos eventually leaves the statue and goes to meet Draifa: despite her being out of focus and the statue still being there, well evident and framed in front of the viewer, she is now the true object of Athos' gaze. What seemed a contingent and unnecessary element of the frame, left out of focus in the background, included in the frame only thanks to the depth of field, is, on the contrary, a diegetic, technical device that moves the narrative plot forward and starts the transition to the next scene. Moreover, Draifa is walking in the same direction as Athos; thus, her movement helps to stress the incongruity between the camera movements of the subjective shot of the statue and that of Athos. Under the appearance of the typical, accidental 'reality effect,' the opaque, distant silhouette of Draifa is actually a formal device with a merely diegetic, rather than mimetic, function.

Fig. 44 – Bertolucci, *Strategia del ragno* (1969).

The presence of Draifa has the further effect of, once again, emphasizing the statue's role as something more than the object of looking: by taking the statue's place as the true object of Athos' sight, Draifa also deflects the attention of the audience from it, making it somehow invisible despite its excessive dimension, almost occupying the entirety of the frame. The statue sees rather than being seen. The spectator's centered, detached point of view is also included in this general chaos of identities and roles, as they identify with the son's perspective on the statue and Draifa, and, at the same time, they are the off-screen object of the statue's gaze. Every role and position is constantly shifting, never fixed and defined once and for all.

The subject is always shown to be simultaneously the object of the *other's* gaze. Looking is always a subjective act. This scene is, I think, in dialogue with another similar sequence, demonstrating the same thing: in *Strategia*, looking outside at the surrounding space always simultaneously coincides with looking inside the self. After scratching out the name of the father from his tomb, Athos comes back home and starts to wash his face, thus, in a way, repeating the effacing gesture on his face. Waiting for him on his bed, he finds the boy living with Draifa. While Athos is washing his face, the boy goes behind the mirror over the sink: when Athos raises his head to look at the boy, the reflection of his face on the mirror interposes itself between the two. Athos' looking at the boy, is also a looking at himself.

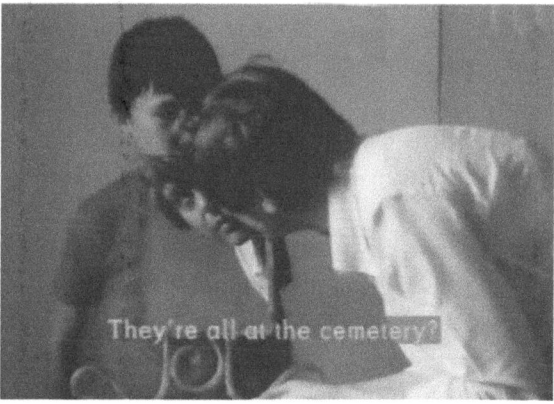

Fig. 45 – Bertolucci, *Strategia del ragno* (1969).

The scene perfectly mirrors the previous one of the statue, with the boy taking Draifa's place behind the statue and the statue being replaced by Athos' mirror image. Moreover, Athos appears to be well-enframed by the mirror, while his gaze goes beyond the limits of his delimited, 'squared' double. Athos looks at the boy, and he is looked back at both by the boy and by his reflection in the mirror. By interposing itself between subject and object, the framed image in the mirror obstructs the mutual gaze between the boy and Athos by means of another gaze: the self-reflexive gaze of Athos in himself. The image of the self half eclipses that of the other: the looking at the real is always filtered through and blurred by the projection of the self upon what they are seeing. Thus, nothing can be contingent, fortuitous and meaningless under the gaze of the subject who emplots and enframes reality within a coherent whole. Everything is given meaning according to the self's particular, unique point of view. Every detail exists only insofar as the self assigns a precise function to it in relation to his position and the rest of the whole. That is why Athos Magnani's identity is nothing but a plot to be read and an enigma to be pieced together. It is exactly this way of looking at reality and at history that is disrupted in these two scenes: the self is always, at the same time, its opposite, the other looking from the other side of the mirror.

Through the typical steps and turns of a crime story narrative structure, it unveils the plot that grounds Athos Magnani's identity as hero. Then, it disrupts a plot by means of another plot. *Strategia* fetishizes plot because, parallel to the fragmentation of the teleological progress of the *récit*, there is, as we have seen, the deconstruction of the ideal, rationalized space of Tara-Sabbioneta. The son's enquiry aims towards closure—i.e., towards the enframing of his father in a finalized form—while the author constantly pushes the solution to the enigma further back; by continuously disorienting the subject searching, thwarting his relation to the surrounding space, displacing his detached, centered point of view from which he is dissecting the mysterious identity of the father. The linear perspective shots and the constant enframing of characters within windows, doors, picture frames, arcades, gates, and mirrors visually translate the emplotment of Athos Magnani as hero of the resistance: the perspective turns him into a monument, materialized memory. *Strategia*, nevertheless, shows emplotments and enframings as only transitory moments of a dynamic process that never reaches finalization and closure. Athos Magnani, at the end of the movie, escapes a definitive, uncomplicated classification into clear-cut categories, remaining an unnamable character in between villain and hero, traitor and martyr, fascist and partisan, father and son, past and present. Thanks to this open ambivalence and lack of closure, such a character guarantees a potentially never-ending *plaisir du texte* to the reader/spectator, who, never provided with the final solution to the *enigma*, can never cease their search for meaning.

From Lili Marleen to Athos Magnani, my investigation has shown that, already from the immediate postwar years, the fascist character was an object difficult to enframe and to emplot because it simultaneously triggers a genre-based kind of emplotment—melodrama, crime story—and disrupts it because of its traumatic ambiguity as both enemy and fellow citizen, self and other, author and hero. The fascist character has a fundamental narrative function in the plot as the perfect type of villain, and, at the same time, they are something more and other than a mere villain, blurring the boundaries that separate them from the hero of the story. This is a formal process that, already active during the postwar years of neorealism, will reach full maturation in the sixties and seventies, when the Italian convulsed political situation will make explicit how the memory and legacy of the Second World War was still an open, unfinalized discourse and unclosed wound. A second generation of filmmakers—Vancini and Bertolucci are the examples in this chapter—will expand and bring to the foreground the disruptive function of the fascist character, the impossibility of looking back at that trauma from a perfect, detached eye, aiming to demonstrate how «the official cult of antifascism has simplified the past in order to produce a reassuring history.»[363] The fascist character is bound to be enframed in a *flawed* form that activates a process of estrangement and defamiliarization: it 'lays bare the device,' sabotaging the

---

363 Forgacs, "Generations, History and Film in Italy," 194.

supposed transparency of a documentary and historical explanation of the past, both in literature and film. In fact, *La lunga notte* is a study of testimony: the eyewitness is represented as a spectator, and testimony is a cinematic experience. The tragedy of war was perceived as a *spectacle* from the beginning, already by the generation who directly experienced it. The closeness to those events does not entail a better, unfiltered knowledge. *Strategia*, as Moravia in *Il conformista* already did in 1949, searches for self-knowledge and the psychoanalytic experience, equal to a reading practice: the truth about history and the self has the shape of a narrative plot- both tragic and low-brow.

The fascist disrupts objectivity and teleology, demonstrating how the memory of the past is a flawed discourse and not a linear perspective, leading to an objective account and a clear-cut categorization of history.

CHAPTER 5
Standing in the Way of Narrative Exchange and Desire: a Reading of the Fascist Character in *Una questione privata* by Beppe Fenoglio.

Marcello in *Il conformista* shapes his life as a coherent narrative in order to justify a crime, only to later find out that the plot structuring his destiny was nothing but a tragic misinterpretation of past events. Athos Magnani in *Strategia del ragno* hides his identity behind a plot that could be read, at once, as the story of a hero or that of a traitor.

In these two cases, as in all the other ones previously analyzed, the fascist character, the spy, and the traitor undeniably entertain a particular, one-of-a-kind relationship with the narrative plot. In fact, they seem to both trigger and thwart the causal sequence of narrated events. These are characters that enable within the text the emplotment of life in the generic *topoi* of melodrama and crime story and that, nevertheless, simultaneously escape closure and finalization into a reductive definition. They appear to allow structure and to defy it at the same time. The author makes of them an unproblematic use, treating them as puppets, as those stereotypical characters that a particular genre tradition endows with a specific, pre-assigned narrative function. Villains, traitors, femme fatales, spies, and rivals in love are the plethora of secondary, fascist types that let romance access the text and disrupt, alter, and deviate the realism of a too autobiographical, diaristic representation of the civil war. In this case, their narrative function prevails over the role they played in historical reality: the language of genre wins over objectivity.

Nevertheless, the historic contingency of fascists and their role in triggering traumatic memories of the civil war exceeds the predetermined finalization carried on by genre memory and shows them to be, on the contrary, the site of *affect* in the text, the dynamic entities undermining the emplotment that they initially facilitated. Plots with fascists undeniably share similar premises, being, most of the time, structured around an absent and absolute cause. *Il conformista* is based on a contingent event wrongly believed to be a necessary cause; in *Strategia del ragno*, the son's enquiry and quest are potentially never-ending and without solution since the cause they were trying to clarify is highly paradoxical, ambivalent and double-faced.

The fascist character seems to transform the plot into the quest for a truth that is missing. The effect of this cause is the tale itself, the story that is told to the reader because everything in the plot seems to originate from the presence of a secret. On the one hand, the mystery triggers the quest and thus the tale; on the other, without the quest, there would not be any tale at all, and so the end is something that the plot, in general, both aspires to and delays. The fascist character is, then, what eases and stimulates the narrative process by introducing secrecy and a lack in the text. At the same time, though, the fascist is also what prevents the mystery from being solved and the absent and absolute cause from being found and revealed. Borrowing words that Todorov uses to describe Henry James' art of fiction, in plots with fascist characters, the presence of truth is incompatible with the tale:

> Le mouvement de James est double et, en apparence, contradictoire (ce qui lui permet de le recommencer sans cesse): d'une part, il déploie toutes ses forces pour atteindre l'essence cachée, pour dévoiler l'objet secret; de l'autre, il éloigne sans cesse, le protège—jusqu'à la fine de l'histoire, sinon au-delà. L'absence de la cause ou de la vérité est présente dans le texte, plus même, elle en est l'origine logique et la raison d'être; la cause est ce qui, par son absence, fait surgir le texte. L'essentiel est absent, l'absence est essentielle.[364]

Like James in the above quotation, authors such as Moravia, Pavese and Bertolucci use fascist characters to endow their texts with secrecy, mystery, and enigma, that is to say, with the clichés of non-realist genres, such as melodrama and the crime story, which trigger the desire to know an absent, hidden cause. Somehow, though, they also let finalization fail; they sabotage and disrupt closure,

---

364 Tzvetan Todorov, *Poétique de la prose* (Paris: Seuil, 1971), 83.

thus postponing indefinitely the attainment of a fixed, static truth and meaning. In Peter Brooks' dynamic-energetic model of narrative plot, the fascist character would have this contradictory function of trigger and obstacle of the narrative desire for an end that would determine meaning once and for all:

> Plot itself stands as a kind of divergence or deviance, a postponement in the discharge which leads back to the inanimate. For plot starts (or must give the illusion of starting) from that moment at which story, or "life," is stimulated from quiescence into a state of narratability, into a tension, a kind of irritation, which demands narration. I spoke earlier of narrative desire, the arousal that creates the narratable as a condition of tumescence, appetency, ambition, quest, and gives narrative a forward-looking intention. [...] The ensuing narrative — the Aristotelian "middle" — is maintained in a state of tension, as a prolonged deviance from the quiescence of the "normal" — which is to say, the unnarratable — until it reaches the terminal quiescence of the end. [...] The narrative must tend toward its end, seek illumination in its own death. Yet this must be the right death, the correct end. The complication of the detour is related to the danger of short-circuit: the danger of reaching the end too quickly, of achieving the im-proper death. [...] *The desire of the text (the desire of reading) is hence desire for the end, but desire for the end reached only through the at least minimally complicated detour, the intentional deviance, in tension, which is the plot of narrative.* [italics mine] [365]

The fascist character offers to the author the temptations of the genre tradition, of genres more interested in a postponement of truth that would keep alive, and suspended, the narrative desire, rather than in a direct, documentary and faithful account of past events.

In this chapter, I intend to investigate what this involvement of the fascist character with narrative desire entails and what exactly it enables within the emplotted space of the text. I believe that *Una questione privata,* the last unfinished and posthumous novel by Beppe Fenoglio, is a very interesting case study, given its extremely linear — almost reminiscent of Boccaccio — structure. I will argue that the short novel is mainly about a missing storyteller and a hero's wish to be his listener. The absolute and absent cause is, in this case, a speaker, an author whose potential message needs to be unearthed. *Una questione privata* is the scene of a failed discourse, of

---

[365] Peter Brooks, *Reading for the Plot* (Cambridge, Massachusetts: Harvard UP, 1984), 103-104.

the silence which resists the reader's wish for the end, the quest for a speech act that the necessary presence of a fascist character leads irreparably astray.

At the center of the plot lies, once again, an enigma that the hero strives to decipher. The story is set in the Langhe Hills during the civil war between fascists and partisans in November 1944. Milton, the protagonist, is a young partisan, a *badogliano* to be exact, i.e., belonging to one of the non-communist factions of the Italian Resistance. The readers encounter him for the first time *in medias res*, when he looks from afar and eventually decides to approach the house where Fulvia, the woman he fell in love with, used to live when she was evacuated from a too-dangerous Turin in 1943. He met her back then through his best friend, and now fellow partisan, Giorgio Clerici, and the three began to spend more and more time together until Milton had to join the army and leave. Now, he finds the villa empty, with the exception of the old governess, who suddenly recognizes him. She tells him that Fulvia went back to Turin and that she will probably never come back as the family has decided to sell the house. Allowed by the governess to look around the abandoned rooms of the villa, a sort of tomb to his eyes, Milton is haunted by the memories of the past, of the moments he shared there with his beloved, remembering the signs of a passion that he never quite openly disclosed to her, preferring to give her indirect hints and allusions through songs and, most importantly, books he suggested she read. His love was, then, a message she had to decipher behind the lines of *Tess of the d'Urbervilles* by Hardy or *Morella* by Poe, a message she probably never interpreted the right way. The series of flashbacks is interrupted now and then by the governess's answers to Milton's questions until she confesses to him that she has always liked him more than his friend Giorgio because Giorgio started to visit Fulvia alone more and more often after Milton left. Furthermore, while she could always overhear Milton and Fulvia speaking when they were alone in her bedroom, on the contrary, she could not hear anything when Fulvia was alone in the room with Giorgio:

> Loro due non li sentivo mai parlare. Io origliavo, non ho nessuna vergogna a dirlo, origliavo per dovere. Ma c'era sempre un silenzio, quasi non ci fossero. E io non stavo mai tranquilla. Ma non dica queste cose al suo amico, mi raccomando. Si misero a far tardi, ogni volta più tardi. [...] Non dico che abbiano fatto il male...[366]

What happened between his best friend Giorgio, the most handsome man of Alba, and Fulvia, the woman Milton fell in love with? Milton is overcome by a frantic desire to know, to ask Giorgio if he and Fulvia betrayed his friendship and his love. Once again, at the outset of the plot, there is a scene of secrecy, a mystery only peered through and overheard through walls, as we have seen was the case of *Un eroe del nostro tempo* by Pratolini, for example, with Virginia spying on Sandrino's orgasm at the beginning of the novel. In this case the secret is caused by silence, and the mystery is alluded to, more exactly, by the *lack* of voices, by a listener missing her speaker. At this point, Milton's furious quest for truth starts, but in the meantime, Giorgio has been captured by the *Repubblichini* and awaits in prison a too-obvious death sentence. The night before, a surreal, uncommonly thick fog misled him directly into the arms of a fascist battalion. The only chance Milton now has to let Giorgio speak and finally let him explain the truth is to find a fascist soldier to exchange with him. His desperate search against time, as Giorgio can be executed at any moment, is unsuccessful, as neither the *badogliani*, the more moderate side of the resistance, nor the *rossi*, the communist and most 'unscrupulous' faction, have imprisoned a fascist recently. At this point, an old peasant woman shows him the neighboring house where a fascist sergeant often comes to encounter his lover, a tailor. The portrayal of the collaborationist woman is, once again, the stereotypical, excessive one of a prostitute driven by an abnormal sexual want:

---

[366] Beppe Fenoglio, *Una questione privata* (Einaudi-Gallimard: Torino, Parigi, 1992), 1023. «I never heard those two talking. I eavesdropped, I am not ashamed to tell you that, it was my duty. But it was always silent, as if they weren't there. And it worried me a lot. But please don't tell your friend. They'd stay up late, later and later all the time. [...] I am not saying they did anything wrong.» (Beppe Fenoglio, *A Private Affair,* translated by Howard Curtis (London: Hasperus Press Limited, 2006), 17, 19.

> È una lurida, l'hai già capito, e questo che fa adesso con questo sergente è poco o niente in confronto a quello che ha fatto prima. Basti dirti che prima dei vent'anni aveva già abortito tre volte. È la più porca di Canelli e di tutti i dintorni e non so se girando tutto il mondo se ne trova una più porca. […] Ha messo tanto male fra mia figlia e mio genero, e mio genero, che non è di queste parti, ha avuto il torto di credere a quella là invece che a noi che gli giuravamo che non era vero niente. Ma ora finalmente l'ha capita e con mia figlia vanno meglio di prima, prima che quella lurida cercasse di avvelenarci. […] E lo fece per pura malvagità, forse perché non poteva sopportare di essere l'unica vera porca dei paraggi e così si è inventata una compagna, ma se l'è solo inventata.[367]

Just as for Milton, the war has turned into a private affair between him and Giorgio, so for this woman, the conflict has become the occasion to take personal revenge against the degenerate, perverse, evil rival neighbor who tried to seduce her daughter's husband. Another secondary love triangle in the background accelerates the main one towards its end.

Milton seems blessed by luck as, that same afternoon, the sergeant shows up on the street, and he is able to surprise and kidnap him. Milton tries to reassure him about his destiny by saying that he does not have any intention to kill him and that, on the contrary, he wants to exchange him for a friend, and the sergeant attempts to escape. Milton is forced to shoot him dead. After having spent a night with his fellow partisans, during which a disturbing story is recounted of partisan violence, reprisal and sexual depravation — the shaving of a female collaborator's head and the consequent group masturbation by some of the partisan perpetrators —, he starts to think again about what the governess has told him, starting even to doubt what he heard and to realize that perhaps he might have misunderstood her words. He decides, then, to go back to

---

[367] Fenoglio, *Una questione privata*, 1092. «She's a dirty cow, you've already understood that, and what she's doing now with this sergeant is little or nothing compared with what she did before. Just think, before she was twenty she'd already had three abortions. She's the worst bitch in Canelli, and in the whole area, I don't think you'd find a worse bitch if you went all round the world. […] She caused a lot of trouble between my daughter and my son in law, and my son in law, who isn't from around here, made the mistake of believing her instead of us, even though we swore to him that there was nothing to it. But at last he realised it, and things with my daughter are better than before, before that dirty cow started making our lives a misery. […] And she did it out of pure wickedness, maybe because she couldn't bear to be the only real cow in the area, and so she invented a companion, but she only invented her.» 98.

Fulvia's house and to interrogate the governess, to listen to her one more time. However, on his way there, he bumps into a troop of fascists. After an endless, breathless chase, his body encrusted with blood and mud, he falls lifeless at the border of the woods. Here, the plot ends, or, better, it is left unfinished by Fenoglio, who was to die himself, unexpectedly, aged 41.

The plot of *Una questione privata* is centered on an exchange of prisoners, which is a recurrent *topos* throughout Fenoglio's work. In fact, this last exchange repeats two previous ones. The most direct source is the episode in *Il partigiano Johnny II*, when Johnny tries, without success, to exchange a fascist sergeant in order to free his friend Ettore. In contrast, in *L'imboscata*, the exchange is a successful one, a framed narrative remembered and told by the partisan Maté. If we add to these antecedents the slightly different rewritings of the same scene in the two preliminary drafts of *Una questione privata*, the episode becomes a true palimpsest calling for an intertextual analysis that inevitably exceeds the boundaries of the single, uncompleted novel. Thus, the exchange of prisoners in *Una questione privata* has a surplus of value that the other previous variations do not have, first of all, because Fenoglio finally turns this scene into the main episode of the novel's plot, into its true Pythagorean upsilon and the decisive turning point. The exchange is now what Moretti defined as 'the moment of truth.' This means that also the character of the fascist sergeant gains meaning and a function he never had before in Fenoglio's work. In fact, compared to the twin scenes in *PJ II* and *L'imboscata*, the exchange of *Una questione privata* has a specific, unprecedented cause. More than being a mere swap between two people, it entails an exchange of a different nature: a linguistic trade. Milton, in exchange for the fascist, is asking for a message, for a discourse, for truth. He desires to exchange silence for words in order to give that absence of words, maliciously interpreted by the governess, a clear, unequivocal meaning.

Una questione privata, I believe, can be read as a story about language, the quest of a listener in search of the lost, absent speech of an author. It is a novel about an unfinalized, unconsummated message that fails to reach its end and its final target because of the highly problematic presence of a fascist character. The fascist is in *Una questione privata* a medium, the mode of speech, the frame of dialogue, that the addresser and addressee would need in order to send and receive to convey a message. Once again, the critical move to consider the fascist character as the main object of analysis allows for an altogether new approach to a text too often read in the same manner. The fascist character is not the *other*, the object of the author's discourse, but he is the necessary material that would make that discourse possible and that, nevertheless, ends up sabotaging it. He is the key to the solution of a riddle and, at the same time, the character that will preserve the enigma.

During the years of philological debate over the correct date of composition of *Il partigiano Johnny*, the main focus of critics has been the extravagant nature of Fenoglio's language—characterized by an unusual mix between English and Italian—at times seen as the climax of his art, at other times as an inner, work in progress, as jargon. What Maria Corti and Maria Antonietta Grignani have defined as Fenoglio's «*ricerca della lingua*»[368] or «*questione della lingua*»[369] constitutes the narrative plot of *Una questione privata*, a novel mainly about the doomed quest for the right language to describe the past, about the impossible mimesis of reality and about a language lacking reference to the one truth is trying to convey. That *Una questione privata* concerns the communication of a message between a speaker and a listener is also confirmed by Fenoglio's tendency to reinforce the phatic aspect of dialogues and to insert illocutionary modules in the last version of the novel, as noted by Enrico Testa:

> La riscrittura mira inoltre ad un rinforzo degli aspetti fàtici ed emotivi della lingua del dialogo con il conseguente inserimento di moduli allocutivi. [...] Al medesimo progetto stilistico pare appartenere anche l'utilizzo dei puntini sospensivi, icona del *gramma* destinata a dar segni delle esitazioni e delle reticenze della voce.[370]

Milton's motive, the cause that drives his quest, is directly related to the style of Fenoglio's prose. The written language of the novel

---

368 Maria Antonietta Grignani, "Virtualità del testo e ricerca della lingua da una stesura all'altra del *Partigiano Johnny*," *Strumenti Critici*, 36-37, (October 1978): 275-331, 275.
369 Maria Corti, *Beppe Fenoglio. Storia di un "continuum" narrativo* (Padova: Liviana, 1980), 20.
370 Enrico Testa, *Lo stile semplice* (Torino: Einaudi, 1997), 301 and footnote.

is modified in the sense of a progressive approximation to the oral, common language. Both author and hero share the same tendency towards an oral speech act, the wish to listen to a voice and to the important news it is ready to send.

A confirmation of the centrality of the quest for language and of the exchange of an oral message comes from the first draft of the novel, which has a different beginning from the third and posthumously published version. Even though in this early draft Milton does not want to free Giorgio in order to hear from him the truth about Fulvia — the love subplot is completely absent — the story begins, not by chance, in my opinion, with a double messenger. After having seen Giorgio being transported to jail on a jeep, an unknown boy runs to tell the news to his mother, who, in turn, runs to inform first her husband and, finally, Giorgio's mother, only to find out the news has already reached her. The boy, Fenoglio writes, «aveva una grossa notizia da portare.»[371] *Una questione privata,* then, begins with the passing of information from person to person by means of oral communication. Although this incipit disappears in the second draft of the novel, and in the third, the theme of the passing of a message does not lose any of its importance, but rather it is amplified by the addition of the Milton-Giorgio-Fulvia love triangle and by Milton's need to hear an explanation from Giorgio. Now, in between the two friends stands the character of Sergeant Alarico, *repubblichino* of the infamous San Marco squad, whose function, meaning and qualities evolve too throughout the different and successive rewritings of *Una questione privata.*

Alarico appears for the first time in *L'imboscata,* and his role in that project, eventually abandoned by Fenoglio in order to write *Una questione privata,* is slightly different. First of all, his name is not yet Alarico but Goti. Now, Alaric was the king of the Goths (*Goti*), the barbarian late invaders of Northern Italy, responsible, among other factors, for the fall of the Roman Empire. Fenoglio, then, changes the name of the fascist character from the name of a people

---

[371] Fenoglio, *Una questione privata. Prima redazione* in Maria Corti, ed. by, *Beppe Fenoglio-Opere,* Vol. I (Torino: Einaudi, 1978), 1721. «The boy had to bring an important news»

(Goti) to the first name that stands for that people and represents its entirety (Alarico), that is to say, from the plural to the singular, from the universal to the particular. The change of name from Goti to Alarico, from the people to its king, stands for a new symbolic resonance. In *Una questione privata,* in fact, the fascist character is important precisely because of his reference value, because Alarico signifies another, Giorgio, the fascist character being then the necessary means of the oral communication, the sign referring to a content (Giorgio's truth).

To be true, the functions and the names of the other characters at play in the exchange of prisoners — namely Milton, Giorgio and Alarico-Goti's 'tailor' lover — also undergo interesting variations in being displaced from *L'imboscata* to *Una questione privata*. A comparative reading of the two different forms that the scene of the exchange of prisoners has in *L'imboscata* and *Una questione privata* will, once more, highlight the fascist character as the true dynamic variable of the text. The two unfinished novels, then, share the same complex constellation of characters rotating around the figure of the fascist. What defines their roles is, ultimately, their *relationship* to the fascist character. The function that one character has with regard to the fascist's function in *L'imboscata* is taken by another character of the constellation in *Una questione privata*. Instead of helping to create binary, Manichean, static oppositions, sergeant Alarico-Goti triggers the carnivalesque relativity between identities and the crossing of boundaries between the characters' static narrative functions. Despite appearing as endowed with a very schematic, merely formal, narrative function — an almost fairytale one, that of being the *instrument-object* allowing the hero to reach his goal — the fascist character has a much more disruptive-excessive mission towards form.

In *L'imboscata*, the exchange of prisoners and the fascist sergeant's liaison with a collaborationist woman are two distinct, separate episodes. The exchange of prisoners does not have anything to do with Milton and with Alarico-Goti, but it is a very marginal episode remembered by Maté regarding the partisan Sceriffo and a fascist tenant, described as malnourished, with glasses and with a pimply face. The woman who has a relationship with Alarico-Goti is in *L'imboscata*, a teacher, not a tailor. Her story — it even has a subtitle of its own: *la storia della maestrina di San Quirico* — is orally narrated to a group of other partisans by Jack, a real storyteller reminiscent of Conrad's *Heart of Darkness*:

> venite a sentire la storia di una maestra. Una storia che merita. Una maestra fascista fino alle unghie. [...] Questa maestra era una fanatica rara, nel senso che non si limitava alla politica nuda e cruda ma sognava di fare un figlio con Mussolini. [...] Edda si chiamava. Come la figlia di Mussolini.[372]

The actual story is absent from *L'imboscata*. Nevertheless, Fenoglio will insert the secondhand narration into *Una questione privata*, where the character of the collaborationist Edda splits into two different women: the tailor lover of Alarico Goti and the 'impertinent teacher.' I am talking, of course, of the violent episode of the 11th chapter, when a group of red partisans shaves the head of the collaborationist teacher as an alternative, milder punishment to the cold-blooded execution advocated by Alonso, the Spanish Civil War veteran. This time, it is Maté who narrates her story, while — a detail not to be overlooked — Milton is absent, half asleep in another room, cursing about the fascist first found and then fatally lost and trying to repurpose his now abruptly aimless existence. Maté begins the story in this way:

> - Ci risiamo con le maestre? — disse Maté. — Attenti, ragazzi, alle maestre perché è una categoria col fascismo incarnato. Io non so che gli abbia fatto il duce a quelle, ma nove su dieci sono fasciste. Io potrei raccontarvi di una maestra, di *una per tutte*.
> - E racconta.
> - Fascista fino alla punta delle unghie, continuò Maté. — Era una di quelle che sognavano di fare un figlio con Mussolini. Ed era anche cotta per quel porco di Graziani.
> - Un momento, — fece Pinco. — Era giovane, era bella? È importante saperlo subito.

---

372 Fenoglio, *L'imboscata*, 885. «Come closer to listen to the story of a teacher. A story that deserves to be heard. A teacher who was fascist to her fingertips. She was a true fanatic, normal politics wasn't enough for her: She was the kind who dreamed of having a child with Mussolini. Her name was Edda, like Mussolini's daughter.»

> - Era sui trent'anni, — specificò Maté, — ed era una bella pianta di donna. Un po' robusta, un po' mascolina, ma ben messa e ben distribuita come carne. E soprattutto aveva una carnagione magnifica, una *vera seta*.[373] [*italics* mine]

Later, she will be defined as a «*fenomeno curioso,*»[374] an oddity difficult to grasp and frame fully. Moreover two details already point to the other version of her in *Una questione privata*. The detail of her silky skin — the only feminine feature of an otherwise overly masculinized body — will, I believe, expand into her tailoring profession in the later novel. A specific part of her will be used to define her whole. Her character from *L'imboscata* to *Una questione privata* expands by means of metonymy, as Alaric is the individual who represents the whole of a people.

Furthermore, Maté tells her story as exemplary of all the other same stories of fascist collaborationist teachers: *una per tutte*, a part of the whole. Thereby, the story of the teacher is a synecdoche, as the fascist sergeant chased by Milton will be. Narrative desire, according to Peter Brooks, exactly works as a perpetually extended metonymy that is «condemned to saying other than what it would mean, spinning out its movement toward a meaning that would be the end of its movement.»[375] The teacher and the sergeant somehow embody the inchoation of the narrative impulse, the desire to tell the story and the simultaneous impossibility of finalizing it, to find the right closure, to arrest the metonymic chain.

Indeed, the teacher's sin, her guilt, is that she speaks too much; she cannot keep her tongue from conveying fascist propaganda, from insulting the partisans, from yelling that fascists should either

---

[373] Fenoglio, *Una questione privata*, 1111. "Are we on about schoolmistresses again?" Maté said. "beware of schoolmistresses, boys. Schoolmistresses are like Fascism personified. I don't know what the Duce did to them, but nine out of ten are Fascists. I could tell you about a schoolmistress, one that can stand for all of them." "Go on" "Fascist to her fingertips," Maté continued. "She was the kind who dreamed of having a child with Mussolini. And she was smitten with that bastard Graziani, too. "Wait a minute," Pinco said. "Was she young and beautiful? That's the first thing we need to know." "She was about thirty," Maté said, " and she was a fine figure of a woman. A bit sturdy, a bit masculine, but nicely built, curves in all the right places. Best of all, she had wonderful skin, just like silk." 120.

[374] Fenoglio, *Una questione privata*, 1112. «a curious phenomenon» 121

[375] Brooks, *Reading for the Plot*, 56.

exterminate them all with machine guns or, in a climax of brutality, burn them all alive with flame throwers, until one day, their patience extinguished after many attempts to warn her to stop, a group of red partisans decides to visit her house and finally execute her. Maté, though, disturbed by the atrocity of what would be a cold-blooded murder, convinces his leader Max to commute the punishment to the shaving of her head, as Tito's men were doing to Slavic women sleeping with fascists:

> Intanto l'avevano presa e la insaccarono su una sedia, a cavalcioni. La gonna le montò su, mostrava mezze le cosce. Sarebbero piaciute a te, Pinco, che sei per la sostanza e la profondità. Le aveva potenti come quelle di un corridore ciclista. Polo aveva già impugnato le forbici, ma la maestra dibatteva la testa perché Polo non potesse lavorarci e infatti Polo dovette chiamar due perché gliela tenessero ferma. Le forbici erano grosse e senza filo, il taglio veniva male e faticoso. Comunque Polo tagliava e cominciava ad apparire il cranio. Ragazzi, non assistete mai alla rapatura di una donna, non vedetele mai la zucca, non cercate nemmeno di figurarvela. È la più brutta patata che ci sia, e l'impressione si allarga a tutto il resto del fisico. Però, per quanto orribile, è una cosa che inchioda. Eravamo tutti fissi, come ipnotizzati, e la maestra non si ribellava più, ma continuava a insultarci e maledirci, con una voce ormai rauca che faceva anche più effetto. Qualcuno dei nostri uscì alla chetichella, tornò fuori dal camion. La maestra faceva ancora qualche mossa di sofferenza o di senso e la gonna le montò più su, ora mostrava le giarrettiere. […] La maestra era ormai esaurita, ora gemeva solo più, come una bambina. […] Lei la maestra in testa non la potevi più guardare. Quasi tutti i nostri se l'erano filata.[376]

---

[376] Fenoglio, *Una questione privata,* 1114-1115. «In the meantime they'd grabbed hold of her and were pushing her down onto a chair so she was sitting astride it. Her skirt rode up her legs, showing half her thighs. You'd have liked them, Pinco, you prefer them solid. Hers were strong like a racing cyclist's. Polo had already grabbed the scissors, but the schoolmistress was thrashing her head around to stop Polo from doing his work and Polo had to ask two of the others to hold her still. The scissors were big and blunt, they were really difficult to cut with. But Polo kept cutting and the skull was starting to show. Boys never watch a woman having her head shaved, never wait till the skull appears, don't even try to imagine it. It's really ugly, like a potato, and it makes the rest of her body look ugly too. But however horrible it is, there's also something you can't take your eyes off. We were all staring at her, as if we were hypnotised, and the schoolmistress had stopped struggling, but she kept on calling us names, and her voice was all hoarse now, which had even more of an effect on us. Some of us sneaked outside to where we'd left the lorry. The schoolmistress was still moving around, with pain or disgust, and the skirt went riding up her thighs even higher, until we could see her garters. […] The schoolmistress was

The woman's body is little by little unveiled and shown to the collective male gaze of the partisan audience. The humiliated and mutilated body of the hysterical woman is the forbidden object of everyone's desire, causing an ambivalent reaction of simultaneous repulsion and attraction in the bystanders-executioners. While, in fact, the narrator now retrospectively comments that the spectacle of a woman's shaved head should not be seen by anyone, back then, when the event was happening, the onlookers' gaze had already been diverted down by the progressive exposure of the woman's womb, arousing their sexual desire. That view pushes them to go out and masturbate immediately. The woman's body has a double target and attracts two different kinds of spectators: the thighs, seen by the partisans, the direct witnesses of the scene; the shaved head, i.e., the object of Maté's and Fenoglio's description. Each one of these two gazes entails a different interpretation and meaning of the female collaborator's body. As seen by the partisans, the woman is, first and foremost, a sexual object: the scene, which started as a reprisal, ends up being a delayed, indirect sexual act between the victim and perpetrators. The sexual appeal of the female body is stronger than their political and ethical ideals, and the reprisal loses, in their view, the political meaning the war had assigned to it.

On the contrary, the author's effort, through Maté's narrating voice, is to channel the reader's attention to the 'mutilation,' the ugliness of her now unappealing body, thus trying to trigger moral disgust and disapproval towards the partisans' violence. The slow debasing of the teacher's body — she is always described as something other than a woman: as a male cyclist with strong, muscular thighs, her head turns into a pumpkin and a potato, and finally, as a crying infant — is unethical to watch, but it is also, simultaneously, erotic. The brutal nakedness of the head is something that should never be witnessed, according to the author-narrator; however, the only ones to see it are, in the end, the readers because almost all of the actual bystanders are looking at something else right below.

---

exhausted now and moaning like a child. [...] As for the schoolmistress, you couldn't look at her head any more.» 124-125.

Their objectification of the female body is unethical, the fact that they see it not as the victim and enemy but as the object of their compulsive, private, individual, sexual desire, misreading her for something that she should not be. This is a mistake similar to Milton's private love quest. However, in a way, they listen to the author-narrator's ethical, moral warning of never looking at such a spectacle, while the scene is represented with extreme realism to the reader. He directly addresses his audience: «Ragazzi, non assistete mai alla rapatura di una donna, non vedetele mai la zucca, non cercate nemmeno di figurarvela.»[377] Although they should not even try to imagine how it looks, the narrator does not spare them a detailed description of the 'crime,' even mentioning that the fingers of the improvised 'hairdresser' became purple from the pressure on the metal scissors. Cutting hair without the consent of the client is not an easy task and takes real time and effort.

The body of the teacher escapes a unique finalization and turns into a double target, a dynamic object that triggers multiple, qualitatively divergent kinds of gaze. It is impossible to look at the fascist correctly: each one of the two gazes is wrong. Looking at her head is right insomuch as it does not sexually objectify her, but it is wrong insomuch as it gives pleasure to the spectator by shaming her. Looking at the thighs is wrong because it is unethical sexual abuse, while it is right insomuch as it avoids, ignores, the other politically charged violation of the victim's body. Once more, the fascist character refuses to be enframed by the uncomplicated assignation of meaning that would derive from a direct, straightforward, not deviated gaze. She says and shows too much.

In *L'imboscata,* too, the teacher is the object of desire of multiple male subjects: Milton, his fellow partisan Jack, Goti and, last but not least, Giorgio Clerici. Her function overlaps with that of the tailor in *Una questione privata*, but her textual space is larger. Moreover, the relationships with the other characters will shift and change in the later work. Milton needs Edda Ferrero to reach Goti; this time, though, his goal is not to exchange him for Giorgio but to kill him. During his visits to the *maestrina* – in order to gain her trust and get

---

377 Fenoglio, *Una questione privata*, 1114

strategic information about Goti—Milton seems to fall for her, as Jack accuses him of being more interested in her panties than in Goti's gun. Goti, in turn, is convinced that he will eventually marry her. The plot gets even more intricate as Milton informs his superior, Nick, that Edda and Goti have an appointment for tomorrow at three. She will tell him that she wants to break up because she is in love with another man:

> - ora ti spiego perché la maestrina gli ha fissato questo appuntamento.
> - Sì, disse Nick prendendo un'altra sigaretta.
> - Per dirgli che tra loro tutto è finito.
> - Benissimo.
> - Si è innamorata di un altro. Non uno dei nostri. Uno sfollato, un nascosto, un neutrale.
> - Peccato, — disse Nick.
> - Si chiama Giorgio Clerici e vive imboscato a Mangano.
> - Tu lo conosci?
> - Di vista, — disse Milton. — Questo Giorgio Clerici fa sul serio con la maestra ed è disposto a sorvolare sulla relazione col fascista ma esige che lei tronchi subito. E la ragazza ha dato appuntamento al fascista per dirgli le cose come stanno e addio.[378]

This is the first time Giorgio Clerici is mentioned. He and Milton do not know each other and Giorgio is not even a partisan but hidden, evacuated, neutral, a draft dodger. The only characteristic he will keep in *Una questione privata* is this absence from the scene, this hiddenness. Milton plans to prevent Edda from going to that appointment and to force Giorgio Clerici to go to the appointment in her place and to kill the fascist so that he can redeem himself from his two crimes: having fallen for a collaborationist woman and for being «uno *strano* tipo di neutrale.»[379] Edda occupies the position of Fulvia as the apex of the love triangle, as she is, in a way, desired both by Milton and by Giorgio. They, moreover, share the same object of desire with Sergeant Goti-Alarico, who, in *Una questione privata*, will be the mere instrument to get to Giorgio. The fascist and Giorgio exchange positions as in *L'imboscata*, Giorgio's narrative function is to let Milton reach the fascist, while in A *Una questione privata*, the exact opposite happens: Milton needs Alarico to arrive

---

378 Fenoglio, *L'imboscata*, 995.
379 Fenoglio, *L'imboscata*, 996. «a strange neutral type.»

at Giorgio. The intertextual comparison between Fenoglio's last work and its closest source shows how the boundaries between heroes and villains are crossed, their identities exceeding the limits of a static narrative role and function, which, on the contrary, mix with one another. Characters are the temporary textual site enabling narrative functions to work in the novel's plot. Their evil or good are not absolute finalizations but only fleeting, dynamic, open consummations. Each one of the characters at play in the love triangle at the center of the exchange of prisoners temporarily takes the place of the other, thus shifting narrative function and role as now object of desire, now subject, as hero or villain, victim or persecutor.

Giorgio Clerici is in *Una questione privata,* the most handsome man in Alba, the privileged son of a rich bourgeois family. Among partisans though, nobody loves him because of his solitary nature, his authentic repulsion of the others' company. He seems to be at ease only with Milton:

> Giorgio pareva sopportare il solo Milton, coabitava solo con Milton. Quante volte, dormendo nelle stalle, si erano stesi l'uno accanto all'altro, stretti l'uno contro l'altro, in una intimità la cui iniziativa partiva sempre da Giorgio. Siccome Milton dormiva d'abitudine ricurvo a mezzaluna, Giorgio aspettava che si fosse sistemato e poi gli si stringeva e adattava, come in un'amaca orizzontale. E quante volte, svegliatosi prima, Milton aveva avuto tutto l'agio di considerare il corpo di Giorgio, la sua pelle, il suo pelo…[380]

The above passage clearly makes the friendship between Giorgio and Milton—and their love for Fulvia—a more nuanced and complex one. Thus, Giorgio, Milton and Fulvia might be the three faces of the same but different desire that would turn Milton's quest into one motivated by double jealousy, a desire for Fulvia and Giorgio at the same time. Each one of the three characters is at once the object and subject of desire, as in *L'imboscata,* with the only difference

---

380 Fenoglio, *Una questione privata,* 1039-1040. «The only person Giorgio seemed able to stand, to get along with, was Milton. How many times, sleeping in cowsheds, they had lain down next to one other, bodies close together. The initiative always came from Giorgio. As Milton always slept curled in a half moon, Giorgio would wait until he had settled and then squeeze up against him and adapt to the same shape, as if the two of them were lying in a hammock. And how many times, waking up first, Milton had lain there looking at Giorgio's body, his skin, his hair…», 36-37.

that here Fulvia replaces the collaborationist Edda, whose relationship with Alarico-Goti becomes an episode on its own. Characters are in constant flux and the narrative space is a still negotiable field. Far from being stereotypical minor characters of the subplot, the two fascists, Edda and Alarico-Goti, are still present as the heroes of the main plot, and the five figures constantly interchange and intertwine positions with respect to the desire that triggers the action of both novels.

In *Una questione privata,* a minor episode of *L'imboscata,* and *PJ II* — the exchange of prisoners — and a minor character — Sergeant Alarico-Goti — are displaced to the center of the plot: they are the 'moment of truth' of the entire story. This is because Alarico-Goti, I will argue, is not only the mere *instrument* that the protagonist needs to reach the end of his journey, the means through which Milton can satisfy his desire, but has the further function to be what enables the narrative desire of both author and reader to move forward and to avoid reaching an untimely end.

The fascist is a medium that both author and hero are sharing: the key to resolving the enigma from Milton's point of view, the key to keeping the enigma unsolved and the text still 'open' and unfinished from the author's, and the reader's, perspective. In both cases, the fascist is a sign that potentially could lead to a final meaning for the hero, which potentially could mean something else for the author.

When Milton finally captures the fascist, thanks to the perfect mathematical synchrony of their encounter, the main problem seems to be the fascist's silence. He either refuses altogether to answer Milton's questions and when he is forced to speak, he only utters 'yes, yes:'

> - Vorrai sapere ciò che ti farò, — gli disse.
> Il sergente tremò e tacque.
> [...]
> - Hai sentito? Dì qualcosa.
> Non rispondeva.
> - Di' qualcosa!
> - Biascicò un paio di sì a testa rigida.
> - [...]
> - Hai capito? Parla.

- Sì, sì.
- [...]
- Intesi?
- Sì, sì
[...]
- Parla.
- Sì, sì.
- E di' qualcos'altro che sì, sì.
[...]
- Hai capito?
Annuì con la testa.
- Tu servi a una cosa sola. Te ne sei convinto? Parla.
- Sì, sì.[381]

If Edda's vice in *L'imboscata* was an unbridled tongue, Alarico now has the opposite vice: he is *too* silent. While Milton considers the fascist to be the intermediary between him and Giorgio's voice — the missing piece that would eventually allow him to hear the truth about that other silence in the room alluded to by the governess at the beginning — Alarico disrupts every chance of dialogue. The key to solving the mystery turns into a mystery himself. Milton cannot even look at his face:

> Milton si portò tutto su un lato per adocchiare la faccia dell'uomo che aveva preso. Ma dopo, a causa dei gomiti spianati all'altezza del viso e per l'ondulamento del passo, non poté dire d'aver colto di più che una spera d'occhio grigio e il naso, piccolo e marcato. Non ne fu contrariato, in fondo non gli interessava. La sua faccia non gli interessava come non avrebbe interessato il comando fascista di Alba che l'avrebbe riscattato. Non importava nemmeno che fosse un graduato: bastava che fosse un uomo, con indosso una certa divisa. Ma che uomo, e che divisa! Milton esaminava con soddisfazione, quasi con dolcezza quel corpo greve ed elastico ed era, per la prima volta, in amicizia con quella uniforme, amico persino degli scarponi sui

---

[381] Fenoglio, *Una questione privata*, 1098. « "You'll be wanting to know what I am going to do with you," he said. The sergeant trembled, and said nothing. [...] "Do you hear? Say something!" The sergeant did not answer. "Say something!" "He muttered the word 'yes' a couple of times, without moving his head. [...] "Got that? Say something." "Yes, yes." [...] "Do you understand?" "Yes, yes." [...] Say something." "Yes, yes." "And say something else apart from yes, yes." [...] Got that?" He nodded. [...] "I need you for one thing, and one thing only. Don't you realise that by now? Say something." "Yes, yes."» 103-105.

quali camminava al traguardo fissato da lui Milton. Che grossa moneta di scambio, quale capacità di acquisto rappresentava![382]

Milton does not even care that Alarico has a body, or even a face. The only thing that seems to count is the fascist green-grey uniform, not its contents but what is covering it. During the head-shaving scene, the true pole of attraction of the bystanders' gaze was the female body, the shameful, horrible nakedness of the head and the parallel erotic, allusive but forbidden nakedness of the womb. On the one hand, the scene with a female collaborator was centered around the unveiling of the bodily content and the impossibility of looking at it in a correct, ethical way. In this scene, on the other hand, with another fascist as the victim, the male body is completely superfluous, and the focus shifts to the covering, veiling the contents. The object of Milton's gaze is the uniform and the fascist character has a value only insofar as he has acquired at that moment an exchange value. The fascist body is completely dematerialized and acquires the volatile, aleatory meaning of money. His only importance and function is to signal and refer to something else as the involucrum of an enigma and as the metonymic function of language. Everything is shown in a moment of unfinalized transition: characters' identities, functions and desires, the author's narrative and the communication of Giorgio's truth.

Una questione privata is structured around the necessity of supposing a direct correspondence between signifier and signified: the fascist *means* Giorgio, and their relation is a finalized sentence. This necessity, though, is short-circuited by the sudden, unexpected

---

[382] Fenoglio, *Una questione privata,* 1097. «Milton went over to once side to get a good look at his captive's face. But afterwards, because the sergeant was holding his elbows by the side of his face and because he was swaying from side to side, he could not have said he had caught more than a patch of grey ear and a small, well-defined nose. He was not bothered, deep down he didn't care. He didn't care about the man's face any more than he cared about the Fascist command in Alba that was going to redeem him. He didn't even care that he had stripes on his uniform. All that mattered was that he was a man, wearing a certain uniform! But what a man and what a uniform! Milton looked with satisfaction, almost gently, at that heavy but agile body, and for the first time he felt friendly towards that uniform, even towards those boots in which he was walking towards a goal that he, Milton, had set. What a fine bargaining counter he was, what a valuable commodity!» 104.

death of the fascist. What was supposed to close a gap is now widening it. The uncomplicated equation misses, the *moneta di scambio* misses its reference value, its closure and the finalization of meaning slips indefinitely, as an open-ended message suspended in the gap between listener and storyteller.

The sergeant does not trust Milton's words of reassurance, so he attempts to escape, and this is the reason why Milton finally pulls the trigger. The death of the fascist has two consequences: it keeps the enigma and the plot alive, delaying the closure of the narrative, and it originates the chain of signifiers and the metonymic slippage of meaning. The fascist character, in the end, functions as the bar separating the signifier from the signified, as the *phallus* according to the Lacanian model:

> [The phallus] Far from incarnating the unambiguous literal meaning behind things, symbolizes rather the incessant *sliding* of signification, the very principle of movement and displacement which on the contrary *prevents* the chain (or the text) from ever stopping at a final, literal, fixed meaning. The phallus, far from being a real object, is in fact a *signifier*.[383]

The fascist, as the Lacanian phallus, is a special kind of signifier, insomuch as it incarnates the semiotic bar which bars the subject's attempt to look at the signified, to access its meaning, to enframe and finalize the metonymic chain. Paradoxically the fascist becomes the crucial character of the novel exactly by threatening it with insignificance, by disrupting the delivery and reading of Giorgio's truth, i.e., of the signified. It is because the fascist dies and the character's reference value is lost that there is a story at all:

> There is a story *because* there is an unreadable, an unconscious. Narrative, paradoxically, becomes possible to the precise extent that a story becomes *impossible* – that a story, precisely, *"won't tell."*[384]

The failed exchange relegates Giorgio's story to an inaccessible silence. However, the absence and very impossibility of hearing his story makes the narrative possible by keeping both enigma and

---

383 Shoshana Felman, "Literature and Psychoanalysis" in *Literature and Psychoanalysis. The Question of Reading: Otherwise* (Baltimore: The Johns Hopkins University Press, 1977), 172.
384 Idem, 143.

desire in a state of open, unconsummated, dynamic transition. The silence of the hero allows the author to speak. The censorship of Giorgio's truth keeps all the others' identities in a state of constant flux, lack of meaning, and staggered approximation to a conclusive classification.

Una questione privata is structured around a sign without object, around the gap that separates language from reality, the impossibility of enframing its truth in a consummated form. As the exposed, tortured body of the female collaborator is an object that is necessarily looked at wrongly, the body of the fascist sergeant is unreadable: it can only be read as the inaccessibility of meaning, as bar/uniform hiding its contents and always representing something else. The object of *Una questione privata* is not the past historical events but, rather, the impossibility of finding the right language to access and rightly convey their meaning. Furthermore, the moment of truth, the moment of crisis, coincides in the text with the fascist character.

Maria Corti, at the end of her triptych on Fenoglio in *Metodi e fantasmi* — using Tynianov's terminology — invites future scholars to determine for each one of Fenoglio's works the dominant factors deciding the general orientation of the work. In my opinion, then, the dominant factor of *Una questione privata* is the oratorical orientation, the prominence given by the author to storytelling situations, starting with Milton's attempt to hear Giorgio's story — made inaccessible by the death of the fascist — ending with the story of the teacher collaborator. In fact, the shaving of her head is told by Jack as a framed narrative while Milton, the protagonist of the main plot, is absent. He is in the next room; he could overhear the story, but he is in a state of deep agitation, thinking about the real sense of the governess's words:

> Ho il cervello disintegrato. Ma bisogna che mi riconcentri. Che ha detto la custode? Ha proprio detto quelle parole riguardo a Fulvia e a Giorgio? Non me le sarò per caso sognate? Ma sì le ha dette. Ha detto "…" e ancora "…" Riesco ancora a rivedere le pieghe della sua bocca mentre lo diceva. Ora, non può darsi che io abbia capito male? Che vi abbia dato un senso anziché un altro? Ma no, il senso era quello, quello era l'unico senso possibile. […] Voglio sperare che abbia parlato seriamente, in spirito di verità, purché non mi

abbia fatto costruire un mondo di dubbio e di sofferenza su certe parole dette tanto per dire, approssimativamente.[385]

The framed story recounted by Jack—about an unwatchable scene—is not even heard by the protagonist. The head shaving scene, then, does not have any connection to the main plot, and its only function is its orientation towards the reader outside the text to disrupt the mythical narrative of an unproblematic, absolutely good resistance. How, in fact, can Milton not react to what is told a few steps from him? The scene narrated by Jack also disrupts the space around him, and the boundaries separating outside from inside and the limits dividing the framed story from the frame appear on the verge of collapsing. In fact, Milton's indifference and non-hearing of the story being told inside another room next to him repeats the other partisans' outside the room where the woman's head has been shaved. Their avoidance of the gaze parallels Milton's avoidance of eavesdropping on the framed story.

Another fascist character is diverting, short-circuiting his attention back to the beginning, to another story and to another storyteller whose message he is now starting to doubt. The death of the fascist sergeant Alaric and the consequent loss of reference value of the signifier and exchange value of the 'currency' result in a potentially infinite multiplication and dispersion of the original meaning that once seemed to him so unequivocal. The governess's message turns into ellipsis and silence, that is to say, into that very same silence that the governess was trying to interpret when Giorgio and Fulvia were locked alone inside the bedroom. The ambivalence and approximation of language leave everything in

---

[385] Fenoglio, *Una questione privata,* 1116. «But Milton was not asleep. He was thinking again about the housekeeper in Fulvia's villa, and he could feel his brain disintegrating. 'Could I have got it all wrong? Have I been exaggerating? Did I understand her correctly, interpret her words correctly? My brain has disintegrated, I need to concentrate. "What did the housekeeper say? Did she really say those words about Fulvia and Giorgio? Or did I dream it? No, she said them. She said "…" and then "…". I can still see the lines round her mouth as she said it. But could I have misunderstood? Could I have thought she meant one thing when she meant another? But no, that was what she meant, that was the only possible meaning. […] I like to think she spoke seriously, in a spirit of truth and wasn't just making me build a world of doubt and suffering on certain words she said approximately, just for the sake of it.» 126-127.

unfinalized transition and flux, truth being an elliptical and unnamable matter. While trying to sleep in the next room, Milton is not overhearing the story told in the actual space near him, but he is eavesdropping the past silence in Fulvia's bedroom, i.e., in the space of the governess' framed story of the beginning. All the stories around Milton are, then, silences, mysteries and riddles. The signified of these tales remains inaccessible to Milton, whose enquiry, now aimless, has no other solution than turning backward and inverting its orientation from the end to the beginning: from Giorgio's cell to Fulvia's bedroom, both absent spaces of silence.

Milton and the reader share the same desire to know, the desire to reach the end of the quest, to arrive at Giorgio and to solve, from the perspective of the end, the meaning of the beginning and the middle of the plot. The inaccessibility of Milton's object of desire results in the paradoxical satisfaction of the reader's *passion du sens*, their desire for the text. Because if an end is reached, the text ceases to exist. The diversion that the plot moves forward needs to remain open and unfinalized for the longest possible time, postponing over and over the transmission of a definitive, uncontestable truth. Narrative desire is a paradox: the wish to know the end motivates the reader's journey in a text, while the pleasure of reading needs the text never to conclude.

The death of the fascist sergeant Alaric precisely enables, in *Una questione privata,* narrative desire to acquire narrative shape, to be not only the theoretical mechanism of every plot but also the particular, concrete realization of a resistance, historical novel. The incessant metonymic slippage of the meaning of narrative plot, as theorized by Peter Brooks following Lacan and Freud's *Beyond the Pleasure Principle,* is the plot of *Una questione privata*, a novel more oriented towards the complex transmission of a message than towards the message itself. The fascist character both allows and thwarts narrative transference: it makes possible a discourse about the traumatic, difficult memory of the Italian civil war exactly by meaning something else, by avoiding a direct, diaristic-realistic account of those events, that is to say, by nurturing the reader's passion for and of the text with the hybridization of realism with melodrama, romance, tragedy and the detective story.

Narrative discourse never finds its closure, as it is left open in the uncertainty of a *sense* that the more it approximates the truth, the more it fails to find a static definition and name:

> Narratives portray the motors of desire that drive and consume their plots, and they also lay bare the nature of narration as a form of human desire: the need to tell as a primary human drive that seeks to seduce and to subjugate the listener, to implicate him in the thrust of a desire that never can quite speak its name—never can quite come to the point—but that insists on speaking over and over again its movement towards that name.[386]

Alaric, the sergeant-lover and Edda, the tailor-teacher, are particular, unique types of fascist characters since, as we have noted above, their disruptive function is the result of multiple shifting and displacements between the other supposedly good characters at play in the exchange of prisoners plot. In fact, other fascist characters in Fenoglio's work do not possess the same dynamic quality of the two enemies and victims of *Una questione privata*. The fascist character does not always escape finalization and refuses to be enframed. At times, instead, it remains a cliché, a stereotypical figure perfectly enframed in a kind of description that seems to be directly inherited from 19th-century realism. Nevertheless, in these minor fascist characters, whose main function in the text is that one of being described, of embellishing the author's prose as mere exercises of style, it is possible to observe the recurrence of some of those constant formal features that all the fascist characters analyzed so far in this study have shown to share. The fascist triggers certain genres of emplotment and description without, though, ending up disrupting realism and escaping the enframing into an unconsummated form. The following are exquisite examples of perfectly enframed forms of fascist characters, whose static natures will help us to grasp with more clarity the dynamic nature of the last two fascist characters of Fenoglio's creative path.

In *Il partigiano Johnny I*, there is a moment that breaks with the exuberant, unique linguistic creativity of the work: the description of the partisan Kyra. His portrait and background story have the rhythm and tension of the *feuilleton*, the melodramatic choice of the

---

386 Brooks, *Reading for the Plot*, 61.

lexicon, and a pathetic tone that interrupts the swift, ironic, at times, expressionist quality of the rest of the novel. Although the depiction occupies a short textual space, and it will be cut from *PJ II*, Kyra, the partisan expert on machine guns, is a magnificent tragic figure and all the charm of the character, Fenoglio writes, derives from a certain perennial sadness in his eyes, betraying a mysterious, inner knot that Johnny wants to decipher. In short, he is an enigma:

> E Johnny s'acuiva in quell'indagine, tutto il restante materiale umano interessandolo poco o niente, all'infuori di Pierre e di Michele. Finché Pierre gli sciolse cautamente l'*enigma*: era un segreto dei capi, gli uomini ignoravano, e Johnny doveva tenerselo: uno sgarbo a Kyra era assolutamente inconcepibile.
> Kyra aveva un fratello maggiore, e ufficiale del presidio fascista di Asti. E, disse Pierre, era buono per i fascisti come Kyra era buono per loro. [...]
> *Tragicamente* per Kyra, la fraternità, sempre formidabile, era per lui l'*upmost and utmost*. Come se non bastasse che egli nutrisse per il fratello maggiore l'amore riverenziale classico ed antico, l'altro era il suo eroe, il suo modello inattingibile per rispetto eppure sempre presente per amore: era il suo ispiratore, il suo comandante, il suo ingegnere, per cui Kyra semplicemente gioiva di essere l'operaio. [...]
> E Johnny poteva vederselo benissimo, attillato nella sua fosca uniforme, un monumento, contro la selciata sfondità della caserma astigiana, di marzialità e di sex-appeal fascisti.[387] [*italics* mine]

---

[387] Fenoglio, *Il partigiano Johnny I*, 577. «And Johnny was curious to get to the bottom of it—all the remaining human material interesting him little or nota t all except for Pierre and Michele. Until Pierre cautiously solved the *enigma* for him—it was a secret known to the officers, the men knew nothing of it, and Johnny was to keep it to himself: a discourtesy to Kyra was absolutely inconceivable. Kyra had an elder brother and he was an officer in the Fascist garrison in Asti. And, said Kyra, he was as lucky for the Fascists as Kyra was for them. [...] Tragically for Kyra, brotherhood, which is always something formidable, was *upmost and utmost* for him. AS if it were not enough that he nourished for his brother the reverential love that was both classical and ancient, the other was his hero, his model—unreachable because of respect and yet always present out of love: he was his inspiration, his commander, the one who had fashioned him for whom Kyra was simply delighted to be the workman who religiously carried out his plans. The other had planned, invented, constructed in every detail Kyra's enthralling, amazing adolescence. [...] And Johnny could very well imagine him slim in his dark uniform, a monument, against the cobbled background of the barracks in Asti, of martial bearing and Fascist *sex-appeal*.» Beppe Fenoglio, *Johnny the Partisan* (London: Quartet Books, 1995) 145-146.

Kyra's enigma is, then, the background figure of his older brother, a fascist officer. Their fratricidal relationship summarizes the fratricidal war that splits and frames them and that has turned the two brothers into the red and black squares of a brutal roulette: the victory of one means the defeat of the other.

Kyra's brother is the type of fascist belonging to an older generation that Fenoglio usually compares to a new, sadistic and violent generation of fascists. In *L'imboscata*, for example, the old, good and fair Colonel Profeti is substituted by the much more violent duo of Venturi and Chiaradia, implying the beginning of an even more ferocious policy and treatment of prisoners. The former is compared to a tiger, while the latter is referred to as a hybrid animal creature, both hyena, or fox, and reptile:

> Se Venturi è la tigre, Chiaradia…
> - La volpe, — anticipò Perez.
> - La jena. Un rettile. Venturi fa le sortite, le azioni e i rastrellamenti, Chiaradia si occupa degli interrogatori, delle torture e degli assassinamenti. Chiaradia è il più sporco e assoluto delinquente che abbia mai infangato la terra. Alle donne degli arrestati che vanno a supplicarlo, prima porta via la borsa e gli ori e poi le salta. E siccome è sifilitico fino agli occhi le appesta tutte mentre le fa vedove. Anche delle bambine di quei disgraziati si fa fare qualcosetta. Anche dalle bambine, sì.[388]

In this perfectly crafted miniature, the hyperbolic portrayal of Chiaradia seems displaced directly from a fairy tale or folk legend. More than a real officer, his features partake something of the evil witch, of the demonic villain transmitted by the folk tradition. As the collaborationist tailor-lover in *Una questione privata* will be *lurida*, he is a dirty receptacle of all human vices: thief, pedophile, rapist, and murderer. His corruption, besides being metaphorical, is also a real, actual sickness of his body: like the reluctant witness-collaborator in *La lunga notte del '43*, Chiaradia is syphilitic. One of the main constant traits of the fascist character is the disfigured, deformed body, a physical corruption and distortion which translates their absolute, ideal, moral perversion literally: they are the embodiment of evil, and they carry with them the visual, evident mark that the 'beast' has left on them. The fascist body is, then, objectified

---

388 Fenoglio, *L'imboscata*, 983-984.

by a physical detail marking their flesh, now by a limp, now by a venereal disease, now by a shaved head. A single trait, as an icon or emblem, visually defines their entire negative, evil personality. The emblematic, almost filmic, quality making straightforwardly evident their inner nature, is confirmed also by two other descriptions in *Il partigiano Johnny*. First, the leader of the red partisans Némega, an ex-fascist that Johnny despises, is said to have a face very similar, except for the «incisioni del vizio,»[389] to that of Osvaldo Valenti, the famous Italian star of fascist cinema who infamously joined the RSI and was eventually executed by a partisan firing squad. The juxtaposition of the partisan's and the actor's faces exemplifies Johnny's negative opinion of the communist leader as a false, equivocal and ambiguous figure, drawing an even wider line between the *badogliani* and the reds, respectively, the good and the wrong sectors of the right side. Second, a few paragraphs earlier, a fascist prisoner seems to make faces that «*pulcinellescamente*»[390] resemble those of Totò «nel diabolico, tremolante disegno intimo di far cadere l'arma dal boja per riso convulsivo.»[391] Laughter is, indeed, another recurrent attribute of fascist figures in Fenoglio's works.

At the beginning of *Primavera di bellezza*, there is another fascinating episode structured around a fascist character. The flashback of the high school is largely centered on Arduino, Johnny's lonely classmate, a Nazi and fanatical adorer of Hitler. Arduino is sitting in the first row, and Johnny, then, looks at him from behind as his later alter ego, Milton will stare at his prisoner Alaric. The fascist cannot be looked at face to face, but mostly from behind, from a limited perspective:

> Johnny guardò avanti, alla forte nuca forforosa di Arduino nel primo banco, vestito di nero, il bastone appeso allo scrittoio, la gamba anchilosata fuori tutta, riversa nel breve passo tra fila e fila di banchi. Arduino non si voltava mai indietro, ma Johnny poteva ugualmente indovinare la sua *ironia* per quei vani accoramenti antifascisti, vedere il *sorriso* che gli allargava il volto tutto mite e gli stringeva gli occhi azzurri. Non era fascista, Arduino, ma

---

389 Fenoglio, *Il partigiano Johnny*, 489.
390 Idem, 487.
391 Idem, 488.

> nazista: [...] le sue speranze erano le speranze tedesche, le sue vittorie quelle tedesche, tedeschi i suoi dolori e lutti, benché finora non ne avesse provati e fosse pienamente convinto che non gliene sarebbero toccati mai. Era tremendamente, gloriosamente solo, tutta la classe schierata con Johnny, antifascista e tedescofoba. [...] Così Arduino era solo, ma con lui stavano Varsavia e Narvik, gli stukas e gli U-boote, e quella ferrata compagnia cresceva giorno per giorno, a ogni edizione di giornale e radiotrasmissione; ma Arduino taceva sempre e *sorrideva* nel vuoto. Si incastrava di tre-quarti nel suo banco consacrato, appendeva il bastone, depositava la gamba nel passaggio e sorrideva. [...] Al finis Arduino usciva sempre ultimo: ritirava la gamba allo scalpitante esodo dei compagni e *sorrideva*, a occhi bassi. Essi lo sogguardavano appena, i perdenti. Poi Arduino raccoglieva le forze e si trascinava fuori. [...] Le compagne lo salutavano oblique e affettuose, perché era nemico di Johnny e della maggioranza e adoratore di Hitler, e un ragazzo disgraziato per la vita, e aveva occhi belli e cavallereschi. [392] [*italics* mine]

Despite Arduino being just a young boy, his figure has the stature of a 19th-century character that can be found in Balzac or Tolstoy. His stoic loneliness and isolation, his smile of supposition and implicit superiority, and his beautiful and chivalric eyes contribute to sculpting a portrait that is half a stereotype and half the masterpiece of pure 19th-century realism. Like Tarcisio in Rossellini's *Era notte a Roma,* and like almost all of the fascist characters we have so far encountered, he has physical defects, i.e., a flawed body: first, a stiff leg that forces him to walk with a cane; second, scurfy hair. Like the name Alaric, Arduino has particular and meaningful resonances too: first, the Arduino family was infamously massacred by the black brigades in Turin on the night of March 12th 1945; second, Arduino d'Ivrea was king of Italy in the 11th century and a figure idealized by the Risorgimento as a precocious paladin of the Italian liberation.

Through Arduino, the spatiotemporal dimension of the novel breaks its limits. It arrives to embrace other exotic continents, and one suddenly seems to be reading one of Verne's adventure novels more than a resistance story. One day, in fact, Fenoglio writes:

> In un punto dell'Atlantico del Sud tre incrociatori inglesi incocciarono la corazzata tascabile tedesca «Graf von Spee». Arduino *sorrise*: divoratore di tutte le pubblicazioni militari germaniche diffuse in Italia, sapeva che la Spee era nettamente superiore a quegli altri in velocità e gittata delle artiglierie. E

---

392 Fenoglio, *Primavera di bellezza,* 345.

sorrideva, opponendo la sua nuca rocciosa ai marosi di speranze che i compagni-nemici spingevano avanti. Il professor Monti spiegava inutilmente Bergson. Bergson, Le Rire, chi riderà?[393]

Fenoglio even provides the scholarly source of Arduino's tendency to smile: Bergson's *Laughter*. The sinking of the Spee was the first naval battle of WWII and the first defeat for Germany, and Fenoglio registers it indirectly through the effects on Johnny's young, somehow 'noble,' Nazi classmate: the defeat signs scars the face of the enemy, triggering the tragic commutation of a confident smile into the silent sobbing shaking his «vasta debole schiena.»[394] The author perfectly enframes Arduino in this episode because he can observe his hero from the privileged point of view of the end, taking advantage of what Bakhtin calls an excess of seeing: the author and the reader know how the war ended. Arduino's laughter then looked at retrospectively, loses all its meaning of arrogance and snobbery, provoking, on the contrary, an empathic bond between the reader and him. From the vantage point of the end, Arduino's laughter is the absurd, paradoxical reaction of a victim who stoically smiles despite his loss. Fenoglio's preference for losers, for Hector over Achilles, is well known. In the high school episode, the framed figure of the disgraced Arduino turns *Primavera di bellezza* into a bildungsroman, adding to the plot a sort of prologue that encloses inside itself a miniature version of the future conflict. Johnny's class is, in fact, a battleground divided into rival factions and also a parliament, with its majority and minority.

The fascist character opens up the plot to exotic scenarios, absolute evil monsters, fratricidal tragedies and the formative, anticipatory years of school education. However, contrary to Alarico-Goti and the collaborationist tailor-teacher Edda in *Una questione privata* and *L'imboscata,* these characters are exquisite, consummated moments of mimesis that never interfere with the diegesis of the main plot, never escaping the author's excess of seeing and consequent enframing in a static easily recognizable stereotypical form. The last part of *Il partigiano Johnny II* becomes, thanks to the

---

[393] Idem, 346.
[394] Fenoglio, *Primavera di bellezza*, 348.

enigmatic presence of a fascist character, a spy-detective story. After having escaped the fascists chasing him after the fall of Alba, Johnny finds shelter in the abandoned house of an older woman, a supporter and helper of partisans who is now in jail. Although in the village and the forest surrounding it, fascist *rastrellamenti* are much less frequent, the new oblique menace to Johnny's clandestine hideout comes from the insidious eyes of spies. There are, in fact, spies everywhere, surveilling with their untraceable, masked gaze the solitary, snowy hillside trails:

> Viviamo tra le spie, le spie sono fra noi gente Cristiana come tanti demòni. [...] Esistono le spie. Non ci avevo mai creduto, nemmeno nei romanzi e nel cine. Ma esistono. Vorrei scoprirne una e sta certo che qualunque morte le facessi fare non ne sarei soddisfatto.[395]

Spies are ghostly, imaginary demons that people cannot tell are real or not. Alternatively, like the characters of novels and films, they seem to belong more to fiction than history. They cannot be true.

One night, after dinner, some peasant neighbors — in the typical storytelling context of oral communication — tell Johnny a story of something that has recently happened to them:

> Il giorno in cui importa parlare, — disse, — io ero via, ero alla fiera di Cossano, una fiera come son le fiere di questi tempi. Così la donna era sola in casa, a parte i bambini, e stava cucinando, perché era l'ora in cui io, secondo l'intesa, stavo ripassando il torrente di ritorno. Lei stava cucinando e di necessità stava di fronte a quella finestrella, — ed indicò l'apertura inferriata. — Alzando a caso gli occhi, vede una faccia, faccia d'uomo, *inquadrata esatta nella finestra*.
> - Io quasi ci rimasi per lo spavento, — interloquì la donna, — e poi dovetti mettermi seduta e non mi riuscì di riprendermi, e lui tornando non trovò pranzo fatto.
> L'uomo alla finestra era un negoziante di pelli di coniglio.[396]

The wife believes the mysterious salesman to be a spy. The account of the riddle begins as a typical gothic short story: the face of a stranger suddenly appears, perfectly enframed, in the kitchen window, thus unexpectedly scaring the woman, who reacts as if she had seen a ghost. Then, the spy is doubly enframed, first, by the

---

395 Fenoglio, *Il partigiano Johnny II*, 793.
396 Fenoglio, *Il partigano Johnny II*, 823.

spatial limits of the setting, by the window's frame, second by the genre of the mystery tale itself, and by the genre of the tale within the tale. Realism and the ghost story are masterfully intertwined by the author in this short passage, built around a real vision of a spy, of a historical, true event, narrated as the second-hand account of the surreal apparition of a phantasm. Moreover, the short story perfectly enframes the fascist spy, not only spatially but also within its complex temporality. The momentous apparition of the ghostly face is enframed by the temporal realism and teleology of the little novella: the woman, home alone while the husband is at a nearby fiera, sees the phantasm while making dinner for the returning husband, who, in turn, will not find any dinner when he is back home. The apparition of the spy breaks the temporal teleology of the tale and results in the final realistic detail-notation that ends the story: the wife's failure and inability to cook the dinner, caused by the shock of the unexpected, sudden vision. The trajectories of the two characters, the wife's and the husband's, are perfectly synchronized: she starts to work in the kitchen at an agreed hour, when her husband is simultaneously crossing the river on his way back. The vertical temporality of the spy's apparition causes a delay in the horizontal teleology of the other two temporalities, short-circuiting their synchronization.

The woman saw something bizarre in the stranger's face, something wrong that she could not quite explain in the salesman's smile:

> E quello che più l'ha spaventata è stato il sorriso.
> - Che genere di sorriso? — s'informò Johnny ma la donna accennò che non era assolutamente in grado di descriverlo.
> Parlò l'uomo: — Le sorrise da farle spavento, da gelarle il sangue, ecco che genere di sorriso. Da allora ne abbiamo parlato per notti e notti nella nostra stanza, nel cuore della notte, coi figli addormentati sodi. Ed era anche un po' strabico, dice la donna, pochissimo però, un vizio dell'occhio che gli era di bellezza anzi che di bruttezza, dice la donna. E sebbene fosse molto giovane, all'incirca della vostra età, partigiano, aveva una striscia bianca di capelli nel mezzo degli altri nerissimi. — Ho potuto vedergliela bene, — disse la

donna,—perché per il caldo della salita si era un po' tirato su il passamontagna.[397]

Arduino's laughter reappears on the uncanny face of the spy, a true visual enigma that escapes the wife's attempt to name and describe it. The genre of the laughter is the unnamable affect escaping finalization and definition, causing the shocking reaction of the woman. The effect of that lack of description, of that inability to find the right words, has its own temporality of latency: it lasts, in fact, for many more nights, and it triggers multiple storytelling occasions in the secreted, enclosed space of the bedroom; in the heart of the night, while the children are asleep. Once again, the author-narrator uses a vocabulary typical of the inherited genre tradition of the gothic mystery tale. In addition to the smile, the woman's memory kept only two more details of that face. First, a weird kind of squint, more a mark of beauty than of ugliness. Second, a lock of white hair, out of place in, and in contrast with, the extreme darkness of the rest of the man's hair. The face of the spy is a surface covered by tricky signs that defy uncomplicated decipherment. In it, bodily vices are signs of a disturbing beauty, not of depravation. Once more, the fascist's body has a faulty, ambiguous attractiveness that confuses the woman and challenges the mimetic function of her speech.

Later on in the novel, Johnny encounters the vendor of rabbit skins. Before killing him though he hesitates, doubting the truth of the woman's discourse, because: «tutto può attendersi, in fantasia, da queste donne di collina che passano la vita in feconda seclusione, nell'unica ed esaltante compagnia dell'ingannevole vento.»[398] Like Milton in *Una questione privata,* he doubts the discourse of the governess, in that case, the possibility of a melodramatic love triangle, this time the ghost story-like apparition of a spy. Face to face with the salesman, Johnny asks him to smile as a final confirmation of the story he heard: the unnamable laughter that was marking the face in the window, and that ended up marking the woman's memory is the certain, inescapable sign and proof that the

---

397 Fenoglio, *Il partigiano Johnny II*, 824.
398 Idem, 848.

storyteller was right. Johnny recognizes in that laughter the same confused and, at the same time, chilling, veiled allusion to the evil that caused the woman's shock and black-out.

The face of the fascist is a riddled surface that triggers a tale within the tale with the perfect, circular structure of a gothic novel taking place in a typical neorealist setting and ending with a tragic recognition scene. Milton will not be able to look at his prisoner's face because his meaning is only his exchange value, his potential, temporary meaning as Giorgio, as someone else's face. On the contrary, Johnny encounters the spy face to face, the enemy's face being covered with meaningful signs alluding to his evil nature. In the former text, the fascist, once he has lost his exchange value, will automatically lose also every reference value, resulting in the open-endedness of Giorgio's discourse, which will forever evade closure. In the latter, the fascist signifies something specific, and the recognition of the smile as a reference to what the woman meant in her account allows Johnny to kill him and to give the tale within the tale a proper end and finalization. Even though, as I mentioned earlier, the fascist character of Alarico-Goti is a special and unique case in Fenoglio, the character of the spy-vendor of rabbit skin confirms too, once more, how these kinds of character excite the narrative desire of heroes, authors and readers. They enhance framed stories that interact with the genre of the framing novel and dramatize the act of its transmission and the overall capacity of its word to signify and straightforwardly refer to a traumatic past still lacking closure and a commonly agreed meaning.

BIBLIOGRAPHY

Albertoni, Ettore, Antonini, Ezio, and Palmieri, Renato. *La generazione degli anni difficili.* Bari: Laterza, 1962.

Althusser, Louis. *The Underground Current of the Materialism of the Encounter.* New York: Verso, 2006.

Amendola, Giorgio. "Il tribunale speciale e l'antifascismo all'interno" in *Fascismo e antifascismo (1918-1936) Lezioni e testimonianze,* 217-246. Milano: Feltrinelli, 1962.

Antonicelli, Franco., ed. by., *Trent'anni di storia italiana. Dall'antifascismo alla Resistenza.* Einaudi: Torino, 1961.

Argentieri, Mino. "La notte di Rossellini," *Cinema 60,* no.3, (Set 1960).

Argenton, Mario. "L'esercito partigiano, " *Mercurio,* (May 1945).

Bakhtin, Michail. "Author and Hero in Aesthetic Activity." In *Art and Answerability – Early Philosophical Essays by M.M Bakhtin.* Austin: University of Texas Press, 1990.

Bakhtin, Mikhail. *L'autore e l'eroe nell'attività estetica. In Michail Bachtin e il suo circolo Opere 1919-1930* Milano: Bompiani, 2014.

Bakhtin, Mikhail. *Problems of Dostoevsky's Poetics* (Minneapolis: University of Minnesota Press, 2014.

Bakhtin, Mikhail., *The Dialogic Imagination : Four Essays.* Austin: University of Texas Press, 1981.

Bakhtin, Mikhail. *Rabelais and His World.* Bloomington: Indiana University Press, 1984.

Baldelli, Pio. "Il Processo di Verona e il problema dell'interpretazione cinematografica della storia contemporanea." *Cinema 60,* no.35, (May 1963).

Bárberi Squarotti, Giorgio. "Pavese o la fuga nella metafora." *Sigma,* no. 3/4, (Dic 1964).

Barthes, Roland. *S/Z.* Paris: Editions du Seuil, 1970.

Barthes, Roland. *Le Plaisir Du Texte.* Paris: Éditions du Seuil, 1973.

Basso, Lelio. "Le origini del fascismo." In *Fascismo e antifascismo (1918-1936). Lezioni e testimonianze,* 9-43. Milano: Feltrinelli, 1962.

Battaglia, Roberto. *Risorgimento e Resistenza.* Roma: Editori Riuniti, 1964.

Battaglia, Roberto. *Storia della Resistenza Italiana.* Torino: Einaudi, 1964.

Battaglia, Roberto. "La resistenza italiana: lo sviluppo dell'intervento armato fino all'insurrezione." In *Fascismo e antifascismo,* 472-498. Milano: Feltrinelli, 1962.

Bayman, Louis. *The Operatic and the Everyday in Post-War Italian Film Melodrama.* Edinburgh University Press, 2014.

Benedetto, Croce. *Scritti e discorsi politici (1943-1947).* Napoli: Bibliopolis, 2010.

Bernstein, J. M. *The Philosophy of the Novel – Lúkacs, Marxism and the Dialectics of Form.* Minneapolis: University of Minnesota Press, 1984.

Bertolucci, Bernardo. *La mia magnifica ossessione. Scritti, ricordi, interventi (1962-2010),* ed. by Fabio Francione e Piero Spila. Milano: Garzanti 2010.

Bianchi, Pietro. "La morte sulla via Emilia," *Mercurio,* (May 1945).

Bianco, D. Livio. *Guerra partigiana.* Torino: Einaudi 1954.

Biasin, Gian Paolo. *The Smile of the Gods; a Thematic Study of Cesare Pavese's Works.* Ithaca: Cornell University Press, 1968.

Bo, Carlo. "L'ideologia del regime". In *Fascismo e antifascismo (1918-1948). Lezioni e testimonianze.* Milano: Feltrinelli, 1962.

Bobbio, Norberto. *Profilo ideologico del Novecento italiano.* Torino: Einaudi, 1986.

Bobbio, Norberto. Introduction to *Leone Ginzburg – Scritti.* Torino: Einaudi, 1964.

Bocca, Giorgio. *Storia dell'Italia partigiana.* Bari: Laterza, 1966.

Bocca, Giorgio. *La Repubblica di Mussolini.* Bari: Laterza, 1977.

Boggione, Valter. *La Sfortuna in Favore : Saggi Su Fenoglio.* Venezia and Alba, Italy: Marsilio; Fondazione Ferrero di Alba, 2011.

Boitani, Piero. *Riconoscere è un dio.* Torino: Einaudi, 2014.

Bosworth, R. J. B. and Dogliani, Patrizia. (Eds) *Italian Fascism. History, Memory and Representation.* Macmillan, St. Martin's Press: Basingstoke, New York, 1999.

Bresciani, Marco. *Quale antifascismo?.* Roma: Carocci, 2017.

Brooks, Peter. *The Melodramatic Imagination.* New Haven: Yale University Press, 1976.

Brooks, Peter. *Reading for the Plot.* Cambridge: Harvard University Press, 1992.

Brownie, Nick and Hillier, John. Edited and translated by. *Cahiers du Cinema 1968-1972. The Politics of Representation.* Cambridge: Harvard UP, 1992.

Calamandrei, Piero. *Uomini e città della Resistenza.* Milano: Linea d'ombra, 1994.

Calvino, Italo. *Il sentiero dei nidi di ragno.* Torino: Einaudi, 1964.

Calvino, Italo. "Il midollo del leone". In *Una pietra sopra. Saggi, vol I.* Milano: Mondadori, 2007.

Calvino, Italo. *Ultimo viene il corvo.* Milano: Mondadori, 2002.

Calvino, Italo. "Le donne di Messina". In *Saggi, vol I.* Milano: Mondadori, 2007.

Canfora, Luciano. *La sentenza. Concetto Marchesi e Giovanni Gentile.* Palermo: Sellerio, 1985.

Caruth, Cathy. *Unclaimed Experience Trauma, Narrative, and History*. Baltimore: Johns Hopkins University Press, 2010.

Cases, Cesare. *Patrie lettere*. Torino: Einaudi, 1987.

Cases, Cesare. *Su Lukács. Vicende di un'interpretazione*. Torino: Einaudi, 1985.

Cases, Cesare. *Il testimone secondario. Saggi e interventi sulla cultura del novecento*. Torino: Einaudi, 1985.

Casetti, Francesco. *Dentro lo sguardo*. Milano: Bompiani, 1986.

Casetti, Francesco. *Bertolucci*. Firenze: La nuova Italia, 1978.

Cassola, Carlo. *La Ragazza Di Bube*. Torino: G. Einaudi, 1960.

Colonello, Aldo and Del Col, Andrea. *Uno storico, un mugnaio, un libro. Carlo Ginzburg, il formaggio e i vermi (1976-2002)*. Trieste: Edizioni Università di Trieste: Trieste, 2003.

Comolli, Jean-Louis. *Cinema Against Spectacle* edited and translated by Daniel Fairfax. Amsterdam: Amsterdam UP, 2015.

Connerton, Paul. *Come le società dimenticano*. Torino: Einaudi, 2010.

Contini Bonaccossi, Sandro and Racchianti Collobi, Licia. *Una lotta nel suo corso. Venezia*: Neri Pozza, 1954.

Cook, Eleanor. *Enigmas and Riddles in Literature*. Cambridge: Cambridge UP, 2006.

Corti, Maria. *Beppe Fenoglio. Storia di un "continuum" narrativo*. Padova: Liviana, 1980.

Corti, Maria. *Il viaggio testuale*. Torino: Einaudi, 1978.

Croce, Benedetto. "La gioventù italiana". In *La libertà*, I, no. 1, 11 marzo 1944 now in *Scritti e discorsi politici I*. Napoli: Bibliopolis, 2010.

Culler, Jonathan D. *Flaubert : The Uses of Uncertainty*. Aurora, Colo.: Davies Group, 2006.

Dalle Vacche, Angela. *The Body in the Mirror – Antifascism after May 1968*. Princeton: Princeton UP, 1992.

De Felice, Renzo. *Il Fascismo – le interpretazioni dei contemporanei e degli storici*. Bari: Editori Laterza, 1970.

Dombroski, Robert S. *Properties of Writing : Ideological Discourse in Modern Italian Fiction*. Baltimore: Johns Hopkins University Press, 1994.

Dronke, Peter. *Fabula*. Leiden and Köln: E.J. Brill, 1974.

Dronke, Peter. *Dante and Medieval Latin Traditions*. Cambridge: Cambridge UP, 1986.

Elsaesser, Thomas. "Tales of Sound and Fury: Observations on the Family Melodrama." In Grant, Barry Keith., ed. by. *Film Genre Reader*. Austin: University of Texas Press, 1986.

Felman, Shoshana. "Literature and Psychoanalysis." In *Literature and Psychoanalysis. The Question of Reading: Otherwise*. Baltimore: The Johns Hopkins University Press, 1977.

Felman, Shoshana. *Testimony : Crises of Witnessing in Literature, Psychoanalysis, and History*. New York: Routledge, 2013.

Fenoglio, Beppe. *Una questione privata*. Torino, Paris: Einaudi-Gallimard, 1992.

Fenoglio, Beppe. *Una questione privata. Prima redazione*. In Maria Corti, ed. by, *Beppe Fenoglio-Opere*, Vol. I. Torino: Einaudi, 1978.

Ferrari, Gloria. "Metaphors and Riddles in the Agamemnon." In *Classical Philology*, Vol. 92, No. 1 (Jan., 1997).

Foa, Vittorio. *Il cavallo e la torre*. Torino: Einaudi, 1991.

Foa, Vittorio. "Le strutture economiche e la politica economica del regime fascista." In *Fascismo e antifascismo*, 266-286. Milano: Feltrinelli, 1962.

Focardi, Filippo. *Il cattivo tedesco e il bravo italiano. La rimozione delle colpe della seconda guerra mondiale*. Bari: Laterza, 2013.

Foot, John. *Italy's Divided Memory*. New York, NY: Palgrave Macmillan, 2009.

Fortini, Franco. "La luna e i falò," in "Letteratura contemporanea", no. 1, year 1, (1950).

Fortini, Franco. "Diario di un giovane borghese intellettuale," in *Il Politecnico*, 39 (December 1947), 34; reproduced in Marco Forti and Sergio Pautasso (ed.) *Il Politecnico. Antologia critica*. Milano: Lerici, 1960.

Francastel, Pierre. *Peinture et societé*. Paris, Lyon: Audin, 1984.

Francovich, Carlo. *La resistenza a Firenze*. Firenze: La Nuova Italia, 1962.

Gadda, Carlo Emilio. *Eros e Priapo*. Milano: Adelphi, 2016.

Garosci, Aldo. *Gli intellettuali e la guerra di Spagna*. Torino: Einaudi, 1947.

Gavin, Dominic. "Myths of the Resistance and Bernardo Bertolucci's *Strategia del ragno* (1970)" in *California Italia Studies*, 4 (2), 2013): 24.

Ginzburg, Carlo. *Miti emblemi spie – morfologia e storia*. Torino: Einaudi, 1986.

Ginzburg, Lydia. *On Psychological Prose*. Princeton: Princeton University Press, 1991.

Gobetti, Piero. "Elogio della ghigliottina." In *La Rivoluzione Liberale. Saggio sulla lotta politica in Italia*. Torino: Einaudi, 1964.

Gottlieb, Sidney. *Roberto Rossellini's Rome Open City*. Cambridge, UK; New York, NY, USA: Cambridge University Press, 2004.

Grignani, Maria Antonietta. "Virtualità del testo e ricerca della lingua da una stesura all'altra del *Partigiano Johnny*," *Strumenti Critici*, 36-37, (October 1978).

Hammet, Ian. "Classification and Change: The Function of Riddles." In *Man*, New Series, Vol. 2, No. 3, (Sep, 1967).

Hein, Laura Elizabeth. *Living with the Bomb : American and Japanese Cultural Conflicts in the Nuclear Age*. Armonk, N.Y.: M.E. Sharpe, 1997.

Heath, Stephen. "Narrative Space." In *Narrative, Apparatus, Ideology. A Film Theory Reader* edited by Stephen Heath, New York: Columbia UP, 1986.

Holquist, Michael. Introduction to *Art and Answerability. Early Philosophical Essays by M.M Bakhtin*. Austin: University of Texas Press, 1990.

Holquist, Michael. *Dialogism*. New York: Routledge, 2002.

Jameson, Fredric. *The Antinomies of Realism*. New York: Verso, 2013.

Jameson, Fredric. *The Political Unconscious*. Ithaca: Cornell University Press, 1981.

Jameson, Fredric. *Valences of the Dialectic*. London: Verso, 2010.

Kermode, Frank. *The Genesis of Secrecy : On the Interpretation of Narrative*. Cambridge: Harvard University Press, 1979.

Kermode, Frank. *The Sense of an Ending ; Studies in the Theory of Fiction*. New York: Oxford University Press, 1967.

Kliger, Ilya. "Heroic Aesthetic and Modernist Critique: Extrapolations from Bakhtin's «Author and Hero in Aesthetic Activity," *Slavic Review*, Vol. 67, No. 3 (Fall, 2008).

Kliger, Ilya. and Maslov, Boris, ed. by,. *Persistent Forms*. New York: Fordham University Press, 2016.

Kline, T. Jefferson. *Bertolucci's Dream Loom : A Psychoanalytic Study of Cinema*. Amherst: University of Massachusetts Press, 1987.

LaCapra, Dominick. *Writing History, Writing Trauma*. Baltimore: Johns Hopkins University Press, 2001.

L.p. "Era notte a Roma," *Cinema Nuovo*, n.149, (Jan-Feb, 1961).

Lajolo, Davide. *Il voltagabbana*. Milano: Il Saggiatore, 1963.

Levi, Carlo. *L'orologio*. Torino: Einaudi, 2014.

Lizzani, Carlo. "Il processo di Verona — dramma di corte," *Cinema nuovo*, no. 161, xii, (Feb, 1963).

Longo, Luigi. *Sulla via dell'insurrezione nazionale*. (Roma: Editori Riuniti, 1971).

Loshitzky, Yosefa. *The Radical Faces of Godard and Bertolucci*. Detroit: Wayne State University, 1995.

Lucente, Gregory L. *Beautiful Fables : Self-Consciousness in Italian Narrative from Manzoni to Calvino*. Baltimore: Johns Hopkins University Press, 1986.

Lukács, György. *The Historical Novel*. Lincoln: University of Nebraska Press, 1983.

Lukács, György. *Saggi sul realismo*. Torino: Einaudi, 1950.

Lukács, György. *Theory of the Novel*. Cambridge, MA: MIT Press, 1971.

Lukács, György. *The Meaning of Contemporary Realism*. London: Merlin Press, 1963.

Machiavelli, Niccolò. *Il Principe*. Torino: Einaudi, 1961.

Malaparte, Curzio. *La pelle*. Milano: Adelphi, 2010.

Manzini, Gianna. "Aspetti di un viale," in *Mercurio*, December 1945.

Mazzoni, Guido. *Theory of the Novel*. Cambridge, MA: Harvard UP, 2017.

Meneghello, Luigi. *I piccoli maestri*. Milano: Rizzoli, 2013.

Moravia, Alberto. "Il conformista." In *Opere Complete, vol. 8*. Milano: Bompiani, 1975.

Moretti, Franco. *Il romanzo di formazione*. Torino: Einaudi, 1999.

Moretti, Franco. *The Way of the World*. London-New York: Verso, 2000.

Moretti, Franco. *Segni e stili del moderno*. Torino: Einaudi, 1987.

Mutterle, Anco Marzio. *L'immagine arguta : Lingua, stile, retorica di Pavese*. Torino: G. Einaudi, 1977.

Noventa, Giacomo. *Tre parole sulla resistenza*. (Milano: All'insegna del pesce d'oro, 1965.

Panofsky, Erwin. *Perspective as a Symbolic Form*. New York: Zone Books, 2003.

Parise, Goffredo. *Il prete bello*. Milano: Adelphi, 2011.

Parri, Ferruccio. "Introduzione," *Mercurio*, (May, 1945).

Pautasso, Sergio. "Cesare Pavese," *Sigma*, (1964).

Pavel, Thomas G,. *The Lives of the Novel : A History*. Princeton: Princeton University Press, 2013.

Pavese, Cesare. *Il mestiere di vivere*. Torino: Einaudi, 1952.

Pavese, Cesare. *Saggi letterari*. Torino: Einaudi, 1951.

Pavese, Cesare. "Il carcere." In *Tutti i romanzi*, edited by Marziano Guglielminetti. Torino: Einaudi, 2000.

Pavese, Cesare. "Il diavolo sulle colline." In *Tutti i romanzi* edited by Marziano Guglielminetti. Torino: Einaudi, 2000.

Pavese, Cesare. "L'adolescenza." In *Saggi letterari*. Torino: Einaudi, 1951.

Pavese, Cesare. "La casa in collina." In *Tutti i romanzi*, ed. by Marziano Guglielminetti. Torino: Einaudi, 2000.

Pavese, Cesare. *La luna e i falò*. Torino: Einaudi, 2000.

Pavone, Claudio. *Una guerra civile. Saggio sulla moralità della resistenza*. Torino: Bollati Boringhieri, 1991.

Pesce, Gaetano. *Senza tregua. La guerra* dei GAP. Milano: Feltrinelli, 1967.

Pietra, Italo. "Oltrepò, vita santa," *Mercurio*, (May, 1945).

Pratolini, Vasco. *Un eroe del nostro tempo*. Milano: Rizzoli, 2013.

Prono, Franco. *Bernardo Bertolucci : Il conformista*. Torino: Lindau, 1998.

Propp, Vladimir. *Morphology of the Folktale*. Austin: University of Texas Press, 1968.

Pugliese, Stanislao G.. *Carlo Rosselli : Socialist Heretic and Antifascist Exile*. Cambridge, Mass.: Harvard University Press, 1999.

Quazza, Guido. "Storia della Resistenza e storia d'Italia. Ipotesi di lavoro," *Rivista di storia contemporanea* (Jan 1, 1972).

Quazza, Guido. *Resistenza e storia d'Italia*. Milano: Feltrinelli, 1976.

Revelli, Nuto. *La guerra dei poveri*. Torino: Einaudi, 1962.

Rhodes, John David and Gorfinkel, Elena. *Taking Place. Location and the Moving Image*. Minneapolis: University of Minnesota Press, 2011.

Ricœur, Paul. *The Course of Recognition*. Cambridge, Mass.: Harvard University Press, 2005.

Ricœur, Paul. *Soi-Même Comme Un Autre*. Paris: Seuil, 1990.

Ricœur, Paul. *Temps et Recit*. Paris: Seuil, 1984.

Rigoletto, Sergio. *Masculinity and Italian Cinema : Sexual Politics, Social Conflict and Male Crisis in the 1970s*. Edinburgh: Edinburgh University Press, 2014.

Rondi, Brunello. "Era notte a Roma," *Flimcritica*, n.95, (Mar, 1960).

Rosselli, Carlo. *Liberal Socialism*, edited by Nadia Urbinati and translated by William McCuag. Princeton: Princeton UP, 1994.

Rosselli, Carlo. *Socialismo liberale*. Roma-Firenze-Milano: Edizioni U, 1945.

Rousso, Henry. *Le Syndrome de Vichy*. Paris: Seuil, 1987.

Salvadori, Massimo. *Breve storia della resistenza italiana*. Firenze: Vallecchi, 1974.

Salvadori, Massimo. *Storia della resistenza italiana*. Venezia: Neri Pozza, 1955.

Santner, Eric L. *Stranded Objects : Mourning, Memory, and Film in Postwar Germany*. Ithaca: Cornell University Press, 1990.

Sartre, Jean-Paul. "L'Enfance d'un Chef." In *Le mur*. Paris: Gallimard, 1939.

Satta, Salvatore. *De profundis*. Milano: Adelphi, 1980.

Schoonover, Karl. *Brutal Vision – The Neorealist Body in Postwar Italian Cinema*. Minneapolis: University of Minnesota Press, 2012.

Sebald, W.G. *Storia naturale della distruzione*. Milano: Adelphi, 2004.

Secchia, Pietro. *I comunisti e l'insurrezione*. Roma: Edizioni di Cultura Sociale, 1954.

Shklovsky, Viktor. *Theory of Prose*. Champaign & London: Dalkey Archive Press, 1990.

Shklovsky, Viktor. *Una teoria della prosa*. Milano: Garzanti, 1966.

Sorrell, Alan. *Reconstructing the Past.* Totowa, N.J.: Barnes & Noble Books, 1981.

Spriano, Paolo. *Storia del Partito Comunista Italiano.* Torino: Giulio Einaudi editore, 1990.

Steimatsky, Noa. *Italian Locations.* Minneapolis: Minnesota UP, 2008.

Strada, Vittorio. "Introduction." In Lukács, György and Bakhtin, Mikhail., *Problemi di teoria del romanzo.* Torino: Einaudi, 1976.

Tellini, Gino. *Il romanzo italiano dell'Ottocento e Novecento.* Milano: Bruno Mondadori, 2000.

Testa, Enrico. *Lo stile semplice.* Torino: Einaudi, 1997.

Tilliette, Xavier. "Il Cristo di Malaparte," *Filmcritica*, n.18, (Nov, 1952).

Todorov, Tzvetan. *Poétique de la prose.* Paris: Seuil, 1971.

Todorov, Tzvetan. *A French Tragedy : Scenes of Civil War, Summer 1944.* Hanover: Dartmouth College : University Press of New England, 1996.

Todorov, Tzvetan. *Les Genres du discours.* Paris: Seuil, 1978.

Togliatti, Palmiro. "Sul movimento Giustizia e Libertà." In *Lo stato operaio*, 5, No. 9 (September 1931).

Togliatti, Palmiro. *Opere.* Roma: Editori Riuniti, 1984.

Tynianov, Yuri. "The Ode as an Oratorical Genre," *New Literary History*, Vol. 34, No. 3. (Summer 2003): 565-596.

Tynianov, Yuri. *The Problem of Verse Language.* Ann Arbor: Ardis Publishers, 1981.

Valeri, Nino. "La marcia su Roma." In *Fascismo e antifascismo*, 105-119, Milano: Feltrinelli, 1962.

Valiani, Leo. "Il Partito d'Azione nel Comitato di Liberazione Nazionale per l'Alta Italia." In *Fascismo e antifascismo*, 588-594. Milano: Feltrinelli, 1962.

Vernant, Jean-Pierre, Vidal-Naquet, Pierre. *Myth and Tragedy in Ancient Greece.* New York: Zone Books, 1990.

Vittorini, Elio. "Eugenio Curiel," *Mercurio*, (May: 1945).

Wagstaff, Christopher. *Il conformista.* London: BFI / Palgrave McMillan, 2012.

Ward, David. *Antifascisms : Cultural Politics in Italy, 1943-46 : Benedetto Croce and the Liberals, Carlo Levi and the "Actionists."* Madison: Fairleigh Dickinson University Press, 1996.

White, Hayden. *Metahistory.* Baltimore: Johns Hopkins University Press, 2014.

White, Hayden. *The Content of the Form : Narrative Discourse and Historical Representation.* Baltimore: John Hopkins University Press, 1987.

White, Hayden. *Figural Realism : Studies in the Mimesis Effect.* Baltimore: Johns Hopkins University Press, 1999.

Woloch, Alex. *The One vs. the Many*. Princeton: Princeton UP, 2005.

Zangrandi, Ruggero. "I giovani e il fascismo." In *Fascismo e antifascismo*, 209-216, Milano: Feltrinelli, 1962.

Zinni, Maurizio. "Uomini in nero: il Fascismo nel cinema italiano (1945-1962)." In *Cinema a passo romano*, edited by Pietro Cavallo, Pasquale Iaccio, Luigi Goglia. Napoli: Liguori, 2012.

Zinni, Maurizio. *Fascisti di celluloide – la memoria del ventennio nel cinema italiano. (1945-2000)*. Roma: Marsilio, 2010.

Zunino, Pier Giorgio. *La Repubblica e il suo passato*. Bologna: Il Mulino, 2003.

FILMOGRAPHY

Bertolucci, Bernardo. *Il conformista*. Mars Film, Marianne Productions, Maran Film. Italy, France, West Germany, 1970.

Bertolucci, Bernardo. *Strategia del ragno*. Rai, Red Film. Italy, 1970.

Camerini, Mario. *Due lettere anonime*. Lux Film, Ninfa Film. Italy, 1945.

De Santis, Giuseppe. *Caccia tragica*. ANPI, Dante Film. Italy, 1947.

Godard, Jean-Luc. *Made in USA*. Anouchka Films, Rome Paris Films, S.E.P.I.C. France, 1966.

Lang, Fritz. *Hangmen Also Die!* Arnold Pressburger Films. USA, 1943.

Lang, Fritz. *Cloak and Dagger*. Warner Bros., United States Pictures. USA, 1946.

Lizzani, Carlo. *Il processo di Verona*. Duilio Cinematografica, Orsay Films. Italy, 1963.

Lizzani, Carlo. *Il gobbo*. Dino de Laurentiis Cinematografica, Orsay Films, Globe. Italy/ France, 1960.

Malaparte, Curzio. *Il Cristo proibito*. Excelsa Film. Italy, 1951.

Malle, Louis. *Lacombe, Lucien*. Nouvelles Éditions de Films (NEF), Universal Pictures, Vides Cinematografica. France/ West Germany/ Italy, 1974.

Maselli, Francesco. *Gli sbandati*. CVC. Italy, 1955.

Montaldo, Giuliano. *Tiro al piccione*. Ajace Produzioni Cinematografiche, Euro International Film (EIA). Italy, 1960.

Ratoff, Gregory. *Lancer Spy*. Twentieth Century Fox. USA, 1937.

Rossellini, Roberto. *Era notte a Roma*. International Goldstar, Dismage. Italy/France, 1960.

Rossellini, Roberto. *Roma città aperta*. Excelsa Film. Italy, 1945.

Rossellini, Roberto. *Il generale Della Rovere*. Zebra Films, Gaumont. Italy/France, 1959.

Salce, Luciano. *Il federale*. Dino De Laurentiis Cinematografica. Italy, 1961.

Vancini, Florestano. *La lunga notte del '43*. Ajace Produzioni Cinematografiche, Euro International Film. Italy, 1960.

Wajda, Andrzej. *Ashes and Diamonds*. Zespól Filmowy "Kadr."Poland, 1958.

Zampa, Luigi. *Anni difficili*. Briguglio Films. Italy, 1948.

Zampa, Luigi. *Anni facili*. Ponti-De Laurentiis Cinematografica. Italy, 1953.

Zampa, Luigi. *Anni ruggenti*. Incei Film, SpA Cinematografica. Italy, 1962.